PLANNING SUPPORT
S Y S T E M S

Integrating
geographic information systems,
models,
and
visualization
tools

Richard K. Brail and Richard E. Klosterman, editors

ESRI PRESS
REDLANDS, CALIFORNIA

ESRI
  Planning Support Systems: Integrating Geographic Information Systems, Models, and Visualization Tools
  ISBN 1-58948-011-2

First printing: June 2001

Printed in the United States of America.

Library of Congress Cataloging-in-Publication Data
Planning support systems : integrating geographic information systems, models, and visualization tools / Richard K. Brail and Richard E. Klosterman, editors.
      p.   cm.
   Includes bibliographical references (p.   ).
   ISBN 1-58948-011-2 (pbk.)
      1. Land use-Planning-Data processing. 2. Information storage and retrieval systems-Land use.
   3. Regional planning-Data processing. 4. Geographic information systems. Brail, Richard K.
   II. Klosterman, Richard E.
   HD108.15.P574 2001
   333.73'13'0285—dc21   2001003074

Published by ESRI, 380 New York Street, Redlands, California 92373-8100. This book was published with the cooperation and assistance of the Center for Urban Policy Research, Rutgers University, New Brunswick, New Jersey.

ESRI PRESS books are available to resellers worldwide through Independent Publishers Group (IPG). For information on volume discounts, or to place an order, call IPG at 1-800-888-4741 in the United States, or at 312-337-0747 outside the United States.

Contents

Acknowledgments

The following chapters were originally published elsewhere:

Klosterman, Richard E. Planning Support Systems: A New Perspective on Computer-aided Planning. *Journal of Planning Education and Research* 17:1 (1997), pp. 45–54. © Association of Collegiate Schools of Planning. Reprinted by permission of Sage Publications, Inc.

Harris, Britton and Michael Batty. Locational Models, Geographic Information and Planning Support Systems. *Journal of Planning Education and Research* 12 (1993), pp.184–198. © Association of Collegiate Schools of Planning. Reprinted by permission of Sage Publications, Inc.

Klosterman, Richard E. The What-If? Collaborative Planning Support System. *Environment and Planning B: Planning and Design 26* (1999), pp. 393–408. Reprinted by permission of Pion Ltd., London.

Hopkins, Lewis D. Structure of a Planning Support System for Urban Development. *Environment and Planning B: Planning and Design 26* (1999), pp. 333–343. Reprinted by permission of Pion Ltd., London.

Introduction

Planning support systems (PSS) have arrived in concept and in application. Urban planners, policy makers, and citizens now have the means to visualize alternative futures for their cities and regions. In this book we explore planning support systems that couple analytic tools and computer simulation models with visual displays. These systems focus on land-use and transportation development options and on the environmental and fiscal consequences of these choices. We expect that their use will become widespread in the next decade, assisting both professionals and the public as all interested parties come to better understandings of the consequences of planning and programmatic decisions.

There are reasons why such a collection of papers on planning support systems is timely. First, the rapid evolution of hardware has made it possible to design, construct, and test complex computer programs that simulate complex systems such as cities and regions. We have moved far away from the early days of batch processing computing in the 1950s and 1960s. Interactive environments are powerful and nearly ubiquitous today, and over the early decades of the twenty-first century the visualization tools and models presented here will become commonplace—not just as specialized "toys" run by specialists, but as fully integrated systems requisite to the urban planning process. Second, there has been a corollary development in computer software. We are finally seeing significant developments in 3-D visualization software as well as continuing evolution in the analytic capacity of GIS. We fully expect these developments to continue, and can foresee the widespread use of virtual reality tools that enable citizens to "surf" their cities.

Third, there is the incredible growth in the availability of data and information resources. The rapid growth of an information-generating industry has fed on hardware and software developments. An excellent example is the use of TIGER street and facility networks in the United States. These topologically correct line files, first used in the 1990 U.S. census, have proven invaluable to planners and analysts, representing a comprehensive picture of communities from the perspective of their roads and railways. There has also been incredible development in satellite imaging, with resolutions as fine as one meter now available, meaning—to put it another way—that individual vehicles can be counted in a parking lot.

Finally there is the Internet, which has shown the potential for group interactions. Chat rooms are one example, and even the coeditors of this volume know couples who have met on the Web and formed lasting relationships. At another level, interest groups use the Internet to disseminate information and opinions. In the most expansive sense of a Web-enabled planning support system, the broader community would be able to visualize the results of alternative future planning scenarios over the Web and explore the effects on their quality of life and on the environment. These four themes—hardware, software, data, and the Internet—act as the catalysts to the rapid evolution of planning support systems.

This book is divided into three sections. We first explore the roots of planning support systems and then expand on the concepts by describing how such systems could be implemented. In this first section there are four chapters that move from a general introduction to specific recommendations on how to construct a system. In the second section we explore a variety of planning support systems that simulate current and future conditions using a variety of methodological approaches. Each chapter illustrates a different approach to a planning support system. Together they represent a powerful affirmation of the possibilities of such systems. The last section of the book focuses on visualization. As used here, the term "visualization" refers to the concepts and applications applied to graphic objects displayed and manipulated on computer screens for individuals and groups. Both general concepts and technically specific programs and tools are discussed here.

SECTION 1: AN OVERVIEW OF PLANNING SUPPORT SYSTEMS

The first chapter is by Richard Klosterman, a coeditor of this volume. He presents an overview of planning support systems that sets the stage for understanding the discipline's conceptual heritage. Klosterman focuses on the evolution of PSS in the context of the intellectual progression of planning across decades. He suggests that the prevailing perspective of planning moved from the applied science approach in the 1960s through a focus on the political process in the 1970s to an emphasis on communication in the 1980s. The development of planning support systems follows this evolutionary path. The urban models that were of central interest in the 1960s are still important today as the basis of scenario building and impact estimation. While it is unclear whether PSS measurably supports planning in the political arena in definable ways, it is certainly true that the visualization components of PSS aid in communicating broadly. Within this context we can "see" as well as numerically analyze the effects of planning decisions, and we can discuss our responses with others in the broader community. As Klosterman writes: ". . . rationality is based not on pure logic and the abstract evaluation of evidence but rather on informed consensus formed by a community of individuals in a particular place and time." In this sense we have moved to the 1990s and beyond with planning as "collective design" as the defining theme. The rapid development of the Web and of group-based decision tools are two indicators of this focus on the community as a fulcrum around which planning decisions revolve. Planning support systems are central to this process.

Britton Harris and Michael Batty focus on the growth in the use of GIS in planning and its capacity and limitations relative to PSS. The authors suggest that GIS per se is not PSS. The development of a decision support system is a multifaceted enterprise that is built on four foundations: mathematical theories, theories focusing on the structure and behavior of urban entities, theories of the planning process, and theories of spatial representation. A planning support system needs to incorporate a wide body of knowledge and use a broad range of data sources; this concern, however, is not within the general purview of GIS, particularly the data required by the models to simulate the interactions among agents and the flows that occur both at a point in time and over time. GIS is essential to the organization and display of information, but needs to be complemented by theories and models from a broader perspective. In this volume we will see planning support systems built on a variety of theoretical bases while integrating GIS into the overall framework.

Harris, a founding father of planning support systems, further develops the concept in his chapter on sketch planning. He lays out the issues surrounding the development of computationally robust tools to assist the planner, and presents a broad picture of the difficulties in doing plans that must consider complex data and modeling efforts as inputs to the exploration of alternative scenarios. While the use of formal optimization procedures to solve planning problems may not be possible, Harris believes that we ought to systematically search for better solutions that are guided by optimization principles. The development of a satisfactory sketch-planning process involves the recognition by both planners and the public that scenario building and analysis must balance the search for optimal solutions against resource constraints.

Lewis Hopkins follows up the Harris paper by fleshing out the sketch-planning process as a basis to a planning support system. He forwards a new concept—the geographical modeling system (GMS)—that attaches systematic modeling processes to spatial objects. An urban GMS would include populations, facilities, locations, and networks. Hopkins then builds his conception of a planning support system on the GMS. The PSS contains an extensive set of components, including, among others, the actors, their activities, and facilities within which these activities occur. These components are manipulated within workspaces that contain a variety of views: sketches, maps, models, and scenarios, among others. Hopkins builds on Harris's idea of sketch planning by delineating the types of activities that can lead to scenario generation and analysis. Hopkins makes a crucial distinction between scenarios that test ideas and plans that lay out intended actions.

SECTION 2: SIMULATION AND SCENARIO CONSTRUCTION

In the second section we look at those modeling systems that simulate urban futures and permit the evaluation of alternatives and the construction of scenarios. Basic to decision support is the capacity to test alternatives and to make judgments based on these alternatives. To conduct these alternative analyses we use models that can project demographic, economic, and land-use changes in cities and regions into the future, and which can estimate the effects of these changes.

We will present a variety of approaches to doing simulations and scenario evaluations at the urban scale. The models presented are drawn from a variety of intellectual traditions. Some are derived from the work of Ira Lowry, others from the discrete choice theory, and yet others are built within a GIS framework. One system is based on the recent developments in chaos and complexity theory. Many of these models allocate aggregate areawide projections of population and jobs to subareas. Depending on the model's purpose, these areas may be as extensive as a multicounty region or as small as a rural enclave located among forests and farms.

We start with a chapter by Stephen Putman and Shih-Liang Chan that has roots in the early classical work of Ira Lowry that modeled household and job location. Following is a chapter by Tomàs de la Barra that integrates spatial interaction and discrete choice theory. Both models have evolved over time and have been used widely. In his chapter, John Landis presents three models, all of which use GIS as a data organization and analysis tool. Eliot Allen presents a planning support system that uses a variety of indicators to assess alternative scenarios. Paul Waddell outlines his approach to models that include explicit consideration of land markets. Richard Klosterman describes *What If?*, a modeling framework that permits the generation of alternative land-use futures given user-defined choices. Michael Kwartler and Rob Bernard conclude the section with a complex modeling system that integrates two- and three-dimensional visualization and analysis with multiagent simulation.

Models focusing on the land-use, transportation, and demographic elements of urban landscapes have had a long and varied background. It is no surprise that these models of complex urban systems arise with the commercial development of the computer in the 1950s. Buoyed by the then-amazing capacity of computers to actually project small-area population, employment, and land-use types, model builders had great hopes that the era of "scientific planning" had begun. This optimism ran up against the very complex social concerns and needs of the Great Society initiatives in the late 1960s and against the hard reality of exactly what the models could and could not do. The initial enthusiasm of the 1950s and 1960s about the benefits of modeling complex urban systems was replaced by pessimism in the 1970s. The 1980s and 1990s saw a rebirth in model development with the rapid growth in computer technology, the proliferation of computerized databases, and the evolution of supporting tools such as GIS.

The first paper in this section, by Stephen Putman and Shih-Liang Chan, discusses METROPILUS, which is the result of the integration of earlier research on simulating regional development and GIS. Putman has a long history of work with simulation models. Starting in the 1970s, Putman and associates developed the Integrated Transportation Land Use Planning system (ITLUP). While the transportation model component has seen little application, the two land-use models, DRAM and EMPAL, have been widely used. DRAM (Disaggregate Residential Allocation Model) simulates the location of households within a region, while EMPAL (Employment Allocation Model) locates jobs. This pair of models has been adopted as a regional forecasting tool by many planning agencies.

In their paper, Putman and Chan outline the roots of DRAM/EMPAL and the subsequent use of this framework in METROPILUS. The conceptual basis of DRAM and EMPAL lies in spatial interaction theory. Distance to jobs, measured as time or cost, in conjunction with land availability and the socioeconomic characteristics of households, defines residential locational choices. For job location the predictive variables include travel impedance and the current locations of jobs and residences. The model structure of METROPILUS is purposively designed to require a small set of input variables in order to run the model. The authors discuss the possibility of including additional predictors, but argue that additional model inputs would require a more extensive data collection effort for each future update. For example, a forecast horizon could be thirty or forty years and all input variables would have to be projected forward over this period.

Tomàs de la Barra has also constructed an operational land-use and transportation modeling system, Tranus. However, while Putman's work has focused on households and jobs, de la Barra has a model system with three modules—land use, transportation, and evaluation. The model is particularly strong in delineating the interactions between activities, land uses, and the transportation system, using a broad economic framework. Both the real estate market on the supply side and land-use activities on the demand side are modeled, interacting with the demand for and supply of transportation resources. De la Barra illustrates the use of Tranus in Swindon in the United Kingdom, and shows how the modeling system can be used to test plan scenarios. For example, the "trend" land-use option for Swindon consumes over 10 percent more fuel for transportation purposes than alternative plans, an important policy consideration when dealing with issues like fossil fuel consumption and global warming.

The third paper in this set is by John Landis. He has developed a series of regional models in California that broke new ground by using GIS to both integrate and analyze data. Landis reports on three model systems in his chapter. His first effort was the California Urban Futures Model (CUF). This model system consisted of four submodels. The first, a population growth submodel, projected aggregate growth for counties and cities. The second submodel used a series of GIS layers, such as land-use, accessibility, or environmental conditions, to produce a single layer of "developable land units" (DLUs). The third submodel allocated growth to the DLUs while the fourth submodel handled annexation and incorporation.

Landis replaced CUF with CUF II in order to deal with a broader range of land uses beyond the residential and to introduce historical experience into the simulation. One major structural change was the move from vector-based polygons to raster-based grid cells. This change was made to simplify computation. CUF II also permitted different types of land uses to compete against each other, and allowed redevelopment and infill as well as development on vacant properties.

The third model in the Landis suite is the California Urban and Biodiversity Analysis Model (CURBA). This model system is grid-based like CUF II and focuses on habitat loss in rural areas. There are three submodels in CURBA. The urban growth submodel predicts growth at the county level based on past trends. The policy simulation submodel simulates alternative development scenarios, while the habitat submodel evaluates the effect of development on vegetative land cover and the fragmenting of habitat areas. CURBA extends Landis' regional modeling efforts to focus on the environmental consequences of land-use decisions. Landis confirms the general suspicion that models sometimes produce surprising and counterintuitive results. As you will see in his chapter, environmentally focused policies may not always be the best solution. There is a clear evolutionary path in the Landis work that is well described here. The chapter is a good example of how the modeling process can evolve in response to both research findings and to new applications.

Eliot Allen of Criterion Planners/Engineers, Inc., is the author of the chapter on INDEX, an ArcView®-based planning support system that permits the user to explore alternative scenarios based on the ranking and weighting of indicators. There are three application areas where INDEX has been used: long-range alternatives analysis, project evaluation, and periodic monitoring. INDEX is not intended as a tool to dynamically model complex urban systems, like other models in this book. Rather, over seventy local governments have used it widely to assess various land-use plans. INDEX has found an important role as a sketch-planning tool for integrated land-use and transportation systems, using recent interesting research on the relationships of design, density, and travel behavior.

Paul Waddell offers a different perspective on modeling. He argues for treating urban development as a dynamic process with explicit consideration of land markets and supply–demand interactions. The model system, called UrbanSim, has been developed for regions in Hawaii, Oregon, and Utah. Like other efforts, the model uses random utility theory and logit models, and disaggregates the results to zones within the region. UrbanSim is closely coupled to the urban transportation modeling process. The model includes access between residences and jobs as both an input to location choice and an output of transportation investment decisions. Impressively, the land development process—both revenues and costs—is incorporated in the model. UrbanSim, as other model systems have done, also uses GIS for both data inputs and display. Waddell breaks with the tradition of proprietary models by placing UrbanSim in the public domain and by making the model available over the Web.

Richard Klosterman has developed a model called *What If?* that proposes an alternative approach to exploring urban land-use futures. The model requires the user to enter a set of policy choices that define a possible future for the study area. When run, the model will project future land-use patterns that are directly related to the selected policies. Developed within a GIS framework, *What If?* determines the suitability of various parcels for different classes of land use, computes the amount of demand, then allocates this demand to the most appropriate parcels. The planner or policy maker can make choices about the region's future and see the simulated land-use pattern. Various policies can be tested to see expected land-use consequences. Policies prioritizing agriculture preservation, for instance, may produce a radically different land-use future than policies that emphasize economic development. In the exploration of such scenarios, *What If?* becomes a uniquely useful tool for considering implications and consequences of policy options.

The final paper in this section presents a highly integrated approach to modeling and scenario evaluation. CommunityViz is an ambitious effort at building a complex planning support system with a strong visual component. The model system combines two- and three-dimensional views of landscapes, structures, and roadways with multiagent simulations. CommunityViz was initially developed for the Orton Foundation for smaller communities in Vermont to assist them in evaluating planning and regulatory choices as they grew. The user can simultaneously move around a community in both two and three dimensions, and view existing and proposed buildings. As changes are made to the community, the effects on schools, infrastructure, and the environment are calculated.

There are three components of the CommunityViz system. The Policy Simulator is a multiagent simulation model based on complexity theory that operates at the individual or household level. Agents in the model replicate the decisions made by community residents. They respond interactively to land-use and facility changes as the community develops, and can "learn" from their interactions with other agents and the environment. The Scenario Constructor permits the user to create land-use alternatives and evaluate them in terms of estimated effects. It works within an ArcView two-dimensional framework and is connected to both the Policy Simulator and to TownBuilder 3D, the three-dimensional module of CommunityViz. This powerful display system can represent photorealistic communities and allow the user to "fly" around the landscape. The three modules of CommunityViz are synchronized so that changes in any one module are shown immediately in the others: placing a new residence on the landscape in Town-Builder 3D generates the additional effects of this residence in the Scenario Constructor module. CommunityViz demonstrates that we can build highly visual and interactive planning support systems that produce both two- and three-dimensional outputs.

What can we learn from these model-building and simulation efforts? We see varying conceptual approaches, methodologies, and overall designs. Both aggregate and disaggregate models are presented, and there are a variety of perspectives on the need for and role of empirical data. We see that it is quite possible to construct a planning support system that projects to the future across various scenarios and at different geographic scales. Models deal with alternative land development patterns and work at both the broad metropolitan level and for small communities. Finally, we see that it is possible to integrate the outputs of these models with different types of visual presentations. It is to these visual components of planning support systems that we turn next.

SECTION 3:
VISUALIZATION

This third section focuses on visualization, and contains four chapters. The first is by Richard Langendorf, who provides us with a basket of visual tools useful in a broad range of enterprises including planning and design. He suggests that living in a complex world requires the exploration of multiple perspectives and a variety of information resources. Visual tools can provide perspective and dramatically aid in understanding our environment. Langendorf first discusses application software useful in visualization, covering GIS, CAD, 2-D and 3-D modeling, and virtual reality, among other topics. He then introduces the concept of an "information workspace," within which each of us operates, and the more expansive idea of an "information landscape," the broad information world within which we visually navigate. Langendorf takes us on a journey through visual tools and concepts and develops a perspective on how we might use these devices to do planning support.

Michael Shiffer has the second chapter in this section, and presents several related, visually based applications focusing on collaborative community planning. An early adopter of technology, Shiffer has used a wide variety of visualization tools in planning situations. In his work we can see the use of the newest technology available at the time, and the willingness to continually adopt newer technologies as they become available. Shiffer's strong interest in using visualization tools in novel ways is demonstrated by his experiments with the computer simulation of traffic and airplane noise. While obvious in retrospect, the concept of letting the computer show pictures of highway traffic that correspond with the widely used "level of service" statistical measure of congestion was a groundbreaking idea. In the airport noise experiment, community residents were able to see airplanes take off and simultaneously hear corresponding noise levels based on a chosen distance from the airport.

Beyond being an early adopter of technology, Shiffer has built a conceptual framework that outlines how we can use "spatial multimedia" in planning. He defines spatial multimedia as the integration of video, sound, and text in a distributed environment. Within this broad, general concept there are specific components. For example, spatial annotation refers to the ability of computer users to place comments on maps and graphics. These comments may be in the form of audio, video, text, or sketches. Shiffer has focused on using visualization tools at both individual and community levels. His "Collaborative Planning System" places spatial multimedia in front of groups, where they can respond to and interact with issues and ideas of concern.

William Jepson, Robin Liggett, and Scott Friedman have the third chapter in this section. They present work going on at the Graduate School of Architecture and Urban Planning at the University of California, Los Angeles (UCLA). Researchers at UCLA began exploring the use of computer technology in the early 1970s. While the early potential for realistic and practical computer aids to the urban design process was difficult to realize, recent advances in technology now make it possible to do very creative projects. The authors demonstrate their work with some extraordinary projects, including "Virtual Los Angeles," a model of the entire Los Angeles basin. Of particular importance is the development of an integrated visualization environment using a variety of software that encompasses both two- and three-dimensional worlds.

Michael Batty and colleagues at the Center for Advanced Spatial Analysis (CASA) at University College London have the concluding chapter, which focuses on a variety of ways to visualize urban environments. Their interest is in state-of-the-art techniques for constructing three-dimensional visualizations of cities. They suggest correctly that 3-D has emerged as the preferred medium for displaying the world, and that there is a rapidly escalating momentum toward broad-scale use for a variety of purposes. Within the broad area of urban visualizations there are various approaches and methods. Software systems are designed for different types of visual output—2-D, 3-D, or multimedia. These systems also work at different levels of abstraction: some contain very detailed visual replications of buildings and landscape, while others work at a more generalized scale. Data entry varies from fully manual to highly automated systems. Finally, the systems use a variety of distribution methods including the Web. Batty and colleagues present different visualizations from around the world. Examples include Tokyo, New York, and London. While Jepson and colleagues have built Virtual Los Angeles, CASA is developing Virtual London. This concluding paper argues persuasively for the potential of visualization, and points to the need for designers of planning support systems to think carefully about how to most appropriately display the results of analysis and communicative planning.

CONCLUSION

Planning support systems are (or at least can be) useful tools for the planner, public officials, and the community. We began this introduction by pointing to hardware, software, data availability, and the Internet as underlying thematic elements to the development of planning support systems. The chapters in this book clearly confirm the fact that the rapid evolution in hardware capacity has been matched by the design of sophisticated software for simulation, mapping, and visualization. We can expect to see even more powerful systems in the future. In particular we can expect that much of the effort in the next few years will center on the development of fast and powerful three-dimensional systems that are fully integrated with simulation models, and which use massive data sets efficiently.

While we will not discuss data sources in detail in this volume, the need for extensive collection and analysis of information useful to a PSS is evident. Emerging critical issues in PSS research will center on data availability, storage, and access. To what degree will we want to use highly disaggregated household-level behavior and preference data for modeling and analysis, as required in CommunityViz? How will we store, manage, and access the huge data sets now emerging from high-resolution satellite imagery and from the outputs of real-time transportation system monitoring, as found in Intelligent Transportation Systems (ITS) applications?

The Internet comprises perhaps the most important area of research. In this book, Batty and colleagues, as well as others, discuss the Internet and the Web at some length. Waddell's UrbanSim model is on the Web in downloadable form. Increasingly we will look to the Internet to provide PSS services to the community; a "hook," however, is needed to get citizens to look to it for community building. In a culture emphasizing promotion of self and personal success, we can question whether citizens will "tune in" and deal with public questions rather than bidding on a new piece of electronics or organizing their next vacation. There are two sets of dynamics that might affect an individual's decision to become involved with community-based decision making framed by a planning support system. The first set is a "push" and the second a "pull." These forces may provide a potential tool in support of meaningful public dialogue.

There is the push to seek solutions that emerges from having to face environmental issues and threats. There is the continuing growth in the acceptance of global warming as reality. The popular press has introduced the concept and addressed the issues (see *The New York Times,* June 12, 2000). If some of the predictions about sea rise are proved correct, then coastal regions will face severe challenges and ameliorative planning will take on new urgency. Also, the era of relatively cheap energy may be coming to an end, and we may face serious decisions about how we wish to consume the remaining stocks of nonrenewable resources. There is another push from the locational decisions made by households and individuals. Suburban sprawl has been a defining trend for decades in the United States, but there are indications that young professionals are looking to the cities again. "Smart growth" is a response to dissatisfaction with congestion and pollution and a perceived decline in the quality of life. Perhaps these issues, among others, will push citizens to seek planning solutions. If so, then Web-enabled planning support systems need to be ready.

There also can be a corollary pull from a well-designed and visually interesting planning support system operating on the Internet. Planning and public policy issues and programs are often abstruse and not of great interest to the broader public. While talk radio waxes heavily about traffic congestion in urban centers, there is little general interest in the federally mandated and locally based transportation improvement program (TIP) document that underlies infrastructure investment in the United States. The rapid development of computer visualization tools, such as those envisaged by Langendorf and Shiffer and demonstrated by others in this volume, will permit citizens to "see" the consequences of planning choices and public investment decisions. Perhaps citizens will tune in along with policy makers, and we will see a level of broader community involvement. We can anticipate that as citizens are both pushed and pulled to explore planning options, the field will be set for more extended public debates.

In the chapters that follow you will be exposed to wide-ranging ideas as well as operational simulation models. Hopefully this book will stimulate your interest in planning support systems, and encourage you to both contribute to the development of these tools and to use them wisely.

Richard K. Brail

Paper 1

Planning Support Systems: A New Perspective on Computer-aided Planning

RICHARD E. KLOSTERMAN

UNIVERSITY OF AKRON

AKRON, OHIO

ABSTRACT

A new perspective on computer-assisted planning has been emerging in the last decade. By tracing the evolving view of planning—"applied science" in the 1960s, "politics" in the 1970s, and "communication" in the 1980s—and the likewise evolving concern of the information sciences with *data* and electronic data processing (EDP) in the 1960s, *information* and management information systems (MIS) in the 1970s, and *knowledge* and decision support systems (DSS) in the 1980s, a foundation is laid on which the increasingly popular topic of planning support systems (PSS) can be seen as a continuation of these trends toward an even broader concern with *intelligence* and collective design.

This paper begins by arguing that the continuing failure of planners to use computers extensively for core planning functions results less from the limitations of their hardware and software than from a limited understanding of the proper role these tools should play in planning. After a review of the changing perceptions and techniques underlying current explorations, the paper concludes by briefly considering the implications which this view has for PSS design and implementation.

AN ALWAYS-IMMINENT REVOLUTION

Computer use in planning began during the 1960s in an optimistic era of steadily increasing real incomes, a widespread faith in the efficacy of science and technology, and the emergence of new academic fields such as operations research, urban economics, and regional science. This general optimism was reflected in professional practice by ambitious federally funded attempts to develop large-scale metropolitan land-use/transportation models and integrated municipal information systems (Hemmens 1971; Government Data Systems 1971; Kraemer 1974; Putman 1979). In planning academia it was revealed by the popularity of the systems view of planning and the rejection of earlier views of "planning as design" for new models of "planning as an applied science." For some, the computer offered "a tool of such revolutionary new potential that it may have an effect of redefining the process of planning itself" (Harris 1968a, 223).

This optimism was severely tested in the 1970s with the spectacular failure of the large-scale urban models, the early municipal information systems, and all attempts to develop policy-relevant computer-based models (Brewer 1973; Danziger 1977; Lee 1973; Greenberger et al. 1976). Sophisticated analytic tools such as mathematical programming once assumed to provide the foundations for a new "science of planning" were found to be increasingly inappropriate for public planning applications. These critiques reflected a more fundamental attack on the "rational planning model" generally assumed to underlie all attempts to use computers in planning.

Planners' faith in computer technology was reborn in the 1980s with the development of microcomputers that made advanced information technologies and computer-based methods readily available to professional and academic planners the world over. Microcomputers are now found on nearly every planner's desk, courses in "computer applications" are a standard part of planning curricula, and a wealth of literature on microcomputer applications in planning has appeared (Klosterman 1992, 251–53). These developments have again led technological optimists to ask whether "planning can survive much longer in its present form" (Openshaw 1986, 68).

The 1990s have witnessed yet another "revolution in information technology" resulting from the general availability of geographic information systems (GIS). Planning schools are now rushing to offer GIS courses to satisfy overwhelming student demand; the academic and professional literature is filled with GIS articles; planning conferences are dominated by GIS sessions; and some authors claim that "[v]irtually anything a planner does can be done with GIS" (Robert Lima, quoted in Juhl 1994:8).

In spite of this continued optimism, it is clear that the oft-foretold revolution in computer-aided planning has yet to occur. Most planners may now have microcomputers on their desks but the available evidence suggests shallow (if broad) use. That is, while many planners use computers, they use them primarily for general-purpose office functions such as processing documents, monitoring budgets, and maintaining records, finding only limited applicability in those practices that are unique to planning such as forecasting, analysis, and evaluation (Klosterman 1992, 251).

Even in the area of GIS, the available information suggests that this increasingly popular technology is still being used primarily for routine operational and management tasks such as permit processing, collecting and maintaining land-related information, and preparing thematic maps. There is little evidence that GIS is being widely used for planning analysis or evaluation (Wiggins and French 1990; Wiggins 1993). The reasons for this will be examined more fully below.

RETURN TO FUNDAMENTALS

Over the last three decades, expensive, fragile, remote, and hard-to-use "mainframe" computers have been replaced by small, inexpensive, and easy-to-use microcomputers that get faster, cheaper, more powerful, and easier to use every year. The development of fast, high-resolution, full-color display and output devices has spawned spectacular advances in computer-aided design and drafting (CADD), GIS, and visualization. Equally dramatic improvements in the capacity and speed of data storage and communication devices, from local area networks (LANs) to the Internet, have made a wealth of digital information readily available to practicing planners in the smallest planning agency and firm. Perhaps most important, entirely new kinds of software—most notably electronic spreadsheets, sophisticated database management systems, and graphically oriented, multitasking operating systems—have made possible a flexible and interactive style of computer manipulation unimaginable only ten years ago.

Planners' continued failure to use computers more fully in their professional practice in the face of these rapid—and accelerating— developments suggest that the most important constraints to computer-aided planning must lie in the "soft" side of the "technology package": technique, organization, and knowledge (Danziger et al. 1982, 3–5; Masser and Campbell 1991). Some authors suggest the problem lies in the "wicked" nature of planning problems and the fact that local governments provide spatially distributed public goods and services that are difficult to describe concretely for computer processing (Dueker 1982, 61; Rittel and Webber 1973). Others point to the mismatch between the structured outputs produced by traditional planning models and decision makers' less formal and unstructured information needs (Langendorf 1985, 422–424). Others highlight the diversity of planners' analytic needs and application areas in a small and poorly funded public-sector market which provides little incentive for developing computer tools that serve those needs (Klosterman and Landis 1988, 365). Still others point to the isolation of planners from local government information systems developed primarily to serve operational and administrative needs (Arbeit 1993; Worrall 1987).

More fundamentally, recognizing that technology (in the narrow sense of computer equipment) is not the problem suggests that the search for an appropriate role for computer-based information and methods in planning must begin not with a particular technology (or set of technologies) but rather with a conception of planning. This perspective is based on the often-repeated observation, "If the only tool you have is a hammer, everything looks like a nail." The implication in this context is that starting with a particular technology such as GIS or expert systems and then seeing how this tool can be applied to planning threatens to distort the nature of planning. It does so almost inevitably—and unconsciously—by focusing attention on those aspects of planning for which a particular tool is appropriate and neglecting other aspects for which it is less appropriate.

Starting with a particular technology also implies that the role of advanced information technologies in planning is shaped largely by developments outside of planning (primarily business and the home entertainment industry) and not by the particular needs of planning. Starting with a particular technology also does not guide the search for new technologies or help identify ways in which new and existing tools can best be integrated into planning practice. Instead, it takes current technology largely as given and molds planning to fit the technology.

These observations are particularly relevant to the current fascination with GIS among planning academics and practitioners. The popularity of GIS—both within and outside of planning—is due largely to the fact that it is a "chameleon technology" which provides basic functions for collecting, maintaining, analyzing, and displaying spatially related information that is extremely useful for a wide range of public- and private-sector applications. However, this general applicability comes at the expense of particular capabilities that are required for specialized applications such as planning (Harris and Batty 1993, 185). The particular advantages—and limitations—which GIS provides for planning will be discussed briefly below.

These considerations further suggest that while no single technology alone can provide all of the capabilities planners need to carry out their professional responsibilities, a range of different technologies might be used together to provide capabilities that no single tool can provide on its own. Recognizing this, several authors have adopted Britton Harris' (1989) concept of planning support systems as an appropriate model for combining a range of computer-based methods and models into an integrated system that can support the planning function (Harris and Batty 1993; Borgers and Timmermans 1991; Holmberg 1994; Janowski and Richard 1994; Rugg 1992; Scholten and Padding 1990; Taylor 1991).

Although the concept of PSS has been defined in several ways in the literature, it will be initially defined here as broadly as possible to include all current and future technologies useful for planning. This does not mean a PSS will include all computer-based tools and methods used by planners; this definition excludes general-purpose software tools for word processing, report presentation, internal budgeting, and the like that planners use just as other professionals do. Instead, it includes only the computer hardware, software, and related information *used specifically for planning* (i.e., the information technologies planners use to perform their unique professional responsibilities as planners).[1] Identifying these responsibilities and refining this preliminary definition of PSS will be a primary concern of the remainder of this paper.

EVOLVING VIEWS OF COMPUTER-AIDED PLANNING

Suggesting that attempts to define the appropriate role for information technology must start with a conception of planning leads directly to the perennial question, "What is planning?" This is a fundamental (and perhaps unresolvable) issue that cannot be examined in detail here. Instead, the following discussion briefly reviews evolving views of planning and its relation to information technology and computer-based methods. The concluding section of the paper draws on these developments to suggest a useful definition of planning and of planning support systems.

PLANNING AS APPLIED SCIENCE

The introduction of computers into planning in the 1950s and 1960s was part of a more fundamental transition from the profession's traditional concern with the design of the physical city to a new focus on the quantitative techniques and theories of the social sciences. Guided by Mannheim's vision of planning as a rational process that applies scientific knowledge and techniques to the management of public affairs, planners abandoned the advocacy of professional visions of the desirable future for the ideology—if not the reality—of value-neutral policy evaluation and the metaphors of the market and pluralist political science. With this, the dominant perception of planning changed from an image of "planning as design" to "planning as an applied science."

This paradigm shift was reflected in planning education by the addition of new students, faculties, and departments from outside the traditional schools of design, and by the abandonment of the once ubiquitous design studio for the now equally prevalent courses in research design, statistics, and quantitative techniques. It was revealed most dramatically in the world of professional practice by the popularity of computer-based urban transportation models, integrated municipal information systems, and the large-scale urban models referred to previously.

The "applied science" model defined rationality in instrumental terms as finding the best means (actions or policies) for achieving desired ends, and planning as an iterative process of defining problems, identifying goals, generating alternatives, and evaluating available alternatives with respect to designated goals. As suggested in table 1, computers were assumed to play an important role in this task by collecting and storing the required data, providing systems models that could describe the present and project the future, and helping unambiguously to identify the best plan from the range of available alternatives (Harris and Batty 1993, 187).[2]

TABLE 1. EVOLVING VIEWS OF PLANNING AND INFORMATION TECHNOLOGY

1960s	System Optimization	"Planning as applied science" Information technology viewed as providing the information needed for a value- and politically neutral process of "rational" planning
1970s	Politics	"Planning as politics" Information technology seen as inherently political, reinforcing existing structures of influence, hiding fundamental political choices, and transforming the policy-making process
1980s	Discourse	"Planning as communication" Information technology and the content of planners' technical analyses are seen as often less important than the ways in which planners transmit this information to others
1990s	Collective Design	"Planning as reasoning together" Information technology seen as providing the information infrastructure that facilitates social interaction, interpersonal communication, and debate that attempts to achieve collective goals and deal with common concerns

Underlying this image was an implicit general systems theory which viewed cities as complex dynamic systems made up of hierarchical subsystems and planning as a rational procedure for optimizing overall system properties, such as utility or welfare. The knowledge required to simulate urban system functions was assumed to be provided by the new fields of urban economics and regional science. Techniques for selecting the optimal action or policy from the available alternatives were likewise assumed to be derived from then-new analytic procedures such as operations research and linear programming that had proven so effective in military and space applications.

This "applied science" model of planning was assumed to be equally appropriate for individuals (the "planner"), private organizations, and public agencies (the "planning agency"). It was further assumed that: (1) information is a "value-" and "politically neutral" resource; (2) more information is always better; (3) the planner's most important role is providing more and better information that can inform and improve the policy-making process; and, more fundamentally, that (4) a clear distinction could be made between the "objective" facts stored in a computer and the "subjective" opinions and values of individuals and groups. All of these assumptions were severely criticized during the 1970s with the emergence of a new conception of "planning as politics."

PLANNING AS POLITICS

Planners discovered in the 1970s that public policy making is fundamentally different from personal or corporate decision making. In the private sector, overall goals and objectives such as maximizing profits or increasing market share are reasonably well defined, reliable information on available alternatives can be collected with little difficulty, and the resources required to achieve designated goals are centrally controlled. None of these conditions applies in the public sector, making it extremely difficult to define—let alone achieve—collective goals and objectives (Rittel and Webber 1973).

Planners also recognized that planning is not—and cannot be—value free. With this came a realization that computer-based information and analytic techniques are themselves inherently and inevitably political, reinforcing existing structures of influence, increasing the power of administrators and technical experts, and transforming the nature of planning and policy analysis. The sheen of "objective authority" imparted by the value- and politically-neutral language of technical objectivity was found to inevitably hide inherently political choices in the selection of data and the analysis, presentation, and distribution of results, hiding fundamental political choices within supposedly technical analyses unfathomable to outsiders (Klosterman 1987; Dutton and Kraemer 1979).

The second assumption on the proper role of information in planning was likewise found to be much less straightforward than planners had initially thought. Information needs and the appropriate strategies for dealing with this information have been found to be defined not by public policy issues *per se* but rather by the way these problems are defined, by prevailing conceptions of policy goals, and by the available means for achieving these goals (Cartwright 1973; Christensen 1985; George 1994).

The seemingly straightforward conversion of information from paper records to digital form can itself have important political and legal implications. Data stored in digital form in a GIS can be used to generate information—for instance the location of all land parcels within a kilometer of a hazardous waste site—that would be extremely difficult to obtain when the same data is recorded in handwritten entries stored in file cabinets. As a result, the greatly enhanced ability to store and access information that GIS provides increases the potential for information abuse and misuse, raising fundamental issues of data security, reliability, and responsibility (Aronoff 1989, 269–77).

The introduction of more accurate and more current information can also *increase* public policy conflicts by revealing issues previously hidden from view and fueling policy debates based on conflicting interests and values. These systems are of course extremely useful for revealing previously unrecognized inaccuracies and conflicts in existing paper-based property records. However, they provide little help in correcting these problems, because errors are often embedded in legal documents that cannot be altered on technical grounds, without some kind of legal procedure (Obermeyer 1994; Werle 1984, 199–202).

Experience has also demonstrated that the social sciences have failed to provide the rigorously tested and empirically confirmed knowledge required to guide the policy-making process (Bernstein 1976, 24–44; Keyfitz 1982; Rein 1976, 52–74). Optimization techniques such as linear programming have been found to be very useful for dealing with well-defined, narrowly technical problems but largely inappropriate for most planning and public policy issues (Strauch 1974; Harris 1989, 88–89). Underlying these largely practical concerns was a more general attack on the "rational planning" that dominated planning theory throughout the 1970s.

PLANNING AS COMMUNICATION

The realization that planning was political was enriched during the 1980s by a new generation of "ethnographic" studies of planning practice. These studies revealed that planning involves much more than the collection and provision of information that can (presumably) improve the policy-making process. Planners of course prepare plans and do analyses. However, they also negotiate; bargain; explain; argue about planning rules, changes, and permissions; and administer rules and regulations. Quantitative analysis and related information technologies play an important role in these activities. But so does advice-giving, storytelling, myths, and the other metaphors and rhetorical devices planners use to communicate their ideas to others (Forester 1980; Harris 1989, 86–87; Innes 1990; Krieger 1981; Mandelbaum 1991).

These studies suggest that planning cannot be merely a politically neutral instrumental means for achieving designated ends. Instead it is an inherently political and social process of interaction, communication, and social design. In this perspective, the *way* in which planners transmit information may be more important than *what* they say. For example, quantitative analyses, no matter how well meaning and technically "correct," expressed in bureaucratic terms and technical jargon, all too often separate planners from the planned-for, reduce public access to information, increase the public's dependency on technical experts, and minimize planners' ability to learn from the public (Forester 1989). These problems are only increased as planners' technical tools become more sophisticated and their language becomes more esoteric.

This new "communications" view of planning suggests it should not be viewed primarily as an abstract decision process attempting to optimize overall system goals such as the community welfare. Instead, it must be seen as including an interactive, open, and ongoing process of intersubjective communication and collective design in which planners help the relevant community "make sense together while living differently" (Healey 1992). On this view the planning activity is grounded in two realms of rationality: (1) the "collective common sense" and collaborative attempts of groups "deciding and acting" together; and (2) the formalized knowledge and the self-reflective consciousness of autonomous individuals (Alexander 1988).

The emergence of the "communications" view of planning is supported by related developments in the broader realms of social and ethical theory. Philosophers now recognize that "social" facts and values are both culturally defined and can both be defended and criticized in ways that parallel the "objective" methods of science. With this have come new attempts to broaden the narrow "positivist" view of reason based on scientifically constructed empirical knowledge to include all realms of discourse. In this view, rationality is based not on pure logic and the abstract evaluation of evidence but rather on an informed consensus formed by a community of individuals in a particular place and time (Brown 1988; Healey 1992, 150–52; Fischer 1990, 217–63; Klosterman 1978; Klosterman 1983).

These developments in the field have been accompanied by equally fundamental but largely independent changes in the prevailing views of the proper role of information technology in public- and private-sector organizations. As shown in table 2, these developments can be viewed broadly as an evolving concern with: (1) *data* during the 1960s, (2) *information* during the 1970s, and (3) *knowledge* in the 1980s.[3]

TABLE 2. EVOLVING CONCERNS OF INFORMATION TECHNOLOGY

1960s	Data	"Observations which have been cleaned, coded, and stored in machine-readable form" Primary concern of electronic data processing (EDP) which promoted efficient transaction processing to improve operational tasks
1970s	Information	"Data which has been organized, analyzed, and summarized into a meaningful form" Primary concern of management information systems (MIS) which integrated diverse data sets to serve management needs
1980s	Knowledge	"Understanding based on information, experience, and study" Primary concern of decision support systems (DSS) which facilitated semistructured decision making to support executive decision making
1990s	Intelligence	"Ability to deal with novel situations and new problems, to apply knowledge acquired from experience, and to use the power of reasoning effectively as a guide to behavior" Possible concern of planning support systems (PSS) which will promote discourse and interaction to facilitate collective design

EDP AND DATA

In the 1960s the infant computer industry was concerned mainly with the handling of *data* (i.e., direct observations which have been cleaned, coded, and stored in machine-readable form).[4] Computer-based information systems were devoted almost exclusively to electronic data processing, the automation of existing manual procedures and the computerization of vast amounts of routine data previously stored on paper. The goal was improving routine operations by facilitating efficient transaction processing, integrating data for related functions, and generating tabular summary reports ("computer print-outs") useful for improving day-to-day operations. The prevailing technology was batch processing of custom-designed, single-purpose, transaction-based information systems on mainframe computers. Public-sector applications included the computerization of day-to-day operational functions such as payroll, accounting, and property tax assessment (Huxhold 1991, 5–9).

MIS AND INFORMATION

In the 1970s the emphasis changed from data to *information* (i.e., data which has been organized, analyzed, and summarized into a meaningful form). The primary concern shifted from the efficient processing of data for operational needs to management information systems (MIS) and the structuring and synthesis of data in forms that could serve management needs. The principle systems objectives became the integration of EDP tasks by organizational function, the processing of information queries, and the generation of summary reports based on a comprehensive database. At the same time, the technology evolved to include minicomputers, relational database management systems (RDBMS), and computer-based mapping. Public-sector applications included the development of urban information systems (UIS), geographic information systems (GIS), and land information systems (LIS) that together provided the integrated information required for management functions such as permit processing, code enforcement, infrastructure management, and transit operations. These management functions continue to be the primary use of most urban GIS/LIS systems (Grimshaw 1988; Huxhold 1991, 64–126).

DSS AND KNOWLEDGE

The emphasis changed again in the 1980s from information to *knowledge* (i.e., to understanding based on information, experience, and study). The change in emphasis reflected decision makers' desire for analytical modeling capabilities and for more interaction with solution processes than were provided by management information systems of the 1970s. Stimulated by Gorry and Morton's seminal paper, an entirely new type of system—decision support systems (DSS)—emerged, generating a substantial body of theory and a large number of applications (Gorry and Morton 1971; Keen and Morton 1978; Sprague and Carlson 1982; Sprague and Watson 1986).

Two primary features characterize the DSS of the 1980s. First, they are composed of three components: a user interface, a database, and a model base. Together, these three components are designed to provide a framework which integrates (1) all relevant information from a wide variety of sources with (2) the full range of analytical and statistical modeling tools, and (3) a graphical interface that conveys information in a readily understandable form to decision makers. The primary design objective is providing flexibility and quick response in an easy-to-use system that could be adapted to the evolving needs and styles of system users.

More important, decision support systems differ from previous MIS approaches in being deliberately designed to deal with ill- or semi-structured decisions. For well-structured problems, the fundamental variables of concern and the relationship between these variables are easy to identify and measure and, thus, to represent in a mathematical or computer model. In contrast, semi- or ill-structured problems have aspects which are partially qualitative in nature and requiring value judgments, in part because decision makers are unable—or unwilling—to articulate clearly the objectives of the analysis or the characteristics of desired solutions (Gorry and Morton 1971; Langendorf 1985, 424).

DSS are designed to help deal with poorly structured decisions by facilitating a decision process which is iterative, integrative, and participative. They are iterative because they allow decision makers to systematically generate and evaluate a number of alternative solutions, gaining insights which are introduced as inputs to help guide further analyses. They are integrative in that they incorporate decision makers' substantive knowledge along with the quantitative data provided by the models to evaluate alternatives across a broad range of pertinent criteria. And they are participatory by permitting decision makers to examine the consequences of employing different information and modeling approaches, and to choose alternate decision criteria, objectives, and constraints.

The principles underlying the DSS model have been revealed most clearly in the public sector by the spatial decision support systems (SDSS) developed by Paul Densham and others (e.g., Armstrong and Densham 1990; Densham and Rushton 1988). SDSS are designed to support decision making related to complex spatial problems such as determining the optimal location for service centers—elementary schools and fire stations, for example. As their name implies, they incorporate three spatially related components of a traditional DSS: a database containing a variety of spatial and nonspatial data, spatially related analytic and simulation models, and a user interface that generally includes a GIS. The GIS generates and stores the required spatial data used as input data for the analytic models. The models take the required data from the database, use it to conduct the required analysis or simulation, and store model outputs in the database. GIS and other data visualization software are then used to display the model results, generally in map form.

TOWARD A PLANNING SUPPORT SYSTEM

The parallel (if largely unrelated) developments in the spheres of planning and information systems technology together provide the foundations for a richer conception of the role which advanced information technologies can play in planning. In planning, earlier views of planning as an "objective" and "value-neutral" tool have been replaced by an increasingly sophisticated appreciation of the inherently political nature of the planning process. With this has come the realization that planning is best seen as including not only the activity of an isolated individual or organization but also—and perhaps more importantly—as an ongoing process of social design, dialogue, and debate in which planners, public officials, and the public attempt to decide together how to best manage the collective concerns of society (Healey 1992). In the realm of information technology, the evolving concern with operational data, management information, and then executive-level knowledge has moved the perceived role of information technology further up the organizational pyramid and from routine, well-structured concerns to increasingly less-routine, less well-structured, and much more difficult issues (Huxhold 1991, 12–22).

As shown in table 2, these developments suggest a possible next evolutionary stage which will go beyond a concern with supplying the knowledge needed to support executive decision making at the peak of the organizational pyramid, to providing *intelligence,* the ability to deal with novel situations and new problems, to apply knowledge acquired from experience, and to use the power of reasoning effectively as a guide to behavior. This approach would expand the role of information technology beyond the organization to address inter-organizational issues of information sharing and mutual learning. It suggests that PSS should be designed to facilitate *collective design,* social interaction, interpersonal communication, and community debate which attempt to achieve collective goals and deal with common concerns.

This is of course an extremely idealized and abstract view of what planning support systems are and should become. However, it does suggest that PSS, like current DSS (and SDSS), should be designed to provide interactive, integrative, and participatory procedures for dealing with nonroutine, poorly structured decisions. However, as a *planning* system, it must also pay particular attention to long-range problems and strategic issues, as well as explicitly facilitate group interaction and discussion; this is in contrast to DSS and SDSS, which are generally designed to support shorter-term policy making by isolated individuals and organizations.

It also suggests that PSS must not be seen as a radically new form of technology that will replace the software tools planners currently find on their desks. Instead, it must take the form of an *information framework* that integrates the full range of current (and future) information technologies useful for planning. This perspective recognizes that the design of a *planning* support system must start with the application—planning—and not with a particular technology (or technologies) and should use all available tools appropriate for serving the particular needs of planning. It also recognizes that most planning problems are composed of different problem areas which often have their own suitable technologies, and that any comprehensive PSS must utilize a full range of different technologies, each appropriate for a particular type of function (Han and Kim 1989, 301).

PSS should also not be viewed as a closed "black box" collection of computer models which can accept raw data and automatically generate master plans, forecast future land-use patterns, or identify optimal policies and actions. Instead, it must be seen as providing the *information infrastructure* for planning that facilitates interaction among planners, and between planners and other actors, both within and outside of government. The PSS must contain structured and accessible information (not just raw data) about the real-world features of concern to the public, along with a full range of software tools for analysis, forecasting, and decision making. It must also support a continuous and interactive process of analysis, design, and evaluation that constantly integrates new information generated as analytical results redefine design issues and the elaboration of design issues generates new demands for analytical information (Harris and Batty 1993, 189; Rugg 1992, 223; Schuur 1994, 102).

THE ROLE OF GIS

The heart of any PSS will undoubtedly be a GIS. The GIS will serve first as a display and communication device, producing maps and charts that describe past and present conditions and model outputs that suggest alternative futures. However, its spatial analysis capabilities will also play an essential role in generating new spatially referenced information required by the computational components of the system.

However, a PSS cannot consist of a GIS alone. It must also include the full range of planners' traditional tools for urban and regional economic and demographic analysis and forecasting, environmental modeling, transportation planning, and predicting future development and land-use patterns. It must also include other technologies such as expert systems (Han and Kim 1989), decision support aids such as multiattribute utility theory (Lee and Hopkins 1995), hypermedia systems (Shiffer 1992), and group decision support systems (Armstrong 1993; Finaly and Marples 1992).

GIS alone cannot serve all the needs of planning because the current generation of "general-purpose" systems cannot easily accommodate the particular informational, computational, and display needs of planning. Among other things, planning requires (1) information that is effectively "aspatial" at a particular level of analysis (e.g., regional population and employment levels and trends for the analysis of a city and its components); (2) information over time (e.g., population, employment, and land-use data for the past, present, and possible futures); and (3) measures of spatial interaction (e.g., the number of trips between zones). None of these can be easily incorporated into current GIS (Harris and Batty 1993, 190).

Planning analysis and forecasting also requires computational procedures that go beyond the standard database manipulation and Boolean functions of most GIS. These needs include the ability to (1) compute cross products, manipulate matrices, and conduct statistical analyses; (2) estimate system parameters and derive solutions iteratively; and (3) support analytical and design functions which incorporate goals, objectives, costs, and benefits (Couclelis 1991; Harris and Batty 1993, 189). Until recently, GIS has also been unable to produce basic data displays such as bar graph and scatter charts, or to integrate maps with graphic images, sound and video clips, and other display media. They are still unable to produce specialized graphic displays such as population pyramids that are particularly useful for planning.[5]

As a result, it is highly unlikely that all of the computational needs of planners will be incorporated into standard GIS packages. Instead, planners will have to adapt existing GIS tools to meet their needs. Traditional programming languages can be used to develop spatial analysis and modeling tools entirely independent of commercial packages. A combination of sophisticated GIS "macro" commands and traditional programming languages also can be used to develop analytic models closely linked to full-featured GIS "toolkits" such as ArcInfo™ (Batty and Xie 1994a; Batty and Xie 1994b). Alternatively, a GIS can be used to prepare maps and perform spatial analyses when loosely coupled to other software tools, such as electronic spreadsheets, which provide the computational functions GIS does not offer with data transferred as needed from one software platform to another.[6]

INCONCLUSION[7]

The ideal PSS is as easy to define as it will be difficult to implement. The perfect PSS would be a fully integrated, flexible, and "user-friendly" system that allows the user to (1) select the appropriate analysis or forecasting tool from an "intelligent digital toolbox" that helps the user identify the most appropriate methodologies and tools for dealing with a particular task; (2) link the appropriate analytic or projection model to the required local, regional, or national information stored—or accessed—through the PSS; (3) run the appropriate models to determine the implications of alternative policy choices and different assumptions about the present and the future; and (4) instantaneously view the results graphically in the form of charts, maps, and interactive video/sound displays. The process would ideally be done interactively and in real time, using models and associated attribute and mapped data available locally or remotely over the Internet. The system would incorporate both qualitative and quantitative decision aids, as appropriate, facilitating voting, ranking, and group interaction (Finaly and Marples 1992, 99; Harris 1989; Rugg 1992, 225; Holmberg 1994, 11–14; Harris and Batty 1993, 193–94).

Many of the required analytic and display modules have been developed and are available, at least in prototype form, somewhere. The important—and difficult—task is integrating these modules into a coherent system that serves the needs of planners. To do this, standardized formats will have to be developed for data storage, access, and interchange; efforts in this direction have begun, such as the development of the federal government's spatial data transfer standard (SDTS). Software tools will have to be identified or developed that can deal with particular tasks, utilizing data stored in standard formats or generated by the analytic modules. Analytic and display models must then be combined into an integrated package and new linking/data exchange tools must be developed that can transfer data from one software tool to another.

This paper has not attempted to provide a well-structured blueprint for guiding these developments, either now or in the future. Issues of systems design and implementation can only be resolved slowly and painfully over time as planning scholars and practitioners develop the tools and experience that will make the PSS ideal a reality. In this way, the paper ends inconclusively, leaving unanswered a host of extremely difficult and important theoretical and practical questions of determining the best ways in which the array of available and emerging information technologies can be integrated into a comprehensive system to support the needs of planning. Crucial issues of funding, coordination, training, and data dissemination are also left untouched.

Nevertheless, the paper has attempted to provide a general framework within which these developments can occur and a vision of where they should be directed. The vision begins by recognizing that the search for an appropriate role for information technology in planning must begin not with technology but with planning, and must strive to adapt available technologies to the particular needs of planning. Emerging conceptions of planning as collective design suggest that planners' computer-based tools must be directly accessible to the public and address issues they are most interested in—e.g., exploring the likely social, fiscal, and environmental impacts of alternative development proposals—in ways they can readily understand. If this vision is correct, advanced information technologies may finally take their place at the center of professional planning practice, supporting community planning in its fullest and richest forms.

AUTHOR'S NOTE

The author gratefully acknowledges the comments and suggestions offered by Ernest Alexander, Seymour Mandelbaum, James Mars, and several reviewers.

NOTES

[1] Defining PSS to include "all of the technologies used by planners" is equivalent to defining planning as "everything that planners do." This definition of planning is too broad because it includes not only the things planners do as planners but also the things they do as private citizens (e.g., their interaction with family and friends) or even in violation of the norms of planning (e.g., taking bribes). It is also too narrow because it excludes the activities of persons who may not be identified as planners but who carry out planning functions (as they may be defined in a particular case). Similar definitional problems plague an overly broad—and narrow—definition of PSS.

[2] This "rational" model still underlies many views of the proper role of computers and related technologies in planning (Webster 1993; Webster 1994; Batty 1995, 27–28).

[3] This four-part distinction between data, information, knowledge, and a new stage of intelligence discussed later in the paper is adapted—in a modified form—from similar concepts proposed by Harris (1987, 4).

[4] The following discussion draws on similar discussions in Hopple 1988: 6–7 and Mannheim 1987: 122–23.

[5] A comprehensive review of more fundamental "postpositivist" critiques of GIS is provided in Sui 1994.

[6] Ding and Fotheringham 1992; Harris and Batty 1993, 189–91. These alternative strategies are evaluated in Sui 1994, 258–60.

[7] The idea of ending a paper with a section titled "inconclusion" is adapted from Britton Harris.

REFERENCES

Alexander, Ernest R. 1988. After rationality. *Society* 26(1):15–19.

Arbeit, David. 1993. Resolving the data problem: A spatial information infrastructure for planning support. In *Proceedings: Third International Conference on Computers in Urban Planning and Urban Management*, ed. Richard E. Klosterman and Steven P. French. Atlanta: Georgia Institute of Technology.

Armstrong, Marc P. 1993. Perspectives on the development of group decision support systems for locational problem-solving. *Geographical Systems* 1:69–81.

———, and Paul J. Densham. 1990. Database organization strategies for spatial decision support systems. *International Journal of Geographical Information Systems* 4(1):3–20.

Aronoff, Stanley. 1989. *Geographical Information Systems: A Management Perspective*. Ottawa: WDL Publications.

Batty, Michael. 1995. Planning Support Systems and the New Logic of Computation. *Regional Development Dialogue* 16(1, Spring):1–17.

———, and Yichun Xie. 1994a. Modeling Inside GIS: Part 1: Model Structures, Exploratory Spatial Analysis. *International Journal of Geographic Information Systems* 8(3):291–307.

———, and Yichun Xie. 1994b. Modeling Inside GIS: Part 2: Selecting and Calibrating Urban Models Using ARC/INFO. *International Journal of Geographical Information Systems* 8(5):451–70.

Bernstein, Richard J. 1976. *The Restructuring of Social and Political Theory.* Philadelphia: University of Pennsylvania Press.

Borgers, Aloys, and Harry Timmermans. 1991. A Decision Support and Expert System for Retail Planning. *Computers, Environment and Urban Systems* 15:179–88.

Brewer, Gary D. 1973. *Politicians, Bureaucrats, and the Consultant: A Critique of Urban Problem Solving.* New York: Basic Books.

Brown, Harold I. 1988. *Rationality.* London: Routledge.

Cartwright, Timothy J. 1973. Problems, Solutions, and Strategies: A Contribution to the Theory and Practice of Planning. *Journal of the American Institute of Planners* 39:179–87.

Christensen, Karen S. 1985. Coping with Uncertainty in Planning. *Journal of the American Planning Association* 51(1):63–73.

Coucelis, Helen. 1991. Geographically Informed Planning: Requirements for Planning-relevant GIS. *Papers in Regional Science* 70:9–20.

Danziger, James N. 1977. Computers, Local Government, and the Litany to EDP. *Public Administration Review* 37:28–37.

———, William H. Dutton, Rob Kling, and Kenneth L. Kraemer. 1982. *Computers and Politics: High Technology in American Local Governments.* New York: Columbia University Press.

Densham, Paul, and Gerald Rushton. 1988. Decision Support Systems for Location Planning. *Behavioral Modeling in Geography and Planning,* ed. Reginald G. Golledge and Harry Timmermans, 56–90. Beckenham: Croom Helm.

Ding, Y., and A. S. Fotheringham. 1992. The Integration of Spatial Analysis and GIS. *Computers, Environment and Urban Systems* 16:3–19.

Dueker, Kenneth J. 1982. Urban Planning Uses of Computing. *Computers, Environment and Urban Systems* 7:59–64.

Dutton, William H., and Kenneth L. Kraemer. 1979. Automation of Bias: Computer Models and Local Government Budgeting. *Information Privacy* 1:303–11.

Finaly, Paul N., and Chris Marples. 1992. Strategic Group Decision Support Systems—A Guide for the Unwary. *Long Range Planning* 25:98–107.

Fischer, Frank. 1990. *Technology and the Politics of Expertise.* Newbury Park, CA: Sage Publications.

Forester, John. 1980. Critical Theory and Planning Practice. *Journal of the American Planning Association* 46:275–86.

————. 1989. *Planning in the Face of Power*. Berkeley, CA: University of California Press.

George, R. Varkki. 1994. Formulating the Right Problem. *Journal of Planning Literature* 8(3):240–59.

Gorry, G. Anthony, and Michael S. Scott Morton. 1971. A framework for Management Information Systems. *Sloan Management Review* 13:56–70.

Government Data Systems. 1971. USAC: Federal Funding for Municipal Information Systems. *Government Data Systems* 1:6–24.

Greenberger, Martin, Matthew A. Crenson, and Brian L. Crissey. 1976. *Models in the Policy Process: Public Decision Making in the Computer Era*. New York: Russell Sage.

Grimshaw, D. J. 1988. The Use of Land and Property Information Systems Information. *International Journal of Geographic Information Systems* 2:57–65.

Han, Sang-Yun, and Tschangho John Kim. 1989. Can expert systems help with planning? *Journal of the American Planning Institute* 55:296–308.

Harris, Britton. 1968a. Quantitative Models of Urban Development: Their Role in Metropolitan Policy-making. In *Issues in Urban Economics,* ed. Harvey S. Perloff and Lowdon Wingo. Baltimore: Johns Hopkins Press.

————. 1987. Information is Not Enough. *URISA News* 90:4–5, 23.

————. 1989. Beyond Geographic Information Systems: Computers and the Planning Professional. *Journal of the American Planning Association* 55:85–92.

————, and Michael Batty. 1993. Locational Models, Geographical Information, and Planning Support Systems. *Journal of Planning Education and Research* 12:184–98.

Healey, Patsy. 1992. Planning through Debate: the Communicative Turn in Planning Theory. *Town Planning Review* 63:143–62.

Hemmens, George, editor. 1971. *Special Report 97: Urban Development Models*. Washington, D.C.: Highway Research Board, National Research Council.

Holmberg, S. C. 1994. Geoinformatics for Urban and Regional Planning. *Environment and Planning B: Planning and Design* 21:5–19.

Huxhold, William E. 1991. *An Introduction to Geographic Information Systems*. New York: Oxford University Press.

Innes, Judith Eleanor. 1990. *Knowledge and Public Policy: The Search for Meaningful Indicators,* second expanded edition. New Brunswick: Transaction Publishers.

Janowski, P., and L. Richard. 1994. Integration of GIS-based Suitability Analysis and Multi-criteria Evaluation in a Spatial Decision Support System for Route Selection. *Environment and Planing B: Planning and Design* 21:323–40.

Juhl, Ginger M. 1994. Getting on the GIS Career Track. *Planning* 60(7, July):8–11.

Keen, Peter, and Michael S. Scott Morton. 1978. *Decision Support Systems: An Organizational Perspective*. Reading, MA: Addison–Wesley.

Keyfitz, Nathan. 1982. Can Knowledge Improve Forecasts? *Population and Development Review* 8:729–51.

Klosterman, Richard E. 1978. Foundations for Normative Planning. *Journal of the American Institute of Planners* 44:37–46.

———. 1983. Fact and Value in Planning. *Journal of the American Planning Association* 49:216–25.

———. 1987. Politics of Computer-aided Planning. *Town Planning Review* 58(4):441–52.

———. 1992. Evolving Views of Computer-aided Planning. *Journal of Planning Literature* 6(3):249–60.

———, and John Landis. 1988. Microcomputers in U.S. Planning: Past, Present and Future. *Environment and Planning, B: Planning and Design* 15:355–68.

Kraemer, Kenneth L. et al. 1974. *Integrated Municipal Information Systems: The Use of the Computer in Local Government*. New York: Praeger.

Krieger, Martin. 1981. *Advice and Planning*. Philadelphia: Temple University Press.

Langendorf, Richard. 1985. Computers and Decision-making. *Journal of the American Planning Association* 51:422–33.

Lee, Douglas B., Jr. 1973. Requiem for Large-scale Models. *Journal of the American Institute of Planners* 39(3):163–87.

Lee, Insung, and Lewis D. Hopkins. 1995. Procedural Expertise for Efficient Multi-attribute Evaluation: A Procedural Support Strategy for CEA. *Journal of Planning Education and Research 14* (4, Summer):255–69.

Mandelbaum, Seymour J. 1991. Telling Stories. *Journal of Planning Education and Research* 10(3):209–14.

Masser, Ian, and Heather Campbell. 1991. Conditions for the Effective Utilization of Computers in Urban Planning in Developing Countries. *Computers, Environment and Urban Systems* 15(1):55–67.

Obermeyer, Nancy J. 1994. Spatial Conflicts in the Information Age. *1994 Annual Conference Proceedings: Urban and Regional Information Systems*.

Association, Volume I, ed. Mark J. Salling, 269–82. Washington, D.C.

Openshaw, Stan. 1986. Towards a New Planning System for the 1990s and Beyond. *Planning Outlook* 29:66–69.

Putman, Stephen. 1979. *Urban Residential Location Models*. Boston: Martinus Nijoff.

Rein, Martin. 1976. *Social Science and Public Policy*. New York: Penguin Books.

Rittel, Horst, and Melvin Webber. 1973. Dilemmas in a General Theory of Planning. *Policy Sciences* 4(2):155–69.

Rugg, Robert D. 1992. A Feature-based Planning Support System. *Computers, Environment and Urban Systems* 16:219–26.

Scholten, H. J., and P. Padding. 1990. Working with Geographic Information Systems in a Policy Environment. *Environment and Planning B: Planning and Design* 17:405–16.

Schuur, J. 1994. Analysis and Design in Computer-aided Physical Planning. *Environment and Planning B: Planning and Design* 21:97–108.

Shiffer, Michael J. 1992. Towards a Collaborative Planning System. *Environment and Planning B: Planning and Design* 19:709–22.

Sprague, R. H., and E. D. Carlson. 1982. *Building Effective Decision Support Systems*. Englewood Cliffs, NJ: Prentice–Hall.

———, and H. J. Watson. 1986. *Decision Support Systems: Putting Theory into Practice*. Englewood Cliffs, NJ: Prentice–Hall.

Strauch, R. E. 1974. *A Critical Assessment of Quantitative Methodology as a Political Analysis Tool*. Santa Monica, CA: Rand.

Sui, Daniel Z. 1994. GIS and Urban Studies: Positivism, Post-positivism, and Beyond. *Urban Geography* 15(3):258–78.

Taylor, Michael A. P., 1991. Traffic Planning by a "Desktop Expert." *Computers, Environment and Urban Systems* 15:165–77.

Webster, C. J. 1993. GIS and the Scientific Inputs to Urban Planning. Part 1: Description. *Environment and Planning, B: Planning and Design* 20(6):709–28.

———. 1994. GIS and the Scientific Inputs to Urban Planning. Part 2: Prediction and Prescription. *Environment and Planning, B: Planning and Design* 21(2):145–57.

Werle, James W. 1984. Problems in Automating Traditional Land Records Data. *Computers, Environment and Urban Systems* 9:199–202.

Wiggins, Lyna L. 1993. Diffusion and Use of Geographic Information System in Public Sector Agencies in the United States. Les Worral, ed. *Spatial Analysis and Spatial Policy Using Geographic Information Systems*. London: Belhaven Press.

———, and Stephen P. French. California Planning Agency Experiences with Automated Mapping and Geographic Information Systems. *Environment and Planning, B: Planning and Design* 17(1990): 441–50.

Worrall, L. 1987. Population Information Systems and the Analysis of Urban Change. *Town Planning Review* 58:411–26.

Paper 2 Locational Models, Geographic Information, and Planning Support Systems

BRITTON HARRIS

EMERITUS PROFESSOR OF CITY AND REGIONAL PLANNING

UNIVERSITY OF PENNSYLVANIA, PHILADELPHIA

MICHAEL BATTY

DIRECTOR, CENTRE FOR ADVANCED SPATIAL ANALYSIS

UNIVERSITY COLLEGE LONDON

ABSTRACT Geographic information systems (GIS) are becoming widespread in management and planning, affecting the very organization and operation of the planning process itself. In this paper, we address the problems and potential of such systems, particularly in relation to the analytical, predictive, and prescriptive models on which strategic planning processes are based. Current GIS are not rooted in the sorts of functions which drive these processes, and here we will identify the difficulties and possibilities for developing more appropriate GIS which are sensitive to the simulation, optimization, and design activities which define spatial planning. To this end, we will describe the development of planning support systems (PSS) in which a wide array of data, information, and knowledge might be structured, and within which GIS development must take place. We will identify the sorts of urban system and locational models which characterize strategic planning and whose data demands might be accommodated using GIS. Our critique of GIS is positive and constructive in that we are concerned to embed GIS in planning processes in the most appropriate way. In conclusion, we will identify a series of requirements which PSS must meet.

INTRODUCTION

"Information . . . ," says Theodore Roszak (1986), ". . . is an idea whose time has come," and nowhere is this more evident than in the development of GIS in planning and management. GIS technology seems to be invading all corners of the planning environment, despite the often dubious nature of such systems in meeting the requirements of the planning task. This paper will address what we consider to be the most important problem involving the response which planning must give to the development of GIS. It rests on the need to develop appropriate frameworks in which GIS can be used sensitively and accurately, and the need to see GIS as part of a wider system of methods in an environment which we call a planning support system. This paper will attempt to articulate the nature of the problem of developing such a system, and will pose the critical requirements which such a system must meet if it is to be truly integrative (i.e., linking GIS and related information systems technologies to the wide range of computer analysis, modeling, and design techniques which have been developed during the last thirty years).

At the outset, we must be clear about the domain of planning we are addressing. In essence, our ideas for GIS and PSS are restricted in scope to planning rather than management, although we are well aware that much GIS technology has been developed for the latter. The specific problems we see relate to the fact that GIS has been developed with few task domains in mind, and in this context relate to both management and planning. We will define *planning* as the premeditation of action, in contrast to *management,* which we see as the direct control of action. Decision making considers the conclusions of planning, and translates them into norms and instructions which govern the management process. It is thus evident that management requires current knowledge of the state of the social or physical system in and on which it is acting. Such current knowledge is based directly on current data, organized in an information system. But planning, too, requires such systems, and in practice these may be one and the same—although their use and function might be very different. In this paper, we will restrict our ideas to planning which we sometimes call strategic or spatial planning. This restriction does not mean that we have no interest in planning as management, but simply that we need to limit our concern to that type of planning for which computation involving locational models has been developed during the last half century.

Spatial planning offers a substantial contrast to management. The concerns of planning are far more long-term. A major consideration of planning is the avoidance of unintended consequences while pursuing intended goals. Both intended and unintended consequences arise out of the propagation of effects throughout the system for which planning has been undertaken, over time, space, and function. In order to assess these consequences, planning needs methods for making conditional predictions based on alternative hypothetical decisions. Both the research establishing the capability to make such predictions, and the mechanisms by which scores of predictions can be made and examined, call for extensive computational resources and sophisticated simulation modeling. While this process involves geographic organization of the data, and deals with spatial relations, it cannot cope with constant shifts of geographic definitions and concepts. It operates far more effectively with a single predefined area system, or a carefully planned and partially hierarchical system in which computation at different scales with aggregation and disaggregation are possible for well-defined purposes.

The planning processes we are concerned with here are intended to answer very general "what-if" or hypothetical questions, and by changing the hypotheses and sifting the results, to arrive at recommendations for many coordinated aspects of future development. Some types of GIS have claims made about their ability to answer similar questions, but on examination, the support for these claims proves disappointing. Most what-if questions which GIS can deal with involve physical map representations. They do not deal with large-scale simulation and the effects of interaction at a distance whose models involving these concepts require very extensive computations. Most GIS, in fact, turn out to be directed to very different problems. These views now require more specific development, which we approach through a discussion of the broad character of a possible planning support system for spatial planning and decision making.

In a nutshell, our view is that GIS, properly considered, are defined in a way which provides very important types of support and control to many other systems and many activities, but that they are sufficiently limited by their intrinsic nature to fail if they are used as the main tools of analysis in planning. They support the organization of information in certain ways, but not necessarily in ways which then support every type of knowledge or intelligence. A profession like planning may unduly limit itself if it accepts the idea that GIS can discharge all or most planning tasks; even analytical geographic research may find itself limited in scope if it relies solely on GIS. Conversely, the designers of GIS should avoid the presumption that their systems are a universal panacea for problems of spatial data management, analysis, and planning. Not only is this presumption unfriendly to the neighboring disciplines in which GIS are used, but any ultimate failure of GIS to solve all problems could react against their acceptance for problems in which they perform well.

It must be said that to a large extent this potential difficulty arises out of the attitudes of commercial vendors of GIS software more often than out of those disciplines of geography and computer science from which such generic ideas have originated. All of these problems flow quite naturally out of the basic orientation and the corresponding strengths of GIS. The best of these systems maintain an attitude of strict responsibility toward the accurate maintenance and manipulation of geographic information, in digital and computable forms. Systems which do this well may be compromised for other uses by the intense demand for heavy computation which this approach imposes. The cumbersome nature of GIS in approaching other computational tasks can give GIS a bad name. Yet an effort to simplify the treatment of geography as the basis for an operational system which supports another approach, can weaken the treatment of geographical and topological relations. If this is done under the name of GIS, it too engenders disrepute, limiting its impact and generating disillusion with computation as an approach to planning.

This issue can be stated more exactly. The greatest strength of GIS is in creating new information and combining diverse sources of geographic data (both purely geographic and comprised of geographic attributes) through the process of overlays; this requires large geographic files and extensive processing. The other processes which use geographic data generally work with fixed definitions of area systems and devote their computational efforts to statistical computations, managerial use of large data files, and simulation. The processes which transform information into statistics and simulation are completely different from the processes which transform geographic data on maps or their computer representation. For GIS, the geography of space comprises the foreground, while for other processes it should be in the background, but correctly represented and well controlled. Both approaches may meet again when results are presented and maps need to be drawn.

These bald introductory remarks run ahead of our argument. We will therefore begin to develop our position from a somewhat different vantage point. First we will sketch out the kind of computer environment or landscape in which GIS is being developed and in which contemporary planning must now operate. To this end, we will describe the evolution of the current generation of GIS and related systems with a view to explaining their role in planning, while at the same time indicating the types of planning process in which such systems might be useful. We will then outline the types of system theory and models, formal and informal, which planners use to help in articulating and analyzing problems, forecasting outcomes, and designing solutions. These models and the substantive theory from which they are derived generate strong requirements for data which is informative in terms of the characteristics of the systems they address, and in this context, we have already anticipated that GIS used in relation to such models can be fairly limited in their support for planning.

We will then deal with the problems posed by the planning process itself, the ways in which planning is based on goals and objectives which are optimized (at least in part) through designs, and the types of information required to serve and advance such processes. If current GIS fall short of the requirements of urban system models, they barely consider the much wider set of requirements posed by the planning process. The sorts of data required in representing goals and objectives, costs and benefits, and the ways in which such data is transformed by the planning process, hardly exist in GIS, and thus an important conclusion from our argument will involve requirements for both information systems and the wider planning support system in which GIS can be embedded. Finally we will define a number of key requirements for planning support and will conclude by suggesting how such systems might be designed.

THE NEW LANDSCAPE OF INFORMATION

In reviewing the computerization of society over the last half century, there is a strong tendency to emphasize the development of hardware and software and to neglect the increasing volume of raw and processed data which society has at its disposal. Computers have obviously brought in their wake a dramatic increase in data, although we know little about the general form of such data and its impact on everyday life. It is clearly easier to chart the development of hardware along the path of miniaturization and software along the path from numerical coding to visual abstraction than it is to measure and classify the way data on every aspect of society has increased and diversified. Yet even casual reflection suggests that this growth has been as haphazard as it has been dramatic, while its impact is increasingly opaque.

A general approach to handling data, however, is ever more urgent as we are about to cross a threshold in which computers and data banks are connecting up through burgeoning networks of communication. Yet even the impacts of the most general and pervasive of data sources—such as those found, for example, in personal finance and credit—are difficult to gauge, and there is little knowledge concerning the inconsistencies, problems of coordination, and accuracy and bias of the data that is being assembled. The landscape of information which this data supports is one which is barely charted, rapidly changing, and highly uneven. From the viewpoint of science, it is easy to sense but hard to measure how data is changing the way we think, theorize, and generate new ideas. Rapid changes in the intellectual landscape are difficult to evaluate, and only when the dust settles will it become clear whether the many new ideas which the computer revolution is spawning are truly new. At present it is hard to know when, if ever, this era of rapid change will stabilize. Moreover, a central problem which we will continue to face is the mismatch between the types of data which are being collected and processed and the data which we require for particular intellectual tasks. One aim of this paper is to explore this dilemma with respect to the various information systems and their data which are currently being developed for spatial decision making in general and urban and regional planning in particular.

This new landscape is characterized by the development of information systems, the best specified of which are those which deal with recording, processing, and communicating spatial data. These systems are referred to generically as geographic information systems, although this term covers a wide variety of software systems dealing with data at different spatial scales, over different time spans, and with different conceptions of use in mind. At the outset we must distinguish such generic systems from actual systems which are being developed and applied to planning, and in this paper we will concentrate on generic systems appropriate to the various activities and functions of planning. GIS deal with two general categories of data.

First there is data which characterizes the intrinsic structure of the spatial system in question; this relates to the geometric and topological structure of space. Such data is represented in two-dimensional digital form, sometimes three. Related to this is attribute data of two types: data describing the physical features of geographic space, and socioeconomic data pertaining to various elements of space and their aggregation. In fact, most systems developed to date are strongly oriented towards the representation of space using digital data and many of their functions involve the manipulation of space. The analysis of socioeconomic attributes is based on spatial manipulations, such analysis often being entirely concerned with the display of data. The origins of GIS in computer mapping are thus revealed and their use for mapping is still one of their main tasks. Here we will explore the problems posed by using such systems in planning where the functions required are somewhat different from those which characterize the current generation of GIS.

It is tempting to compare the growth of GIS with the development of word processing a decade or so ago, for undoubtedly the 1990s was a period when graphics or picture processing became widespread. But GIS are somewhat more specialized in focus despite the fact that they are being applied to a wide variety of professional tasks. At the finest scale, these systems merge into those developed for computer-aided design and drafting, while at larger scales, they relate to remote sensing. Across many scales, various types of image processing are being developed to complement their use. Nevertheless, the dramatic growth in the use of such systems is still surprising in the face of their simplistic nature. In fact, it is likely that because such functions are so elemental in their emphasis on the representation of maps, they enjoy widespread popularity; but this poses major problems for application areas such as urban planning, where such systems are required to interface with complex models set in sophisticated problem-solving, design, and decision-making processes. Parker (quoted in Forrest 1990) calls GIS ". . . a chameleon technology . . . ," suggesting that its power depends upon the technology being so adaptable. But this generality is being secured at the expense of tailoring such systems to specific functions, and it rests on the questionable assumption that all practical contexts which make use of these techniques have similar requirements with respect to spatial data.

There is another issue here and this involves the difference between data and information. Martin Shubik (1979) cogently remarked ". . . ours is a data-rich but information-poor society." In fact, it is the functions to which information systems are put which transform data into information, and thus the extent to which such systems inform relates to the functions which they enable. GIS are based on elaborate functionality which relates to their manipulation of spatial geometry and topology; many of their processing operations involve filtering, generalizing, overlaying, and aggregating points, lines, and areas which represent space. This in itself is informative with respect to how space can be structured, but it is rarely backed up by any substantive model of the system of interest or the problem in question. When socioeconomic attributes are added to such systems, the physical geometry of spatial representation drives the way such attributes are processed and displayed. It could thus be argued that from the point of view of the design of new systems which resolve or alleviate current problems, such information systems are of less use than are those more specific systems in which the nature of the problem and the way it is to be addressed form the rationale for spatial representation.

Information systems for planning must be constructed with at least three interrelated bodies of theory in mind: theories of computation; social and functional theories of the systems being planned; and the theory of planning (Harris 1991a). To this we should add a fourth based on the theory of spatial representation or description. In general, we will suggest that these four approaches to the spatial world determine the framework which we are calling planning support systems. We will argue in this paper that existing GIS and related information systems fall far short of the requirements for such planning support (Harris 1989). PSS are somewhat broader than those decision-support systems which exist in management, while they are variously referred to as spatial decision-support systems (Densham 1991), creativity-support systems (Manheim 1986) and suchlike. Most contemporary GIS have been developed with theories of spatial representation and of computing or processing in mind, but there are few which have sought to develop their functionality with substantive systems and their design or planning in mind. In this sense, then, the current generation of GIS are likely to be unsuited to many planning tasks. This is not a criticism of GIS per se, but simply a statement of their limitations. One goal of this paper is to develop a critique of present systems and to suggest how they might be improved, adapted, and rebuilt to the tasks and requirements of contemporary planning. We will begin with a description of how GIS has evolved.

THE EVOLUTION OF GEOGRAPHIC INFORMATION SYSTEMS

In the 1950s and 1960s, the paradigm which most influenced the development of urban planning was based on an implicit general systems theory. Cities and regions were considered to be complex systems whose structure could be understood in terms of hierarchies of subsystems, spatial or otherwise, embedded within dynamic frameworks whose equilibrium properties were assumed to be quite tractable. Planning such systems was seen to be a matter of optimizing some general systems property such as utility or welfare, and the ideal type of system model embodied such optimization in terms of system behavior (Harris 1959). In cases where such optimization was clearly not systemwide, planning was seen as akin to introducing some control mechanism into the system of interest. This characterization was clearly an "ideal type" in that nowhere did any real city or regional system closely approximate this type of functioning. In fact, this view of system models merely pointed the direction towards optimization; although systems could be developed in terms of optimality, such models were seen as simply informing the wider and more significant process of planning, which in turn existed as part of a still wider political reality.

In this context, then, planning embraced systems models, and these models were, in turn, regarded as embracing the information systems useful in making them operational. The relationships between information, model, and planning, however, were structured in a sequence beginning with description and understanding, continuing through the survey and information systems design, in turn being enhanced through system modeling, and then moving into a design phase in which alternative plans were generated and evaluated. The two-phase nature of this process was, and continues to be, referred to variously as "analysis–synthesis," "problem–solution," "simulation–optimization" (Simon 1969). When this process was explored and applied in the context of land-use/transportation planning some three or more decades ago, it was predicated on the basis of a rational technocracy in which the requisite data for planning could be obtained, system models producing informed understanding based on this data developed, and best plans selected unambiguously from a wide range of relevant alternatives (Batty 1979).

The ensuing reality was somewhat different. The initial enthusiasm for computerized modeling and planning was quickly tempered by the difficulties of collecting the relevant data, by the sheer extensiveness of the task in terms of data representation, and by the difficulty of developing appropriate system models (Brewer 1973; Lee 1973). Problems pertaining to the selection of the best plan also plagued the process, but it was the shift in the perspectives of the planners and decision makers which most undermined these developments. The shift from planning as a process of optimizing spatial location in terms of limited efficiency to one based on broader-based issues of equity, as well as the increase in uncertainty posed by global crises of energy and economy, increased skepticism concerning its use. During the 1970s, when this style of planning became less fashionable, the intellectual high ground came to be dominated not by planning theory but by questions of ideology and social theory. During the last twenty years, however, the practice of planning has become ever more pragmatic as it has attempted to respond to and embrace new fads and fashions (Batty 1989).

It is behind this cloak of pragmatism that geographic information systems have developed. The computer revolution, which began to make itself widely felt in a personal context with the development of the microcomputer from the mid-1970s, was clearly essential for advances in graphics which enabled computer mapping to become routine. Once such mapping became possible, then its demand became widespread. In parallel, the increase in spatial data—spurred on by the existence of a technology to support it—and the ever-increasing bureaucratic needs of a complex society created an enormous demand for appropriate information systems. In particular, the storage and processing of local administrative and population census data, and the increasing availability of digital data from agencies dealing with map production, were instrumental in the development of GIS.

As planning became more pragmatic and managerial, the demand for data systems relating to facility location and scheduling, to resource management and conservation, to property and tax registration and so on increased the need for GIS (Densham and Rushton 1988). In short, such systems developed in response to all these trends and needs. GIS were developed in as simple a form as possible so that they could be adapted to a wide variety of basic tasks from computer mapping to simple data classification, across a range of scales and for diverse system types. For example, Forrest (1990) lists over sixty distinct systems and problem areas to which such GIS might be applied, with examples as diverse as navigation and political redistricting. Furthermore, such systems have acquired more and more the characteristics of toolkits in that their design embodied enough flexibility to accommodate a wide range of problem types (Dangermond 1990).

Given the lack of any strong intellectual framework other than cartography within which GIS has been developed, and given the absence of strong institutional constraints, it is easy to understand how developers and vendors of GIS have continually broadened the appeal of their product as a simple general-purpose instrument. This clearly runs counter to the development of task-specific applications, although the existence of a narrow but varied set of applications has meant that the developers have agreed upon standardized ways of inputting and outputting data as well as upon conventions for relational data representation and display. Thus the key issues in the development of GIS have not been on the extension of such systems to task-specific functions but upon improving the representation of spatial data. For example, there has been wide discussion of cartographic analysis within such systems concerning the development of optimal methods and algorithms for spatial search. The representation of spatial data in raster or vector form has conditioned the development of different systems, although more recently, methods for moving between the two forms are being extended to most systems. The question of scale of representation, however, has not been the subject of much analysis to date, although there is significant research in progress (Buttenfield and McMaster 1991).

It is often assumed that a GIS should equally be able to represent data at site-specific scales of the cadastre, to regional scales and above, where thematic mapping is of the essence. At even higher scales, map projections are essential components of GIS, and in many such contexts, the origin of the data from remotely positioned sensors guides their construction and use. Most systems have not been developed with time series data in mind; in fact, this same bias exists in the development of system models in the strategic planning process. The sorts of GIS which we are alluding to here have some difficulty in being adapted to routine problems where data is being continually updated and where real-time access, or at least frequent access, is required. In these domains, for example in land-use zoning control, in emergency service response, in traffic management, and so on, special-purpose information systems combining the functionality requisite for control of the system in question have been designed. Finally, although state-of-the-art GIS are being evolved to embrace raster and vector, network and area representations, as well as sophisticated and general ways of importing and exporting raw and processed spatial data, most systems are oriented towards atemporal spatial problems, or at best, problems in which data is recorded as snapshots in time.

Recently the emphasis in GIS has been upon developing stronger relationships to other widely available software through input and output standardization, and there is now some evidence that some systems embrace more specific functionalities such as those required in land-use planning (Batty 1992). For example, ArcInfo is being extended to contain explicit spatial interaction modeling, while systems such as GIS Plus and TRANSCAD have been designed from scratch with transportation planning in mind. There is both a convergence and divergence occurring. A standardized set of basic GIS operations on digital data together with basic display facilities now characterize all state-of-the-art GIS, while different systems are clearly being developed for specific tasks with regard to the type of planning, problem solving, design, or control associated with the activity in question.

The functionality of the present generation of GIS is thus based on comparatively low-level processing operations which pertain to spatial geometry. As yet there are few high-level functions relating to particular system models and planning tasks embodied in such technologies, although these are being added to several systems at present (Birkin et al. 1990). Where GIS are used in planning, their use in relation to particular stages of the planning process is informal in that they are seen as being useful and efficient storage and display media for spatial data (Huxhold 1991). The range of spatial analytic functions useful for preliminary analysis of data is also fairly limited in such systems, these having to be added through fairly tortuous yet ingenious system macros (Ding and Fotheringham 1992). When it comes to using such systems as a basis for spatial modeling, optimization, or design, their use is informal at best, depending upon the skills of the user in forging a link between the GIS in question and other standardized as well as customized software (Densham 1991).

We can thus conclude that with respect to the planning process and the use of appropriate system models for description, analysis, prediction, and prescription, the current generation of GIS hardly approaches the kinds of functions which planning requires. Many systems, however, do have an important place in more routine, managerial types of planning which do not necessarily require sophisticated functionality. But the kind of planning support system we are alluding to here requires analytical and design functions which incorporate goals, objectives, costs, and benefits. Information generated through the process itself, as issues become better defined and as new data is generated through learning, must also be integrated. For GIS to be truly informative, they must be consistent and strongly linked to problem definition and the system models used to inform the overall planning process. To this end, we will now describe some of the functions of planning support which should ideally be embodied in relevant information systems before we continue with identifying the data and information requirements of relevant locational models.

THE FUNCTIONS OF PLANNING SUPPORT

Planning support systems form a framework in which three sets of ideas and functions are combined. Clearly the tasks which comprise the planning process are part of the structure to be supported by various models or conceptions of the system of interest and the problems which planning aims to resolve. This process generates its own information about the problem and the way it is likely to be alleviated, solved, or resolved. A second variety of information is associated with the system models which are employed to inform the planning process through analysis, prediction, and prescription. Such models are informative insofar as they are able to capture the essential workings of the system in question. A third basis involves systems which are used to transform basic data into information which in turn provides the driving force for modeling and design. Information which is produced during the planning process alters the very process itself and thus must be communicated back to the data systems and models responsible for its generation in the first place. In this sense, information is continually created, destroyed, and transformed as the process proceeds and as the planner cycles purposively and intelligently through its various stages, generating the knowledge necessary for informative planning (Batty 1990).

As we have been at pains to point out, data is not information, and data systems are but the first step in a convoluted chain of transformations which govern the way basic problems are defined and described, goals and objectives for their solution specified, plans and policies generated and evaluated, and the best set of such plans ultimately chosen and implemented. Moreover, the problems which drive the planning process can pertain to many domains, each with different conceptual and operational models in mind and each giving rise to multifarious data requirements. Even in the comparatively narrow domain of urban and regional planning, the types of problems defined can vary widely and there is no basic consensus about the best or most relevant theories and models which define the system of interest. Consequently, data requirements for seemingly similar planning problems can differ radically. Moreover, the plans and policies involved can differ to the same degree. Based on the view that there is never likely to be a completely consistent and general theory or model which encapsulates all the elements of the problem in question, practical planning is likely to embody many styles, many models and their theories, and consequently many differing, sometimes contradictory, sometimes complementary data systems. In short, the notion that there will be a plurality of information systems, models, and planning processes relevant to any single problem is the reality we have to work with (Couclelis 1991).

Nor is information timeless in its definition and use. The problem which motivates the need for planning will be based on some perceived evolution of the system in question, on some temporal divergence between the real and the ideal. Theories and models which are based on substantive ideas concerning the functioning of socioeconomic systems are usually dynamic in some sense and pertain to the process by which the past has evolved to the present. Data informing this evolution is likely to be important. In contrast, planning is about creating ideas and plans which will inform the future. This type of data is speculative and ill-defined, yet it exists throughout the planning process, being created through the use of system models in prediction and prescription.

Information systems, however, generally contain data which pertains to the present. Such data defines the instant in time at which the problem is conceptualized and planning begins, and in this sense is what Harris (1991b) has called the ". . . knife edge between that past and the events still to come . . ." Most GIS, while being highly sophisticated in terms of spatial data, are somewhat crude in their handling of temporal data. This is a bias which emerges from a lack of concern for the wider theoretical and substantive context of the problems and systems in question to which such GIS are being applied. Moreover, appropriate information systems for planning are by no means exclusively spatial in focus. The data required in planning is always a mix of the spatial, aspatial, and nonspatial, a blend of the qualitative and the quantitative, covering a wide range of physical, social, and economic attributes, many of which are not comparable with one another. Moreover, as we have implied, the planning process generates its own data and information about the future which is as significant as data pertaining to the past and the present. GIS are not well adapted to such conceptions, thus implying that these systems can at best only provide useful information with respect to the somewhat narrower aspects of typical planning problems.

The multifarious functions of a planning support system, therefore, define the data which is required, and the way these functions are used determine the channels through which this data is transformed into information. We can interpret information as forming the glue which binds the individual stages of the planning process together. This process can thus be considered to be based upon flows of information which define the purpose of the planning task, and the plan can be seen as the ultimate form of information in its transition from data concerning the problem to that concerning the solution (Le Clercq 1990). Data and system models, as well as procedures which enable the design of solutions to planning problems through plans, thus establish the need for information systems which deal not simply with past and present data but with data which emerges from the planning process itself; this data may be transformations of the original data, collections and organizations of new data whose demand is a result of the process, data which pertains to the future of the systems of interest through prediction and prescription, as well as data which is generated by learning about the problem and by adapting the process to the problem in hand. GIS rarely meet the challenges posed by such diverse requirements, although they still remain a critical part of the planning process and the development of system models which are based on their data.

**LOCATIONAL MODELS
AS A BASIS FOR
PLANNING SUPPORT**

Typical system models which support the urban planning process are derived from a wide range of disciplinary and methodological perspectives. All disciplines have an impact on the study of human systems but here we will mainly focus on those which treat behavior in terms of social and economic characteristics, consistent with the goals of spatial planning. In our treatment of such systems, the concept of a well-developed system structure which can be organized in terms of hierarchies and networks of subsystems, together with system behavior which is equilibrating in some sense, will be central. The dynamic evolution of such systems is usually studied in terms of a balance between various forces: in economics, demand and supply; in ecology, predator and prey; and so on. Here we will deal with models in which such balance is assumed to be the usual condition of the system or at least the state towards which such systems are evolving (Simon 1969).

Location models useful to urban and regional planning emerge from the two traditions of economics, macro and micro, although the richest of such models are those based on human spatial behavior at the micro level; this is where we will begin. The notion of cities as a system of markets in which land is the commodity and rent indicative of the price mechanism is well established in location theory, and the richest such models attempt to simulate the way in which such a spatial equilibrium emerges (Anas 1987). Congestion in the transport systems and wages in the labor market can also be regarded as equilibrating forces. In these models, which now form the basis of most housing market and travel demand models, the demand for land and housing by consumers and producers and its supply by developers is resolved through the price mechanism in which incomes and transportation costs are related to utilities and profits. In this sense, most urban economic models follow the traditions of microeconomics in which consumers maximize utility and producers maximize profit. Thus in a very special sense, these models might be regarded as optimizing and the competitive equilibrium which is ultimately established can usually be interpreted in terms of welfare or consumer surplus. It is assumed that planning enters these systems through mechanisms which resolve various types of market failure where some collective welfare cannot be optimized by the market itself. However, it is fair to say that in the use of these types of model in planning, specific welfare maximization through planning is not normally embedded within the formal mechanism of the models themselves. In short, these models are not usually taken as the formal basis for the optimization. Like most models in planning, they are used to describe, analyze, predict, and evaluate, but not to prescribe.

A well-developed body of theory has been developed in these domains over the last thirty years. Urban economics and travel demand modeling represent the most completely worked out of these domains, although many operational urban models pay some lip service to conceptions of the market. In housing markets, the models developed in the Alonso–Beckmann tradition attempt to explain residential location in terms of utility maximizing, the best developed operational developments being in the work of Anas (1982). Models of retail location too have been well developed in terms of their embedding into dynamic frameworks in which demand and supply are balanced; several operational versions of such models now exist to inform decision makers as to the most appropriate locations for new and expanded retail centers (Harris and Wilson 1978; Fotheringham and O'Kelly 1989). In modeling travel demand, the discrete choice approach in which travelers optimize their utility but randomly over a range of possible values has been well developed since the mid-1970s (Ben Akiva and Lerman 1985), and there are several attempts to link such models to those which were derived more pragmatically as gravitational analogues in a statistical optimizing framework (Wilson et al. 1981). Recently there has been considerable interest in the development of equilibrium travel demand/supply capacity models in which balance can be achieved consistently over trip generation and distribution, modal choice, and route assignment. There have also been attempts to synthesize such models through various optimization schemes which can be regarded as close to one another; for example, through utility, welfare, entropy, likelihood, and related schemes of maximization (Anas 1983).

All these models generate data demands which can be quite formidable in terms of data collection. Spatial interaction in the form of flows between locations relevant to the housing market, the workplace, the retail sector, and other related services are crucial. Incomes, rent levels, and related financial data such as travel costs, fares, derived measures of the value of time, and so on, may be required. This type of data is difficult although not impossible to obtain, and is sometimes provided indirectly through various proxies. But it is rare to see a GIS which handles such data—especially data on interactions and flows. Furthermore, in the development of microeconomic models, data on various types of consumer and producer preferences is important.

The data structures and estimation techniques required in their interpretation are well beyond the scope of any current GIS, for most commercial systems emphasize geometric and physical data rather than data which characterizes some process-based theme.

Data pertaining to the way equilibrium in various land markets is achieved is also useful, implying that any such data scheme would be at least quasi-dynamic in form. As we have already noted, GIS are not well adapted to dealing with temporal data. These types of model also require data which relates activities such as counts of population and employment of various types to counts of physical data such as housing, and to economic data such as incomes and rents. In other words, these models require data from different sources which must be dimensionally consistent—but the whole question of developing GIS with functions which ensure consistency over different data types has hardly been broached. From what we have already said in previous sections, the current generation of GIS do not contain functions which would enable the sorts of model we are describing here to be estimated and used in prediction or prescription. In fact, the only way at present to use GIS to support such modeling would be to transfer relevant input and output of data between such systems and models, and perhaps to use the systems to check data for consistency, to derive new variables for use in modeling, and of course to provide useful media for graphical communication through visualization.

We will continue here to dwell on models of urban subsystems and then indicate how more comprehensive models might impact on GIS. Demographic models are well developed in planning in terms of the natural processes of aging but have not been developed with any rigor in a spatial context. Macroeconomic models of the urban and regional system based on input–output structures with functional and spatial linkages form the basis of the economic subsystem in locational modeling, while a variety of lesser techniques based on locational quotients, shift–share representations, and suchlike pervade the development of urban economic analysis in a practical context. The major problem with such models is that they have been developed separately from the tradition of spatial models and thus do not emphasize interaction or market clearing.

There has in fact been substantial speculation on the ways in which these demo-economic sector models might be integrated with location models of housing, transport, and retail markets, although progress in linking such systems functionally has been slow; links which do exist are pragmatically structured (de la Barra 1989; Batey and Madden 1982; Wegener 1982). The data requirements of such models, too, are not those that are obviously amenable to representation in a GIS, because both demographic and economic models are only implicitly spatial: their categorizations are across age cohorts, occupations, and industry types, and are not usually disaggregated to the physical areas which form the basis of GIS. Where space is considered explicitly in demographic models, it is in terms of migration defining temporal–spatial flows which, as we have seen, is data difficult to handle anyway in the current generation of GIS.

Since the 1960s, there have been many attempts at planning to build and apply more general urban model structures which couple various partial system models together. We have already noted the idea of integrated models in which demographic and economic coupling provides the basis for partial spatial modeling, although earlier and more general attempts in which economic and demographic structures are used to weave the residential, workplace, and retailing subsystems together in functional terms have been widely applied as developments of Lowry's (1964) original Pittsburgh model (Batty 1976; Putman 1983, 1992). These types of model structure have been extended to deal with transportation modeling, too (Webster et al. 1988); various dynamic extensions to such models also exist (Mackett 1983). Recently there have been several attempts to integrate demographic, economic, travel demand, housing market, and spatial interaction models within more general model structures, which in turn have been embedded within dynamic frameworks (Bertuglia, Leonardi, and Wilson 1990).

The data requirements of these models can be formidable, but the problems of linking them to GIS are no different from those already indicated. GIS find it difficult to deal with flow and temporal data, and consequently such models rarely have been linked to such systems. However, the real problem of extending GIS to embrace the functionality required in such modeling relates to the fact that current GIS have not been designed with any iterative capabilities in mind when it comes to extending their functions to deal with equation solving and estimation. Invariably, urban models which seek to model some equilibrium must be solved iteratively, the iterations being some analogue of the way markets clear, of the time involved in moving toward a steady state, or simply of the need to solve many simultaneous nonlinear equations. The idea that GIS might be constructed around such processes has barely been considered to date (Couclelis 1991).

In fact, there is considerable research and development work going on at present that will lead to much better interfaces between GIS and other statistical software and model-based computation. Using macros and other higher level programming structures, it is now possible to begin to develop links between non-GIS software based on standard packages or purpose-built code and GIS itself. Using GIS as a spatial data store and display engine is becoming increasingly possible as the vendors introduce ever more flexibility into their products. Furthermore, there are GIS appearing which are being built around model-based methods, specifically land-use and transportation models, while it is ever more likely that users of GIS will not be content to simply use their GIS for the stated functions—which, as we have implied, are quite limited for planning. The National Center for Geographic Information and Analysis, for example, has a research initiative which is concerned with developing and extending GIS in various ways which lead to computational models better grounded in the sorts of theories relevant to geographers and planners (Fotheringham and Rogerson 1992).

In the sequel, we will begin to describe some of the difficulties of using optimization models in relation to GIS. However, it is worth noting that GIS are quite well adapted to combining variables in spatial form, and one of their main functions is in overlay analysis. The sorts of implicit model which lie behind such operations are somewhat rudimentary, although "overlaying" with a view to finding map areas which meet given spatial constraints and which seek areas where the potential or utility for development is greatest, is a process akin to formal optimization. Other developments in which location–allocation models might be embedded or linked to GIS are being actively explored at present in much the same manner that transportation models are being linked to such systems (Densham 1991). In one sense, it is easier to extend GIS structures to encompass optimization modeling than more complex predictive system modeling which draws from substantive discipline areas. However, in general, linking GIS to system models of all kinds is an activity which has hardly begun, with few urban models taking on the vestiges of GIS and vice versa. Nevertheless, this is an active area of research where there is likely to be some considerable progress over the next decade.

We need to note the relationships between GIS and other models based on ecology and energy which are relevant to urban and regional planning. These models are based more on the functioning of non-manmade systems than on social systems, although there is an essential interaction between both types which is always problematic. In fact, GIS are better adapted at the present time to dealing with models of physical than of socioeconomic systems; systems whose main representation is physical in form can be more easily represented in GIS than the nonphysical whose characteristic variables are often more abstract. For example, it is easier to see how systems whose data pertains to the surface of the earth, such as climate models, models of energy use and pollution, models of global warming, of environmental functioning, and so on can draw on the concepts of GIS—although some of the problems alluded to above, in terms of the substantive functioning of systems, influence their formal use in the context of GIS.

We have been dwelling on the problems of linking models to GIS with the emerging conclusion that such systems and models are not easily embedded within one another. In other words, extending the functionality of GIS to enable complex models to be a part of such systems does not seem like a useful development in other than the most specialized of applications. The implication is that where GIS is to be used to support modeling, such systems should be mainly based on using their representational and graphic capabilities to store, derive, and communicate data rather than extend their usage to modeling. In the same way, it appears that formal models should not attempt to be embedded or embellished with GIS-like functions but should use the power of GIS for purposes of communication and presentation. However, none of this preempts the possibility that new forms of GIS might emerge built around models rather than data. For example, it is easier to build urban models in spreadsheet than in GIS media, for such spreadsheets offer extensive functionality in one-to-one correspondence with their data storage capabilities. GIS-like spreadsheets might find a role in planning support as frameworks for formal modeling, along lines already developed using standard spreadsheets for urban models and related planning techniques (Brail 1987; Klosterman, Brail, and Bossard 1992).

THE REQUIREMENTS OF PLANNING SUPPORT SYSTEMS

Up to this point we have reviewed the growing capabilities for PSS and we have seen that methods are in place for recording, storing, and presenting geographic information from a variety of sources in a reliable, accurate, and usable form. We have shown that models are available which replicate the functioning and often the dynamic development of systems with multiple geographically distributed components and actors performing a variety of functions, pursuing a variety of ends, and obeying numerous social, physical, and biological laws. Finally, we have noted how in many cases the behavior of the actors or the analysis of possible actions leads to some sort of optimal performance or policies for parts of certain systems. This review demonstrates that most of the elements which are needed for a planning support system in urban and regional affairs are already at hand, but not yet in a fully integrated form. The use of appropriate data and computational schemes in GIS is a special weakness. It is our purpose in this section to define more exactly the desirable content and features of a planning support system, and to focus attention on the shortfalls in current practice.

There is obviously a substantial overlap between spatial planning, as it is undertaken in city and regional planning, and geography. Both disciplines (or professions) rest on the study and analysis of spatially distributed systems, and of their growth, development, and change. At the same time, planning goes further, in requiring the management of these systems and the anticipatory premeditation of action regarding them. These activities are akin to policy making, and the need for them arises in both public and private undertakings, in urban and rural settings, and in man-made and natural systems. With respect both to replicating system behavior and to anticipatory action, planning and geography simultaneously draw ideas from economics, although they are somewhat in conflict with it (Harris 1991b). The principal conflict, which we can but note here, arises over the claim of many economists that market forces alone (perhaps with some remedial legislation to tax, subsidize, or regulate such irregularities as externalities) can automatically drive behavior to appropriately optimal conclusions. If this were so, then planning would be largely irrelevant and economic geography in certain aspects redundant, because market forces would determine the shape of geographic development and the optimal allocation of resources. It could thus be claimed that a competitive equilibrium is both the best plan and the best explanation for human geographic distributions.

This view suffers from some obvious limitations. We have to assume that human and institutional behavior follows closely the description given in microeconomics. Spatial distributions and spatial separation call for a redefinition of equilibrium, as does the long-term permanence of investment in buildings, structures, and improvements to the land. Most important, however, is the many-sided situation in which public investment and spatial separation together lead to economies of agglomeration and of scale, large works are indivisible, reciprocal externalities cannot be disentangled, and both private production and public goods have large fixed costs so that marginal cost is below average cost. All of these situations lead to lumpiness, full or partial monopolies, and the possibility of multiple local equilibria in the allocation of resources and the development of locational patterns. Even if all possible economic measures have been taken to ensure that equilibrium states are locally optimal, multiple stable equilibria imply multiple optima.

The existence of multiple local equilibria has enormous consequences for the actuality and the theory of geographic location and spatial planning. Any given local optimum may be far from an optimum optimorum, so that a high level of benefit resulting from the play of market forces is either a matter of accident or a matter of planning, or both. Problems of prediction and economic justification which arise out of chaos in the environment (that is, the unpredictability of complex deterministic systems) are exacerbated by the possibility of catastrophes, or sudden discontinuities in development (Bertuglia, Leonardi, and Wilson 1990). These discontinuities arise, in a space of continuous responses to change, out of the folding of the response surface which corresponds with multiple optima. In computational terms, it is exactly this multiplicity of local optima which makes the problem of global optimization completely intractable. In this situation, there are two principal requirements for planning, which devolve onto any planning support system:

- First, since system optimization (which equates with the automatic generation of plans) is impossible, the search for good plans must be by way of an informed process of trial and error which generates alternatives and prepares them for testing. This is often called sketch planning.

- Second, planning and policy making need extensive tools for tracing out the consequences of alternatives, since otherwise there is no way to compare alternatives on the basis of their costs and benefits, and no way to look for means of improving or replacing alternatives.

These tools can now be provided in a computer-based environment, using models which simulate the development, performance, and equilibrium properties of hypothetical systems. However, present-day information systems do not permit us to trace these consequences far enough over time, space, or function.

In addition to these two basic requirements, there are others which are related to them, to the process of planning, and to the state of the art of computer simulation and information systems; we will list these as follows:

- We must be able to trace the effects of all possible measures which may be included in a plan, and their combinations.

- We must be able to reproduce all effects which may be of interest in evaluating the achievement of any desired objectives—not only efficiency and economic effectiveness, but equity, amenity, diversity, environmental protection, and many others.

- Simulations must encompass very large systems because planning must avoid unintended consequences, which are generated over space, time, and function in ways which escape narrowly focused evaluations.

The demands on geographic and related information systems are extensive and we can define these as follows:

- The geographic content of spatial decision making is essential, and must be stored in terms which are relevant to these decisions and the associated models—such as quantitative measures of interaction time and cost.

- Visually accessible and in some cases interactive displays of inputs and outputs are needed because visual effects and synoptic overviews of relationships are essential to planning.

Similar requirements extend to public information, public education, and public participation in the planning process; the information system must interrelate actively with simulation methods which are used to trace the effects of plans.

Planning support systems will operate in a changing environment, in which they will be put to many different uses, and in which experience should be rapidly accommodated in expanding and altering the capabilities of the system:

- A PSS should be designed to extend to the outer envelope of potential and feasible uses, from planning management through functional planning (such as transport, housing, retail trade, and environmental conservation), to comprehensive planning and zoning.

- A PSS should be especially cordial to the entering of new plans or modification of old ones, and at various levels of specificity, in the process of sketch planning.

The planner should be supported in experimental approaches not only in generating plans themselves but also in planning method, in the definition and measurement of the objectives of plans, and in the interpretation of behavior and the type and style of models to be used. Therefore,

- PSS should be available for public use, both as to methods and as to data.

- A PSS should accommodate research, allowing the introduction of new methods of simulation, new sources of data, new flows of work, and new measurement and presentation of outputs.

- The use of the systems should as far as possible be self-teaching.

- They should be adaptable to a wide variety of situations, levels of information, size and type of area being planned, and styles of planning.

And last but not least,

- The models and methods embodied in the PSS should be understandable to the user and, in Einstein's (1955) immortal phrase, be ". . . as simple as possible, but not more so."

**OPTIMIZATION AND
PLANNING SUPPORT
SYSTEMS**

It is possible, but not perhaps appropriate here, to turn all of the fore-going into a set of specifications for producing a PSS. This is an act of research design in which we are interested, but for which we see the importance of numerous centers of design and innovation. Having said all this, we may still turn our attention to a few issues which will need to be debated, tested, and constantly reviewed in initial designs and their later revisions, and which our own experience has called forcibly to our attention. An issue regarding the employment of economic principles in modeling which is often of major importance is the representation of the behavior of people, households, and firms. Partly this issue turns on the concept of "economic man" and the importance of non-economic motivations, and partly it turns on the uniformity or diversity of behavior. These issues are linked. While economic forces are important, they may not be wholly determinative of behavior; and while there is much uniformity in modern life (and indeed in all social affairs), there is some diversity which may not be economically explainable. The paradigm of free enterprise itself contradicts the rules of microeconomics and their drive toward uniformity. We believe for our purposes in the use of discrete choice or gravity models to represent this diversity, but we recognize that it can be reproduced by devices like the application of linear programming to a succession of choice situations (Anas 1983; Wilson et al. 1981).

Our insistence on a flexible and even skeptical attitude toward economic doctrine is not to be taken too far. We recognize the very great importance of the economic consequences of plans both for the public polity and for the beneficiaries of plans. Indeed, we regard market measurements of plan performance, when they can be made available, as being of very great value. At the same time we continue to recognize the public (and private) importance of non-economic bases for decision, and feel that these have an inescapable role in planning. Issues of multiple criteria for choice amongst plans can however become very troublesome. As the number of criteria increases, standard methods become combinatorially explosive (Harris 1967). Some criteria tend to evade quantification. It is a fact of political life that planners do not make final decisions, and that the public, their representatives, and other decision makers often have undeveloped or unexpressed criteria which become effective only in the face of actual or imagined choices. Such unknown criteria perforce cannot be part of any systematic evaluation, and their existence is a powerful argument for the preparation of alternative plans or schemes, with closely comparable measurable values.

This precept, which has its roots in traditional land-use planning and in the arts, runs entirely counter to the rules of science and of economic optimization. In science (as in religion) there is generally only one correct theory to explain a given phenomenon, and in economics a unique optimum is reached by a slow ascent to the summit, so that it is very similar to other close-to-optimal solutions. This situation changes drastically when there are many local optima. In the solution, for instance, of the Koopmans–Beckmann problem of quadratic programming (which fits the problems of factory layout and new-town zoning), there may be many local optima which differ greatly from each other yet have very similar values. This can be verified by experiment, with well-defined specifications for local optima and for measures of the values of arrangements and the differences between them. The important consequence is that certain very different plans and policies (for example, for urban transport or for health care) can potentially be clearly discriminated between not on the basis of expected performance, but only on the basis of aesthetic, moral, or political considerations.

The generation and testing of a large-scale and complex plan by the general methods we have outlined is feasible but potentially difficult. The rapid growth of computing power and the potential improvement in methods will reduce this difficulty. However, the process of finding a number of alternative good plans which are in the nature of possible local optima is apt to be more difficult. It is at present and for the foreseeable future more in the nature of an art than of a science. We believe that the key to reducing this difficulty and improving the art lies in a division of labor between the planner and the computer. The planner should be in a position to generate many plans which are in their fundamental features structurally different, but in which a minimum number of specific decisions have been taken. The computer should be able to undertake the detailing of the plans as required, and it is this overall requirement which every PSS should meet.

The essential way in which this should be done is by a set of design or planning rules which the computer would apply. These might have many different forms, among which the planner could choose in operating the system. One of the most immediately attractive is an optimizing procedure which determines locations and allocations for a functional subsystem according to one of several predetermined methods. This approach evades the difficulty in general system optimization by dividing the larger system into subsystems which can be separately optimized once certain planning decisions have been taken (Simon 1969). These planning decisions are parts of the planner's structural scheme, or they result from the prior optimization of some other subsystem. Many of these optimizations would often use market simulations and could produce economic measurements of performance. A few examples will distinguish some of the varied approaches to this problem.

Good economic models exist (as we have discussed) of house choice and housing markets, for which rents or prices are endogenous and the state of the market determines the choices and the utility levels of the households of different types and with different levels of income, as they result from market clearing. This model can be used in a variety of modes: with general equilibrium or with incremental changes; with a preexisting or a built-to-order housing stock; with zoning or with market determinations of housing type and lot size; with taxes, subsidies, travel costs, distributed employment, neighborhood characteristics, and other influential factors. If there are no built-in externalities such as social preferences in location or advantages in agglomeration, this model leads to a unique equilibrium which is optimal given the surrounding circumstances. Obviously it can be used in many different ways as a market model, and it can be modified to respond to various forms of public control and allocation in a socialist or mixed market, and to measure their impacts.

Detail trade and services can be located by many different types of models which assume some sort of balance between the advantages of shopping in larger centers or establishments and the disadvantages of traveling longer distances. The location of shopping under these models is often not mediated by a price mechanism, but measurements of the costs of operation and the levels of consumer satisfaction can be devised. Still other classes of activity such as facilities for public safety, health, education, and some services like post offices may be located according to optimizing procedures which take into account non-economic standards like response time, suitable size of facility, user convenience, and so on. These facilities must be located in relation to the present and prospective demand for services, and are only indirectly controlled by economic considerations. The techniques available for optimizing their location come from geography, operations research, functional engineering, and planning practice.

We are aware that the coordination of facilities such as these with a geographic information system so as to provide a planning support system of real utility is a major undertaking. It will involve the coordination of existing methods in a new software environment, and use of such a PSS should and will lead to the recognition of a need for new and presently unforeseen inventions and changes. As we have tried to indicate, it should lead to an environment in which research and practice are brought much closer together, and in which many more people in various walks of life, professions, and disciplinary fields become more deeply involved.

CONCLUSIONS

Perhaps the best way to draw our conclusions together is to review, in the light of what we have said so far, the immediately feasible role of a geographic information system in the operation of a planning support system. This can then be contrasted with the work of the PSS itself, and some indication of future cooperation and possible convergence of the two streams may be spelled out. Lying behind the work of GIS and PSS in regional and metropolitan planning, there must be another system which is essentially nongeographic with respect to the region being studied. Such a predictive system would deal with future trends in population growth and age composition, in- and out-migration, family formation, industrial composition, productivity, income, and many other factors disaggregated by population and industry groups, but not usually by areas within the region. While this system is needed to support planning, we do not here consider it part of the PSS we have been developing, although it is quite clearly another PSS. Without diverting the reader onto yet another track, it is worth noting that our conception of the general environment of planning is based on several interacting and overlapping PSS with perhaps some meta- or higher level PSS, ordering and organizing those at lower levels. This is a notion that we will explore in future work.

The GIS in this partnership would then control the definitions of geographic areas, of channels of communication, and of point or small-area locations. It would be used to define a set of basic elements at the lowest spatial disaggregation which would be used by the PSS. GIS functions could be actively used by the PSS to aggregate these elements into larger areas in the hierarchy. The GIS would act as the display engine for the PSS, producing maps and charts summarizing the operations of the PSS. The contribution of the GIS could go far beyond this. The overlay capabilities of the GIS could be used to generate variables relevant to the work of the PSS but not directly accessible to it, such as the average slope or elevation of each area, or the proportion of areas in floodplains. The GIS should be able to extract other information and features, such as the number and condition of structures, or the description of a hierarchy of movement channels to be used in transport or utility planning. The present state of the region by small areas could be specified in terms of land and facility valuations, population, employment, and any other attribute data presently known to the GIS.

The PSS by contrast would be largely concerned with design and simulation in strategic planning. It could readily accept the input of new facilities and of new regulations which would affect the functioning of the region and the behavior of its occupants, and thus would be appropriately used in simulations. Most importantly, it would be able to act on inputs of population and industrial change, and to trace out the interactions of these changes with the changes in facilities and policies which were being tested. The simulations and design modules of the PSS would deal with residential, commercial, and industrial location, with the planned provision of public facilities, and with the provision of needed utilities or the effects of levels of utility services. Underlying much of the locational simulation, there would be a model of transport interaction which would accommodate policies with regard to mass transit, parking, and transport fees, and which would simulate congestion and the transport response to it. Land-use responses would appear in the modeling of locational behavior. An important feature of a PSS would be its data management capabilities, which would deal with multiple future time periods and multiple alternative plans and their outcomes. This multiplicity of files of attribute information could swamp presently available GIS, and might carry the danger of compromising their data integrity.

The nature of a PSS need not be specified in detail for us to see that the demands of its design and operation are very severe. This suggests that progress could be made more rapidly if prototype PSS were to be developed independently of GIS, but in parallel with it. We believe that the arguments of this paper make such a development not only desirable, but inevitable. Neither the arguments nor the realization of such a development, however, should be interpreted as foreclosing the ultimate inclusion of PSS capabilities within GIS. However, the present lack of available PSS capabilities leads planners to be ignorant of their potential, and this leads to a lack of demand which discourages the vendors of GIS from producing suitable PSS capabilities. Thus their potential realization is blocked. In short, development would probably be more rapid and of higher quality if GIS and PSS followed independent but loosely coupled paths of development for some time to come. To recognize the different character of the requirements for the operation of the two systems in a computer environment does not preclude the possibility that means may be invented to couple them more closely. At this stage, we believe that independent development will tend to define this problem with greater clarity, and thus to lead more rapidly to such a resolution if one is available.

REFERENCES

Anas, A. 1982. *Residential Location Markets and Urban Transportation: Economic Theory, Econometrics and Policy Analysis with Discrete Choice Models.* New York: Academic Press.

———. 1983. Discrete Choice Theory, Information Theory and the Multinomial Logit and Gravity Models. *Transportation Research B* 17:13–23.

———. 1987. *Modeling in Urban and Regional Economics.* New York: Harwood.

Barra, T. de la. 1989. *Integrated Land Use Transport Modelling: Decision Chains and Hierarchies.* London: Cambridge University Press.

Batey, P. W. J. and M. Madden. 1982. Demographic–Economic Forecasting within an Activity–Commodity Framework: Some Theoretical Considerations and Empirical Results. *Environment and Planning A* 13:1067–83.

Batty, M. 1976. *Urban Modelling: Algorithms, Calibrations, Predictions.* London: Cambridge University Press.

———. On Planning Processes. In *Resources and Planning,* ed. B. Goodall and A. Kirby, 17–45. Oxford: Pergamon Press.

———. 1989. Urban Modelling and Planning: Reflections, Retrodictions, and Prescriptions. In *Remodelling Geography,* ed. B. MacMillan, 147–69. Oxford: Basil Blackwell.

———. 1990. Informative Planning: The Intelligent Use of Information Systems in the Policy-Making Process. In *Critical Success Factors: Key to Use of Information Systems-Technology in Local-Regional Planning,* ed. H. Sazanami, 307–56. Nagoya, Japan: United Nations Centre for Regional Development.

———. 1992. Geographic Information Systems: GIS in Urban Planning and Policy Analysis. In Proceedings of the Study Group Meeting on Regional and Global Economic Integration, Development Planning, and Information Technology, *GIS in Regional Development Planning,* ed. H. Sazanami, 27–60. Nagoya, Japan: United Nations Centre for Regional Development.

Ben Akiva, M. and S. R. Lerman. 1985. *Discrete Choice Analysis: Applications to Travel Demand*. Cambridge, MA: The MIT Press.

Bertuglia, C. S., G. Leonardi, and A. G. Wilson, eds. 1990. *Urban Dynamics: Designing an Integrated Model*. London: Routledge.

Birkin, M., G. Clarke, M. Clarke, and A. G. Wilson. 1990. Elements of a Model-Based Geographic Information System for the Evaluation of Urban Policy. In *Geographic Information Systems: Developments and Applications*, ed. L. Worrall, 132–62. London: Belhaven Press.

Brail, R. K. 1987. *Microcomputers in Urban Planning and Management*. Center for Urban Policy Research, New Brunswick, NJ: Rutgers University.

Brewer, G. D. 1973. *Politicians, Bureaucrats and the Consultant: A Critique of Urban Problem Solving*. New York: Basic Books.

Buttenfield, B. P. and R. P. McMaster, eds. 1991. *Map Generalization: Making Rules for Knowledge Representation*. London: Longmans.

Clercq, F. Le. 1990. Information Management within the Planning Process. In *Geographical Information Systems for Urban and Regional Planning*, ed. H. J. Scholten and J. C. H. Stillwell, 59–68. Dordrecht and Boston, MA: Kluwer Academic Publishers.

Couclelis, H. 1991. Geographically Informed Planning: Requirements for Planning-Relevant GIS. *Papers in Regional Science* 70:9–20.

Dangermond, J. 1990. Geographic Information System Technology and Development Planning. *Regional Development Dialogue* 11:1–14.

Densham, P. 1991. Spatial Decision Support Systems. In *Geographical Information Systems: Principles and Applications*, ed. D. J. Maguire, M. F. Goodchild, and D. W. Rhind, 403–12. London: Longmans.

———, and G. Rushton. 1988. Decision Support Systems for Locational Planning. In *Behavioural Modelling in Geography and Planning*, ed. R. G. Golledge and H. Timmermans, 56–90. London: Croom Helm.

Ding, Y. and A. S. Fotheringham. 1992. The Integration of Spatial Analysis and GIS. *Computers, Environment and Urban Systems* 16:3–19.

Einstein, A. 1955. *Essays in Science*. New York: Philosophical Library.

Forrest, E., ed. 1990. *Intelligent Infrastructure Workbook: A Management-Level Primer on GIS*. Fountain Hills, AZ: A-E-C Automation Level Newsletter.

Fotheringham, A. S. and M. E. O'Kelly. 1989. *Spatial Interaction Models: Formulations and Applications*. Boston: Kluwer Academic Publishers.

———, and P. A. Rogerson. 1992. Problems in Spatial Analysis from a GIS Perspective, A Paper Presented at the NCGIA Research Initiative 14: *GIS and Spatial Analysis*. SUNY–Buffalo, New York: NCGIA.

Harris, B. 1959. Plan or Projection: An Examination of the Use of Models in Planning. *Journal of the American Institute of Planners* 25:265–272.

———. 1967. The City of the Future: The Problem of Optimal Design. *Papers of the Regional Science Association* 19:185–95.

————. 1989. Beyond Geographic Information Systems: Computers and the Planning Professional. *Journal of the American Planning Association* 55:85–90.

————. 1991a. Planning Theory and the Design of Planning Support Systems. Paper presented to the Second International Conference on Computers in Planning and Management, Oxford, 6–8 July, 1991.

————. 1991b. Planning, Geography and Economics in Spatial Decision-Making. Paper presented at the Department of Geography, State University of New York, Buffalo, NY, 26 October, 1991.

————, and A. G. Wilson. 1978. Equilibrium Values and Dynamics of Attractiveness Terms in Production-Constrained Spatial-Interaction Models. *Environment and Planning A* 10:371–88.

Huxhold, W. E. 1991. *An Introduction to Urban Geographic Information Systems,* New York: Oxford University Press.

Klosterman, R., R. K. Brail, and E. G. Bossard, eds. 1992. *Spreadsheet Models for Urban and Regional Analysis.* Center for Urban Policy Research, New Brunswick, NJ: Rutgers University.

Lee, D. B. 1973. Requiem for Large-Scale Models. *Journal of the American Institute of Planners* 39:163–78.

Lowry, I. S. 1964. *A Model of Metropolis.* RM-4035-RC. Santa Monica, CA: The RAND Corporation.

Mackett, R. 1983. The Leeds Integrated Land-Use/Transport Model (LILT). *Supplementary Report 805.* The Transport and Road Research Laboratory, Crowthorne, Berkshire, UK.

Manheim, M. L. 1986. Creativity-Support Systems for Planning, Design and Decision Support. *Microcomputers in Civil Engineering* 1:3–14.

Putman, S. 1983. *Integrated Urban Models: Policy Analysis of Transportation and Land Use.* London: Pion Press.

————. 1992. *Integrated Urban Models 2.* London: Pion Press.

Roszak, T. 1986. *The Cult of Information.* New York: Pantheon Books.

Shubik, M. 1979. Computer and Modeling. In *The Computers Age: A Twenty Year View,* ed. M. L. Dertouzos and J. Moses, 285–305. Cambridge, MA: The MIT Press.

Simon, H. A. 1969. *The Sciences of the Artificial.* Cambridge, MA: The MIT Press.

Webster, F. V., P. H. Bly, and N. J. Paulley, eds. 1988. *Urban Land-Use and Transport Interaction: Policies and Models.* Avebury, Aldershot, Berkshire, UK.

Wegener, M. 1982. A Multilevel Economic–Demographic Model for the Dortmund Subregion. *Sistemi Urbani* 4:371–401.

Wilson, A. G., J. D. Coelho, S. M. MacGill, and H. C. W. L. Williams. 1981. *Optimization in Location and Transport Analysis.* New York: John Wiley & Sons.

Paper 3

Sketch Planning: Systematic Methods in Planning and Its Support

BRITTON HARRIS

EMERITUS PROFESSOR OF CITY AND REGIONAL PLANNING

PHILADELPHIA, PA

ABSTRACT

The nature, instruments, and procedures of sketch planning are necessarily similar to, but not identical to, those of planning. Sketch planning itself is similar to sketching as an artist might practice it, but is not primarily interested in representations of specific plans to be fleshed out later. Rather it is concerned with explorations of one or more essential aspects of an issue, a project, a plan-to-be. These explorations serve to both encourage an atmosphere of imaginative improvisation in which means have precedence over ends, and to support later stages of planning, when ends become paramount. This paper seeks first to make clear the differences and similarities between sketching and planning, and second, to describe the ways and means by which sketch planning may systematically be supported and practiced.

INTRODUCTION

Planning is the premeditation of action. Premeditation implies purpose, and the product of this purposeful consideration is a plan. This discussion is thus about the means and processes of making plans.

Sketch planning is a subset of planning, and must follow some of the same rules. The first section of the paper tries to distinguish between the two, but the rules developed later as applied to sketch planning must also apply to planning as a whole, with some possible modifications.

This whole discussion will go beyond sketch planning in general, to discuss the use of sketch planning as a support for planning, and to discuss some of the supports of sketch planning itself. These supports will of course turn out to be supports for planning as a whole, though possibly not as fully developed as may be needed. Conversely, many of the supports for planning which are discussed elsewhere in this volume also support sketch planning, and are not developed here. In what follows, we attempt first to distinguish in principle between planning and its sketches. Then, in the next two sections we discuss two central supports for sketch planning, a critical set of *instruments* and the framework for a set of *procedures*. Finally, we draw some conclusions, in the form of a sketch of sketching which brings together many of the characterizations of the sketch-planning process.

SKETCHING AND PLANNING

When we speak of sketch planning we seem to use an image of the activity of drawing and painting. A sketch may be a prelude to a more complete rendering of the subject, but unlike a maquette in sculpture, it is not a model or smaller copy of the real thing (as one woman said about her model husband). We might do better to think of a sketchbook, in which we find different poses and different ways of looking at an object, and of examining its various details with some care. In the context of the whole, the sketch maker is simultaneously exploring a topic or a cluster of topics, thinking about how the sketcher's vision may be made visible to others, and conducting a self-examination of the ways in which those capabilities in the artist's command may be used to represent the topic. Thus, simple representation is not necessarily the primary objective. Given that the rendering is abstracted from reality, it is tested for its capability of finding the essential aspects of the topic and conveying the artist's view of them so as to capture the viewers' interest, insight, and satisfaction.

In this discussion, the object is a planned and naturally developed pattern of urban arrangements in the future, and thus exists only in the mind of the artist or sketch maker. Where sketches support the subsequent activity of painting and sculpture, the object has often been seen by the artist, or the final work consists of a composite of many realities. Similar sketching supports the production of works of literature and philosophy, and is found in the notes and explorations of mathematicians and scientists. In the visual arts and in literature, the importance of the *deja vu* is often salient, but in music, architecture, urban planning, science, and mathematics it is only a springboard to what might be called the *jamais vu*. In other words, there are two contributions of all these arts: new modes of vision, and new visions. Sketching a plan means sketching things which have never been seen before, or at least have never been seen before in this combination.

In an artist's sketch, the abstraction consists in a sacrifice of detail, often of color as well, of some dimensions including that of depth and of completeness or balance. In sketch planning, as in art, there are necessary additions, not visible in any previous source but arising out of knowledge, imagination, or intended affect. In both sorts of sketch, the knowledge is incomplete, the imagination is in part intended to be factual, tinged with purpose, and in part with affect depending on ideas of beauty, ethics, and a desire for attention.

In the current instance, the "artist" is a collective of planners and publics or their subgroups or individual members. Any number can play, but imagination is individualistic, and orchestration may be less effective than an atmosphere which encourages improvisation.

The resulting sketchbook contains very many more representations of the object of planning than can possibly be realized or even seriously considered as the basis for a final product. Many of the representations are skewed away from reality, and some are contradictory to others. Many are ugly, and many will have been, prior to the sketch, "unimaginable" or incapable of being imaged. Most essential to sketch planning and to the artistry of sketching is the intent (successful or not) to capture in each sketch some or all of the essential aspects of interest in the pursuit of the object through its image.

There is one essential difference between artistry and planning: the artist can walk away from an object and its representation; the planner cannot. Utopia is quite literally nowhere.

The planner engaged in sketch planning faces a serious dilemma. The essential aspects of interest in a plan are fairness, livability, workability, and affordability. Each of these is influenced by the ultimate plan (as it is achieved in reality) at various levels—from the general to the particular. It is no exaggeration to say that every planning objective is impacted by thousands of details in the city's functioning. Such details are influenced by the larger decisions and broader concepts of the plan, but this influence is not direct or unique: planned decisions compete with other influences as well. Yet a sketch of any kind tends to suppress detail. In the case of the artist, some of the detail which is suppressed in a sketch may be suppressed again, or recaptured and altered in the final product. The planner does not have the liberty to provide minute details of development behavior, no matter how consequential it may be, because the micromanagement of the details of a plan defeats many of its original purposes, and cannot be undertaken by the planner.

Properly conceived, sketch planning must face this dilemma and find a way to indicate much relevant detail without expending the time and effort required to make complete plans. The failure to bridge this gap leads to severe limitations either on the basis for judging sketch plans, or on the number and variety of sketches which can be examined. Alternatively, the costs and time expended in planning become exorbitant.

A certain large part of this difficulty is ameliorated by the use of models which trace in some detail the decisions and actions of enormous numbers of participants in urban life. These results permit broad judgments based on the criteria of interest, even though they may be mistaken in a multiplicity of details. The correction of these mistakes or misapprehensions is part of the job of detailing a very limited set of alternative plans (perhaps as few as two or even one), and of the political process of securing public acceptance and legislative or administrative approval. There is an important shift of emphasis here: we hold that *the broad consideration of alternatives belongs in a thorough process of sketch planning, and not primarily in the final stages of plan making.*

This however has one more critical implication. The viewer (either a professional or a member of the public), looking at a sketch plan and its interpretation through models, must cultivate a new way of seeing. Like a viewer of the new school of Impressionism, anyone who looks at a sketch plan must be prepared to sense the reality beneath it, and—it might be hoped—the aesthetic intent underlying the manner in which it is conveyed.

**THE MECHANICS OF
SKETCH PLANNING**

Even given all these assumptions, there remain issues about how sketch planning should proceed. The enemy of free and imaginative sketch planning is the prolonged and tedious preparation of sketches, and the burden of time and cost encountered in extended computer analysis. These have different remedies.

The preparation of sketch plans for analysis involves the translation of proposed changes in a given basic plan into computable formats. Even a completely new plan might be defined in terms of certain basic decisions, with some things held constant—like topography and the standing stocks of buildings and infrastructure. The activities of preparation will require the careful consideration of methods of scenario building, possibly semiautomatic. In addition, this process should be aided by prepared menus of possible actions and means for their injection into the analytic process. With these materials and the experience of preparing them, the preparation of scenarios could be largely automated, and further intervention facilitated. Sketching plans *de novo*, and modifying them in an improvement process, requires much the same in the way of preparation of scenarios, but by definition, the improving modifications are simpler and of smaller scope.

A reduction in the computational burden of exploring sketched plans is an equally complex issue. The burden arises in two different ways. First, the exploration of new starting points and the improvement steps in an optimum-seeking process require very many repeated analyses. Finding the starting plans and the best improving steps depend on the skill and experience of the users, and can be substantially bettered over time. Second, the computational process is demanding because a major focus of analysis is on real-world interactions. The computation involved in interaction goes up at least with the square of the number of interacting elements. To oversimplify, the interactions between pairs of 1,000 zones are 25 times as numerous as the interactions between pairs of 200 zones, and 400 times as numerous as with 50 zones. Interactions among triplets of zones arise for some kinds of interaction, and here the ratios of the burden are 125 and 8,000 in the above cases.

The time consumed in computation greatly extends the process of evaluating alternatives, and its reduction could be the subject of a much longer discussion than is appropriate here. Improved computing speeds and the growth of parallel computing will be of major importance, but it will always be considered appropriate to engage in some simplification to facilitate sketch planning. Given the structure of urban affairs and the goals of planning, the behavior of many different actors and the impact of plans on them is of particular importance. Contrary to many approaches seen in practice, we believe that in sketch planning the most effective reduction in computing time is to be found in retaining a disaggregated classification of actors, while using a somewhat coarser division of areas—that is, zones. This emphasis shortens the time for any embedded transport analysis, but for transport planning itself, this bias is often reversed. Like increased skill in using a system directed to the support of sketch planning, greater efficiency in decisions about the reduction of computation will arise out of experience, and will evolve over time.

We can elaborate this very general overview in several directions.

The mechanics (but not the processes) of sketch planning consist of three easily defined parts: first, specify a set of interventions, a plan, or part of a plan; second, determine the probable consequences or outcomes of this intervention; and third, evaluate these outcomes with reference to the goals being pursued.

There is of course a supervening task which could be thought of as a part of the mechanics: how and whether to expand the exploration with a new set of assumed actions. This is the subject of the second part of this paper.

On reflection, these three parts of the mechanics are not very mechanical and certainly not fully specified. Their scope may be readily outlined in a brief review. The mechanisms must be capable of handling any available or conceivable planning action; there are scores of these, even broadly defined, and thus millions of possible combinations. The analysis must indicate consequences on all relevant policy dimensions; there might be only a single predefined measure of good performance, but more likely there will be as many as a dozen objectives, with criteria by which they can be measured. The kernel of this procedure is the means used to determine the manifold outcomes of the varied components of a plan or proposal. This is a model of some sort, which connects all the elements of the plan, together with their interactions over time, space, and function, with the possible outcomes. We start our discussion with this difficult construct.

There is a very real possibility that the "model" which makes these connections is to be found only in the head of an experienced planner, or in the deliberations of a task force in a planning office, or (with rising improbability) in a legislative body or a public hearing. All of these methods, based on experience or interest, are involved in resolving other issues in addition to predicting outcomes. Because of the selectivity in choosing participants in the process, and their prejudices or self-interest, judgmental methods are prone to bias, and must be used with considerable care.

There are many models with a more formal structure than most kinds of thought experiment. At one extreme is a computer simulation of urban interaction, location, and growth. A model of this type is used to estimate the demand for transportation facilities and the distribution of traffic, congestion, and automotive pollution in large urban complexes. Similar modeling techniques have been extended to the forecasting of regionwide changes in land use as well. At another extreme is the kind of model which might be used by a developer or urban designer—a combination of maps, drawings, and a spreadsheet analysis of costs, building volumes, requirements, and cash flow. At an intermediate scale we might look for computer models which predict the functioning and amenity of neighborhood plans and small new towns like Reston, Columbia, or Levittown; here however we would look in vain, as formal models have not been developed at this scale.

In general, we would conclude that the type of planning being undertaken would determine the character of the model being used. There are however exceptions to this conclusion. These are natural enough but not widely recognized.

First, the various scales interact with each other. A developer or designer with long-term interests would like to know how a given local development fits into a longer-term plan or prognosis. Is the proposed space marketable, or adequate for long-term demand? Would the replication of this design by competitors reduce profitability? From a larger planning point of view, would replication of this type of development be desirable? Would a given planned development be impacted by other, external developments not immediately obvious? Successful or unsuccessful neighborhood and new-town designs influence the entire development of the urban region, by their character and the way they function—and by the drive to replicate successful examples.

Second, and very important for this discussion, is the possibility that each of these scales has the same kind of objects, occupiers, and interactions—and thus that urban functions at different scales could be modeled by skillfully combining primitive but universal computer capabilities. This approach has been outlined by Hopkins (1997, 1998) in a provocative and thoughtful way. It involves not only sketch planning, but we might say, "sketch modeling" on the part of the user. Such a potentiality has long been imputed to a developed GIS system, but with disappointing results. For the present, we will leave this matter open, expecting that models which are developed for sketch planning at any particular scale will meet the need, and that highly flexible and adaptable universal models will be under investigation and test until they are shown to do so as well.

From the viewpoint of sketch planning, a nonjudgmental method of connecting planned actions with their potential consequences creates a black box which is taken for granted in the planning process. Many of the components of the judgmental prediction of consequences will have been entered into the model design, and before proceeding with sketch planning the users are entitled to know the nature of that design judgment. This needed knowledge includes the internal structure and assumptions of the model, and its fit with proposed actions and putative outcomes.

To illustrate the critical nature of internal structure, consider the potential variety in a model of residential locational choices. Most models currently in use employ discrete choice or gravity-like models to account for diverse behavior. The Herbert–Stevens model (1960) uses linear programming, which does not directly produce any diversity of behavior, and the NBER model (Ingram et al. 1972) is a hybrid. Some models have economic constraints which produce estimates of the costs of location to the householder, while others do not. Models have various ways of treating the location of jobs in relation to residence, sometimes not even considering this factor. Some models deal with incremental change, while others project some sort of longer-term equilibrium. (For general surveys of model styles, see Wilson [1974], Harris [1985], Anas [1987], Wegener [1994].)All of these differences may result in different conclusions about the outcome of planned actions, and the sketch planner must be aware of these differences in broad terms. A planner who confects a unique model using a toolkit of model parts becomes responsible for the results of these design choices.

Next, consider the dimensions along which the output of models should be available. In the interests of realism, a model may analyze more dimensions that are needed for judgments, but more commonly the judgments require more dimensions of analysis than the models can provide. For example, the standard transport-planning model, predicting the demand and its distribution in a planned system, is directed toward a planning process in which the principal concern is a kind of efficiency—with an optimal combined public and private cost. But a larger planning process may also be concerned with equity for the poor, for women as householders and workers, and for minorities. Present uses of transport-planning models do not differentiate system users on most of these dimensions, and inadequate attention to mass transportation may implicitly be biased against the poor. In land-use planning, the same effect is produced by a different mechanism; suburban land planning is almost automatically concerned with the interests of middle- and upper-class households, to the exclusion of the poor.

At the other end of the process, the types of action available to land planners together with actions and events which are external to the planners' powers should be accommodated in the model. This has become evident in transport planning, where the consideration of new measures like higher gasoline and parking costs, and compulsory car pooling, have been considered as policy measures but do not necessarily influence the projected behavior in currently operational models. This is equally clear in land-use modeling, where for example changes like federal mortgage guarantees have drastically changed the behavior of locators. A flexible sketch-planning effort will ordinarily come up with many proposed new policies which may not match the capabilities of existing means for projecting their impacts.

We mention briefly the fact that environmental concerns, when considered in the planning process, tend to multiply these difficulties. The objectives must be clearly defined in measurable terms, the actions available or imaginable will enlarge the scope of projecting their effects, and there may be serious difficulties in establishing the connection between acts and their impacts in terms of costs, of social behavior, and of physical consequences.

Given this general outline of the mechanical structure of sketch planning, we need to review briefly some ancillary concerns. Sketch planning is a repetitive activity, in the process of which interested individuals or groups propose new plans or amendments to existing ones and examine their consequences. This repetitive nature of the process suggests three requirements: ease of entering proposals, speedy turnaround in the analysis, and clarity in presenting the outcomes and their relation to the objectives. Each of these requirements poses special problems.

The need for quick turnaround leads to a conflict in the design of models or other processes for predicting outcomes. The desire of specialists in various types of analysis for improved realism and accuracy can lead to an all-out war with speed in computation. This war is being ameliorated by the relentless expansion of computer power, but to an extent this only whets the appetites of the analysts. The effect of this war has resulted in curtailing the scope of transport planning (as described earlier), and to the acceptance of simple land-use models—or rejection of more adequate ones. The variation of concepts and priorities between practitioners and researchers does not facilitate resolving this conflict.

Given some temporary resolution of this difference, and agreement in a given locality or jurisdiction on methods of modeling the impacts of plans, it is within the power of the planners to help shape the two other requirements.

First, inputting new proposals must be largely automated. Making each change by hand can lead only to frustration. Changes range from the particular (such as adding a new highway or transit facility, or locating some important activity) to the general (such as changing zoning arrangements areawide, enacting taxes or subsidies, or prohibiting or requiring selected activities and actions). Many of the general regulations are conditional and locational, such as "Don't permit the sale of liquor within two hundred yards of a school," or "Do not permit industrial buildings on land with slopes over 8 percent." The articulation of changes of this type could effectively be initiated through a dedicated GIS system, but must be translated into the proper form for processing by a model.

Second, the output of modeling must again automatically be processed for study and interpretation. In the usual course of events, this will require translating the raw output into measurements defined by the goals of the plans. At the same time, many of the results are geographically distributed, or the goals are defined in terms of various types of areas and the relations between them. This requires not only calculations and graphic display, but also various types of maps. Once again, we conclude that processing with a dedicated GIS is appropriate.

Needless to say, most of these "mechanical" problems have not been solved, and unfortunately cannot be solved in isolation from each other. This presents a design problem which may be clarified by general discussions like the foregoing, but which must be solved through efforts applied to real problems. This might be done in a single large effort, and perhaps this is appropriate for different types of models— although some of these have been evolving for many years. Since the ancillary activities of input and output are where the planner meets the modeler, we may expect their mechanics to evolve over a period of interaction between the two professions. Ideally, this evolution may meet some other specifications for the improvement of plans in the next section.

DOING THE BEST WE CAN

Planners are said to reject optimization on the grounds that "We don't optimize, we just do the best we can" (Lowdon Wingo, personal communication). This remark might be called an *optimoron*, since an optimum is indeed the best that can be achieved. The resolution of this contradiction lies in the implied emphasis by planners on the limitations and obstacles to what we *can* do. These are in part recognized in the theory of optimizing as constraints, but a less technical view suggests that there are gaps in knowledge, uncertainties, and above all limitations on the resources and time available for doing the best we can. These tend to throw the planners' activities into a realm of bounded rationality, which recognizes certain limits on fully rational optimization.

We must emphasize one aspect of planning which is thought to define its difference from optimizing, and which does indeed undermine any intent to apply optimizing methods to planning. But paradoxically, this factor also undermines the possibility of doing systematic planning itself. I refer to the view of most planners that their activities imply the invention of new actions to solve perceived problems. Optimizing works with a predetermined set of possible actions (whose effects can be predicted). If a new measure is introduced, previous optimizing results must be completely reexamined, but the same may be said of any ongoing planning process. New ideas can invalidate the conclusions of previous work. All this applies to new technologies and social changes as well, and it is somewhat disconcerting to discover that the outcomes of a planning process, however well-conceived, may themselves be a part of the unpredictable future. We proceed without addressing this dilemma directly. But we note that it increases the difficulties of planning, and we persist in the view that planning may be improved by considering the fundamentals of optimizing.

Since planners recognize the importance of improving plans as far as possible, we can regard their methods as a form of optimum seeking. Sketch planning, suitably organized, should be able to explore a very large range of decisions in seeking better plans, while planning proper will select a very few such sketches and be devoted to perfecting them. This means that sketch planning must be controlled and directed in such a way as to avoid a prodigal expenditure of resources. We explore the design of a sketch-planning *process*.

It is perhaps tautological to say that what planners produce is a plan. A plan, however, describes a group of interrelated decisions which can be taken more or less independently of each other. If the decisions were fully independent, then they would belong to separate plans for different functions—but in fact different arenas of planned action share resources and jointly influence outcomes, circumscribing this independence. Conversely, if a group of decisions were completely interdependent they would be a single decision, but one of enormous scope and detail. The problem of finding a good plan is thus one of finding a good combination of decisions which interact but which can be decided separately, and whose consequences are knowable but not explicitly planned. The key word here is "combination," because a relatively small number of decisions implies a very large number of combinations.

By way of illustration, suppose that we can somehow determine that there are, in a given region, twenty possible links which might be added to the regional highway network. (Finding such a small set of possibilities in most regions is unlikely.) Then suppose further that we want to select a subset of these links for construction in the near future. There are over a million such subsets to be considered. Suppose that we decide in advance that just ten out of the twenty links are affordable; then there are still over 192,000 subsets to be considered. Suppose that we have chosen a set of ten links to be constructed; there are over 3.5 million sequences in which they might be built. Of course, all of these choices are constrained by considerations such as the continuity of routes and the connectivity of the system, but for larger systems, the combinatorial explosion is much more severe, and the problem of finding best solutions, or even very good ones, is daunting.

The basic target both in planning and in optimizing is to find a procedure which will identify a best plan—that is, one which eliminates, or proves superior to, all competing alternatives. Planning pursues this objective only insofar as it is deemed feasible, thus eliminating many but not necessarily all alternatives. (Of course the fact that only one or a few plans are presented may mean that other and possibly better plans have been administratively but not substantively eliminated.) Optimizing theory seeks practical means to pursue the target of eliminating all inferior plans to the bitter end, or to show how this pursuit is impractical and to find ways to moderate its difficulty. The methods of optimizing theory have been extensively studied, and provide a favorable starting point for this discussion.

There are three basic methods for optimizing. The first is the improvement of solutions; the second is the construction of solutions in a way which is demonstrably optimal; and the third is the exhaustive enumeration of all possible solutions. In actuality, strict optimization requires that the method of complete enumeration be implicitly embedded in either of the other two methods. At the same time there are short cuts which may make complete enumeration possible with greatly reduced work. In what follows we will discuss and illustrate some methods, as a guide for formulating a viable process of sketch planning.

Throughout, we will emphasize the multiplicity of solutions.

Consider a simple problem of personnel administration: There are N jobs to be filled by N candidates. Each candidate has a different measured aptitude for each job. How shall we assign them in the best interests of the organization? There are N different possible assignments, since the first person can be assigned to N different jobs, the second to $(N-1)$, and so on. For ten jobs and candidates there are 3.5 million assignments, and for twenty, over 2 billion billion. Yet this is a linear programming problem whose solution can be computed in fractional seconds.

This and many other similar problems can be approached by swapping one decision for a better one, and thus eliminating all inferior answers—a method which is pursued persistently in improving plans.

Swapping is likely to fail to find a complete optimum if the different decisions interact with each other with sufficient strength. In the case just discussed, suppose that different candidates have pairwise preferences for interacting (or not) with others, and different pairs of jobs have different tendencies to throw their occupants into interaction. The same problem arises in locating interacting facilities in urban space (Koopmans and Beckmann 1957), or in effectively distributing facilities in a factory or office building. Here, paradoxically, swapping is less likely to provide a best solution, but is more desirable than ever because it provides an approach to a problem which is otherwise intractable.

Any improvement method requires a starting point, and in the case of the more difficult problems, multiple starting points, since in the difficult cases, different starting points may lead to different endpoints, when no further improvement can be expected. Multiple starting points, if thematically different enough, will result in alternative sketch plans.

The constructive method of optimizing requires us to construct a solution, one step at a time. If the end result is to be optimal, each step should be optimal and should leave the whole optimal up to this point. This approach is common in planning practice, but not necessarily with the caveat as to continuing optimality. We provide examples.

The most common constructive approach is the *greedy algorithm*. Here, we take one decision at a time, at each step considering the most effective measure at that point. Concrete examples have a dynamic developmental aspect which is not captured in simple optimizing. For example, a program of building high schools in a growing city could be a series of sequential decisions subject to greedy planning. The first high school might be located near the center, the "best" place, but then the second high school would be off-center, and the two schools would not be in the best combined locational pattern. This imbalance would continue indefinitely, but with diminishing force, as long as the high schools were large and other locators did not follow them.

A better approach is much more restrictive, and is found in the basic idea of *dynamic programming,* that parts of an optimal problem solution are themselves optimal solutions to a smaller problem. This approach has many important applications, such as in finding the shortest path through a transport network, and even some greedy algorithms qualify. In planning, it would enforce the useful idea of "doing the best we can" at every level and elsewhere in the urban system. However, too many minor best solutions are contingent on other external actions which the planner must decide. Nevertheless, in many cases a poor plan of a reduced system means that the whole is not well planned. For example, a poorly planned subcenter or an unbalanced transport system could invalidate the optimality of a regional plan. This situation must be interpreted very carefully, because as we have shown, its converse is not true, and the optimality of parts of a plan in isolation does not guarantee the optimality of the whole.

Planning in general lacks the structure which is used in successful constructive methods—a structure which at least partially predetermines an order of successive decisions, and preserves several alternative lines of partial decisions if they are so far optimal.

We are now left with the possible necessity of explicitly enumerating all possible combinations of actions, in order to ensure that no potential optimum is overlooked. Without identifying special relational structures in the articulation of the plan, this is a cumbersome procedure at best, and in the final analysis it may be necessary to abandon complete enumeration for more approximate approaches.

We will first look at one more formal method, called branch and bound, which does in fact implicitly enumerate all possible solutions by eliminating many which cannot be successful. The two parts of the name correspond with two aspects of a procedure. *Branching* depends on arranging decisions in a tree, with one decision at each level, from which branches go from the alternative choices to the next level, so that all possible combinations will ultimately be explored if the entire tree is examined. Since for many decisions the number of branches multiplies very rapidly, the tree is pruned by a procedure called *bounding;* this means eliminating combinations of decisions whose further development is known to be impractical— a step which is common in planning. This is done, rigorously in optimization and more intuitively in planning, by estimating the lowest possible further cost of decisions not yet made at any point, adding them to the known cost of decisions already made (that is, made tentatively in confecting the plan or sketch), and comparing them to the best known result from some other place or a previously tested plan. For example, the cost of fixed rail transit combined with low-density development could be estimated to be excessive—eliminating one of these features from parts of a plan.

The major difficulty with this procedure is that of estimating the minimum additional net cost of decisions not yet taken. (Of course the last decision examined may drive the cost out of bounds by introducing an ugly, high-cost, or illegal combination.) This procedure is often applied as a form of argument and not a rigorous method, although as we will see, such arguments are likely to be necessary to reduce the time spent in exploration.

In the work of a planning office, branch and bound might be a rough guide to part of the work program, but can hardly be used in its complete detail. Formally or informally, it is desirable to put proposals with strong implications at the top of the list of decisions to be considered. Such broad implications include in the first instance monetary costs, and in addition environmental costs or negative externalities. At the same time, they may include benefits to particular areas or classes of the population; these implications may be strong but difficult to measure, as they often depend on a long chain of reasoning. In this case, some method of detailing the implications of a proposed but possibly partial plan will be needed.

Having reviewed all these methods in some haste, we can now return to the fundamental problems of sketch planning, and finally make a few suggestions for dealing with them. We will distinguish the two broad approaches discussed above, constructive methods and improvement procedures—which would be applied in that order, but need to be discussed in the reverse order.

An improvement procedure, somewhat like planning in general, needs three components: a starting point, an improvement process, and a rule for stopping. The starting point is an initial sketch plan, or a scenario for the principal decisions to be embodied in it. The improvement procedure is usually some form of swapping: altering one decision or one allocation of resources at a time; finding at least a very good swap and executing it; then repeating the procedure. Finding what steps to take next in search of improvements will be informed by the evaluation of the current plan, and the identification of shortfalls, which is analogous to finding a search direction in formal optimization, or to "oiling the squeaking wheel," in common parlance. A stopping rule for the improvement process depends on the recognition of the unavailability of any sufficiently advantageous swap. A stalled improvement process indicates the possibility that a new starting point should be selected.

The potential value of new starting points hinges on one outstanding but often neglected aspect of planning and optimization: the fact that there may be several plans of nearly equal merit, but of such different structures that they cannot be converted into one another by any (or any practical) improvement procedure. In optimizing this is characterized by the recognition of local optima. In planning it is recognized in the differing structure of some interesting cities, in the difficulty of choosing among different approaches, and by the implicit arguments for providing alternative plans. This problem is inescapable, arising as it does out of the existence of externalities, indivisibilities, economies of scale, and public goods. In economics this problem is called *market failure,* in computer science it is called *NP-completeness*, and in planning it might be called *conflicting land uses,* which since they cannot be resolved automatically, require intervention and design.

There is thus a hidden virtue in this impossibility of formal optimization, or of planning based entirely on the inevitability of market forces. It is sometimes recognized in formal optimization that the criteria for searching for an optimum must be restricted and perhaps oversimplified. In planning this is widely understood, and remedies are approached in many different guises. What is perfectly clear in both cases is that if a number of good solutions or plans are offered to the client or the public, new criteria which were put to one side in the interests of simplification or on the basis of narrow economic theory will be resurrected. If a number of alternatives have already been ranked or ordered, these new values may change the ranking. Multiple local optima imply the existence of good alternatives, and their evaluation enriches the planning process by eliciting broader involvement and new points of view. It is essential however that these alternatives have some basic structural differences, rather than relatively trivial variations. The starting points for an improvement process should contain some of these structural differences, which will then lead to different outcomes of these improvements.

A stopping rule for searching out new starting points or continuing improvements is somewhat elusive. It should be based on the possible improvement which might be achieved, but this is fundamentally unknown. It is possible to examine the sequence of earlier alternatives and their degrees of success, and to apply statistical extreme value theory to estimate the probable best degree of future success with additional efforts. This assumes, however, that in some sense all the previous efforts and their potential successors are drawn from the same universe of possible plans. This assumption may be thought to deny the premise of the enterprise, to find something new.

Enough detail has been reviewed at this point to permit a final overall review of the sketch-planning process in the form of some overall observations and admonishments.

CONCLUSION: A SKETCH OF SKETCHING

In trying to frame a procedure for planning, we now recognize the fact that much of the systematic search for better solutions must be organized outside of formal optimization, but be guided by some of its principles. Even so, in the light of our earlier discussion of the mechanics of sketch planning we can recognize that optimization actually occurs on at least two levels, which are the natural reflection of the division of problems into those which are and are not computationally intractable and at the same time more or less resistant to decision by market and behavioral forces. *Planning should focus on the more intractable issues, but the effects of plans are often detailed by simulating some form of optimizing behavior.*

How this should be done in practice could be the basis for many fascinating studies, but with minor assistance in what follows, the reader should attempt to frame a conception of planning and sketch planning based on experience and insight. This process will be given a nudge by painting a contrast between an initially successful effort in transport planning, and the much greater difficulties of land-use planning. This comparison is intended to be instructive but also provocative, in the light of some tension between the transportation and land-use planning professions.

The Chicago Area Transportation Study began its work with a well-developed framework for planning. It defined its own scope too narrowly, first of all in omitting the impact of transport development on land uses. Land-use planning would not neglect the impact of transportation plans, but since the two activities are not on speaking terms, it is impossible to close the loop at this time. CATS and other metropolitan transport studies extensively surveyed the needs and behaviors of the users of the transport system; land-use planners basically lack the information needed to study the present and future behavior of home buyers, renters, and developers—as well as of industry and services. On the basis of these studies, CATS devised methods for estimating user demands for transport services quite accurately, using a combination of statistical analysis, discrete choice models, and optimal decisions for trip making, choice of mode of travel, choice of destination, and choice of routes of travel. Based on this demand, CATS optimized the distribution of congestion in the transport system. Land-use planning has no such large-scale behavioral interpretation of land development.

CATS had a well-developed measure of system performance: the sum of user costs and public costs, which was to be minimized. This made it possible to define improvements—reducing the size of underused facilities or closing them, and increasing the size of congested facilities or creating parallel capacity. Land-use planning has no definition of system planned performance, and thus has no clear indication of how to manage improvements in plans, or when to stop the process. Of course there are more exigent stopping rules than the performance of the planning process—such as reaching the end of budgeted funds, or running into a report deadline; but it would still be useful to know what we are doing, and not always to be governed by these indicators of incomplete success.

CATS used only one well-considered starting plan, which laid a good basis for a motorized transport system but did not properly consider mass transit. This was a professional failure. However, with respect to such starting points, land-use planning has no well-designed initial analysis aside from the many experiential and intuitive views as to what is wrong with the system and some general direction in which it should go. This is thus a good point in our development to leave transport analysis and focus more completely on land use.

Each new starting point is a *scenario*, or list of critical measures which will condition the development of a tentative planned solution to future problems and needs. Each scenario may be expected to lead to a single endpoint, unless new critical decisions in the improvement process are very large, and can be regarded as generating essentially different alternatives. Such decisions belong in the scenarios themselves. Amongst many scenarios, experience should permit a development which will usually result in a unique endpoint or alternative; thus no two scenarios should usually be so similar that a systematic process of improvement will merge them into one.

The selection of critical action measures for scenarios must focus on major decisions. At the start of a planning exercise it may be difficult to ensure that all the determinants of an outcome have been considered, so a general list of default options must be prepared. These may include fixed rules, such as the preservation of historic sites and of open space, or they may include specific rules for change, such as conditions under which zoning may be revised, streets closed or opened, and public services provided or withdrawn.

The improvement process in land-use planning is also less well defined than in transport planning, because there is a wider range of decisions and because the effects of a given scheme are more diffuse, more varied, and more remote from the control of the plan. The decisions in a scenario, as modified in the improvement process, must call on methods described early in this paper to define the consequences of plans. These will include the costs of housing and travel to various segments of the population, the extent of crowding, congestion, and pollution, and the levels of other elements of the quality of life. They will also include the distribution of economic activity and services, and the state of the environment.

It should be apparent that the locational choices of various actors, and the development of many new precincts, within the plan, are not subject to the direct control of the planner, any more than are the travel demands of the public in transport planning. The models which crystallize private decisions into a set of presumed outcomes therefore obviously also decide many aspects of development which are sometimes considered a part of the comprehensive planning activity—even when this is not fully effective. Such models should specify behaviors akin to those in real life which, under the rules of the plan, gain for the actors the most advantageous situations possible. That leads of course to optimal arrangements, subject to the competition of other actors, the influence of other sectors, the rules of the plan, and the knowledge, skill, and resolution of the locators.

Interpreting the outcomes of a plan as detailed in this fashion should enable the planners to measure what outcomes are or are not advantageous to specified groups, what seem to fail to achieve their desired objectives, what imbalances arise, and how general expectations for the scenario are or are not fulfilled. These findings should lead to changes in the scenario intended to overcome their deficiencies. However, since the outcomes are related in a complex fashion to the scenarios, experience in making changes will be required before this process can be expected to go smoothly.

Multiple scenarios, intended to lead to structurally different endpoints, introduce two modifications to the treatment of improvements and the establishment of stopping rules. First, in order to allow time and resources for several explorations, tighter stopping rules should be enforced. (That is, greater improvement should be required on each step, to permit the continuing of the process.) And second, the possibility of improvement is no longer measured only with respect to the current scenario alone, but also in relation to completed explorations of alternatives. Thus if a given scenario is, so far, much less successful than a competing completed scenario, then it should be required to show much higher than anticipated rates of improvement. Then the stopping rule may include a rule for abandoning an alternative.

Experience will show the desirability of an important caveat in generating or changing scenarios—both within a planning agency and whenever these procedures are opened to public participation. The warning has to do with evaluating the effects of proposed actions. Some specific changes may be low-cost and have low impact. These might be generally acceptable, but a wise precaution might be to extend their scope or replicate them, since at a higher level they might have proportionately less impact, or induce more adverse unintended side effects. Conversely, a well-directed change might exhibit low cost-effectiveness because some synergistic additional measures have been neglected. Interactions of both these types are what make planning difficult and interesting, and a good sketch-planning system should extend the experience of both planners and publics in dealing with them successfully.

We finally return to our initial question as to the difference between planning itself and sketch planning. To use a different metaphor than before, we might say that before we get serious about a major purchase, we go shopping. Shopping, like sketch planning, is wide in scope but somewhat superficial. It includes explorations of where to look. It engages in exploring all the same issues which appear in the final purchase. Nevertheless, purchasing proper requires more care, more consideration, and more detailing of actions and requirements. More people may be involved, and more interests may need to be satisfied. Yet when one says, "Let's go shopping," it might be assumed that shopping and purchasing are the same thing. They are not, although one leads to the other and they are hard to separate. Let's go sketching.

REFERENCES

Anas, A. 1987. *Modeling in Urban and Regional Economics.* Chur, Switzerland: Harwood Academic Publishers.

Hopkins, L. D. 1997. From Sketch Planning through Commitment: Progress Toward Planning Support Systems for Urban Development. In *Proceedings of Computers in Urban Planning and Urban Management, v. 2.* Mumbai, India: Narosa Publishing House.

———. 1998. Progress and Prospects for Planning Support Systems. *Environment and Planning B, Anniversary issue* 29–31.

Harris, B. 1985. Synthetic Geography: The Nature of Our Understanding of Cities. *Environment and Planning A* 17:443–69.

Herbert, J. S. and B. H. Stevens. 1960. A Model of the Distribution of Residential Activity in Urban Regions. *Journal of Regional Science* 2:21–36.

Ingram, G. K., J. F. Kain, and J. R. Ginn. 1972. *The Detroit Prototype of the NBER Urban Simulation Model.* New York: National Bureau of Economic Research.

Wegener, M. 1994. Operational Urban Models: State of the Art. *Journal of the American Planning Association* 60:17-29.

Wilson, A. G. 1970. *Entropy and Urban Modeling.* London: Pion.

———. 1974. *Urban and Regional Models in Geography and Planning.* New York: Wiley.

Paper 4

Structure of a Planning Support System for Urban Development

LEWIS D. HOPKINS

PROFESSOR, DEPARTMENT OF URBAN AND REGIONAL PLANNING

UNIVERSITY OF ILLINOIS AT URBANA–CHAMPAIGN

ABSTRACT

The idea of a planning support system, if not the label, has been with us for at least twenty-five years. Many components have been developed, but we lack an underlying structure with which to integrate these components. GIS provides useful tools, but the map concepts on which it is built are insufficient for a planning support system. The structure proposed here builds on elements of geographic modeling and on elements of planning. It works with actors, flows, investments, facilities, regulations, and rights as well as elements familiar in GIS. It includes views and tools for sketch planning, model building, scenario building, evaluation, lineage tracking, and plan-based action.

PLANNING SUPPORT SYSTEMS

Designing computing tools to support planning is an old idea. The Chicago Area Transportation Study used computers to run its models and displayed some of its results as travel desire lines on a primitive cathode-ray tube in the 1950s (Chicago Area Transportation Study 1960). Britton Harris (1960) has long argued for an approach to planning that combines sketch planning—rapid and partial description of alternatives—with state-of-the-art modeling of the implications of these alternatives. He has developed several highly refined computing tools for such modeling. Mel Branch (1971) described an elaborate PSS for "continuous city planning," including the design of a room for collaboration with citizen boards. Most of the tasks we now imagine were included in his proposal, but computing was a minor medium for calculation and not for display or direct interaction. More recently, Harris and Batty (1993) argued for coherent sets of tools for such tasks and labeled them Planning Support Systems (PSS). They identify

> ". . . two principal requirements for planning, which devolve onto any planning support system.
>
> First, since optimization (which equates with the automatic generation of plan) is impossible, the search for good plans must be by way of an informed process of trial and error which generates alternatives and prepares them for testing. This is often called sketch planning.
>
> Second, planning and policy making need extensive tools for tracing out the consequences of alternatives, since otherwise there is no way to compare alternatives on the basis of their costs and benefits, and no way to look for means of improving or replacing alternatives (pp. 193–194)."

New plans for Washington, D.C. (National Capital Planning Commission 1997), and Madrid (Neuman 1997) provide recent examples of sketches that were central in the development of plans. The Portland 2040 planning process in Portland, Oregon, considered alternative development patterns, initially in fairly abstract form equivalent to sketches, then traced out their consequences through the use of models. Portland-area planners also monitor the effects of implementation tools relative to plan intentions, and adjust actions to achieve intentions.

With gradually improving computational power and graphic displays, many computing tools have been developed that are useful in particular planning tasks, but no coherent system that links a wide range of tasks from sketch planning to modeling has been developed. Klosterman (1997a) argues that changing perceptions of how planning works created a moving target for system design. Branch's three-decades-old description is, however, surprisingly consistent with today's conception of planning as involving collaboration and extensive interaction with citizens. Collaboration is fundamental to communicative rationality, and collaborative aspects of PSS have been developed (Armstrong 1994; Shiffer 1992). Ironically, the tremendous success of geographic information systems (GIS) for a broader market has, if anything, distracted us from the development of PSS. The underlying structure of a PSS should be different from that of a GIS because in a PSS we want to manipulate elements of the situation for which we are planning and these elements are not inherently features of maps (Hopkins and Johnston 1990).

The purpose of this paper is to describe an underlying structure for a PSS focused on making and using plans for urban development. The intended scope of tasks includes sketch planning, model building, scenario building, evaluation, lineage tracking, and plan-based action. The two fundamental ideas are that

- the system should be built on a common set of elements of urban development processes, and

- the workspace views and tools should be based on tasks of making and using plans for urban development.

The first implies that the system should be built in object-oriented terms, both in the sense of object-oriented simulation and in the sense of object-oriented programming (Taylor 1990). The second implies that the interface should be open to a full range of planning tasks. In section 2, I will discuss objects and the ways in which an object-oriented approach can support a wide range of tasks from sketching to modeling. In sections 3, 4, and 5 the proposed structure is described from three perspectives: urban development, interface views, and planning tasks. The structure is described in the present tense for simplicity of language, but it is speculative. It has not been implemented, though it is possible with today's technology and knowledge. Some of the views and tools have been implemented as parts of disparate systems and are cited below in discussion of specific aspects of the system.

OBJECT STRUCTURE FOR A PLANNING SUPPORT SYSTEM

The PSS is intended to support both initial thinking and the persuasion required to achieve commitment to actions. These tasks may be undertaken by individuals working alone, by collaboration among experts, or by collaboration of experts with clients or constituencies. It is thus essential that ideas can be developed from simple concepts to specific actions that are fully elaborated and analyzed, without losing track of what has been proposed or assumed.

Sketching an idea about urban development implies quickly describing a set of relationships among urban development activities. We might sketch the major connectors of the existing road network and proposed additions to the network, thinking of these elements as both connecting paths and separating edges. We might locate key groups of people or activities, implying both roles as origins and destinations of trips and as perceptual organizers of social space. Such sketches require objects that denote elements and relationships without specific geographic positions or relationships sufficient to place them on a map. Qualitatively, the sketch may distinguish "blobs" and "edges," but these types of objects denote ideas about urban development, not map features. They have attributes, behaviors, and qualitative spatial relationships with other objects. A class structure of objects that can describe urban development activities without necessarily relating to a map will support sketch planning. The same basic structure of classes of objects can also support modeling and the other tasks of making and using plans.

A geographic modeling system (GMS) structures the elements being modeled in a particular application domain and provides tools to support such modeling. For example, a GMS for ecological modeling (Westervelt and Hopkins 1999) includes (1) individual animals, collections of animals as populations, behaviors of individuals, and interactions with other animals of the same and different species; (2) landscape processes such as plant growth; and (3) tools for manipulating these elements and combining them into models. These elements apply to a particular domain of ecological modeling. They might be incorporated into a more general modeling system that included aspects of urban development, but the key objects for urban modeling are different.

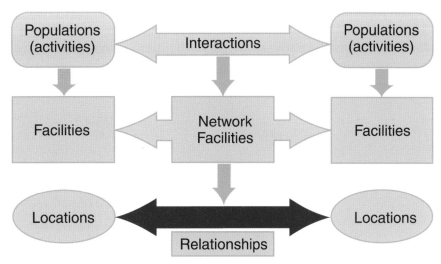

Figure 1. Structure of a geographical urban modeling system.

In its simplest form, a GMS for urban modeling includes locations and the relationships among them and populations and the interactions among them (Hopkins 1997). A more complete view of a modeling system for urban development is shown in figure 1. The activities we wish to model are the behaviors of populations of individuals. These include shopping, working, school, and the trips implied in carrying them out, and yield interactions among populations, where a population may be a collection of individuals or a collection of retail firms. These populations occur in facilities—buildings—and their interactions occur over network facilities—roads, sewers, light rail. The facilities are located in space and the locations have spatial relationships among them. This set of elements can be manipulated in sketch-planning tasks and in implementing spatial interaction models, transportation models, and location–allocation models.

Figure 2 annotates this diagram to show how transportation modeling ideas fit this framework. Facilities are investments, which are durable (long lasting), lumpy (indivisible increments), and costly to reverse. Similarly, network facilities, such as roads or light rail, are investments that change the nature of relationships among locations. Given these facilities in locations, populations made up of individual actors choose locations for housing and choose modes and routes of travel over networks. The UrbanSim model (Waddell 1998) is perhaps the best example of an urban development model built from an object-oriented perspective, and thus adaptable to use in a GMS. Some of the classes of elements, or "objects," that support the UrbanSim model could also support other tasks in a GMS, and in turn in a PSS built on a GMS.

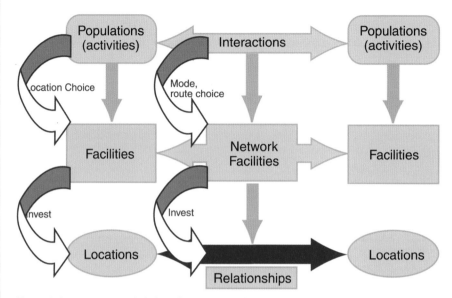

Figure 2. Investments and choices for transportation and land-use modeling.

This framework supports both the consideration of alternative investments and the effects of these investments on housing location choice, retail location, employment location, and spatial interaction. Sketch planning manipulates these investments rapidly and at many levels of abstraction. Models consider patterns of investment that may occur given certain initial conditions and behaviors that may occur given these investments. These elements thus support one major aspect of urban development plans: investments in facilities and infrastructure.

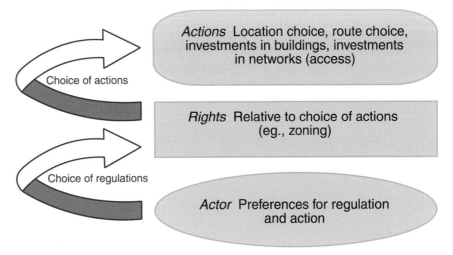

Figure 3. Rights and regulations.

The other major aspect of urban development plans is regulation. A PSS must, therefore, include elements that define rights, which determine the set of available actions, and elements that define regulations, which change the current set of rights. Figure 3 describes these relationships. Actors have preferences of two kinds, preferences for the set of rights in which they act and preferences for actions given these rights (Riker and Ordeshook 1973). Again, the three levels of this diagram highlight consideration of regulations changing rights and of the behavioral implications of such regulations. Sketch plans consider different configurations of regulations. Models trace out their implications as actors respond to them. Both the sketches and the models manipulate the same basic classes of objects.

URBAN DEVELOPMENT ACTIVITIES AND ACTORS

The PSS is built on a data structure and set of elements focused specifically on urban development. Rather than building from a traditional GIS and thus from primitives of map features (points, lines, polygons) or surfaces (raster or grid arrays), the PSS builds from Actors, Activities, Flows, Investments, Facilities, Regulations, Rights, Issues, Forces, Opportunities, and Constraints.

Actors are divided into two major subclasses, individual and collective. Private actors include individuals, firms, and developers, which are described by attributes such as budget, behavioral motivations, and available actions. Collective actors include voluntary groups and governments and are described by such attributes as budget, behavioral motivations, available actions, regulatory authority, and spatial jurisdiction. A collection of individuals constitutes a population. Individuals can also be aggregated into households. We can then, for example, define populations of households demanding retail services, retail providers, developers who might build facilities, and governments with authority to regulate location of retail facilities. Actors can invest and thus change physical capital stock, regulate and thus change rights to act, and behave within an urban system by choosing housing location or exhibiting travel behavior.

Activities are things that actors do (other than make investments or set regulations). Daily activity patterns are the basis for generating trip demands, as in microsimulation of trip-making behavior so as to include trip chaining, for example.

Flows are trips or other interactions generated by an actor (e.g., migration moves, messages, sewage) from one facility to another facility over a network.

Investments change capital stock. In other words, they change capacity and location of facilities. Investments are durable, costly to reverse, and at best partially divisible. An investment lasts for a long time, cannot be changed in location or capacity without additional cost, and cannot be implemented in arbitrarily small increments because of economies of scale in construction and operation. Investments change the capacity of infrastructure, for example by adding lanes to highways, adding new links to highway networks, adding pipes to sewerage networks, adding capacity to water or sewage treatment plants, or building schools or health posts. Private actors make investments such as buildings for housing, commercial, or industrial use. Actors make investments constrained by budget capacity, by rights, and by capabilities to take particular actions.

Facilities represent capital stock, which includes housing, commercial buildings, and industrial buildings as well as roads, sewers, water supply, schools, and health posts. A facility thus has a location and a capacity at a given time. Facilities are sometimes ascribed attributes of demand or supply, but in general such attributes should be ascribed to actors that use the facilities. For example, a household, not the house in which it lives, should be the basis for generating trips to work or shop. The house in which the household lives is more fixed in location than the household and sets the intensity of land use. Similarly, although we could estimate the attractiveness of retail services in terms of size of the facility, attractiveness is more appropriately a function of the size of the retail firms located there. For flexibility of use, however, the PSS supports definition of attractiveness for either the facility or the firm.

Regulations change rights. Regulations define changes in the available actions for individuals, firms, and developers within the jurisdiction of the regulator. Actors with the appropriate jurisdiction and capacity to enforce them can make regulations.

Rights specify the available actions for particular groups of actors, for example residents in a municipality. They specify available actions for individuals, firms, developers, and governments. In the case of governments, rights may be limited by constitutions, for example, a requirement to compensate owners for land, or by higher levels of government, such as legislation by state governments that limits the actions available to municipalities. Rights are imperfectly enforced, which may be affected by the budget of the responsible actors. They include taxes and incentives because these also modify the available actions. Rights define relationships within voluntary groups as well as coercive groups. A downtown business organization, for example, might levy fees on its members to pay for a downtown plan. Enforcement of rights within voluntary groups, however, is different from enforcement in coercive groups.

Issues are concerns about the current or future situation as perceived by actors with relation to Actors, Facilities, Flows, Rights, and Regulations. Issues are identified in early sketching of situations in collaboration with citizens and in evaluating plans with respect to these issues raised initially or additional issues discovered during the planning process.

Forces are relative to populations or facilities and have direction and degree. They might describe directions of perceived growth pressure or perceived social barriers. Again they are useful in framing situations and in evaluation.

Opportunities and constraints provide objects to identify perceived general options and constraints in early stages of sketching the situation. They are described in terms of actors and other elements above.

The above elements suggest a set of object classes. The actual class structure of an implemented PSS would be much more complex, but this set is sufficient to explain the approach to creating a common set of objects useful across planning tasks. Note that manipulation and graphic display of these elements is largely independent of this object structure. The system design could be implemented in association with GIS or with newer ideas of virtual reality or both.

All work is organized into Workspaces, in which the state of current work is saved, at least in the sense of a record sufficient to reconstruct it from the data on which it is based. This approach is similar to other modern software packages. A workspace can include the following types of Views: Sketches, Maps, Models, Scenarios, Multi-attribute Tables, Plans, and Realized Scenarios.

All of these Views use object classes described in the previous section. Thus, an idea for a light rail line exists independent of a particular View. It can be viewed as a Sketch, in which case it merely shows connections among locations. These connections are defined by the names of the locations they connect. The same idea can be viewed as a Map, in which case the named locations are associated with geographic coordinates. A line connecting locations in a Sketch can be assigned a length, a capacity, a mode type, and a construction date, all without any reference to geographic coordinates. These attributes might remain constant across various route alignments, as would results of modeling based on attributes that are independent of alignment. If an alignment were specified as part of a more complete Scenario, the contradiction of assigned length and computed length would be flagged for resolution by computer or human expertise. In this way, ideas can be evaluated at various levels of abstraction.

Thus, "plans-in-the-making" can exist at various levels of abstraction and completeness, which is essential for collaboration. Plans can be described in different languages of discourse by different parties (Williams and Matheny 1995). Even Realized Scenarios, that is, descriptions of the state of the world, can exist distinctly and at various levels of abstraction and thus need not be agreed to by all participants. Two characteristics are crucial to these capabilities: The elements of urban development action must exist independent of any of the particular types of views, and these elements must make sense as things that participants want to talk about and manipulate.

Sketches are diagrams without geographic coordinates. They may identify sets of objects, nonspatial relationships among objects, or qualitative spatial relationships among objects. We can thus, for example, sketch an issues-and-forces diagram in approximate geographic relationships but without geographic coordinates. We can sketch incompatibilities among projects proposed as investments, where relationships have no geographic meaning at all. Friend and Hickling (1987) present examples of a full range of diagrams and sketches useful in making plans.

Maps are the traditional view of a GIS. Objects viewed in Sketches can be elaborated and viewed in Maps, for example, showing existing Issues and Forces, sets of proposed actions, or outcomes. Maps also display patterns of input data and results from Models or Scenarios. Map views have all the capabilities of a traditional GIS. The difference is that urban development objects defined in the previous section may have attributes of spatial extent or location at a particular time; in a GIS the spatial extents or locations are the objects, and only such objects and their attributes can be manipulated. In the PSS, therefore, elements, which can be viewed in Maps, can also be used in other types of Views.

Models are used to construct and calibrate models and to initiate individual model runs. Models are constructed from Actors, Activities, Flows, Investments, Facilities, Regulations, and Rights. Types of models include transportation models, urban development simulations, housing location models, retail trade models, and cohort survival population forecast models. The Model view is a worksheet for use of a modeling language.

Scenarios play out a set of assumptions and proposed actions. At a minimum, a Scenario consists of a set of Investments and Regulations. Usually a Scenario also includes runs of one or more Models to trace out the implications of the initial conditions and actions. In most cases, a Scenario includes several runs of different Models addressing different aspects of a set of proposed actions. For example, a Scenario might start with an existing land-use and infrastructure pattern. A set of assumptions and a set of Investments and Regulations might then be selected. The implications of these assumptions might be discovered by running a simulation model of housing development, a transportation model of interaction each year, a retail facility location model, an air pollution diffusion model, and an accounting model of housing price and affordability. A set of Scenarios in a Workspace may be the basis for constructing and presenting recommended actions that are combined into a Plan.

Multiattribute Tables report performance across a set of attributes of Investments, Regulations, combinations of Investments and Regulations as Plans, and results of Scenarios expressed as Activity patterns, Flow patterns, or predicted Investments. These tables can be manipulated to display and compare alternatives or alternative outcomes or to provide inputs to formal evaluation methods. Four table formats support visual comparison, multiattribute evaluation methods (including equity and fairness measures), cost–benefit analysis, and decision analysis. Each of these requires slightly different information and thus a slightly different format, but the formats are transformable to encourage use of more than one method of evaluation.

Plans are combinations of Investments and Regulations that make sense as strategies for one or more Actors. These Investments and Regulations have costs, fit budgets and jurisdictions, and have expected or contingent times and locations. Plans are distinct from Scenarios in that Plans are statements about intended actions, whereas Scenarios play out assumptions to test ideas. Plans can exist as tentative ideas, as proposals for discussion, as formal drafts, or as formally adopted documents. Plans can include contingent strategies, based on expectations and opportunities to make sequential decisions after uncertain outcomes can be observed. We might test a particular Plan in several Scenarios with different assumptions about initial conditions, exogenous trends, and model parameters.

Realized Scenarios are records of the state of the real world. They provide starting points for simulation Scenarios and provide the monitoring data for Plan-Based Action tools. Rather than presume that there is a single set of observed facts, it is useful to be able to describe the current state and history of development in different ways for different purposes from the perspectives of different participants.

These Views support a full range of planning tasks. They function by sharing common objects that describe urban development actions.

The Tools support the traditional aspects of planning processes—designing options or alternatives, forecasting performance of alternatives, and evaluating performance—as well as communicative processes of collaboration and argument. The categories of Tools are not the same as these aspects, however, because the same Tools are used in several aspects of planning. Sketch-planning tools, for example, are used to design options, to work out their spatial relationships, and to evaluate their compatibility. Models are used to design options, to work out implications, and to generate specific performance measures for evaluation. The set of Tools available changes with the type of View that is active in the Workspace, but many of the Tools are common to several types of Views. Tools are described here categorized by major tasks: Sketch Planning, Model Building, Scenario Building, Evaluation, Lineage/Process, and Plan-Based Action.

Sketch-planning tools work with any of the object types primarily in Sketch, Map, or Plan views. These tools not only place graphic symbols, but use a set of gestures (simplified motions analogous to strokes of a pen) to place objects in relation to each other and to define their properties and the properties of their relationships. These properties can initially be defined in very abstract or incomplete terms, but can be elaborated to support various types of modeling and evaluation. Elaboration tools refine definitions—for example, the proposed time, capacity, and cost of a new road link initially inserted merely as a link. Sketching can be used for efficient description of any kind of idea. Thus sketch-planning tools can be used to describe the "Issues and Forces" in the current situation (Where are we?), to describe desired land-use pattern outcomes in terms of Facilities (Where do we want to be?), or to describe sets of Investments and Regulations that might be implemented (How can we get there?). These tasks play very different roles in the planning process, but the tools needed are very similar. Issues and Forces compiled collaboratively in a Sketch may evolve into a Plan, without encoding the ideas again from scratch. George (1997) implemented sketch tools for describing urban design ideas, but his implementation is not based on a structure that can be generalized to support other types of sketches.

Model-building tools, equivalent to a domain-specific modeling language, work with Actors, Activities, Flows, Investments, Facilities, Regulations, and Rights in order to build, calibrate, and run Models. The modeling capabilities support three types of models implied by the investments, location choices, and interactions in the geographic modeling system diagram in figure 2. First, pure cross-section spatial interaction models, such as transportation models, predict trip flows and link loading given fixed facilities and fixed household locations. Second, marginal adjustment models are quasi-dynamic; they predict, for example, movement of households, but assume that housing stock is fixed. Third, models of urban investment predict investments in physical stocks of infrastructure and buildings and thus predict changes in capital stock over time. Batty and Xie's modeling interface for population density functions (Batty and Xie 1994a; Batty and Xie 1994b) provides these tools for one specific domain. Waddell's UrbanSim (1998) is based on a set of object classes similar to those proposed here.

Scenario-building tools work with all of the object classes to generate Scenarios. The tools focus on selecting data for particular runs of models, constructing comparable data sets to run linked models, interpreting model results as input to other models, and displaying model results. Smart annotation helps to decide which results to display, when to display them, and how to interpret them. For example, a dynamic microsimulation of land development for twenty years will generate too many events and variables to be displayed. Smart annotation tools look for trend changes, discontinuities, and nonrandom (clustered) patterns in space and time and highlight these events and variables. Scenario tools include structured procedures for sensitivity analysis and robustness, modeling to generate alternatives (Brill et al. 1990), and direct manipulation of elements in a scenario in real time as its implications are played out and displayed. The *What if?* PSS includes scenario-building tools for tracing out the implications of specific urban development criteria (Klosterman 1997b), but does not support modeling.

Evaluation tools work with all types of objects, primarily as arranged in Multiattribute Tables, to support various forms of evaluation of outcomes and actions. Tools support structuring of data for discounting over time, for structuring decision trees, and for implementing cost–benefit analysis, cost revenue analysis, decision analysis, and computation of equivalent alternatives. Tools also support sensitivity analysis and comparisons across techniques. An important aspect of evaluation is display of comparative performance in ways that help decision makers to identify improved alternatives through diagnostic or "cognitive feedback" (Lee 1993; Lee and Hopkins 1995).

Process/Lineage tools provide guidance on processes and record the process used. There is not a separate process/lineage view because process advice is embedded in the interface itself and the user cannot modify the lineage record. This advice can be thought of as predicting what sequence of analyses would yield a persuasive argument when viewed retrospectively as the lineage of an argument. The interface incorporates process diagrams, which show what data has been used, what the users have done, what the computer has done, and what options are currently available (Johnston and Hopkins 1994). At any time, a user can request expertise from the system on possible tasks to undertake next or on use of difficult techniques (Lee 1993). Planning involves complex manipulations and analyses of many different types of data. It is important to be able to show what assumptions have been made, what data has been used, and what analyses have been performed. The lineage tools allow the planner to show how an argument or result was constructed, to check that result, and to perform sensitivity analyses of the entire process. This information supports persuasion and responds to counter arguments. It also makes visible the process, which is essential in involving citizens and sustaining their trust.

Plan-Based Action. Plans must be used and plans that have been created with computing support are already encoded in ways that can make implementation more effective. If a plan is constructed as a strategy, a contingent sequence of related actions, then plan-based action requires keeping track of actions that have been taken, outcomes that have occurred, states of environmental variables that were treated as uncertain in the plan, and implications for currently available actions. If the plan calls for sewer expansion in a particular place with a particular capacity, but land development in the sewershed can now be observed to be occurring at much higher densities than expected, then the sewer pipe sizes may have to be increased. If development is occurring faster than expected, then capital improvement projects will have to be built sooner or development timing will have to be regulated. If a regulation is not resulting in intended higher densities, then revised regulations may be required.

More specific definitions of these various tools must be developed as such a system is implemented. These categories of tools give an indication, however, of how the proposed structure can support these various types of tools in a common computing environment.

AN AGENDA FOR BUILDING PLANNING SUPPORT SYSTEMS

The system described here does not yet exist. It was described in the present tense only for simplicity of language. A PSS can and should be based on

1 a common set of objects inherent in urban development processes, and

2 views and tools that share these common objects so as to support a full range of planning tasks.

In implementing prototypes of such a system, we will discover reasons to revise and refine this structure. Such prototypes and trials with users are essential to test and modify these ideas. Although partial prototypes will be useful, they should focus on testing a common underlying structure for PSS, not merely on implementing constituent parts.

ACKNOWLEDGMENTS

Some of these ideas were developed while I was a Fulbright Scholar at the Central Department of Geography, Tribhuvan University, Kathmandu, Nepal, and were presented there; at the 5th International Conference on Computers in Urban Planning and Urban Management in Mumbai, India; and at National Chung Hsing University, Taiwan. The ideas have been refined based on responses to those presentations and discussions with Britton Harris, Shih-Kung Lai, Paul Waddell, and Doug Johnston.

REFERENCES

Armstrong, M. P. 1994. Requirements for the Development of GIS-based Group Decision Support Systems. *Journal of the American Society for Information Science* 45(9):669–77.

Batty, M., and Y. Xie. 1994a. Modelling Inside GIS: Part 1: Model Structures, Exploratory Data Analysis and Aggregation. *International Journal of Geographic Information Science* 8(3):291–307.

———. 1994b. Modelling Inside GIS: Part 2: Selecting and Calibrating Urban Models Using ARC/INFO. *International Journal of Geographic Information Science* 8(5):451–70.

Branch, M. 1971. *City Planning and Aerial Information.* Cambridge, MA: Harvard University Press.

Brill, E. D., Jr., J. M. Flach, L. D. Hopkins, and S. Ranjithan. 1990. MGA: A Decision Support System for Complex, Incompletely Defined Problems. *IEEE Transactions on Systems, Man, and Cybernetics* 20(4):745–57.

Chicago Area Transportation Study. 1960. Chicago Area Transportation Study, Final Report, Volume II: Data Projections. Chicago: Chicago Area Transportation Study.

Friend, J. K., and A. Hickling. 1987. *Planning under Pressure.* Oxford: Pergamon.

George, R. V. 1997. Hyperspace: Communicating Ideas About the Quality of Urban Spaces. *Journal of Planning Education and Research* 17(1):63–70.

Harris, B. 1960. Plan or Projection: An Examination of the Use of Models in Planning. *Journal of the American Institute of Planners* 26(4):265–72.

Harris, B., and M. Batty. 1993. Locational Models, Geographic Information and Planning Support Systems. *Journal of Planning Education and Research* 12(3):184–98.

Hopkins, L. D. 1997. From Sketch Planning through Commitment: Progress toward a Planning Support System for Urban Development. In *Proceedings of the 5th International Conference on Computers in Urban Planning and Urban Management,* ed. P. K. Sikdar, S. L. Dhingra, and K. V. Krishna Rao. Mumbai, India: Narosa Publishing House.

Hopkins, L. D., and D. M. Johnston. 1990. Locating Spatially Complex Activities with Symbolic Reasoning: An Object-Oriented Approach. In *Proceedings of the 4th International Symposium on Spatial Data Handling.* Zurich, Switzerland.

Johnston, D. M., and L. D. Hopkins. 1994. TRAINER: A System for Training Requirements Assessment and Integration with Environmental Resources, contract report to U.S. Army Corps of Engineers Construction Engineering Research lab. Urbana: University of Illinois at Urbana–Champaign.

Klosterman, R. E. 1997a. Planning Support Systems: A New Perspective on Computer-Aided Planning. *Journal of Planning Education and Research* 17(1):45–54.

———. 1997b. The What If? Collaborative Planning Support System. In *Proceedings of the 5th International Conference on Computers in Urban Planning and Urban Management,* ed. P. K. Sikdar, S. L. Dhingra, and K. V. Krishna Rao. Mumbai, India: Narosa Publishing House.

Lee, I. 1993. Development of Procedural Expertise to Support Multiattribute Spatial Decision Making. Ph.D. thesis, Regional Planning, University of Illinois at Urbana–Champaign.

———, and L. D. Hopkins. 1995. Procedural Expertise for Efficient Multiattribute Evaluation: A Procedural Support Strategy for CEA. *Journal of Planning Education and Research* 14(4):255–68.

National Capital Planning Commission. 1997. Extending the Legacy: Planning America's Capital for the 21st Century. Washington, D.C.: National Capital Planning Commission.

Neuman, M. 1997. Images as Institution Builders: Metropolitan Planning in Madrid. In *Making Strategic Spatial Plans: Innovations in Europe,* ed. P. Healey, A. Khakee, A. Motte, and B. Needham. London: UCL Press.

Riker, W. H., and P. C. Ordeshook. 1973. *An Introduction to Positive Political Theory.* Englewood Cliffs, NJ: Prentice–Hall.

Shiffer, M. J. 1992. Towards a Collaborative Planning System. *Environment and Planning B: Planning and Design* 19:709–22.

Taylor, D. A. 1990. *Object-Oriented Technology: A Manager's Guide.* Reading, MA: Addison–Wesley Publishing Company.

Waddell, P. 1998. The Oregon Prototype Metropolitan Land Use Model. Paper read at Transportation, Land Use, and Air Quality: Making the Connection, at Portland, OR.

Westervelt, J., and L. D. Hopkins. 1999. Modeling Mobile Individuals in Dynamic Landscapes. *International Journal of Geographic Information Science.*

Williams, B., and A. Matheny. 1995. *Democracy, Dialogue, and Environmental Disputes.* New Haven, CT: Yale University Press.

Paper 5

The METROPILUS Planning Support System: Urban Models and GIS

STEPHEN H. PUTMAN

CHAIR, GRADUATE GROUP

DEPARTMENT OF CITY AND REGIONAL PLANNING

UNIVERSITY OF PENNSYLVANIA

PHILADELPHIA, PENNSYLVANIA

SHIH-LIANG CHAN

INSTRUCTOR, NATIONAL CHUNG–HSIN UNIVERSITY

TAIPEI, TAIWAN

ABSTRACT

As a future-oriented activity, effective planning depends upon temporally and sectorally disaggregated information inputs. Past, present, and future are all included in what planners would like to know in order to make effective policy plans and decisions. In recent years the confluence of developments in geographic information systems, urban land-use and transportation modeling, and computer hardware has made possible an unprecedented increase in the availability and timely provision of information inputs to planners. Here we describe the integration of a sophisticated set of land-use models, EMPAL and DRAM, with a powerful geographic information system (GIS) software package, ArcView GIS, on a desktop computer in order to provide comprehensive information input to future oriented planning decisions. The combined system, METROPILUS, is currently in use in six major metropolitan areas in the United States.

INTRODUCTION

Planning may be thought of as a process for determining appropriate future action through a sequence of choices (Davidoff and Reiner 1962). To make these choices under uncertain conditions, planners need to collect comprehensive information about the past, the present, and the future. In discussing the relationship between planning and information, Hopkins (1981) argues, even more explicitly, that planning can be perceived as gathering information to reduce uncertainty. From our perspective it really goes without saying that planning practice depends heavily on the availability and quality of information. Moreover, the quality of planning and its decision processes can be substantially improved when the required information is handled appropriately and efficiently. Clearly, then, effective planning requires descriptive, predictive, and prescriptive information inputs (Webster 1993; Webster 1994). As planning is always oriented toward the future, forecasting becomes a necessary part of it. Following through the planning process, planners attempt to understand and define current issues, foresee future developments, and propose feasible plans based on available information. Among the available approaches for meeting the forecasting requirements of planners, urban models can be an efficient and effective support tool.

The evolution of computer and information technology over the last few decades has had a significant impact on the planning profession. Among the technological advancements, after microcomputers, per se, GIS is perhaps the one that has been most attractive to planners. With its powerful capacity for spatial data management, spatial analysis, and visualization, GIS provides planners with new tools to implement their work more efficiently. While many planners have been quick to utilize these new planning tools, it should be remembered that GIS was not originally designed or developed for the planning profession. For this reason, both users and developers have been trying to find ways to make GIS and related technologies more useful in the planning environment. One popular approach involves trying to integrate GIS with applications or functions originating in planning. Planning support systems (PSS) have been the subject of considerable debate in recent years, and have received some benefit from the efforts in this direction. With this in mind, we examine here the basic elements in PSS, and then define our approach to implementation of one such system, by integrating urban models with GIS, to provide improved functionality of planning support. We then discuss the results of initial applications of this system.

GEOGRAPHIC INFORMATION SYSTEMS EVOLVING

In 1963 the senior author of this chapter was involved in the Pittsburgh Community Renewal Program (CRP). One of the major tasks undertaken as part of that project was the development of computer models to forecast the effects, on employment and household location, of the various policies that were to be a part of the CRP. The use of computer-driven pen plotters to draw maps was proposed as well, mainly to display data, but also, ultimately, the results of the various analyses. It was thought that this would provide a valuable and cost-effective supplement to the general activities of the Pittsburgh City Planning Commission under whose auspices the project was being conducted. The mapping was in fact completed, but at a cost which vastly exceeded the initial budget, which made it prohibitive to use such maps as regular analysis tools or aids. The cost of producing maps by computer at that time was such that they could only be used to make a few final maps for "display" purposes.

The same era saw the development of computer software for the production of "printer plots." One of the better-known such packages was SYMAP, which was somewhat easier to use than the pen plotter software, with more rapid response, but accompanied by a substantial degradation of image quality. The results of these programs were still rather slow in coming, and were extremely crude by today's standards, allowing for only the most rudimentary map presentation techniques. Suffice it to say that over the twenty years that followed, a combination of factors led to phenomenal changes. Both conceptual and technological factors were involved, including the development of database systems, computer graphics technology, computer hardware, and the like. These have given us today's remarkably sophisticated and cost-effective GIS software. The capabilities available, for example, in ESRI's rather inexpensive ArcView GIS package, implemented on a microcomputer costing less than $3,000, are capable of producing results that were not even imagined possible during the time of the Pittsburgh CRP.

The notion of large urban or regional data sets, linked or indexed by geographic reference, has provided the basis for a dramatic increase in analytical as well as in presentational capability in urban planning and analysis. Even so, here we are describing the development of potential, of capabilities, rather than of a discrete formal change in the way that urban and regional planning, forecasting, and policy analysis are actually done. It is the concept of the PSS, built upon a

GIS base combined with other analytical capabilities, which points to ways in which major changes in planning practice can be made.

URBAN LAND-USE AND TRANSPORTATION MODELS EVOLVING

The idea of urban models, specifically urban land-use and transportation models or large-scale urban models, originated during the 1950s and expanded during the 1960s—not surprisingly, the decades of important developments in computer technology. For a brief time, urban models were treated as a potential new tool for planning, not only aiding in planning activity, but also carrying the possibility that they might be instrumental in redefining the process of planning itself (Harris 1965). Although they were subsequently criticized as failing to fulfill the ultimate goals of planning (Lee 1973), urban models did not vanish, but continued to be developed and applied, and have reemerged in the past two decades to take a new role in planning activities. A report by ISGLUTI (Webster, Bly, and Paulley 1988), as well as a later special issue of the *Journal of American Planning Association* (1994), addressed recent developments in this field and listed the many models that are currently being applied to help planners in their diverse activities.

In 1963 there were no operational land-use models. The situation in transportation modeling was somewhat different. With the support of substantial funding from the U.S. Bureau of Public Roads (BPR), a package of computer software generally referred to as the BPR Package had been widely distributed to planning agencies and was in nearly universal use for transportation network analysis. This was, of course, not to say that there were no problems with these models. There were many, but a formal structure had already been put in place within which the results of years of theoretical, empirical, and technological progress could be placed as they developed.

Perhaps the earliest attempts at planning agency application of land-use models took place in the early 1960s. An overview of many of the early attempts at residential location models can be found in Putman (1979). After the first decade's work, the two dominant types of models in agency use were the several Lowry model derivatives (Goldner 1971) and the many applications of the EMPIRIC model. The response to this work by both the academic and professional planning communities was ambivalent. Even so, there was still a strong perceived need for modeling tools to address the metropolitan location and land-use forecasting problem.

In 1971 the Federal Highway Administration (FHWA) issued a request for proposal (RFP) for a means of analyzing what it then described as the problem of "premature obsolescence of highway facilities." This project and several that followed allowed the problems of model application and convenience of use to be examined in light of previous successes and failures in land-use modeling. For today's readers it is worth noting that during the time of this work there were no microcomputers; there weren't even any video display terminals. It was a keypunch–punchcard world. In that sense, at that time, ease of use meant comprehensive written documentation, and uniformity of inputs and outputs. Ease of use also meant then, as well as now, that data could be obtained and models calibrated in a straightforward manner.

By the mid-1990s the EMPAL and DRAM models, developed by this author (Putman 1983, 1991, 1995), were the most widely applied land-use models in the United States, having at that time seen actual agency implementation and use in sixteen metropolitan areas. DRAM locates households, while EMPAL locates employers/employees. While these models did not have the most theoretically comprehensive structures that could be imagined, to a very considerable extent they worked, and met many of the user agencies' needs. After the initial model implementation projects, during which the models were installed on agency hardware, calibrated to regional data, and applied in forecasting by the agencies, about half the agencies continued with in-house use of the models as a component of their ongoing land-use and transportation and forecasting analyses.

Models that are useful in urban and regional planning must draw upon numerous perspectives, from areas such as economics, entropy/information theory, random utility theory, mathematical geography, and others. The basic intent of operational urban models is to integrate the activity systems in the urban area according to spatial interactions within a socioeconomic framework. These models can help planners discover urban location problems and test the effects of proposed solutions or policies. Models can provide assistance to planners in performing the functions of analysis, prediction, policy simulation, and impact analysis.

From the viewpoint of rationalism and comprehensiveness, the planning process includes a cycle of problem definition, analysis, goal formulation, operational objectives, generation of alternatives, evaluation of alternatives, and choice of alternatives. This procedure, with the decision to plan, and possible subsequent implementation, turns the cycle into active reality. Sitting in the context of cyclic processes, urban models can provide the requisite information for analysis, operational objectives, generation of alternatives, and evaluation of alternatives. Accordingly, the real world will change in response to the implementation of some specific action, which is based, in part, on the information provided by urban models. The observed information regarding the change will serve as new input for further planning, and model, processes.

FRAMEWORK FOR AN URBAN MODEL/ GIS-BASED PSS

Planning support systems (PSS) have become an increasingly popular topic of discussion with respect to the provision of efficient environments for planning activity. From both the technical and the functional viewpoints, it has been commonly accepted that a PSS should be built on the basis of GIS technology (Harris 1989; Klosterman 1994). At the same time, it has also been argued that a PSS cannot consist of GIS alone. In addition to the GIS core, a PSS must also include a full range of planners' traditional tools. These might include, for example, the tools for urban and regional economic and demographic analysis and forecasting, for environmental modeling, for transportation planning, and for predicting future development and land-use patterns. The idea of integrating urban models and GIS thus arises quite naturally within this context. It becomes possible, as well, to develop an Urban Models and GIS (UM/GIS)-based PSS for planning support (Scholten and Padding 1989; Batty and Harris 1993). To fulfill the functions of planning support, a UM/GIS-based PSS should be composed of at least three modules, or module groups. They are, as shown in figure 1, a Model Knowledge Module, a Model Operation Module, and the Information Transformation/Communication Modules. The data/information exchange engine in the system is provided by other external database management systems (DBMS). As described above, the GIS functionality provides the base for subsequent PSS development, the environment in which the PSS functions will be constructed. Later, we will discuss the relationships among the components and their functions.

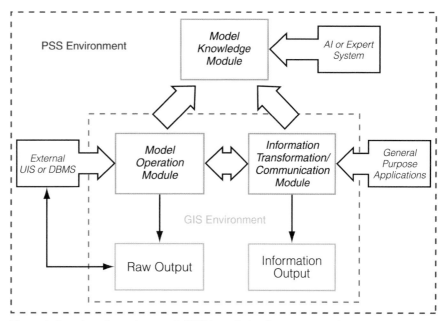

Figure 1. Overview of an urban model/GIS-based planning support system.

Currently available urban models were developed in the context of their own specific initial purposes and theoretical backgrounds. Before attempting to apply them to ongoing planning activity, the users have to know what the models can do, what their limitations are, and how they work. The Model Knowledge Module would serve this function more efficiently and effectively than is currently done through traditional paper documentation. An online system, in conjunction with hard-copy documentation, would provide a better source of such knowledge. Users of the PSS might then query the module for advice such as the most appropriate model to apply under a specific situation, the information requirements for a particular type of analysis, or the means of interpreting the criteria used in model calibration.

This framework follows the flow of information in the planning process, which can be defined as information collection, information organization, and information communication. The Model Operation Module and the Information Transformation/Communication Modules are the two major components of the information production function of the system. The Model Operation Module is a collection of urban models that are necessary for the planning activities of the planning agencies. This module performs both the functions of prediction and prescription, depending on the contents of the models included. The important issue in this system with respect to data management is how to manage and exchange data within the system and with other systems. The issue brings up the necessity for a DBMS to serve as the data management engine in the UM/GIS-based PSS. Once the required information is generated from the analysis processes, planners have to communicate and exchange the information with other entities, which include experts, the public, and/or other PSS. The PSS developed here belongs in the second and third stage. With a further connection to a database management system, DBMS, the overall system would be able to cover a major portion of the several procedures of information production.

**INITIAL DEVELOPMENT
CONSIDERATIONS**

Active development of the specifications for this new system began in the mid-1990s. At that time, sixteen different metropolitan areas in the United States had an ongoing or recently completed EMPAL/DRAM model system application. Prior to these applications, the models had been calibrated for data from more than forty different metropolitan areas worldwide. With this considerable base of experience, as well as the whole range of user responses and comments, we began to develop some sense of the form that the new system would have to take in order to best meet the needs of the majority of users. While there was a considerable range of comment as to what improvements might be desired, the overwhelming majority focused on a desire for greater ease of use. All other possible improvements, including those of enhanced theoretical elaboration, fell much farther back on preference lists.

Over the years, the EMPAL and DRAM models have been implemented on numerous computer systems. They were initially developed on IBM mainframe computers. Many model runs as well as considerable model development took place on IBM 360 series machines. In the early 1980s some runs were done on a Cray supercomputer. In 1981 we provided source code for both models to the Puget Sound Council of Governments for conversion for use on their CDC machines. The last (to our knowledge) mainframe use of these programs was on an IBM 3090 at the University of Pennsylvania (Putman 1992).

The first microcomputer implementation was in 1984 on an IBM PC/AT in Sarajevo, Yugoslavia. The first practical microcomputer implementation was for use in Phoenix, in 1992. The momentum of the Microsoft® Windows® operating system in the 1990s swept software development along with it so that now virtually all the active EMPAL and DRAM applications are on Pentium®-class PCs. To most current users of these models, the PC was the only platform that made any sense for their purposes. Thus one of our first major design decisions was that the new PSS would operate in a PC/Windows environment. In making this decision we had to weigh the benefits of the continuance of multiplatform development and support against the advantages of a focused investment in development solely within the Windows environment.

Next to ease of use, the two most important desiderata from the users were tighter integration of the land-use models with a GIS package, and greater modularity of land-use submodels. The GIS connection was wanted both for input and for output consider-ations. Many planning agencies were moving, or had already moved, to consolidating much of their data-oriented activity within a master GIS environment. Data preparation and manipulation for land-use forecasting analysis would, in that way, be much more efficiently accomplished within an agency's GIS. The outputs could be easily moved to the modeling environment. Planners, per se, were also coming to expect the rich analysis and results display capabilities of a modern, sophisticated GIS package.

From the perspective of longer-term model development efforts, we could see that there were advantages to be had from eventually recasting the forecasting models in a more discretely modular for-mat. This would, first, allow greater flexibility in the testing of alter-native model, or submodel, formulations. In this environment, these sorts of tests could be conducted without having to completely repro-gram complex models in their entirety. In addition, in this form, advantage could be taken of the database underpinning of the GIS to allow the submodels to retrieve, process, modify, and replace data items in the GIS data bank. Operation in this mode would provide an unprecedented degree of model development and testing capabil-ity. It could also provide users with some degree of flexibility of model configuration for their own special application purposes.

Given the situation, one component of the solution was clearly dominant. We decided to use the ArcView GIS software package from Environmental Systems Research Institute, Inc. (ESRI), to provide the GIS and database underpinning for our new METROPILUS PSS. In addition to GIS and DBMS functions, ArcView GIS includes a scripting language, Avenue™, which allowed us to embed our models and associated user interfaces in the system along with additional utility programs. Furthermore, it was easy to develop links to the Microsoft Excel spreadsheet package. This new system is currently providing planners in several large regional agencies with a substantial increase in productivity, flexibility, and ease of use for their urban land-use and transportation modeling.

The prototype for METROPILUS was initially assembled in 1996. Modified versions of EMPAL and DRAM were linked by Avenue scripts. In then-current agency applications, the models were being run by use of long DOS batch files. They were run in DOS, or in a "DOS box" under Windows. The DOS batch files handled the file management tasks. All the models had been designed, from the outset, years earlier, with standard input and output file formats, thus putting the differences in data formats from one application to another outside the model structure. This was one of the factors that made it possible for the models to be applied in so many different regions. This same input and output file consistency allowed the ready adaptation of the models for use in the new PSS. The problem of the system's current "control card" input was temporarily resolved by having Avenue put the user in a text editor environment (e.g., DOS-EDIT or Notepad) for manipulation of the "control card" inputs.

The prototype METROPILUS was used for student projects in early 1997. Inexperienced student users became rapidly proficient in rather sophisticated model applications. This happened much more rapidly than we had ever expected. Further, the system operation within the GIS environment led the students to new and innovative model analyses and output presentations.

As one might expect, ease of use meant different things to different people. For some, ease of use meant a desire for a system that would run, more or less from start to finish, with the pressing of a single button. For others, ease of use meant a better way to get the control card data into the models, a way that would obviate the need to type numerical values in the correct columns of a card image format.

While it is not possible to have a model system which runs from start to finish with the press of a single button (nor is it clear that it would be a good idea in any case), it is possible to move towards having the system take care of most of its own file-accounting details.

A step towards fuller automation to meet the first of these desires was met by use of the Avenue scripts. They were made intelligent in that they could track the forecast year of a given model run, as well as track the ID of each run (e.g., "Baseline," "Policy 1," "Policy 2"). This means the system itself takes care of the tedious accounting process of ensuring that the correct outputs become the correct inputs to subsequent models within a time period, or within subsequent time periods.

The second desire was met by the development of graphical user interfaces (or GUIs) for the input of control card data such as regional forecasts, regional employment and household ratios, equation parameters, and the like. These GUIs, programmed in Microsoft Visual Basic®, are called up by the scripts as needed. In this way the user can select an "Edit Card" box from a drop-down menu whenever control card values need to be reviewed or modified.

As a final matter along these lines, one of the more difficult steps in the application of these models in practice is the Verification process in which the calibrated model set is tested for various types of consistency. An Avenue script has been developed which guides the user through this step. The same is true for the subsequent Validation step, for which a script has also been developed. These will be described in more detail in the next section of this chapter.

THE METROPOLITAN INTEGRATED LAND-USE SYSTEM—METROPILUS

OVERVIEW

The general configuration of the overall METROPILUS PSS is shown in figure 2. The system also integrates spreadsheet software—in this case, Microsoft Excel—to support the descriptive and statistical analysis functions that are not provided in either DRAM/EMPAL or ArcView GIS. The communication between the GIS environment and Excel is performed by dynamic data exchange (DDE).

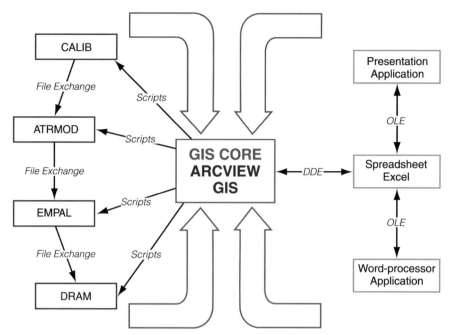

Figure 2. Functional structure of METROPILUS.

The current and fully operational version of this system consists of three main groups of model components. The first group is the models and their associated computational utilities. The second is the set of GUIs, which provide a convenient means of interaction between user and model system. Finally, the third group is comprised of the GIS package and an integral set of customized procedures, or scripts, for implementing the various analysis steps that might be undertaken with the system.

In the models group are newly enhanced versions of EMPAL and DRAM. EMPAL, the Employment Allocation Model, locates employers/ employees. DRAM locates households to place-of-residence and, by use of an internal submodel, LANCON, calculates the land consumption consequences of the previously calculated employment and household location demand.

In addition to these two models there are two major computational utilities. The first of these is CALIB, which uses a modified gradient search technique to calculate the EMPAL and DRAM parameters, or coefficients, that produce the best fit of the model equations to a region's data. CALIB also calculates goodness-of-fit statistics, asymptotic significance t-tests for each parameter, F-test for each complete equation, and location elasticities that give a measure of the location sensitivity to change in each of the independent variables.

The second computational utility is ATRMOD, the attractiveness modification program, which serves two purposes. First, ATRMOD is used to prepare the residual variation from the calibration results for use in subsequent forecasting procedures. Second, ATRMOD provides a systematic procedure for incorporating exogenous information input from local planners and technical advisory groups in order to fine tune the model forecast by the addition of informed local knowledge.

CALIBRATION—CALIB

The calibration process involves fitting the DRAM or EMPAL equations to the data that describes a particular region. The calibrations require one or more indicators of goodness-of-fit of the models to the data. The equation structures of the DRAM and EMPAL models are intrinsically nonlinear, and the data from which their parameters must be estimated is not normally distributed. The procedure used by CALIB to estimate the parameters for these models in their current, aggregate, form is one of gradient search. The partial derivatives of a goodness-of-fit criterion with respect to each specific parameter are calculated and the values of these derivatives determine the direction of parameter search (Putman 1983). The goodness-of-fit measure used is derived from the notion of maximum likelihood as developed in econometrics.

It is important to note that in its usual equation form, the value of the likelihood statistic is dependent on the magnitudes of the data being used. That is, in a region with millions of households, the value will be larger than it will be in a region with hundreds of thousands of households. To deal with this problem a relative measure of goodness-of-fit is used which is analogous to the traditional R2 measure, but which is appropriate to the nonlinear DRAM and EMPAL equations, and to the non-normal distributions of the data. This measure of relative goodness-of-fit is called a likelihood ratio, and has a range such that for a perfect fit, it equals 1.00, and for the worst fit, it equals 0.00. Typical results obtained when fitting DRAM and EMPAL fall between 0.80 and 0.95, and the values are independent of the magnitude of the dependent variables. In figure 3 the main screen of the DRAM calibration card-editing GUI is shown.

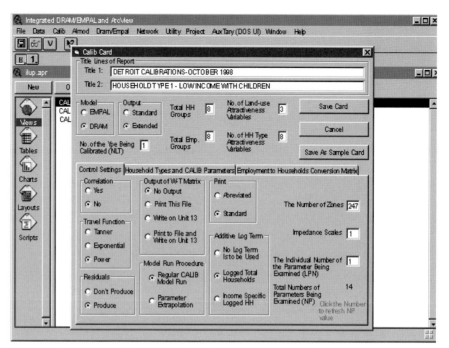

Figure 3. DRAM calibration card.

Estimating the parameters for nonlinear models requires the development of ways to assess their statistical significance which can substitute for the measures more readily calculated in the estimation of parameters of linear models with normally distributed variables. The maximum likelihood estimator, when correctly calculated, is asymptotically normally distributed with its mean equal to the true parameter value, and with a covariance matrix that can be calculated by use of second-order partial derivatives. These derivatives are calculated as part of the parameter estimation procedure, and allow the computation of asymptotic t-statistics that yield an indication of the significance of the individual parameters in the models' equation structures.

In addition to information on the model's goodness-of-fit and statistical significance, it is also important to know the relative sensitivity of each locator to the model's independent variables. Location elasticities measure the sensitivity of household and employment location to changes in the attractiveness variables of the DRAM and EMPAL models. Suppose, for example, that the DRAM location elasticity for the residential land for the low-income households in zone 12 is 0.2500. This means that a 1-percent increase in residential land in zone 12 will result in an 0.25-percent increase in the numbers of low-income households.

The location elasticities are static measures of model sensitivity. This means that when a location elasticity is calculated for a specific attractiveness variable in a specific zone, the values all other attractiveness variables are assumed to remain fixed. That is, in the example above, the only variable that is allowed to change is the quantity of residential land in zone 12. All of the other attractiveness variables in zone 12 are assumed to be fixed, as are the attractiveness variables (including residential land) in all other zones. Because they are static measures of model sensitivity, the location elasticities will change as the values of the DRAM and EMPAL attractiveness variables change (e.g., the location elasticities for forecast years will be different from the location elasticities for the base year).

The value of the location elasticity for a specific attractiveness variable and zone is a function of: (1) the value of the calibrated parameter for the attractiveness variable, (2) the numbers of households or employees in the zone, (3) the magnitude of the attractiveness variable, and (4) the relative attractiveness of other zones in the region. That is, the location elasticities will be larger when the calibrated parameter for the attractiveness variable is large (in absolute value), the number of households or employees is small (relative to other zones in the region), or the value of the attractiveness variable is small (relative to other zones in the region). This information provides a means of assessing, without the need for innumerable model runs, the relative sensitivities of the various locators in the different zones to the different independent variables in the model structure. This knowledge, in turn, provides a means of assessing the likely degree of impact of a specific policy proposal on individual locator-zone combinations.

RESIDUAL PROCESSING, INCORPORATING LOCAL KNOWLEDGE INPUTS—ATRMOD

At the completion of the calibration, or parameter estimation step, several further adjustment procedures must be completed for both EMPAL and DRAM. For both models a set of verification runs must first be performed. In these runs, the calibration data set is used to run the models to determine whether the model replicates the input data. The regional employment control total must equal the sum of the calibration year employment by type.

If the calibration has been properly completed, and the various data files properly prepared, both EMPAL and DRAM will almost exactly replicate the input data as output. While this sounds like a rather trivial matter, in agency application this modeling step confirms the completeness and consistency of the model inputs prior to the expenditure of wasted effort working with erroneous data files.

Another output from the calibration stage is a file of locator-and-zone-specific residuals. These residuals, the unexplained variation from the calibration process, are processed and combined into what are called K-factor files. In addition to providing a basis for investigating the calibration errors for possible spatial bias or outlying values, the K-factors can serve in either or both of two roles in EMPAL and DRAM. First, they provide a mechanism for carrying the calibration residuals forward to the verification runs and, with progressive attenuation, to the forecasts. Second, they provide a means of adjusting the attractiveness of a particular zone for a particular locator type. A sample map, showing the calibration residuals from a preliminary analysis for the Greater Cairo Region of Egypt, is given in figure 4.

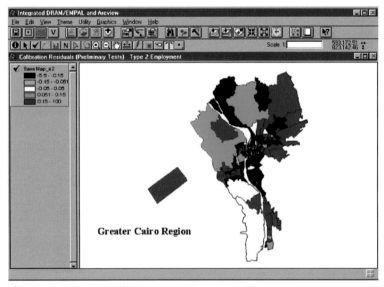

Figure 4. Calibration residuals, greater Cairo Region.

In the first role, the use of K-factors requires that locator-specific K-files (residuals) be saved in the final calibration runs for each locator type. These locator-specific files are then used as inputs to the ATRMOD computer program, which combines them into a single file each for EMPAL or DRAM. This combined file is an input in subsequent runs of either model, and can be attenuated over successive forecast periods as the effects of the base-year residuals are expected to diminish in importance.

In the second role, individual elements of the overall matrix of K-factors can be modified in order to impose a specific increase or decrease in a zone's attractiveness for a particular locator type. In calculating a forecast of a particular employment type, the zonal portion of the region's total employment (of that particular type) is first calculated. The sum of the zonal portions (for a particular employment type) must equal 1.00: they are normalized over the region. These normalized portions are multiplied by the region's total employment for that employment type to yield the forecast of employment by zone.

The zonal attractiveness adjustment procedure provides a tool for people with local knowledge of special circumstances to modify the model. These adjustments are done by attenuating or amplifying the attractiveness of specific locators in specific zones. These attractiveness modifiers act on the estimated zonal portions, before they are normalized and multiplied by the regional employment total.

This part of the model implementation/application process is referred to as the validation step, and involves forecasting from the base year to a time period five years later. Local planners and developers usually have a fairly good idea as to what will be "on the ground" in five years' time (especially if the work using a 1990 base year is being done in 1995, and 1995 is the validation run target year). The K-factors procedure is then used to adjust the zonal attractiveness for individual locator types in order to attempt a close match to the "known" target year. This final step of model tuning is also a way to cope with unusual events that took place during the calibration period.

RESIDENCE LOCATION—DRAM

The earliest version of this model was constructed on the empirical foundation laid by the Lowry model and its derivatives, as enhanced by the entropy-maximizing approach taken by Wilson. Later work has shown the formulation to be equivalent to a logit model of residential location choice, with the actors being aggregated into groups by household type and geography.

In application, DRAM is an aggregate form of a multinomial logit model of location choice. In computational form this yields the functional equivalent of a modified singly constrained spatial interaction model. There are three modifications: (1) a multivariate, multiparametric attractiveness function is used; (2) a consistent balanced constraint procedure is included in the model, allowing zone- and sector-specific constraints; (3) an additive lag term is used for the purpose of informing the model structure as to the prior "use" of each geographic area. The model is normally used for four to eight household categories, defined in terms of income, whose parameters are individually estimated (Putman 1983, 1995). The equation structure currently in use is as follows:

$$N_i^n = \eta^n \sum_j Q_j^n B_j^n W_i^n c_{i,j}^{\alpha^n} \exp(\beta^n c_{i,j}) + (1.0 - \eta^n) N_{i,t-1}^T \qquad (1)$$

where

$$Q_j^n = \sum_k a_{k,n} E_j^k \qquad (2)$$

and

$$B_j^n = \left[\sum_i W_i^n c_{i,j}^{\alpha^n} \exp(\beta^n c_{i,j}) \right]^{-1} \qquad (3)$$

and

$$W_i^n = (L_i^v)^{q^n}(x_i)^{r^n}(L_i^r)^{s^n} \prod_{n'} \left[\left(1 + \frac{N_i^{n'}}{\sum_n N_i^n} \right)^{b_{n'}^n} \right] \qquad (4)$$

where

E_j^k = employment of type k (place-of-work) in zone j

N_i^n = vacant developable land in zone i

$N_{i,t-1}^T$ = total households residing in zone i at time t–1

L_i^v = vacant developable land in zone i

x_i = 1.0 plus the percentage of developable land already

L_i^r = residential land in zone i

$a_{k,n}$ = (regional) coefficient of type n households per type j employees

$c_{i,j}$ = impedance (travel time or cost) between zones i and j

η^n, α^n, β^n, q^n, r^n, s^n, $b_{n'}^n$ = empirically derived parameters

In the earlier formulations of the applied versions of DRAM, all the attractiveness variables were measured in the same time period. In early 1994, the increased availability of the necessary data allowed new formulations to be examined that included a lag term in an attempt to increase forecast reliability.

DRAM is also capable of including additional attractiveness variables in the spatial potential term, equation (4), of the model. To date there has been rather little use of this option in practice, as the inclusion of such variables does require the subsequent development of a means for their updating in forecast runs of the model. Some investigation has been done as to the effects of including residential land value as an additional attractiveness variable, with rather little contribution to the model's overall reliability. Also, there is the additional problem of updating the land value variable as a part of the long-term forecasting procedure. Even so, this work has led to the beginning of the development of a representation of land supply variables for use in future releases of METROPILUS.

LOCATION SURPLUS AS AN OUTPUT MEASURE FROM DRAM

Location surplus is a measure of the aggregate benefit that locating households receive from the attributes of a residential zone. Because household utility can only be measured on an ordinal scale (i.e., it is not possible to determine the monetary value of utility), the location surplus measures should be interpreted as index numbers. The larger the value of location surplus, the more utility households receive from their choices of residential location. The location surplus measures used in DRAM can be derived by using either of two different methods. Both methods produce the same measures and are based on the assumption that households attempt to maximize utility when choosing residential locations. For the first method, the DRAM model is interpreted as a multinomial logit model and the location surplus measure is found by calculating aggregate indirect utility (McFadden 1974, Ben–Akiva and Lerman 1985, Freeman 1993). In the second approach, the location surplus measure is found by directly integrating the DRAM travel demand function (Neuburger 1971, Cochrane 1975, Williams 1976). It is worth noting here that if one follows any of several approaches to the development of an urban land-use model based on urban economic theory (e.g., Alonso's bid-rent theory, or random-utility-based discrete choice analysis (Anas 1982, McFadden 1978), one gets some form of multinomial logit expression for the individual's maximization of his/her location (consumer) surplus. In effect, DRAM operates as a reduced form model of this same approach. A very nice illustration of this is given by Martinez (1992). In DRAM, the location surplus is calculated for each household type in order to compare the relative benefits of policies being tested, in terms of their impacts on each of the household types as well as on the region's households overall.

EMPLOYMENT LOCATION—EMPAL

The computational form of EMPAL is also a modified singly constrained spatial interaction model. There are three modifications: (1) a multivariate, multiparametric attractiveness function is used; (2) a separate, weighted, lagged variable is included outside the spatial interaction formulation; (3) a constraint procedure is included in the model, allowing zone- and sector-specific constraints. The model is normally used for four to eight employment sectors whose parameters are individually estimated (Putman 1983, 1991, 1995). The current equation structure is as follows:

$$E_{j,t}^k = \lambda^k \sum P_{i,t-1} A_{i,t-1}^k W_{j,t-1}^k c_{i,j,t}^{\alpha^k} \exp(\beta^k c_{i,j,t}) + (1.0 - \lambda^k) E_{j,t-1}^k \quad (5)$$

$$W_{j,t-1}^k = (E_{j,t-1}^k)^{a^k} (L_j)^{b^k} \quad (6)$$

and

$$A_{i,t-1}^k = \left[\sum_\ell (E_{\ell,t-1}^k)^{a^k} (L_\ell)^{b^k} c_{i,\ell,t}^{\alpha^k} \exp(\beta^k c_{i,\ell,t}) \right]^{-1} \quad (7)$$

where

$E_{j,t-1}^k$ = employment (place-of-work) of type k in zone j at time t–1

$E_{j,t}^k$ = employment (place-of-work) of type k in zone j at time t

L_j = total area of zone j

$c_{i,j,t}$ = impedance (travel time or cost) between zones i and j at time t

$P_{i,t-1}$ = total number of households in zone i at time t–1

$\lambda^k, \alpha^k, \beta^k, a^k, b^k$ = empirically derived parameters

EMPAL can use additional attractiveness variables such as vacant commercial land or lagged commercial employment density. These variables must be forecast outside the EMPAL and DRAM model structure, and then entered for the appropriate forecast run. To date, experiments including additional variables have always come to the conclusion that while some short-term gain in model reliability might be obtained, updating these variables over a typical 30- to 40-year forecast horizon is extremely difficult.

SUPPLYING THE LAND DEMANDED—LANCON

The current EMPAL and DRAM combined model structure estimates the amounts of land used after calculating overall location demand. EMPAL calculates location demand by employers, followed by DRAM's calculation of location demand by households. LANCON takes both these calculated demands and estimates the actual change in the amount of land, by zone, that will be used by each of the demand categories. If there has been a decrease in demand by a particular demand category, then the land currently in use by that category is released into a pool of land available for any use. If there has been an increase in demand by a particular demand category, then the additional land used by that category is calculated. After the calculations are done for each demand category, the sum of land used is adjusted, by increasing densities, to match the land available for such uses.

The land used by each demand category is estimated in terms of the rate of land use by a locator of that specific demand category, as calculated in equations that are in the form of production functions. The calculation of the rate of residential land use by new household locators in a specific zone is given by the following equation:

$$\frac{L_i^r}{N_i^T} = \kappa_0 \left(\frac{L_i^d}{L_i^d + L_i^v} \right)^{\kappa_1} \left(\frac{L_i^B}{L_i} \right)^{\kappa_2} \left(\frac{L_i^C}{L_i} \right)^{\kappa_3} \left(\frac{N_i^I}{N_i^T} \right)^{\kappa_4} \left(\frac{N_i^4}{N_i^T} \right)^{\kappa_5} \left(L_i^d + L_i^v \right)^{\kappa_6} \quad (8)$$

where

L_i^d = total developed land area of zone i

N_i^4 = number of low-income households in zone i

N_i^4 = number of high-income households in zone i

$\kappa_0, \kappa_1, \kappa_2, \kappa_3, \kappa_4, \kappa_5, \kappa_6$ = empirically derived parameters

The functional forms used to calculate basic land consumption and commercial land consumption have similar structures.

There is, of course, much more that could be said about the general model structure. For example, the link between EMPAL and DRAM provides a mechanism for the region's household income distribution to change as its employment mix changes. The system provides a rich set of outputs in both tabular and graphic form. In addition, its procedures for linking to other software packages give it an extraordinary degree of flexibility.

SAMPLE INFORMATION PRODUCTS AVAILABLE FROM METROPILUS

DESCRIPTIVE INFORMATION

The system provides general descriptive information that can be used by planners to detect potential problems and to explore existing problems. Production and presentation of this information can be accomplished by means of both spatial and nonspatial methods. Some of the functions are built-in features of the ArcView GIS package, but most are provided by the METROPILUS scripts and the connected spreadsheet software. It is also possible to integrate the system with software packages designed to do exploratory spatial data analysis (ESDA). The descriptive information in the system can be displayed by means of distribution maps such as is shown in figure 5, and by means of statistical charts.

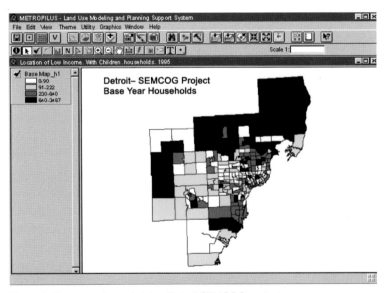

Figure 5. Base-year households—Detroit SEMCOG project.

FORECAST OUTPUT INFORMATION

Forecast information describing future time periods is the major product of the combined planning support system. For each geographic area this forecast information includes: (1) employment location (place-of-work) for each employment type, (2) household location (place-of-residence) for each household type, and (3) land use by land-use category. Outputs can be combined and manipulated. For example, figure 6 shows a spatial comparison between base and forecast years of high-income households in the Atlanta region. With suitable connections to an agency's travel model system, trip distribution and travel cost (or time) forecasts could be produced as well.

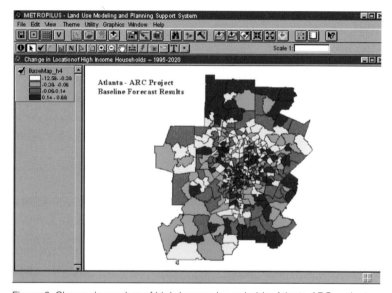

Figure 6. Change in number of high-income households, Atlanta ARC project.

POLICY SIMULATION, IMPACT ANALYSIS, AND COMPARISON

Policy analysis is the task that is most uniquely associated with the use of urban models. It is a little-discussed fact that a relatively simple extrapolation will often give quite acceptable results for an ordinary "plain vanilla" forecast of the future (especially the near future) of some aspect of a region. Extrapolation will not, however, give any consistent means of estimating the effects of changes in different assumptions, parameters, and variables on the forecasts. The development of the accounting components of the scripts in METROPILUS, which manage the naming, manipulation, and archiving of files, make it substantially easier for policy analyses to be done within this system. In addition, the GUIs are designed to make this operation proceed much more effectively than was previously possible. The impact analysis and policy comparison processes are performed within the GIS core and spreadsheet in an interactive way. The system produces the result information in whatever formats are most convenient for the individual users.

For example, figure 7 shows the comparison in household distribution between a proposed highway beltway and a baseline forecast to 2015 in Sacramento. Operating within the ArcView GIS shell makes this sort of presentation, which would have been almost unthinkably time consuming and expensive ten years ago, a simple, quick, and cheap matter for a moderately experienced user of GIS and urban models.

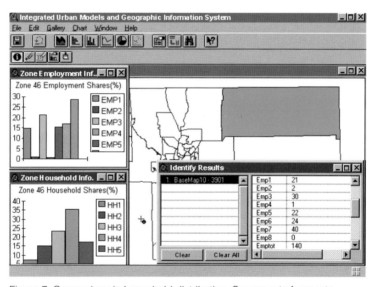

Figure 7. Comparison in household distribution, Sacramento forecasts.

SPATIAL QUERIES

The spatial query function in the system follows Tomlin's (1990) idea of local, focal, and zonal relationships that are analysis-oriented. Local information enables planners to understand the situation or problems of a specific zone or spatial unit; this is the basic location information for planners. Focal information is about the individual zone, or the neighborhood of a specific zone. This type of information is especially useful for identifying the impact of a local facility on its neighbor zones. The last category, zonal information, refers to the complete area. The visual interaction of the spatial query allows planners to have information on both location and attributes simultaneously, which facilitates the understanding of the area of interest. For example, figure 8 shows a zonal information query that includes information on the specific zone, as well as frequency distributions of its employment and households.

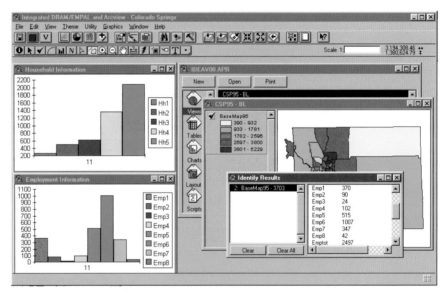

Figure 8. Output of METROPILUS, Colorado Springs.

Spatial query methods available in the system include the selection of single zones selection, multiple zones, neighbors, and travel time intervals. Single and multiple zonal selection retrieves specific information about the selected targets. Neighborhood selection highlights the continuous neighbors of a specific zone. Travel time interval selection allows users to select zones located within a specific travel time interval of a zone (e.g., the zones within a range of thirty minutes' travel time). The query function then displays the corresponding information for the selected zones and can pass that selected portion of the database to the linked spreadsheet for further analysis.

An additional sample of information output is based on the travel cost (or travel time, or composite cost) forecast that comes from the exogenous transportation models. The travel times, measured by minute, may be used to create travel time contours for the planning area. Comparing these travel time isolines from different forecast years makes it easier to observe changes in traffic congestion. For instance, figure 9 illustrates the change of travel time from zone 1 (in the CBD) to other zones, between 1995 and 2010 for Colorado Springs. It shows the increasing travel congestion between zone 1 and other zones in the region.

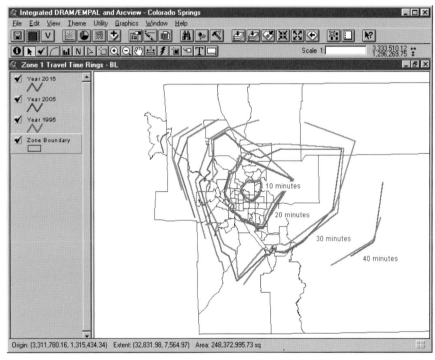

Figure 9. Example of travel time rings, Colorado Springs, 1995 to 2010.

CONCLUDING REMARKS

Our goal in developing METROPILUS was to respond to the expressed desires of planners for more convenient urban modeling software by moving from a concept of modeling to one of planning support. We have described the development and implementation of a computer environment in which planners can efficiently handle information analysis and production. This environment combines a set of urban models with a GIS package and to other procedures. Within the integrated METROPILUS urban model system, descriptive and predictive information is generated. The use of GIS functions in this system allows the predictive information to be presented from the spatial perspective. Our solution to the complex task of developing such a system is a loosely coupled system. This solution, using a scripting language to connect the system components, was selected because of its flexibility. As a result, it provides planning agencies with a convenient path for integrating their current computer-based analytical resources to extend the functions of the system.

Klosterman (1994) suggests that defining what the PSS may be is easy (relatively speaking) while implementing one is hard (an understatement). We have described an important first step toward the development of more complete planning support systems which can be used by urban planners and/or analysts. To achieve the ideal information environment, it will be necessary for planners to refine and extend their understanding of their information needs and to better understand the capabilities of the tools being applied. We have no doubts as to the inevitability of progress along these lines.

REFERENCES

Anas, A. 1982. *Residential Location Markets and Urban Transportation: Economic Theory, Econometrics and Public Policy Analysis*. New York: Academic Press.

Ben–Akiva, M., and S. R. Lerman. 1985. *Discrete Choice Analysis: Theory and Application to Travel Demand*. Cambridge, MA: MIT Press.

Cochrane, R. A. 1975. A Possible Economic Basis for the Gravity Model. *Journal of Transport Economics and Policy* 9:34–49.

Davidoff, P. and T. Reiner. 1962. A Choice Theory of Planning. *Journal of the American Institute of Planners* 28:103–15.

Freeman, A. M. 1993. *The Measurement of Environmental and Resource Values: Theory and Methods*. Resources for the Future, Washington, D.C.

Goldner, W. 1971. The Lowry Model Heritage. *Journal of the American Institute of Planners* 37:100–10.

Harris, B. 1965. Introduction: New tools for Planning. *Journal of the American Institute of Planners* 31(2):90–93.

———. 1989. Beyond Geographic Information Systems: Computers and the Planning Professional. *Journal of American Planning Association* 55:85–90.

Harris, B. and M. Batty. 1993. Locational Models: Geographical Information and Planning Support Systems. *Journal of Planning Education and Research* 12:184–98.

Hopkins, L. 1981. The Decision to Plan: Planning Activities as Public Goods. *Urban Infrastructure, Location and Housing,* ed. Lierop, W. R. and P. Nijkamp. Netherlands: Sijthoff and Noordhoff.

Klosterman, R. E. 1994. Planning Support Systems: A New Perspective on Computer-aided Planning. Paper presented to the 36th Annual Conference of the Association of Collegiate Schools of Planning. November, 1994. Tempe, AZ.

Lee, D. B., Jr. 1973. Requiem for Large-scale Models. *Journal of the American Institute of Planners* 39:163–87.

Martinez, F. 1992. The Bid-choice Land-use Model: An Integrated Economic Framework. *Environment and Planning A* 24:871–85.

McFadden, D. 1974. Conditional Logit Analysis of Qualitative Choice Behavior. In *Frontiers in Econometrics,* ed. P. Zarembka, 105–42. New York: Academic Press.

———. 1978. Modelling the Choice of Residential Location. In *Spatial Interaction Theory and Planning Models,* ed. A. Karlqvist, L. Lundqvist, F. Snickars, J. Weibull, 75–76. Amsterdam: North–Holland.

Neuburger, H. 1971. User Benefit in the Evaluation of Transport and Land Use Plans. *Journal of Transport Economics and Policy* 5:52–75.

Putman, S. H. 1979. *Urban Residential Location Models.* Boston: Martinus Nijhoff.

———. 1983. *Integrated Urban Models: Policy Analysis of Transportation and Land Use.* London: Pion.

———. 1991. *Integrated Urban Models 2: New Research and Applications of Optimization and Dynamics.* London: Pion.

———. 1992. Chaotic Behavior in Models of Urban Spatial Patterns. In *Computer Assisted Modeling on the IBM 3090: The IBM Contest Prize Papers Volume 2.* ed. Billingsley, K. R., Brown III, H. U., and E. Derohanes. Athens, GA: Baldwin Press, University of Georgia.

———. 1995. The EMPAL and DRAM Location and Land Use Models: An Overview. Paper prepared for FHWA, TMIP Land Use Modeling Conference, Dallas, TX.

Scholten, H. J. and P. Padding. 1990. Working with Geographic Information Systems in a Policy Environment. *Environment and Planning B: Planning and Design* 17:405–16.

Tomlin, C. D. 1990. *Geographic Information Systems and Cartographic Modeling.* New Jersey: Prentice–Hall.

Webster C. J. 1993. GIS and the Scientific Inputs to Urban Planning. Part 1: Description. *Environment and Planning B: Planning and Design* 20:6:709–28.

———. 1994. GIS and the Scientific Inputs to Planning. Part 2: Prediction and Prescription. *Environment and Planning, B: Planning and Design* 21:145–57.

Webster, F. V., P. H. Bly, and N. J. Paulley, eds. 1988. *Urban Land-use and Transport Interaction: Policies and Models.* Brookfield, VT: Avebury.

Williams, H. C. W. L. 1976. Travel Demand Models, Duality Relations and User Benefit Analysis. *Journal of Regional Science* 16:147–66.

Wilson, A. G., J. D. Coehlo, S. M. Macgill, and H. C. W. L.Williams. 1981. *Optimization in Location and Transport Analysis.* Chichester, Sussex: Wiley.

Paper 6

Integrated Land Use and Transport Modeling: The Tranus Experience

TOMÁS DE LA BARRA

MODELISTICA

CARACAS, VENEZUELA

ABSTRACT

Tranus is one of the few integrated land-use and transport models currently operational. The model system is an integrated and operational set of three modules—land use, transport, and evaluation. Tranus has its roots in spatial interaction and discrete choice theories, and creates dynamic simulations with feedback loops between the land-use and transport modules. One important component of Tranus is its ability to deal with both the supply of and demand for land. In this paper the overall model design is presented, followed by a discussion of various applications. Tranus can be applied at urban, regional, or national levels. In Swindon, England, alternative land-use and transport scenarios were simulated. Outputs included job and population distributions and changes in floor space, land consumption, and transport energy consumption across the study area.

INTRODUCTION

Integrated land-use and transport modeling has been a matter of concern to academics and practitioners for a long time. Relatively few practical integrated models have been developed, however. The purpose of this essay is to show, by example, that the integrated modeling approach has many advantages over the conventional and dominant practice of the transport-only analysis. We will describe a fully operational integrated model and present a recent application as an example.

The Tranus integrated land-use and transport modeling system contains three modules. The land-use module deals with the location and interaction of activities and the representation of the real estate market. The transport module contains sections on trip generation, combined modal split and assignment and capacity constraint. An evaluation module is the third component of the Tranus system. Tranus can be applied to any scale from urban to regional and national levels. The purpose of the program suite is to simulate the probable effects of applying particular land-use and transport policies and projects, and to then evaluate the social, economic, financial, and environmental effects.

Following descriptions of the overall Tranus design, we will present a recent application in the city of Swindon in the United Kingdom. A final section discusses the practical usefulness of the integrated approach and draws a number of conclusions from the experience.

THEORETICAL FRAMEWORK OF TRANUS

BACKGROUND

In the last two decades, important theoretical and empirical developments have been achieved in the field of activity location and transport analysis. Many of these achievements have occurred in the area of systems analysis, based on a structural and quantitative approach to explain urban and regional phenomena. The origins of spatial analysis go back as far as Von Thünen (1826), but in recent times the work of Hansen (1959), Alonso (1964), and Lowry (1964) can be considered as starting points. The first generation of gravity-type models of the 1960s, and the first operational transport models, were followed by the important work of Wilson (1970), which not only introduced entropy-maximizing techniques to spatial modeling, but also led the way towards integrated land-use and transport analysis. Wilson showed that land use and transport could be represented by means of a common theoretical framework. In input–output analysis, the work of Leontief and Strout (1966) is of major importance, both at national and regional scales.

Tranus is rooted in this tradition, but also draws heavily on the work of Domencich and McFadden (1975) in discrete choice analysis and random utility theory. Although these authors did propose a general model, most of their work and that which followed is centered on the problem of modal choice in transportation, and no specific models were proposed and developed for the rest of the elements of the urban or regional system. In Tranus, this theoretical backbone has been extended to all decision levels, from modal split to assignment, trip generation, the location of activities, and the behavior of real estate developers. A detailed explanation and a good complement to this description of the theory underlying the Tranus system can be found in de la Barra (1989) and in Modelistica (1999). Figure 1 summarizes the way in which Tranus has drawn from the main theoretical streams described above.

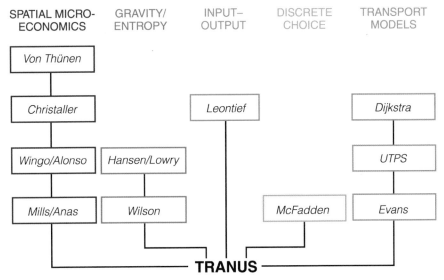

Figure 1. The theoretical *family tree* of Tranus.

INDIVIDUAL AND AGGREGATED CHOICES

In general terms, decision theory describes social processes as a set of decisions made by individuals. The main assumption is that individuals choose rationally between the options available to them. Each individual, faced with a number of options, will rank them according to the degree of satisfaction or *utility* perceived in each case, and will choose the one that provides the greatest utility. On the other hand, utility is a subjective concept—its perception will vary from one individual to another and from one choice to another.

Mathematically, utility can be represented as a utility function for a particular individual, which contains variables describing measurable attributes of each option. Faced with a particular set of options, an individual may be assumed to evaluate each one with the same utility function, and will choose the option that yields the greatest utility. While this concept is the basis of microeconomic theory, it is of little practical value for the urban analyst. It would be impossible to keep track of utility functions for each individual living in a city or region. There is, then, the need for aggregation. Individuals may be grouped according to common socioeconomic characteristics, and options into groups of similar types. Spatial aggregation is important: point location of individuals or firms must be replaced by location in larger discrete areas or *zones*.

Aggregation introduces sources of variability, because individuals within a group are different and perceive utility in different ways. The same can be said about aggregated options and zones. Naturally, if groups are small, variability will be small also. In order to represent variability, random utility adds a random element to the utility function. Utility functions will no longer apply to a particular individual; instead, they will apply to a population of individuals related to groups of options. A population-related utility function must not only contain the aggregate measurable characteristics of each option group, but also random elements.

In the individual case, the utility function is deterministic and produces a unique result: the selection of a specific option (i.e., the one of greatest utility). In the aggregate case, since there are random elements, utility functions are probabilistic, producing a distribution of individual choices among the available groups of options. Mathematically, the probabilistic model is obtained by integrating the joint distribution. Hence, several models may be derived from the general one, according to the particular shape of the distribution. Domencich and McFadden (1975) explored several possible shapes, showing that the most appropriate was the Gumbel distribution, which after integration yields a multinomial logit model.

If logit is the chosen model, then there is one and only one way of measuring the average utility of the population, the logarithmic average of the distribution, also called composite cost or *log-sum* (Williams 1977). Furthermore, if such a model is applied in the context of two different scenarios of future conditions, the difference in utility will be equivalent to the consumers' surplus in traditional economic theory. In Tranus, this general formulation has been improved in several ways, introducing scaled utilities and an improved formulation of the log-sum (de la Barra 1998).

DECISION CHAINS

Thus far we have dealt with one particular choice situation. In an urban or regional system, however, a long and complex decision chain may be established. For example, a typical chain would be:

place of work $\rightarrow$ residence $\rightarrow$ shopping $\rightarrow$ transport mode

Each link along the chain is clearly conditioned by the preceding link. For instance, where to go shopping is a decision conditioned by the place of residence. In order to represent such a decision chain in a set of models, each component must precede the next in the correct order. Each link along the chain has a corresponding model, producing probabilities such as $P(w)$, $P(r)$, $P(s)$, and $P(m)$. In the example above, the number of people that work in a particular zone and travel by bus from the zone in which they live to shop in another zone may be estimated as the number of people that work in that zone multiplied by the residential choice probability, multiplied by the probability that they will go shopping in another zone, multiplied by the probability of choosing a bus. This is a comfortable solution, because it is possible to model each link in the decision chain separately and avoid very large computations.

The problem is more complex than this, however, because each link in the chain may influence the preceding one. In the above example, it could well be that people decide where to go shopping precisely because there is a good bus service. Thus, the choice of transport modes affects the choice of shopping place. Similarly, the choice of residential location may have been influenced by the availability of local shopping facilities.

In order to accommodate this, the process of calculation must begin from the other end, from the last link in the chain, and proceed backward. In the example, we would have to calculate the overall availability of transport from residence to shopping. The way to do this is by calculating the corresponding composite cost or log-sum, producing the overall aggregate utility of all shopping facilities around each residential area. In this way the transport element has been transferred into the shopping-place utility, and eventually into the residential location utility. On reaching the top of the decision chain, the model must reverse direction and proceed again in the original direction, calculating and multiplying the probabilities. This way of calculating composite costs and probabilities is a generalization of nested logit models.

If it were not for variable costs and elasticities, the calculation process would end here. In the above example, if the bus service is used beyond its capacity, the cost of travel (or time) may increase until residents eventually choose other travel options. Because the overall transport utility from the place of residence to the place of shopping will decrease, the probability of shopping in that particular place may also change. This effect may be further transferred to the residential choice. Thus the calculation process becomes iterative, aggregating utilities and estimating probabilities backward and forward several times until a state of equilibrium is reached. Demand elasticities also influence the process. In the example above, if bus services to shopping facilities become congested, some people may travel less, perhaps shopping once a week instead of once a day, and thus generating fewer trips.

STRUCTURE OF THE INTEGRATED MODEL

An explicit dynamic structure relates the two main components of Tranus, land use and transport. The way in which land use relates to transport through time is shown in figure 2, where discrete time intervals are represented as t_1, t_2, t_3, and so on. The land-use and transport systems influence each other through time. Economic activities in space interact with each other, generating flows. These flows determine transport demand within the same time period, and are assigned to the supply of transport. In turn, the demand–supply equilibrium at the transport level determines accessibility, which is fed back to the land-use system, influencing the location and interaction between activities. This feedback, however, does not occur instantly in the same time period, but is lagged. Hence, transport accessibility in period t_1 affects the distribution of flows in the following period t_2. Since there are also elements of inertia in land use from one period to the next, the effects of changes in transport might well take several periods to consolidate.

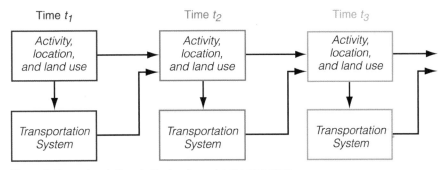

Figure 2. Dynamic relations in the land-use–transport system.

A change in the transport system, such as a new road, a mass transit system, or changes in fares, will have an immediate effect on travel demand, but will only affect activity location, interaction, and the estate market in the following time period. Changes in land use, on the other hand, such as growth in the production of particular economic sectors, a new supply of land, buildings, or investment, will result in modified interactions and change transport demand within the same time period.

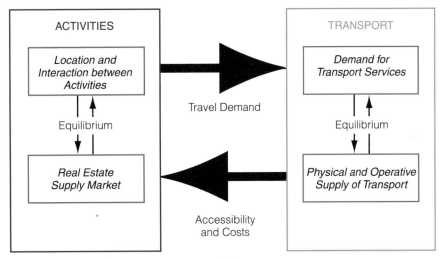

Figure 3. Main components in the Tranus model.

The main components and relationships in the Tranus model are shown in figure 3. There are the activities system and the transport system. Within the activities system there are the location and interaction processes and the supply of real estate. Both subsystems interact. Activities demand land and floor space from the real estate market. The interaction between the two gives rise to equilibrium prices in the form of rents. Apart from the real estate market, the transport system strongly influences activity location. The interaction between activities in space is the main source of travel demand. The transport model takes travel demand from the interactions between activities and assigns it to two classes of supply, physical and operative. The physical supply is made of roads, railways, ports, and so on, while the operative supply represents transport services, such as bus routes, cars, trucks, or rail services.

ACTIVITY LOCATION AND INTERACTION: THE LAND-USE MODEL

The land-use model is basically a spatial input–output model with a very general formulation. Within this structure the user may define a complex model of a region with a detailed representation of the economic and social system, or a very simple one with only the main elements represented. The analyst may determine the structure of the model most suitable to the emphasis and purpose of the study.

In order to define the system, the study area must be divided into internal and external zones. The economy of the area is divided into sectors, such as productive sectors (agriculture, mining, industry, services, etc.), households (by income or size), or physical elements (land or floor space). Each sector in the model has a number of associated attributes, such as production (exogenous or induced), production cost, consumption cost, value added, restrictions, equilibrium price, and others.

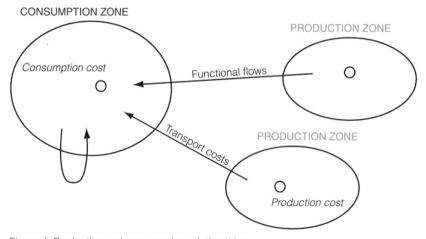

Figure 4. Production and consumption relationships.

Production in one sector and zone requires inputs from other sectors and zones. Sectors are related to each other through demand functions that vary according to the cost of the inputs plus the cost of transporting them from the production zone to the consumption zone. This is a very broad definition, and in fact it allows for the representation of economic transactions, generation of employment, demand for services, and the consumption of land and floor space. These relationships are shown in figure 4. The results of these transactions are flows, represented in origin–destination matrices, which are later transformed into transport demand. For example, the generation of employment from production may lead to trips to work, or the consumption of one productive sector by another may lead to movements of commodities.

The model keeps track of the costs involved in the transactions. The cost of producing one unit of a sector is the sum of the cost of all inputs, plus the cost of transport and any possible value added (including taxes and subsidies). If there are restrictions on the amount of production that may take place in a particular zone and sector, the model simulates an equilibrium price. Typically, land and floor space are restricted to existing stock, and in this case equilibrium prices will represent land values or rents. The model also makes an explicit representation of imports and exports.

The logical sequence of calculations for the activity location model is shown in figure 5 on the following page. The model begins by reading in a set of user-defined parameters and previous time period land-use results. Next, incremental models are applied to the data. Studywide increments are allocated to zones according to the distribution functions, and zone-specific increments are added. This results in a current time data set that governs the rest of the calculations, and allows for the calculation of the attractor variables that will influence the spatial distributions in the main input–output model.

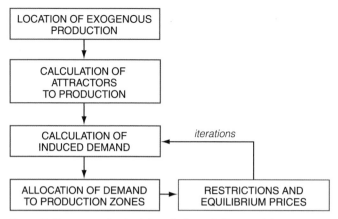

Figure 5. Sequence of calculations in the activities model.

At this point an iterative process is started. Each loop begins by calculating the demand for inputs required to achieve the production allocated in the previous iteration. Demand is calculated on the basis of demand functions, which may be elastic with respect to consumption costs. Once total demand for inputs has been determined for each demand zone and sector, it is distributed to production zones and sectors, according to the utility function and the attractors embedded in the logit model. The distribution process may include imports and exports from/to external zones. Once the distribution has been determined, production costs are calculated as the sum of the cost of the inputs, plus transport costs, plus possible value added.

The next step is to check whether total production by zone and sector satisfies possible constraints. If total production in a constrained sector and zone is greater than the maximum, an equilibrium price is increased, and if less than the minimum, equilibrium price is decreased. It follows that if a particular zone and sector has not been constrained, the equilibrium price will be equal to the consumption cost.

At the beginning of the first iteration only exogenous production (final demand plus exports) will be present. At the end of the process there will be a certain amount of induced production, that is, the production that is necessary to satisfy the demands from the start-up production. In the second iteration, induced production from the final demand plus that of the first iteration is determined and allocated. The iterative process continues until the increments in production become sufficiently small and equilibrium prices have stabilized, making the model converge to an acceptable level. The final results will consist of a set of matrices of flows and the characteristics of each sector: production, consumption, and prices.

For future projections, a supply model is included to represent the expected behavior of land and floor space developers. Developers are assumed to choose among options, just like the demand side does. For instance, developers in a specific zone may choose between developing new land (if available) into high- or low-density residential use or for commercial use. They may also substitute, say, low-density residential land and turn it into commercial, or they may pull down detached houses and replace them with apartments. Such processes are estimated with another set of logit models in which the utility function includes the expected price or rent of the new stock, the price of the stock being replaced, demolition costs, building costs, and so on. Land-use controls may be introduced into the model to constrain this process. For instance, the historical center of a town may be preserved, or prime agricultural land may be kept undeveloped.

THE TRANSPORT MODEL

The activity location/transport interface supplies the transport model with a set of matrices of flows representing potential transport demand, plus possible exogenous trips. The purpose of the transport model is to transform potential demand into actual trips, and to assign them to the transport supply options. The calculation sequence of the transport model is shown in figure 6.

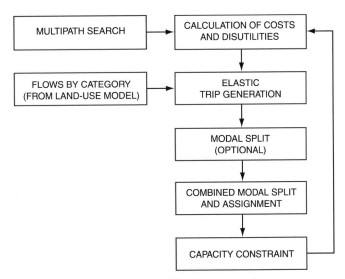

Figure 6. Calculation sequence of the transport model.

The first task of the transport model is to search for a set of *n-paths* connecting each origin to each destination. Paths are a sequence of links and modes that users may combine to perform a trip, representing travel options. Mode combinations represent transfers, which may be subject to specific rules. Also, which modes may be combined by which travel types restrict the choice set. For instance, heavy goods might combine freight trains and trucks, while passengers might choose between passenger modes such as car or bus, or nonmotorized forms (walking, bicycling, etc.).

In order to determine the paths, the transport model must analyze the transport network, defined as a set of interconnected directional links in the form of a graph. Each link is described in terms of its main characteristics: link type, link length, physical capacity, capacity of each public transport operator, and prohibited turns. Link types, in turn, define a number of general characteristics common to all links of the same type, such as speed, charges (tolls), maintenance costs, and the transport administrator in charge of the link. When along a path there is a transfer, possible transfer costs and waiting times are added. Transfers may involve integrated fares. The generalized cost of each path includes out-of-pocket costs (tariffs), values of time, and mode penalties to represent preferences and other non-modeled elements such as reliability, comfort, and so on. The degree of overlapping between paths is calculated to ensure that the results represent *distinct* travel options.

Once all paths have been found, the process of calculation enters an iterative cycle. It begins by calculating both monetary and generalized costs along each path. Generalized costs must be recalculated each time to account for changes in travel and waiting times due to congestion. Composite costs or log-sums are calculated over all paths for each user category.

The next step in the iterative process is trip generation, which transforms the potential travel demand calculated by the land-use model into actual trips at a particular time of the day (peak hour, twenty-four hours, etc.). Trip generation determines the number of trips from an origin to a destination by a particular transport category, as an elastic function of the corresponding composite cost. Elasticity in travel demand means that for a given functional relationship, more trips will be made if there is a reduction in the cost of travel. For example, if a certain number of people live close to their place of work, they might travel more times in a day because, perhaps, they go home for lunch. If a family lives close to shopping facilities, they might travel daily to do their shopping, while if they live in a more isolated location, they might go only once a week. In peak hour analysis, it may be that heavy congestion forces people to travel before or after peak hour. As a result, in each iteration the number of trips will be reduced as congestion builds up. Elastic trip generation also means that if a new transport facility is introduced, a certain amount of induced demand will be generated.

Following trip generation, a modal split stage is offered as an option. This is because the assignment model that follows in the sequence may be used as a combined modal split and assignment procedure, as will be described. The model user, however, may choose to perform a modal split stage first, to split demand, say between public and transit modes, and then use the assignment model to split between the different submodes that may exist within the transit system. In most conditions the modal split stage may be skipped altogether. If used, modal split takes the form of a logit model.

Trips for each category are assigned to the different multimodal paths connecting origins to destinations. Since each path implies a particular sequence of modes and transfers, trips are simultaneously assigned to modes as well as to links of the network. This is carried out by means of another logit model, where the utility functions are determined by the overlapped generalized cost of each path. The combined logit modal split and assignment model is equivalent to the multilevel hierarchical modal split model commonly found in the literature. In this case, however, the model itself automatically builds a highly complex hierarchical tree, a direct consequence of the use of overlapped costs.

By applying vehicle occupancy rates, trips are transformed into vehicles by mode in each link of the network. In the case of transit operators, vehicles subject to fixed routes are assigned directly to the network. Alternatively, the user may ask the model to determine the number of vehicles as a function of demand. In turn, the number of vehicles by operator is transformed into standard vehicles by applying appropriate rates.

The final stage of the iterative process is a capacity restriction procedure, in which travel speeds are reduced and waiting times are increased in every link for each route as a function of demand/capacity ratios. Waiting times take into consideration the frequency of transit services and the demand/capacity ratio in the vehicles themselves. Hence, people waiting for buses will have to wait longer if the vehicles are at capacity. Because the transport network in Tranus is multimodal, capacity constraint takes into account all vehicles, including cars, buses, and possible trucks of various kinds. Capacity constraint also includes the effects of queuing: if a link gets overloaded, speeds in the preceding link along each path are affected accordingly.

The iterative process continues until convergence is achieved. The model is said to have converged if in the current iteration volumes, speeds, and waiting times have changed with respect to the previous iteration values below a convergence target in all links and routes of the network. If the system has not converged, the calculation returns to the estimation of composite costs, because the new travel and waiting times will affect them at a path level, and consequently, at all other levels. In turn, the new costs will affect trip generation, modal split, and assignment, and even the location of activities in a next time period.

Finally, the transport model includes an optional transit supply procedure. For each route, a frequency range may be defined instead of a fixed frequency. The model begins with the minimum frequencies, but in each iteration each route is analyzed to check if demand is greater than capacity. If this is the case, the model evaluates whether the operating conditions of the route improve if frequency is increased. As demand grows through time, the model will increase transit supply accordingly, provided transit operators are able to keep or improve their operating conditions.

THE EVALUATION PROCEDURE

The evaluation of land-use and transport policies requires a base scenario where the policies are not included, and an alternative scenario with the policies included. The scenarios require that Tranus be run at discrete time intervals to the projection year. The differences in the results will represent the net effect of introducing the policies. At the end of the process an evaluation procedure may be applied, comparing the two scenarios across a number of socioeconomic, financial, and, optionally, energy consumption indicators.

Current costs and benefits are arranged in the form of accounts. There are three main accounts: users, operators, and administrators. Users perceive benefits (positive or negative) from land use and transport. Operators of transport services perceive income from the fares they charge to users, and must pay for operating costs. Administrators are the organizations that look after the infrastructure. They may perceive benefits from possible toll or parking charges to vehicles, and must pay for maintenance costs. From the results of the land-use model, it is possible to calculate the amount of energy required for domestic heating or cooling as a function of dwelling size/type and insulation levels. In the case of transport-related energy, the transport model estimates consumption by vehicle type as a function of average vehicle speed in each link.

The evaluation procedure may be complemented in many ways with external procedures that are not part of the Tranus system. For instance, a GIS-based environmental assessment model may be applied to the results of the land-use model. Or pollutant emissions and atmospheric diffusion models can be used to evaluate air quality.

OPERATING CHARACTERISTICS

Care has been taken to make the Tranus system as user-friendly as possible. The centerpiece of the software is a graphical user interface, permitting network editing and graphical output of the simulation runs. The underlying database is robust, object-oriented, and dynamic. All data elements are related to each other in logical ways. For instance, transit routes are related to the road links used. In turn, the route is related to the operator and mode, and the link to the link type and the organization responsible for upgrades and maintenance. The data remains consistent throughout the application, a feature that is complemented by consistency checks on the data. The dynamic feature means that the database understands and relates scenarios. All data is organized around a scenario tree. There is a base year from which all other time periods and scenarios *hang* in logical ways with specific dependencies. If a specific data item is changed in one year/scenario combination, such a change is automatically *inherited* by all dependent year/scenarios downstream.

RANGE OF APPLICATIONS

The spatial modeling system may be applied at any level—urban, regional, or national. There are three main features of the model. First, the general input–output structure permits applications at any scale, from small urban areas through metropolitan regions to statewide, national, or even international levels. A very simple model structure may be designed for a small urban area or for quick strategic applications. On the other extreme, highly complex models may be designed with many activity types interacting with each other and with a detailed description of the real estate market, including floor space by type (residential and nonresidential) and land-use types. At statewide and national scales, complete input–output accountings may be represented, with prices for all sectors, and explicit representation of imports and exports.

Second, the multimodal and intermodal logit assignment models are capable of representing both passengers and freight movements. Third, Tranus is a fully integrated land-use and transport model and is capable of both short-term and long-term projections. Long-term projections require serious consideration of the interaction between land use and transportation, particularly important when dealing with the environmental implications of policies and projects.

Tranus has been used to analyze urban and regional development plans, the impacts of specific projects, new road improvements, transit systems, toll highways, HOV lanes, congestion pricing, railways, ports, and airport facilities. Since 1985 there have been numerous applications, including the metropolitan areas of Caracas, Bogota, Panama City, Santo Domingo, and Buenos Aires. Also, the system has been applied at the national level to transportation networks in Venezuela, El Salvador, Guatemala, Paraguay, and Chile. In the United States, metropolitan models have been developed for Sacramento and Baltimore, and a statewide application was done for Oregon. In Europe, urban models have been built for Lyon, Brussels, Valencia, Swindon, and Inverness, and a national application is being developed for Switzerland. We will describe a recent application in Swindon in the United Kingdom.

THE MODEL OF SWINDON

Swindon is located to the west of London, about an hour away by train. The town and surrounding villages were the subject of a detailed study on land use and built stock, and for this reason the area was chosen as a case study for a research project on integrated land-use and transport modeling with special emphasis on energy consumption. The project was financed by the EPSRC "Sustainable

Cities" program called *An Integrated Building Stock, Transport and Energy Model of a Medium-Sized City.* This was a two-year project, from October 1995 to October 1997. The team was composed of the Open University Faculty of Technology, the University of Manchester School of Architecture, Rickaby Thompson Associates, and Modelistica, which was in charge of the actual modeling work.

MODEL DESIGN

The main innovation in the model of Swindon was the inclusion of floor space types in the model design. Consequently, this is a good example to show how far the Tranus system can go in the representation of complex real estate systems. Figure 7 shows the structure of the land-use model that was adopted. There are three columns: activities, floor space, and land. Activities are in turn divided into employment sectors and households. Employment sectors included agriculture and industry, government, retail and warehousing, office, health, and education. Households were classified into three income groups.

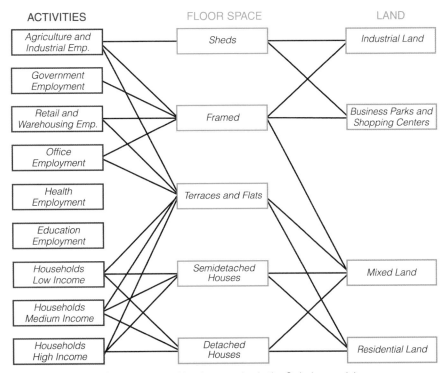

Figure 7. Activities, floor space, and land categories in the Swindon model.

Floor space types were defined to represent the typical types of structures that may be observed in the English built stock, as became evident from available statistics. Sheds represent typically large roof-lit structures preferred by manufacturing industries and warehouses. Framed buildings are mostly multistory side-lit structures, typical of office buildings. Terraces and flats represent a predominantly domestic type characterized by closely packed structures. Semidetached and detached houses are exclusive to residential activities and represent medium and low densities. The lines connecting activities to floor space types represent the demand relationships that were assumed to take place. For instance, the manufacturing industry may choose between sheds, framed, or even terraces and flats, while households may choose between the latter, semidetached, and detached houses.

Four types of land were defined. Industrial land represents the traditional type where manufacturing industry locates. Business parks and shopping centers were defined to represent an emerging type where both modern noncontaminating industry and large shopping facilities may locate. Mixed land is typical of the town center, in which a high-density pattern allows for all types of activities to locate, usually in multistory buildings. The residential land type represents lower densities of a more exclusive type, although some framed structures were allowed. The straight lines connecting floor space with land types represent which types of built forms may locate in which types of land. For instance, sheds may occupy industrial or business parks, while detached houses may choose from mixed or residential land.

This model design allows for many combinations. Households, for instance, may choose to live in a semidetached house on mixed land. A set of penalty factors representing preferences was estimated. When projecting into the future, activities demand increasing amounts of floor space, which in turn imply an increasing demand for land. The model estimated separate equilibrium rent values for floor space and land. Activities, however, must pay for the combination of both.

As demand for space grows, developers may introduce new land and new buildings according to the price signals that they receive. If there is enough land available and prices go up, developers will introduce a new supply of land and floor space until prices drop to previous values. If land becomes scarce, however, densities will tend to increase and substitutions may take place. Activities may consume smaller amounts of floor space, thus requiring less land, and floor space density may also rise. Developers may substitute one type of land for another, such as industrial land for mixed or residential land for business parks. In this model, developers may also substitute one type of floor space for another. They may, for instance, pull down detached houses and build framed structures, or they may turn a large manor house into small flats (demolitions and conversions).

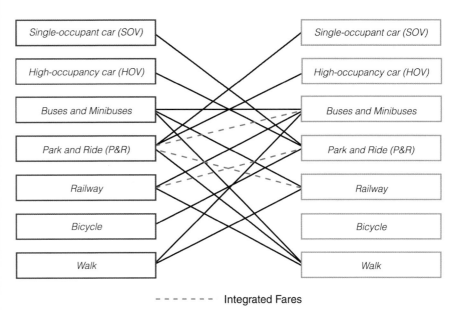

Figure 8. Modal choices and transfers in the model of Swindon.

On the transport side the network was defined in the usual way, consisting of roads and a regional motorway for the base year, plus bus-only lanes, suburban train, cycleways, and park-and-ride facilities for future scenarios. A single mode set was defined, as seen in figure 8, including single- and high-occupancy cars, buses and minibuses, park-and-ride, railway, bicycle, and walking. The figure shows the way in which these modes were allowed to combine and where integrated fares apply. For example, a traveler may drive his car to a park-and-ride facility, take a bus or a train, and finally walk to the destination. In this case the parking ticket includes the bus or train fare. Travelers may also walk or cycle all the way, or they can cycle to a park-and-ride station.

ALTERNATIVE SCENARIOS

Data was collected from the usual sources with the help of the local county. As mentioned, a detailed survey of the built stock was available from a previous study. Energy-use statistics were also available for vehicles and buildings from a national survey. With this information a GIS database was built and the model was calibrated for base year 1991. A single projection was made for 1996 and checked against limited information. Four scenarios were designed and simulated projections were made up to year 2016 at five-year intervals. The scenarios were defined as follows:

Containment and increased density ("Concentrated"). No new land was allowed for development outside the existing urban boundaries of Swindon and surrounding villages. A car-ban area was defined in the town center, eight park-and-ride facilities were introduced, and a network of bus-only lanes was established with integrated fares with the park-and-ride sites.

High-density Dispersal ("Hinterland"). Same as above, except that high-density developments were allowed in the satellite towns around Swindon. A suburban rail service was introduced with integrated fares to some additional park-and-ride sites, connecting some of the satellite towns. The bus-only lane network was extended to reach the satellites.

Limited Peripheral Expansion ("Peripheral N–W"). Same as the Concentrated Scenario in all respects, except that a limited expansion was allowed in the northwest area adjacent to the Swindon urban area. This is a proposal put forward by the local council.

Trend Scenario ("Trend"). Business as usual in that new developments were allowed everywhere, and no changes were introduced to the transport system.

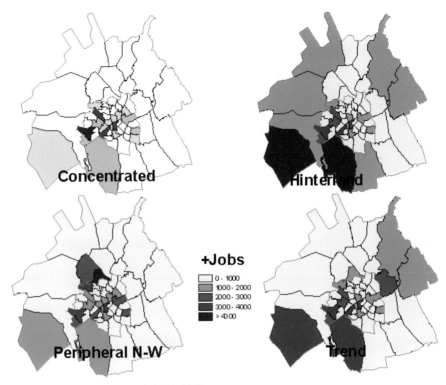

Figure 9. Employment growth 1991–2016.

SIMULATION RESULTS

Results from the simulations are numerous and varied, so that only a few samples are given below. Figure 9 shows employment growth as net differences between 1991 and 2016. The Concentrated Scenario shows little growth outside the urban area, with tertiary activities finding enough derelict industrial land for conversion. The Hinterland Scenario shows much more expansion, with employment going out to the satellite towns. The Peripheral N–W Scenario is similar to the Concentrated Scenario, except that many jobs look for new land in the designated expansion area. The Trend Scenario presents some expansion, not too different from the Hinterland Scenario, but to a limited extent because developers use the industrial land to construct offices and are able to expand the periphery of Swindon.

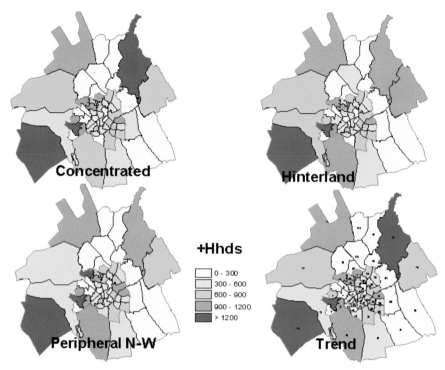

Figure 10. Population Growth 1991–2016.

The location of households shows a different pattern, as shown in figure 10. Ironically, the Concentrated Scenario shows little growth in the Swindon area, with the lowest central residential density of all. This is because jobs concentrate more, causing land rents to increase and pushing households into the periphery. A similar pattern may be seen in all other scenarios, although the proposed expansion in the N–W Scenario is successful in attracting residential growth. The Trend Scenario, as expected, shows the greatest expansion and lowest densities. The Concentrated Scenario fails to fulfill its purpose because it concentrates too much, forcing households out into the periphery and the satellite towns. In all scenarios it was assumed that in the future households will gradually increase their taste for low-density residential land with semidetached and detached houses, and this certainly affects the results.

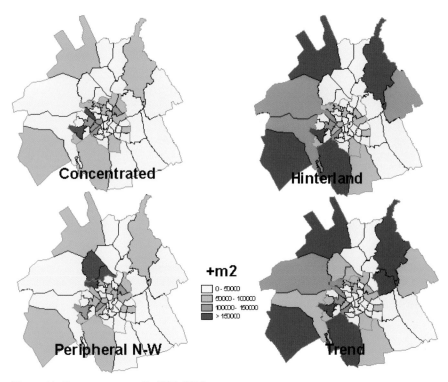

Figure 11. Floor space growth 1991–2016.

The maps of figure 11 show the net growth in floor space from 1991 to 2016. The total amount of floor space differs between scenarios, even if the total number of jobs and households is the same. For the more constrained scenarios, less floor space is developed, since land restrictions cause a rise in land rents that is passed on to floor space; consequently, activities consume less floor space due to elasticities. It follows that the Concentrated Scenario shows the lowest expansion of the built stock. The Peripheral N–W is also constrained, but the N–W development area clearly stands out. When land is allowed to grow in the satellite towns, floor space consumption spreads out, and this trend is more pronounced in the Trend Scenario where there are no restrictions.

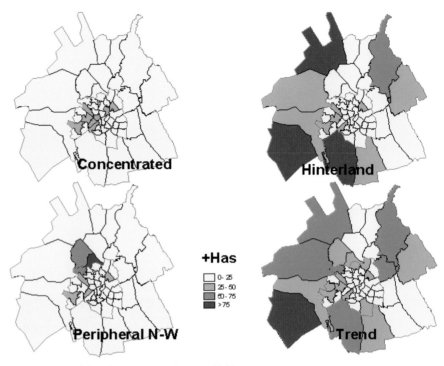

Figure 12. Land development growth 1991–2016.

As expected, land development growth follows the constraints more closely, as seen in figure 12. This is because land is directly subject to the constraints, while floor space may increase even if land is not allowed to grow by increasing floor space density. The total amounts of land consumed in each scenario are summarized in figure 13, which shows that there is a significant increase in the Hinterland and Trend scenarios compared to the other two. At the end of the projection year, the consumption of land in the Trend Scenario is more than 600 hectares bigger than in the Concentrated Scenario, representing 10 percent of the total stock.

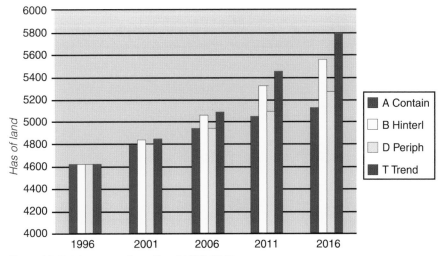

Figure 13. Total consumption of land 1996–2016.

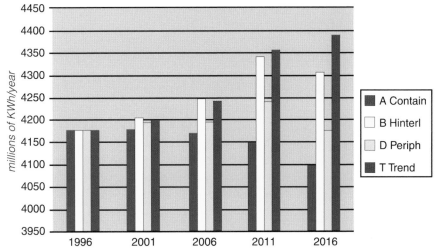

Figure 14. Total energy use in buildings 1996–2016.

Total consumption of floor space also differs by scenario and this is reflected in the estimates of total energy used by buildings presented in figure 14. More compact types (framed and terraces and flats) use less energy compared to the rest (shed, semidetached and detached houses). This results in savings of about 8 percent in energy used by buildings in the Concentrated Scenario compared to the Trend Scenario.

Scenario	1995	2001	2006	2011	2016
A Contain	6.4%	13.1%	13.4%	13.7%	13.9%
B Hinter	6.4%	13.5%	14.3%	15.2%	15.7%
D Periph	6.4%	12.9%	13.0%	13.3%	13.5%
T Trend	6.4%	7.0%	7.2%	8.3%	8.4%

% PUBLIC TRANSPORT (passeng-Km)

Scenario	1995	2001	2006	2011	2016
A Contain	4.1%	8.6%	8.5%	8.5%	8.6%
B Hinter	4.1%	8.5%	8.3%	8.5%	8.7%
D Periph	4.1%	8.5%	8.1%	8.1%	8.1%
T Trend	4.1%	4.2%	4.4%	4.5%	4.7%

% NONMOTORIZED (passeng-Km)

Scenario	1995	2001	2006	2011	2016
A Contain	0	39825	46635	49917	53065
B Hinter	0	37637	43929	50100	55654
D Periph	0	37911	46021	49011	52389
T Trend	0	0	0	0	0

PARK-AND-RIDE TRIPS

Figure 15. Modal split statistics 1996–2016.

Transport results are a mixture of the indirect effects of land-use policies and the direct effects of transport policies included in each scenario. All scenarios except the trend include a car ban in the town center, bus-only lanes, and park-and-ride sites. The modal split statistics (figure 15) show that the Trend Scenario had a modest increase in public transport use in terms of passenger-Km (from 6.4 percent in 1996 to 8.4percent in 2016). The car ban in the town center combined with the park-and-ride sites in all other scenarios becomes evident, doubling the use of public transport and nonmotorized modes. The Hinterland Scenario is the one that achieves the highest use of both. The number of trips involving park-and-ride is considerable in all scenarios.

An interesting conclusion that came from the results is that in spite of the fact that the town center is no longer accessible by car, all travelers perceive benefits, including car users. If travelers are allowed to take their cars into town, they do so and get stuck in traffic jams. If, however, they are forced to leave their cars parked near the center and bus into town, they end up better off, saving time and money. (Incidentally, this policy was successfully implemented in Oxford.)

These policies also have a favorable impact on fuel consumption by vehicles, as may be seen in figure 16. Compared to the Trend Scenario, all alternative scenarios show fuel savings in the order of 160,000 liters per day, a considerable amount considering that Swindon is a medium-size city. Finally, figure 17 shows assigned nonmotorized trips for the Peripheral N–W Scenario compared to the Trend, zooming into the central area where such trips are most common.

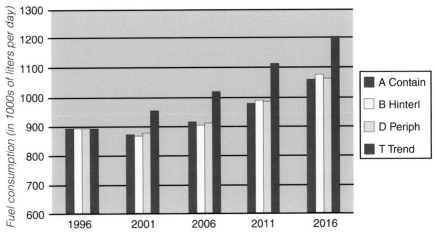

Figure 16. Vehicles' fuel consumption 1996–2016.

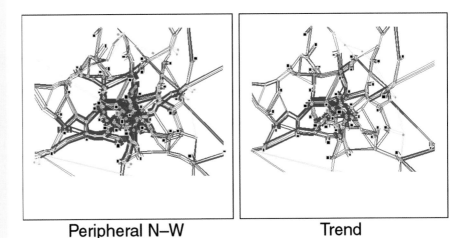

Figure 17. Assigned nonmotorized trips 1996–2016.

CONCLUSIONS

Tranus represents a new breed of integrated model that has many advantages over the more limited and conventional transport-only modeling that has dominated urban and regional planning in the last few decades. The range of policies that may be analyzed is much wider, and reasonable long-term projections are obtained.

In this last decade we have seen considerable advances in theory and software development that make it possible to develop new and better models. The Tranus system described above is one of many such analytical tools that have emerged recently. Such tools are possible in part because of the extraordinary advance in the development of geographically referenced databases, and by a dramatic reduction in costs and widespread availability of data, often through the Internet. Some may choose to call this a revolution of sorts, but even the most moderate analyst will have to admit that the realm of urban and regional planning is going through a process of change. Those who want to stick to the old methods, limiting their analysis to the assignment of cars onto highways, will find it difficult to respond to the new requirements. Government, local authorities, environmental groups, organized neighborhoods, and the public all have increased their expectations.

Paper 7

CUF, CUF II, and CURBA: A Family of Spatially Explicit Urban Growth and Land-Use Policy Simulation Models

JOHN LANDIS

DEPARTMENT OF CITY AND REGIONAL PLANNING

UNIVERSITY OF CALIFORNIA, BERKELEY

BERKELEY, CALIFORNIA

ABSTRACT

Three newer-generation regional simulation models, developed at the University of California, Berkeley, require significant use of GIS concepts and methods. These three models—California Urban Futures I and II (CUF I and II) and California Urban and Biodiversity Analysis Model (CURBA)—show how applied research evolves in response to testing and implementation. The models are all similar in that they work at the site level; use GIS for data manipulation, analysis, and presentation; and are designed for use in actual planning situations. The models differ in internal structure and purpose. While CUF I is vector-based, CUF II and CURBA use a raster data structure. Also, unlike CUF I, CUF II permits different land-use types to bid against each other for a particular location. CURBA's design is similar to CUF II, but focuses on the interactions between land-use change and habitat loss.

INTRODUCTION

Planning is about changing the status quo. For land-use and development planners, this means envisioning alternate future land-use and activity patterns. Planners typically approach the task in one of two ways. The predominant approach, based in planning's design tradition, is to imagine a set of desirable land-use outcomes, and then work *backward* to identify the present-day decisions and policies required to achieve those outcomes. A second approach, based in planning's analytical tradition, is to postulate alternative present-day decisions and policies, and then trace their effects *forward* into the future. This second approach requires the ability to model, or *simulate,* the effects of particular policies and interventions.

Neither approach is inherently better. Both require considerable information, attention to detail, skill, and yes, even guesswork. When the futures being visualized are complex (i.e., involve interactions between multiple policies and activities), are spatially explicit (e.g., refer to particular parcels or sites), and require a high degree of consistency across areas or time periods, urban simulation models can be extremely helpful.

Urban simulation models were first operationalized in the late 1960s. Crude by current standards, they were roundly (and sometimes appropriately) criticized as presumptuous, bloated, inaccurate, resource-consuming, unresponsive to the issues of the day, and devoid of any underlying theory (Lee 1973). Stung by the fury (and the occasional unfairness) of the criticisms directed their way, urban modelers went back into their offices, laboratories, and classrooms to quietly improve their craft.

The late 1970s and early 1980s witnessed steady improvement in modeling theory and methods—most notably the development of probabilistic estimation techniques such as logit and probit, and the application of those techniques to the explanation of individual behavior (Batty 1992, Batty and Xie 1994, Wegener 1994, 1995). By the late 1980s and early 1990s—thanks to ever-increasing computer processing power and storage capabilities—urban modelers were able to manipulate spatial data layers, each including thousands, if not hundreds of thousands, of features and attributes. By the mid-1990s the stage was set for a new generation of more powerful, more useful, and more relevant urban simulation models (Clarke 1996).

This chapter presents the theory, logic, and selected simulation results for three new-generation urban simulation models developed at the University of California, Berkeley. They are (1) the first generation of the California Urban Futures Model, also known as CUF; (2) the second generation of the California Urban Futures Model, known as CUF II; and, (3) the California Urban and Biodiversity Analysis Model, known as CURBA. CUF and CUF II were designed to be used for regional, countywide, and local land-use planning.

CURBA is intended to be used at the regional or county level for integrated land-use and habitat conservation planning.

The three models share several attributes. All three are spatially explicit; that is, they work at site rather than zonal or jurisdictional levels. Thus users can investigate the results of their simulations at a variety of spatial levels, from the backyard to the region. All three models utilize GIS to manage multiple data layers, generate sites, and present results. Last and most important, all three were designed for real-time use by practicing planners and decision makers in framing and evaluating realistic land-use and development policies.

CUF I: A NEW APPROACH TO MODELING URBAN GROWTH

ORGANIZATION AND LOGIC

Introduced in 1994, the California Urban Futures Model (CUF) broke new ground in four areas (Landis 1994a, 1995). It was the first large-scale and operational urban growth model to be spatially explicit. It was the first large-scale urban growth and simulation model to utilize a geographic information system for data integration and spatial analysis, not just display. It was the first operational urban growth and planning model capable of simulating the interactions between public land-use policies and private developers regarding the scale, density, and location of proposed developments. Finally, it was the first large-scale planning model specifically designed to evaluate regional, subregional, and local land-use alternatives.

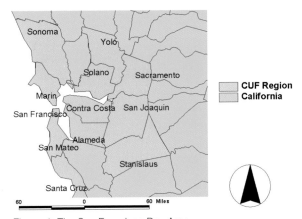

Figure 1. The San Francisco Bay Area.

As its name implies, CUF was designed to simulate future urbanization patterns in California, specifically in and around the greater San Francisco Bay Area (figure 1). CUF is really four linked submodels, run recursively (figure 2).

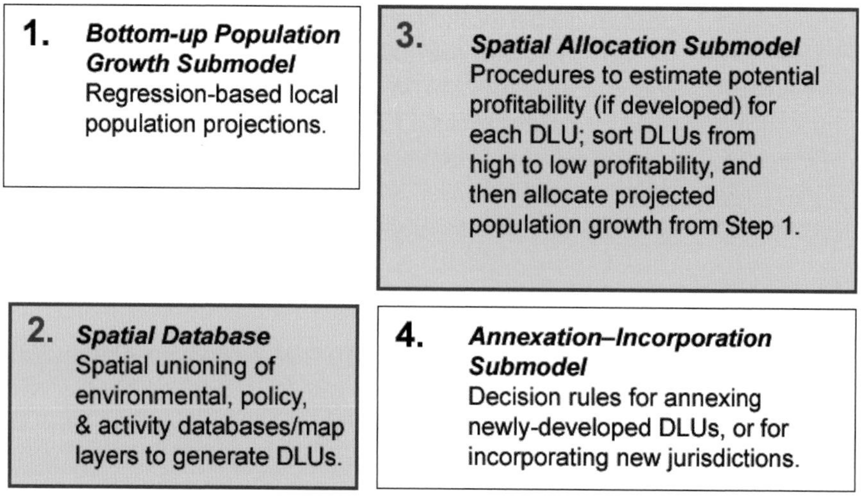

1. **Bottom-up Population Growth Submodel** Regression-based local population projections.	**3.** **Spatial Allocation Submodel** Procedures to estimate potential profitability (if developed) for each DLU; sort DLUs from high to low profitability, and then allocate projected population growth from Step 1.
2. **Spatial Database** Spatial unioning of environmental, policy, & activity databases/map layers to generate DLUs.	**4.** **Annexation–Incorporation Submodel** Decision rules for annexing newly-developed DLUs, or for incorporating new jurisdictions.

Figure 2. CUF model structure.

The Bottom–up Population Growth Submodel. This is the demand side of the CUF Model: it generates five-year population growth forecasts for every Bay Area jurisdiction. The Bottom–up Population Growth Submodel consists of two linear regression equations, one for counties and one for cities. (See Landis 1994 for the variables, their definitions, and regression results.) Unlike top-down models, which project local population growth by distributing regional or county growth totals, the CUF Model projects *each* municipality's growth as a function of its current size, growth history, and growth policies. Unincorporated population is calculated as the difference between projected county population and the sum of city population projections.

The Spatial Database. This is the supply side of the CUF Model. It consists of a series of GIS map layers that describe the environmental, land-use, zoning, current density, and accessibility attributes of all locations in the study region or county. These various layers can either be analyzed individually, or combined into a single GIS layer that includes all relevant attribute information for all locations. The combined layer consists of thousands of irregularly shaped polygons, or *developable land units* (DLUs). DLUs are polygon constructs generated through the geometric union and/or intersection of multiple environmental, market, and policy map layers. The shape and size of each DLU are determined by the values of its component attributes. Neighboring DLUs have one or more different attribute values. An example of a DLU would be an undeveloped site with steep slopes, served by sewers, zoned for light industry, and located less than 500 meters from a major freeway. Depending on the number and complexity of the map layers which are used to generate them, DLUs may range in size from one to several hundred acres. The typical Bay Area county includes 30,000 to 50,000 distinct DLUs. Although DLUs are not parcels, in some locations, they approximate collections of parcels. DLUs are available for development or redevelopment.

The Spatial Allocation Submodel. This submodel is a series of procedures for allocating projected population growth (step 1, above) to appropriate DLUs (step 2). Each run of the Spatial Allocation Submodel involves five steps:

1 All undeveloped DLUs in a county are scored according to their potential profitability if developed in residential use. Potential profitability is calculated as shown below:

Per-acre residential development profit $_{(i,j,k)}$

= Average new home sales price $_{(i,j,k)}$
- Raw land price $_{(j,k)}$
- Hard construction costs $_{(i,k)}$
- Site improvement costs $_{(i,j,k)}$
- Service extension costs $_{(j,k)}$
- Development, impact, service, hookup, and planning fees $_{(k)}$
- Delay and holding costs $_{(k)}$
- Extraordinary infrastructure capacity costs, exactions, and impact mitigation costs $_{(j,k)}$

where: The subscript i denotes the size and quality level of the typical new home in each community as obtained from sales transaction records;

The subscript j denotes the slope, environmental characteristics, and specific location of the homesites, or DLUs; and,

The subscript k denotes the jurisdiction in which the site is located.

2 DLUs regarded as inappropriate for development for environmental, ownership, or public-policy reasons are eliminated from consideration.

3 Remaining DLUs (those which may be developed) within each municipality[1] are sorted from high to low in order of their potential profitability if developed.

4 Within each municipality (or its urban service area) projected population growth is assigned to DLUs in order of profit potential, from high to low. The choice of allocation density rests with the user (the default is the current "market" density), and may vary between model runs. After the model has allocated as much population growth as will fit into the most-profitable DLU, it moves to the next-most-profitable DLU, and so on. The allocation process is complete either when all projected population growth is allocated, or when there is insufficient developable land within the municipality to accommodate forecast growth. Depending on the land-use policy scenario being investigated, the model can collect any unallocated population growth for potential spillover.

5 A similar procedure is used to allocate forecast county population growth (plus any unallocated spillover growth) to unincorporated county DLUs. The allocation process within a county is complete either when all forecast and spillover population growth is allocated, or when there is insufficient developable land within the city to accommodate forecast growth. Unallocated population growth, if any remains, can be accumulated for later reallocation to those counties with available land.

Implicit in these procedures is the assumption that decisions regarding the pattern and timing of urban growth are mostly in the hands of large-scale, profit-maximizing land developers (see Peiser 1992). These decisions are affected by—but not determined by—large-scale public infrastructure investments as well as governmental land-use and environmental regulations.[2] In this sense, the CUF Model has a distinctly California flavor. Land developers and homebuilders are assumed to be price-takers with respect to both new home sales prices and raw land prices.

The Annexation–Incorporation Submodel is the final component of the CUF Model. It is a series of decision rules for annexing newly developed DLUs to existing cities, or for incorporating clusters of DLUs into new cities.

Once the data and parameters required for the model have been assembled, any number of alternative policy scenarios may be easily and quickly tested. "Running" a CUF Model scenario consists of filling out a computerized *form* indicating specific development prohibitions, regulations, or incentives to be applied to particular areas. Individual scenarios take about two minutes to run per county, even in counties with more than 30,000 DLUs.

In summary, the CUF Model "grows" each county and its constituent cities by determining how much new development to allocate to each DLU during each model period as a function of the profitability of developing that DLU as housing, the characteristics of the DLU itself, population growth pressures, and a series of user-specified development rules.

APPLYING THE CUF MODEL: THREE REGIONWIDE SCENARIOS

The CUF Model was developed to test alternative growth management scenarios for the 14-county greater Bay Area region.[3] Initial testing focused on three regionwide scenarios:

Scenario A. Business as Usual. This baseline scenario assumed that development patterns in the Bay Area would continue to be guided by the preferences of the private market, subject to existing, locally based growth and development policies. Hillside and wetland development would be allowed, as would development beyond existing urban service areas. Development policies and restrictions would not be coordinated between neighboring cities, or within counties. Population growth which could not be accommodated within municipal boundaries would be allowed to "spill over" into unincorporated areas.

Scenario B. Maximum Environmental Protection. This second scenario assumed the coordinated adoption of stringent environmental protection policies by all Bay Area municipalities. These policies included (1) prohibitions on the development of hillsides with slopes in excess of 15 percent; (2) prohibitions on the development of areas identified as wetlands; (3) prohibitions on the development of sites identified as "prime" and "unique" agriculture by the California

Farmland Mapping and Monitoring Project (CFMMP); and (4) changes to local zoning ordinances requiring that the average density of new residential development be equivalent to average existing residential densities. Under this scenario, cities would grow at their historical densities, rather than those determined in the market.

Scenario C. Compact Cities. This scenario assumed the countywide adoption of policies designated to promote compact and contiguous development forms. It assumes that new residential development should occur in and around existing urban centers. To promote such a goal, this scenario assumed the regionwide adoption of three sets of policies (1) that all new residential development would occur at a minimum average density of 4,500 persons per square kilometer (approximately 18 persons per acre); (2) that all cities would adopt policy requiring that 20 percent of their projected population growth in the form of "infill" development; and (3) that new "greenfield" development be limited to sites within 1,000 meters of existing city boundaries. The Compact Cities scenario also prohibited the development of hillsides, wetlands, and prime and unique agricultural lands outside city sphere-of-influence boundaries. Growth which could not be accommodated within these rules was to be channeled into predesignated "new towns."

In terms of implementation, all three scenarios are quite reasonable. Even the most stringent scenario, *Scenario C: Compact Cities,* calls for only modest increases in residential densities and infill levels. And while absolute prohibitions on the development of steep slopes and wetlands *(Scenario B: Maximum Environmental Protection, and Scenario C: Compact Cities)* might seem extreme to some, in reality, most steeply sloped areas and many wetland parcels are not particularly attractive to residential developers. Programmatic feasibility aside, only *Scenario A: Business as Usual,* can be regarded as politically feasible. Repeated suggestions of increased regional coordination aside, there are currently no planning agencies or institutions anywhere in California able to coordinate zoning and land-use policies among cities, let alone among counties.

Summary results for the three scenarios are presented in table 1. For the entire study region, a total of 163,012 acres of currently undeveloped land would be required to accommodate projected population growth through the year 2010 under *Scenario A: Business as Usual.* Under *Scenario B: Maximum Environmental Protection,* that total would fall slightly to 147,468 acres. Under *Scenario C: Compact Growth,* it would fall further to 106,779 acres. Under *Scenario A,* new development would occur at a regionwide average density of 17.5 persons per acre. Under *Scenario B,* new development densities would rise slightly to 19.4 persons per acres, and under *Scenario C,* they would rise to 26.8 persons per acre.

TABLE 1. 2010 CUF MODEL LAND DEVELOPMENT PROJECTIONS FOR 3 SCENARIOS

County	Existing Developed Acreage 1990	Forecast Population Growth, 1990–2010	Additional Acres Required for Development			Average Growth Density (persons/acre)		
			Scenario A: Business as Usual	Scenario B: Maximum Environmental Protection	Scenario C: Compact Cities	Scenario A: Business as Usual	Scenario B: Maximum Environmental Protection	Scenario C: Compact Cities
Alameda	135,732	258,030	12,306	12,602	8,624	21.0	20.5	29.9
Contra Costa	132,841	305,322	23,376	19,051	11,935	13.1	16.0	25.6
Marin	40,500	107,533	4,991	5,708	2,693	21.5	18.8	39.9
Napa	18,705	81,948	8,772	6,252	3,830	9.3	13.1	21.4
Sacramento	133,483	398,261	27,972	28,367	23,079	14.2	14.0	17.3
San Francisco	na	na	na	na	na	na	na	na
San Joaquin	43,094	262,478	11,638	9,291	9,316	22.6	28.3	28.2
San Mateo	72,573	58,847	49	49	49	1201.0	1201.0	1201.0
Santa Clara	177,121	362,478	11,861	8,031	230	30.6	45.1	1576.0
Santa Cruz	27,552	151,858	13,146	14,282	6,721	11.6	10.6	22.6
Solano	42,847	158,027	8,080	6,375	5,090	19.6	24.8	31.0
Sonoma	60,292	302,724	20,509	19,521	17,272	14.8	15.5	17.5
Stanislaus	43,885	349,537	16,630	12,750	14,851	21.0	27.4	23.5
Yolo	22,115	62,524	3,682	5,189	3,089	17.0	12.0	20.2
Total	950,740	2,859,567	163,012	147,468	106,779	17.5	19.4	26.8

Projections of additional land consumption and density vary more widely for individual counties than for the region as a whole. Under *Scenario A: Business as Usual,* for example, 23,376 additional acres of suburban Contra Costa County would be developed by 2010. *Under Scenario B: Maximum Environmental Protection,* that total would fall to 19,051 acres; and under *Scenario C: Compact Growth,* it would fall to 11,935 acres. In San Mateo County, by contrast, the same results would be obtained under all three scenarios.

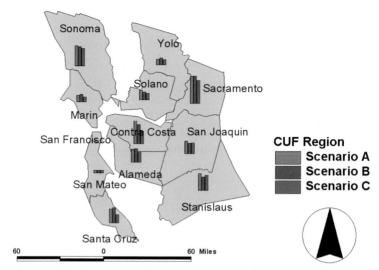

Figure 3. CUF Model results. Acres required under the three scenarios.

Some results are unexpected. For example, because it would shift development outward from parcels that are environmentally sensitive but contiguous to existing development, *Scenario B: Maximum Environmental Protection* would actually result in greater land consumption in Alameda, Marin, Sacramento, and Yolo counties than would *Scenario A: Business as Usual.* In much the same vein, *Scenario C: Compact Growth* would have less effect in three of the four Central Valley counties (Sacramento, San Joaquin, and Stanislaus) than in the core Bay Area counties—mostly because the former are already fairly compact. The ability to produce results which may be unexpected *a priori,* but which are nonetheless plausible, is one hallmark of a useful simulation model. These are but a smattering of CUF Model simulation results. For additional examples see Landis (1995).

Readers should note that these results are all aggregations of individual site-level development allocations. This ability to "zoom in" so that users can view model and simulation results at almost any level of interest—from backyard to region—is perhaps the most useful and outstanding feature of any spatially explicit urban simulation model. Of course, resolution is not the same thing as accuracy. Whatever the model and whatever the use, land-use planners and decision makers need to understand something of how these types of models work (and do not work) so that they can more fully evaluate what they are viewing.

Like many pioneers, CUF was a little rough around the edges. It could simulate the preferred locations of residential but not commercial or industrial land uses. It could simulate the land-use effects of regulatory policies, but not public infrastructure investments such as highways or transit extensions. Real estate prices, to the extent that they played any role, were entirely exogenous. Development that could not be allocated simply spilled over into neighboring jurisdictions (subject to user-specified limits), rather than feeding back into the allocation process through higher land or structure prices. CUF's biggest shortcoming, however, was that the process for allocating prospective development was based on a series of uncalibrated decision rules, rather than historical experience.

The CUF II Model was developed to remedy these shortcomings (Landis and Zhang 1998a, 1998b). Unlike its predecessor, CUF II includes multiple land uses—residential, commercial, and industrial. CUF II, moreover, allows different land uses to effectively "bid" against each other for preferred sites. Redevelopment and infill development are allowed as alternatives to greenfield development. Most important, rather than being based on untested decision rules, land-use allocation procedures are calibrated against historical experience.

The logic of the CUF II model is shown in figure 4. CUF II differs from its predecessor in two fundamental ways. First, instead of irregularly shaped DLUs, the CUF II model decomposes space into 1-hectare (100-by-100-meter) grid cells.[4] Each grid cell has the same location and dimensions across all map layers. This makes it easier and faster to overlay and compare different map layers. In terms of size, 1-hectare grid cells are small enough in size to capture the detailed fabric of urban land use, but large enough to avoid problems of data "noise."[5] On the negative side, grid cells are entirely artificial. They lack physical, economic, or legal reality. Unlike parcels, they are not transacted. Nor are they directly regulated. Thus, they are not themselves the subject of development or redevelopment decisions.

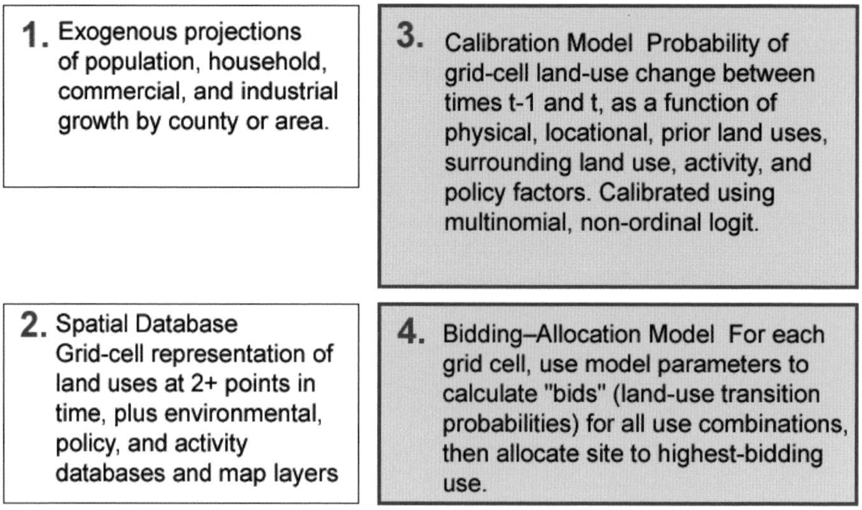

1. Exogenous projections of population, household, commercial, and industrial growth by county or area.

3. Calibration Model Probability of grid-cell land-use change between times t-1 and t, as a function of physical, locational, prior land uses, surrounding land use, activity, and policy factors. Calibrated using multinomial, non-ordinal logit.

2. Spatial Database Grid-cell representation of land uses at 2+ points in time, plus environmental, policy, and activity databases and map layers

4. Bidding–Allocation Model For each grid cell, use model parameters to calculate "bids" (land-use transition probabilities) for all use combinations, then allocate site to highest-bidding use.

Figure 4. CUF II Model logic.

The second difference between CUF II and the original CUF Model goes to the heart of the way projected urban activities are allocated to sites. Whereas the original CUF model allocated residential users to irregular sites (DLUs) in order of their potential profitability, the CUF II Model allocates land using activities to 1-hectare sites (grid cells) on the basis of estimated land-use change probabilities. These probabilities are calculated using statistical equations calibrated from observed land-use changes. Separate probabilities are calculated for each potential land-use change for every undeveloped and developed grid cell.

The use of separately estimated land-use change probabilities offers several advantages. It makes it possible for different activities (e.g., residential, commercial, and industrial growth) to bid against each other for preferred sites. It also makes it possible to simulate redevelopment—that is, the reuse of previously developed sites. It offers the potential for a much richer set of spillover possibilities. Perhaps most important, it allows the CUF II model to simulate the urban growth and land-use effects of potential infrastructure investments such as highways and transit lines.

CALIBRATING THE CUF II MODEL

The CUF II Model considers nine categories of observed land-use change:

1 Undeveloped to single-family residential

2 Undeveloped to multifamily residential

3 Undeveloped to commercial (retail and office)

4 Undeveloped to industrial

5 No change in undeveloped status

6 Change from (previously developed) nonresidential to residential

7 Change from (previously developed) noncommercial to commercial

8 Change from (previously developed) nonindustrial to industrial

9 No change in previously developed status

For calibration purposes, past land-use changes are observed as discrete changes in grid cell land-use classification between 1985 and 1995. The observed category changes (the dependent variable) are compared with a series of independent variables using a multinomial logit estimator.[6, 7] (The CURBA Model, explained in the next section, is calibrated using a binomial logit model.)

Unlike most multinomial logit models which are ordinal in form (i.e., the categories which make up the dependent variables can be ordered or ranked), the CUF II model makes use of a *non-ordinal* logit estimator to predict land-use change. This means that no one type of land-use change may be presumed, *a priori*, to be universally superior to any another. In some situations, for example, commercial land uses may be found to be superior to residential land uses. In other situations, residential land-use change may be observed to be superior to commercial land-use change.[8] It is the use of a nonordinal logit estimator that allows different land uses to later compete against each other for preferred sites.

The generalized form of the multinomial logit model of site-level land-use change is:

$$\text{Prob}[i|l] = \{\exp(\beta_0{}' + \beta_1{}'x_{l1} + \beta_2{}'x_{l2} + \ldots + \beta_m{}'x_{lm})$$
$$\Sigma_{+1,L}\, \exp(\beta_0{}' + \beta_1{}'x_{l1} + \beta_2{}'x_{l2} + \ldots + \beta_m{}'x_{lm})\}$$

where: $\text{Prob}[i|l]$ is the probability that each site *i* is developed or redeveloped to use *l*,

x_{lm} are explanatory, or independent variables associated with each site *i*,

β_m are the logit coefficients (to be estimated) associated with land use *l* and variable x_{lm};

and l is the full set of land use changes.

Logit analysis *can* be used to model discrete phenomena like land-use change. Whether it *should* be used for that purpose is a slightly different matter. In order for the calibrated land-use change equations to be reliable—that is, to be free from bias—we must make two assumptions about the process of land-use change itself. The first is that all of the actors and agents involved in the development process—landowners, developers, builders, households, and businesses—must act independently of each other. This assumption is intended to rule out the possibility of oligopolistic or strategic behavior.[9]

A second assumption revolves around the presence, or more specifically, the lack of presence, of agents. Discrete choice analysis has traditionally been used to model the behavior of identifiable agents like individuals or households[10] (Ben–Akiva and Lerman 1984, Domenich and McFadden 1975, McFadden 1974). In the case of land-use change, the agents of interest are actually land buyers and sellers. Potential buyers must decide—based on current and expected site and market conditions—whether to bid for a particular parcel. Given the same information, potential sellers must decide whether or not to accept any of the bids offered them. Because it tracks sites rather than transactions, the CUF II Model lacks agents. To sidestep this problem, we invoke the idea of competition. Specifically, we argue that in competitive markets (e.g., those with few barriers to entry), the characteristics of particular agents do not affect outcomes. Whether developers are well-capitalized or poorly capitalized, whether they specialize in residential development or retail development, whether their experience is local or national—in a competitive market, these factors should be of less importance than the strength of the demand for urban development and the availability of appropriate sites.[11]

To make the analysis computationally manageable, separate logit models were calibrated for undeveloped and previously developed land in each of eight Bay Area counties. Hectare-scale land-use data was provided for 1985 and 1995 by the Association of Bay Area Governments (ABAG). Each logit equation takes the following general form:

The various independent variables were projected to affect the probabilities of land-use change as follows:

Pr [Land use change$_{ijkl}$] = f {initial site use, demand factors, site accessibility and distance characteristics, physical and development cost constraints, policy factors, relationships to neighboring sites}

where: Pr[Land use change$_{ijkl}$] indicates the probability that site i in community j changed from land use k to land use l between 1985 and 1995;

i indicates each site;

k, the initial (1985) land use of site i, is either undeveloped or developed; and l, the terminal (1995) land use of site i is either single-family residential, multi-family residential, commercial, industrial, or else is unchanged from the initial use.

Initial Land Uses: Conventional urban economics holds that commercial and industrial uses are generally of a "higher order" than residential uses. That is, they are capable of generating higher land rents. If this is true, previously developed residential sites should, all else being equal, be more likely to be redeveloped into commercial or industrial uses. By the same logic, previously developed commercial or industrial sites are unlikely to be redeveloped into residential use.

Demand Factors: The probability that sites will be developed or redeveloped will depend in large measure on the strength of the demand for space. We measured demand in two ways: (1) as the rate of household growth or change during the previous five years (1980–85); and (2) as the rate of job growth or job change during the previous five years. Both variables were measured at the city level; all sites within a city were presumed to be subject to comparable demand pressures. Assuming that population and employment growth causes land conversion (and not vice-versa), we expected the estimate coefficients of both variables to be positive. Two other demand measures were entered to account for possible scale effects: (3) the initial number of households in the city as of 1985; and (4) the initial number of jobs in the city, also as of 1985.[12] We included a fifth demand side variable, the jobs–households ratio, to test the hypothesis that the balance between jobs and housing in a community might somehow affect land-use change.

Accessibility and Distance Effects: Economists have long contended that the demand for sites (as measured by land prices and densities) should be strongest near major city centers, principally for reasons of minimized (work trip) transportation costs. The San Francisco Bay Area has three regional employment centers (San Francisco, Oakland, and San Jose) and many more subcenters (e.g., Walnut Creek, San Ramon, Pleasanton, Fremont, Santa Clara/Sunnyvale, Palo Alto, San Mateo, Hayward, Berkeley, Richmond, Fairfield, Vallejo, and Santa Rosa). To capture the effects of regional accessibility on land-use change, we used GIS to measure the Euclidean distance from every hectare site to downtown San Francisco, and to downtown San Jose.[13] If development really does favor more accessible locations, we would expect the coefficients of these two measures to be consistently negative.

Accessibility can be also be measured more generally. Regardless of trip destination or purpose, activities located near major freeway interchanges or transit stations have a higher level of generalized accessibility than activities located farther away. Because of this, we would expect such sites to be in greater demand, and thus, to face greater development and redevelopment pressures. To test this hypothesis, we measured the aerial distance from every site to the closest freeway interchange and/or BART stations.[14] To the extent that proximity to regional transportation facilities encourages land-use change, we would expect the coefficients of these two measures to be negative.

Physical and Cost Constraints: A site's physical characteristics may affect its general developability or its developability to particular uses. Slopes were estimated for each site from USGS DEM (digital elevation model) data. To allow for nonlinearities and threshold effects, we coded slope into five 0/1 dummy variables, corresponding to five slope classifications: 1- to 2-percent slope; 3- to 5-percent slope; 6- to 9-percent slope; 10- to 15-percent slope; and 16-percent or greater slope. Because of the higher costs associated with hillside development, we generally expect to observe a negative relationship between the dummy variables denoting steeper slopes and the probability of site development.[15, 16]

In theory, developers who propose projects inside existing urban cores (often called infill) should be able to take advantage of existing infrastructure capacity to a greater extent than developers who propose more far-flung projects. To capture this effect, we used GIS to measure the linear distance from each site to the nearest sphere-of-influence boundary.[17] The greater this distance, we assume, the higher the cost of providing required infrastructure and urban services.[18]

Policy Factors: Most constraints to development are political, not physical. Just about every local government in California utilizes zoning to stipulate which uses and densities are permitted where.[19] Similarly, California municipalities are supposed to designate their ultimate "build-out" boundaries as "spheres of influence." In practice, local policy constraints are rarely absolute. Zoning can be and frequently is changed. Indeed, experienced developers typically look for under-zoned properties in the hope of changing their zoning to a higher, and thus more profitable, use. Likewise, depending on the county, sphere-of-influence boundaries may be easily extended.

Because of the cost and difficulty of obtaining, digitizing, and coding accurate, up-to-the-minute zoning maps for every jurisdiction, we did not include zoning variables in the model. We did, however, determine whether each site was within a current sphere-of-influence boundary.[20] All else being equal—and notwithstanding the laxness with which current sphere-of-influence requirements are sometimes implemented—we expect that vacant sites outside sphere boundaries would be less likely to be developed.

Using digital maps of farmland quality published by the California Farmland Mapping and Monitoring Project, we determined which undeveloped sites were located on prime farmlands.

Adjacent Use Effects: All else being equal, we would expect site land uses to be strongly affected by the pattern of neighboring or adjacent uses. We would expect, for example, that a vacant site surrounded by residential uses would be more likely to be developed into residential or retail use than into office or industrial use. Likewise, we might expect that a vacant site surrounded by commercial uses would more likely be developed into commercial use than into single-family residential use. Five variables denoting the share of neighboring sites in each major land use (single-family, multifamily, commercial, industrial, and transportation) were included in each model.[21]

Interuse Externalities and Proximity Effects: Different land uses generate both positive and negative externalities. Indeed, the desire to mitigate negative externalities is the principle rationale behind zoning. Externalities need not be negative, however. A shopping center located near a large subdivision or apartment building is the beneficiary of a positive spillover—in this case, a large potential market.

To test for the presence and importance of interuse externalities, we used GIS to measure the Euclidean distance from each site to the nearest commercial site, industrial site, and public-use site. To the extent that the negative externalities associated with a combination of uses exceed the positive externalities, we would expect the estimated coefficients of these variables to be negative. Conversely, a positive coefficient would indicate that the positive externalities associated with proximity between uses exceed the negative externalities. Finally, to the extent that proximity effects and interuse externalities do not matter, we would expect the variable coefficients not to be statistically significant.

Table 2 summarizes the various independent variables used in the CUF II Model. Overall, the various models of vacant land-use change fit the data reasonably well (table 3). Model "fits" range from a high of 99.0 percent for Napa County (meaning that the model correctly predicted 99 percent of all observed 1985–95 grid cell land-use changes) to a low of 92.2 percent for Contra Costa County. As a group, the models do best at predicting which vacant sites are most likely to remain vacant. For vacant-to-single-family residential land-use changes, the goodness-of-fit measures vary from a high of 48.3 percent in Solano County (meaning that the model correctly predicted only about half of vacant-to-residential land-use changes) to a low of 21.6 percent in Sonoma County. For vacant-to-commercial land-use changes, the goodness-of-fit measures vary from a high of 78.8 percent in Napa County to a low of only 12.4 percent in Contra Costa County. Goodness-of-fit measures for vacant-to-industrial and vacant-to-multifamily land uses vary even more widely.

TABLE 2. GOODNESS-OF-FIT RESULTS FOR CUF II

Independent Variables	Description
Demand Variables	1980–85 % employment change (by city) 1980–85 % household change (by city) 1980 Households (by city) 1980 Employment (by city) Jobs/Household ratio—1980 (by city)
Distance Variables	Site distance to San Francisco (in 200m increments) Site distance to San Jose (in 200m increments) Site distance to freeway interchange (in 200m increments) Site distance to nearest BART station (in 200m increments)
Physical and Cost Constraint Variables	Slope1: 1–2% site slope (dummy variable) Slope2: 3–5% site slope (dummy variable) Slope3: 6–10% site slope (dummy variable) Slope4: 11–15% site slope (dummy variable) Slope5: >15% site slope (dummy variable) Distance to sphere-of-influence (in 200m increments)
Policy Constraint Variable Adjacent-Use Variables	Prime agricultural land (dummy variable) Within sphere-of-influence (dummy variable) % of adjacent grid cells in Residential use % of adjacent grid cells in Commercial use % of adjacent grid cells in Industrial use % of adjacent grid cells in Public use % of adjacent grid cells in Transportation uses Hectares of vacant land within 200m
Interuse Externality and Proximity Effect Variables	Distance to nearest commercial use (in 200m increments) Distance to nearest industrial use (in 200m increments) Distance to nearest public use (in 200m increments)
Initial-Use Variables	Initially in residential use Initially in commercial use Initially in industrial use

TABLE 3. GOODNESS-OF-FIT RESULTS FOR CUF II

Goodness-of-Fit Results: Percent of Vacant Land-use Changes Correctly Predicted					
County	Vacant to Single-family	Vacant to Apartments	Vacant to Commercial	Vacant to Industrial	Remain Vacant	All Vacant Sites
Alameda	30.39%	18.29%	57.45%	44.88%	97.39%	94.78%
Contra Costa	31.76%	10.39%	12.39%	6.12%	95.95%	92.22%
Marin	25.66%	na	41.18%	na	99.22%	98.42%
Napa	40.60%	100.00%	78.79%	47.83%	99.51%	99.04%
San Mateo	37.88%	16.67%	35.76%	21.43%	99.04%	98.10%
Santa Clara	27.86%	20.69%	39.70%	22.44%	98.08%	96.00%
Solano	48.32%	31.25%	37.38%	25.76%	98.71%	97.38%
Sonoma	21.62%	16.28%	24.92%	23.55%	98.53%	97.02%

County	Redevelop to Residential	Redevelop to Commercial	Redevelop to Industrial	No Change	All Developed Sites
Alameda	24.71%	49.30%	36.00%	95.95%	92.31%
Contra Costa	21.10%	6.90%	63.64%	96.97%	94.17%
Marin	0.00%	0.00%	na	98.83%	99.68%
Napa	23.46%	2.63%	16.67%	95.66%	91.77%
San Mateo	21.40%	10.00%	66.67%	96.85%	93.93%
Santa Clara	14.70%	9.60%	14.08%	95.52%	91.43%
Solano	18.67%	25.71%	50.00%	97.87%	95.85%
Sonoma	18.57%	18.90%	12.50%	97.87%	95.85%

The eight redevelopment models also explain overall rates and patterns of redevelopment—or more precisely, the lack of redevelopment—reasonably well. Overall model fits vary from a high of 95.8 percent for Solano and Sonoma counties to a low of 91.4 percent in Santa Clara County.[22] As with the vacant-land models, the redevelopment models are far better able to explain the lack of redevelopment activity than particular use-to-use changes.

The models generate a plethora of coefficients, one for each variable and outcome. See Landis and Zhang (1998) for a more detailed presentation and discussion of the parameter estimates.

SIMULATING THE LAND-USE BIDDING PROCESS

Once calibrated, the parameter estimates can be used to calculate multiple land-use change probabilities—one for every category of land-use change—for every grid cell. For the purposes of activity allocation, these probabilities serve as *site bids*.[23] That is, for every site, higher land-use change probabilities correspond to higher site bids. Once site bids are estimated, the allocation process is fairly straightforward. For each site, the calculated probabilities are compared, with the "winning" land-use change being the one with the highest bid. To the extent that the probability associated with no land-use change (either from undeveloped or developed status) exceeds the probability of land-use change, a site will remain in its initial use. This is exactly analogous to the situation in which a prospective buyer's bid price falls short of a seller's reservation price.

Site Land Use Change Probabilities

Sites

A	B	C	D	E	F
G	H	I	J	K	L

Pr [Undev. > Single-family]

| .81 | .75 | .70 | .65 | .60 | .62 |
| .88 | .79 | .68 | .66 | .62 | .55 |

Pr [Undev. > Commercial]

| .78 | .70 | .65 | .60 | .84 | .84 |
| .73 | .68 | .66 | .62 | .83 | .87 |

Pr [Undev. > Industrial]

| .70 | .65 | .76 | .82 | .82 | .83 |
| .77 | .66 | .62 | .55 | .86 | .73 |

Pr [Developed > Single-family]

| .05 | .08 | .01 | .25 | .99 | .09 |
| .54 | .36 | .75 | .35 | .56 | .42 |

Pr [Developed > Commercial]

| .65 | .60 | .62 | .80 | .75 | .70 |
| .66 | .62 | .55 | .85 | .73 | .68 |

Sites Sorted by Land Use Change Probabilities

Rank	Site	Change	Probability
1	E	Developed. > Single-family	0.99
2	F	Undev. > Single-family	0.88
3	L	Undev. > Commercial	0.87
4	K	Undev. > Industrial	0.86
5	J	Developed. > Commercial	0.85
6	F	Undev. > Commercial	0.84
7	F	Undev. > Commercial	0.84
8	K	Undev. > Commercial	0.83
9	F	Undev. > Industrial	0.83
10	E	Undev. > Industrial	0.82
11	K	Undev. > Industrial	0.82
12	A	Undev. > Single-family	0.81
13	D	Dev. > Commercial	0.8
14	H	Undev. > Single-family	0.79
15	B	Undev. > Commercial	0.78
16	H	Undev. > Industrial	0.77
17	C	Undev. > Industrial	0.76
18	I	Dev. > Single-family	0.75
....			
....			
59	A	Developed. > Single-family	0.05
60	C	Developed. > Single-family	0.01

First Cycle Allocation

Step	Site	Allocation
1	E	Single-family
2	F	Single-family
3	L	Commercial
4	K	Industrial
5	J	Commercial
6	F	Already Allocated
7	F	Already Allocated
8	K	Already Allocated
9	F	Already Allocated
10	E	Already Allocated
11	K	Already Allocated
12	A	Single-family
13	D	Commercial
14	H	Single-family
15	B	Commercial
16	H	Already Allocated
17	C	Industrial
18	I	Single-family
....		
59	A	Already Allocated
60	C	Already Allocated

Figure 5. CUF II site allocation schematic.

Bids can be compared across sites as well across potential uses. To the extent that the vacant-to-residential land-use change probability associated with site A exceeds that of site B, then site A will be developed in residential use prior to site B. The ability to compare probabilities between both uses and sites makes it possible to address issues of development spillover—that is, what happens to development when a preferred site is either unavailable, or else reserved for a higher-probability use. Figure 5 outlines the logic of the bidding process; further details are described in Landis and Zhang (1998).

CURBA: INTEGRATING URBAN LAND-USE AND HABITAT CONSERVATION PLANNING

CURBA—the California Urban and Biodiversity Analysis Model—pushes the ideas behind the CUF II Model in yet another direction. CURBA, like CUF II, is a spatially explicit model of land-use change, calibrated at the hectare level. But whereas CUF II focuses on different types of urban land-use change and is indifferent to habitat quality, CURBA focuses on different types of habitat, and their relationships to urban land-use change in general. CUF is meant to be used in predominantly urban counties. CURBA is intended for use in predominantly rural counties where development and habitat loss are crucial issues. So far, CURBA Model data sets and models have been developed for eight California counties in three ecoregions: Santa Cruz and Monterey counties along the Central Coast; Stanislaus, San Joaquin, and Sacramento in the Central Valley; and El Dorado, Placer, and Nevada in the Sierra Nevada.

The CURBA Model consists of three major components (figure 6): An *Urban Growth Model,* which includes procedures for calibrating countywide logit equations describing past urbanization patterns, and for using those equations to construct future development scores; a *Policy Simulation Model,* consisting of procedures for simulating how alternative development policies might alter future urbanization patterns; and a *Habitat Patch Evaluation Model,* for evaluating the impacts of those patterns on habitat integrity.

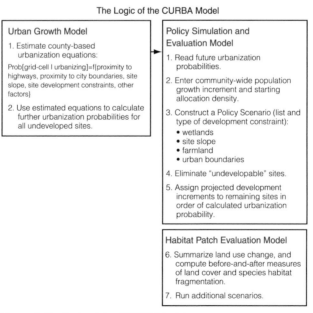

The Logic of the CURBA Model

Urban Growth Model

1. Estimate county-based urbanization equations:

Prob[grid-cell I urbanizing]=f{proximity to highways, proximity to city boundaries, site slope, site development constraints, other factors}

2. Use estimated equations to calculate further urbanization probabilities for all undeveloped sites.

Policy Simulation and Evaluation Model

1. Read future urbanization probabilities.

2. Enter community-wide population growth increment and starting allocation density.

3. Construct a Policy Scenario (list and type of development constraint):
 • wetlands
 • site slope
 • farmland
 • urban boundaries

4. Eliminate "undevelopable" sites.

5. Assign projected development increments to remaining sites in order of calculated urbanization probability.

Habitat Patch Evaluation Model

6. Summarize land use change, and compute before-and-after measures of land cover and species habitat fragmentation.

7. Run additional scenarios.

Figure 6. The logic of the CURBA Model.

THE URBAN GROWTH MODEL

Like CUF II, the CURBA Model makes use of a logit estimator to explain observed changes in urbanized land between two points in time. The observations consist of all undeveloped 1-hectare grid cells in the initial year. The dependent variable can take on two values: a 1, indicating that a grid cell was urbanized between the initial and terminal years; or a 0, indicating that it was not. The independent variables include both spatial and nonspatial factors. The model specification takes the following general form:

Prob [undeveloped grid-cell i = f { grid-cell proximity to highways facilities, slope is urbanized between and other natural constraints to development, 1986 and 1994] proximity to jurisdictional boundaries, local growth policies, recent population and job growth}

Figure 7 reports on the results of the "best parsimonious model" for each of the eight case-study counties. This is the specification that includes the fewest independent variables yet produces the highest overall goodness-of-fit.

Dependent Variable: Likelihood of Urbanization between 1986 and 1994									
Independent Variable	Expected Coefficient Sign	El Dorado County	Monterey County	Nevada County	Placer County	Sacramento County	San Joaquin County	Santa Cruz County	Stanislaus County
City 5-year growth rate	+		0.0291						
Distance to city limits (meters)	-						3.9937	-0.032	
(meters)	-	-0.354	-0.0724	-0.119	-0.188	-0.1325	-0.028		
Distance to major highway (meters)	-				-0.036	-0.0183		-0.005	
Distance to Roseville (meters)	-				-0.004				
Locally-important farmland	-								
Pct. of neighboring cells in urban use	+		-0.2829						-0.5155
Percent slope	-	-0.097		-0.103			-0.271	-0.156	-0.2037
Within census-designated place (0/1)	+								
Within city limits (0/1)	+					0.892			
Within FEMA floodzone	-					-1.7361		-1.746	
Within Rocklin city limits (0/1)	+				1.925				
Within Roseville city limits (0/1)	+				1.786				
Within Salinas city limits (0/1)	+		2.4147						-0.0689
Within sphere-of-influence (0/1)	+						1.6686		1.2718
Within wetland area (0/1)	-	-2.775							
Intercept		0.083	-1.5191	1.53	-0.799	-1.0325	-5.43	-2.905	0.883
Goodness of fit measures									
Log-likelihood ratio		#####	13,271.0	#####	#####	34,578.0	#####	#####	19,145.0
Chi-squared		#####	8,499.0	#####	#####	15,336.0	6,421.0	#####	14,062.0
Pct. concordant predictions		95.7%	94.0%	90.8%	94.4%	90.8%	84.4%	84.7%	94.1%

Figure 7. CURBA Model results, selected counties.

Two relationships stand out for all or almost all counties. All else being equal, sites near existing urban development (or, in the case of Santa Cruz, near city limits) tend to be developed before more distant sites. Second, flat and nearly flat sites tend to be developed before steeper sites. The roles of other factors varied between counties. Highway proximity served to encourage urban development in Nevada, Sacramento, and Sacramento counties. In Sacramento and San Joaquin counties, areas outside flood zones were developed ahead of sites inside flood zones. In Monterey and Stanislaus counties, free-standing vacant sites were more likely to have been developed than sites surrounded by other urban uses. In Placer County, sites in the cities of Rocklin and Roseville were developed ahead of sites in other cities. In Monterey County, sites in fast-growing cities and within Salinas city limits were developed ahead of other sites.

Their parsimonious structure notwithstanding, all eight models do a surprisingly good job explaining 1986–94 urbanization trends. The El Dorado County model, for example, explains fully 96 percent of observed site-level urbanization. Even the worst model, for San Joaquin County, explains more than 84 percent of observed urbanization.

Once the various logit models have been checked and compared, the estimated coefficients are used to calculate future urbanization probabilities for all remaining undeveloped grid cells. These probabilities range from a high of 1 (indicating development is certain) to 0 (indicating the impossibility of future development). The calculated urbanization probability grid is then exported to the Policy Simulation and Evaluation Model in ArcInfo export format.

THE POLICY SIMULATION AND EVALUATION MODEL

The Policy Simulation and Evaluation Model consists of a series of ArcView GIS commands and scripts and is designed to make it easy for users to simulate and then evaluate multiple local growth policies. The first step in constructing and evaluating a growth policy scenario is to import and display the calculated urbanization probability grid as shown in figure 8 for Santa Cruz County.

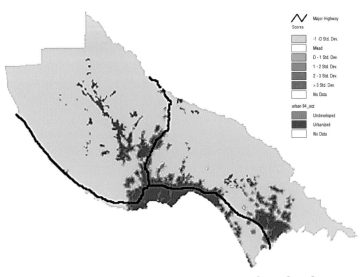

Figure 8. Calculated development probability scores, Santa Cruz County.

The next step is to enter the increment of population growth to be allocated to suitable grid cells, and the minimum allocation density, in persons per hectare.[24] Gross development densities are estimated by dividing county population levels by the number of urbanized grid cells. Unless otherwise specified, projected population growth may be allocated to suitable grid cells anywhere within a subject county.

Policy scenarios can be constructed. Grid cells may be excluded from future development—regardless of their calculated probability scores—on the basis of excessive slope; whether they are in a designated wetland or flood zone; their agricultural class; their proximity to a river, stream, highway, or road; and their proximity to particular jurisdictional boundaries, including city limits and sphere-of-influence lines. The effect of precluding a grid cell from development is to shift the population growth which might otherwise have been allocated to it to some other, lower-scoring grid cell. Policy scenarios can also be constructed by specifying alternative allocation densities. Once a particular policy scenario has been fully specified, the CURBA Model displays a summary map of developable and undevelopable grid cells.

Next, the CURBA Model allocates projected population growth to the remaining developable sites, in order of their calculated development probabilities. The allocation process proceeds until all required sites have been developed, or until no more sites are available, or until some user-specified minimum development probability threshold has been reached. Once the allocation process has been completed, the CURBA Model reports the average allocation density and displays a map showing the resulting growth allocation. The resulting growth allocation is then compared with various habitat designations.

HABITAT PATCH EVALUATION MODEL

After generating an alternative development scenario, the CURBA Model allows users to analyze the impacts of projected development patterns on vegetative land cover and habitat fragmentation and thus, indirectly, on habitat quality. Digital vegetation maps and associated species lists were obtained from the California GAP Analysis Project at the University of California, Santa Barbara. For each vegetation and species class, as requested by the user, the CURBA Model calculates the following before-and-after habitat fragmentation measures:

1 *Total patch area,* of a given vegetation class or species.

2 *Percent of Landscape:* This is a specific habitat's share of total undeveloped (or landscape) area. It is obtained by dividing total habitat area by total landscape area. Higher values mean that the landscape is composed of fewer distinct habitat types, and, all else being equal, suggest a lower level of biodiversity.

3 *Number of Patches:* This measure is a count of the number of distinct (nonadjacent) areas, or "patches," of a particular habitat type. For a given total habitat area, a larger patch count indicates greater habitat fragmentation, and thus reduced habitat quality.

4 *Maximum and Minimum Patch Size (in hectares):* These are a measure of the area of the largest and smallest patches of a specific habitat type. All else being equal, larger patches are preferable to smaller ones.

5 *Mean Patch Size (in hectares):* This is the typical, or average, patch size for a particular habitat type. It is obtained by dividing total habitat area by the number of patches. Larger mean patch sizes are almost always preferable to smaller ones.

6 *Patch Size Variance and Standard Deviation (in hectares):* These measure the distribution of habitat patch size. A small variance and standard deviation indicates that distribution of patch sizes

clusters around the mean. A large variance and standard deviation indicates a wide variety of patch sizes.

7 *Patch Density:* This is the number of habitat patches of a particular type per 100 hectares of landscape. As an indicator of habitat quality, lower patch densities are preferable to higher ones.

8 *Largest Patch Index:* This is the area of the largest patch of a particular type divided by the total landscape area. An index value close to 1 (or 100 percent) indicates that most of the landscape is composed of a single habitat patch. Depending on the type of habitat, this may be a positive indicator of habitat quality, but a negative indicator of biodiversity.

9 *Total Edge:* This is the total (outside) perimeter of patches of a particular habitat type. Higher amounts of edge permit easier movement across habitats types.

10 *Average Edge–Area Ratio:* This measure is the ratio of total patch edge (or perimeter) to total patch area. Higher edge–area ratios are typically associated with greater patch fragmentation, or with long and narrow patch shapes.

11 *Edge Density:* This measure is the ratio of total patch to landscape area.

The extent to which particular habitat fragmentation values are associated with habitat quality and biodiversity varies by area, habitat type, and species. CURBA Model users can choose to analyze all habitat types, or just selected ones. They can also analyze multiple habitat types according to common vertebrate species.

SANTA CRUZ PILOT STUDY

To demonstrate its capabilities, we used the CURBA Model to test the effects of three growth policy scenarios on projected urban development patterns and habitat fragmentation in Santa Cruz County for the year 2010. According to the California Department of Finance, the population of Santa Cruz County is projected to increase by approximately 50,000 persons between 1995 and 2010. At the county's current average density of 20 persons per hectare, an additional 2,500 hectares (or approximately 6,250 acres) will be required to accommodate this level of population growth.

Where this growth goes and how it impacts Santa Cruz habitats will depend, in part, on how Santa Cruz County's four incorporated governments[25] choose to regulate private development. For the sake of simplicity, we assumed all four municipal governments together with Santa Cruz County would act in concert on a common set of policies. Three distinct scenarios were tested using the CURBA Model (figures 9a, 9b, 9c).

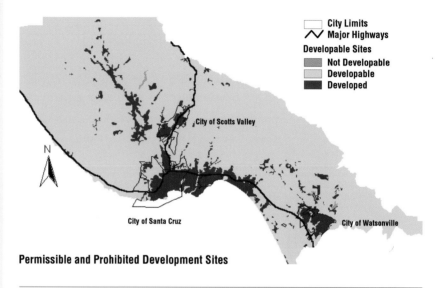

Permissible and Prohibited Development Sites

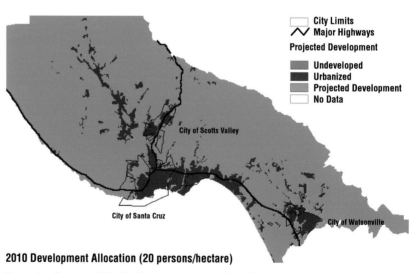

2010 Development Allocation (20 persons/hectare)

Figure 9a. Scenario SC1, No Constraints, Santa Cruz County.

Scenario SC1, entitled *No Constraints,* permits urban development to occur just about anywhere in Santa Cruz County, except on wetlands. Urban development is permitted on all types of farmlands, within flood zones, adjacent to rivers and streams, on hillsides of any slope, and outside existing sphere-of-influence boundaries.

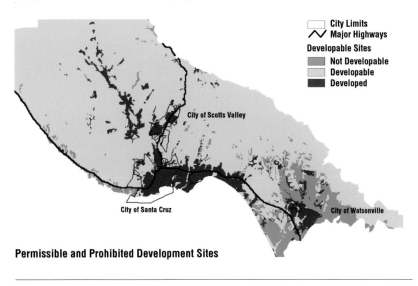

Permissible and Prohibited Development Sites

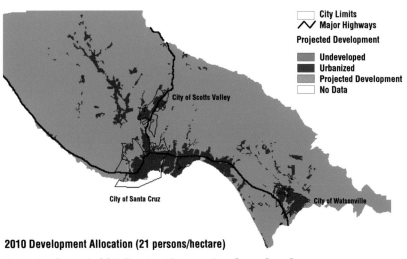

2010 Development Allocation (21 persons/hectare)

Figure 9b. Scenario SC2, Farmland Preservation, Santa Cruz County.

Scenario SC2, entitled *Farmland Protection,* assumes the adoption of zoning and other regulatory policies which would preclude the development of prime and unique agricultural lands, as well as farmlands classified as being of importance to the state and local economy. Scenario SC2 would also prohibit development on wetlands. Other hazard areas and environmental resources such as flood zones, riparian zones, and hillsides would be unprotected.

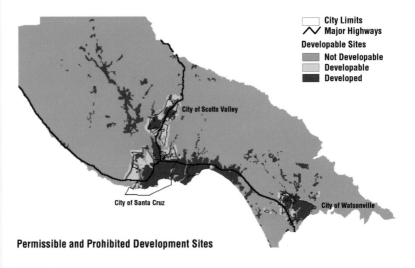

Permissible and Prohibited Development Sites

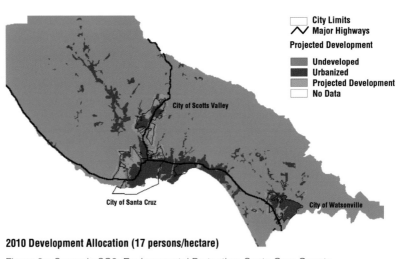

2010 Development Allocation (17 persons/hectare)

Figure 9c. Scenario SC3, Environmental Protection, Santa Cruz County.

Scenario SC3, entitled *Environmental Protection,* would impose numerous limits on new development throughout Santa Cruz County. Development would be prohibited from occurring on wetlands, within FEMA-designated flood zones, on sites with slopes greater than 10 percent, and within 100 meters of a river stream. Development would also be limited to sites within 500 meters of existing sphere-of-influence boundaries. To further reduce land consumption, Scenario SC3 assumes the adoption of a development density floor of 25 persons per hectare—a level 20 percent higher than the current countywide average density.

Figures 9a through 9c present the results of the various scenarios. The top panel of each figure shows which sites are to be considered developable and undevelopable given the constraints imposed under each scenario (development is allowed in the yellow areas, but precluded from the red ones). The bottom panel presents the growth allocation results for each scenario; existing development is in dark gray; projected new development is in red.

Under *Scenario SC1: No Constraints* (figure 9a), almost every undeveloped site in Santa Cruz County is considered developable (top panel). As the bottom panel shows, however, projected new development will tend to favor sites at the edges of existing cities, particularly Watsonville. These locations are flat, and are well served by existing infrastructure, especially regional highways. They are also less likely than more distant sites to arouse political opposition to sprawl.

The effect of adopting policies designed to protect farmland (figure 9b: *Scenario SC2: Farmland Protection*) is to place most of the county's coastal and southern areas off limits to development. The areas east of Watsonville, in particular, which comprise some of California's best farmland, would be protected from development. The effect of these constraints (compared to Scenario SC1) would be to shift more new development northward to the outskirts of Santa Cruz and Scott's Valley, and to the unincorporated areas of Felton and Ben Lomand.

Because Santa Cruz County is so hilly, and contains hundreds of miles of stream bed, the effects of limiting development on hillsides and in riparian areas (as well as in prime and unique agricultural areas) is to place most of the county off-limits to development. This is the result shown in the top panel of figure 9c, which summarizes the results for *Scenario SC3: Environmental Protection.* The effect of these constraints is to shift projected new development to those few remaining areas judged to be the least environmentally sensitive. This includes areas surrounding the city of Scott's Valley, areas to the northwest of Santa Cruz, and a few "infill" sites north of Watsonville. Thus ironically, one of the primary effects of adopting policies designed to protect the environment would be to shift much of the county's prospective growth to Scott's Valley, a city known for its small-town, environmentally-friendly character.

We note that these are scenarios, not forecasts. The extent to which the development patterns we have identified under the various scenarios would ultimately depend not on which conservation programs and regulations are adopted, but on how those regulations are administered.

Regardless of which of the three scenarios are pursued, the vegetation types likely to be most affected by projected urban growth are Agriculture and Upland Redwood Forest (table 4). Under *Scenario SC1: No Constraints,* projected urban growth would consume 902 hectares of Agricultural land cover and 405 hectares of Upland Redwood Forest land cover. Under *Scenario SC2: Farmland Protection,* Agricultural land-cover losses would decline to 447 hectares, while Upland Redwood Forest losses would rise to 620 hectares. Agricultural land-cover losses would decline somewhat further under *Scenario SC3: Environmental Protection,* while the loss of Upland Redwood Forest would increase to 1,232 hectares. On a percentage basis, the loss of Agricultural land cover would range from a high of 4.4 percent under Scenario SC1, to a low of 1.8 percent under Scenario SC3. The maximum percentage loss of Upland Redwood Forest, 2.5 percent, would occur under Scenario SC3.[26]

TABLE 4. HABITAT LOSS, ALTERNATIVE YEAR 2010 DEVELOPMENT SCENARIOS, SANTA CRUZ COUNTY

Vegetative Land Cover Type	Initial 1994 Land Area Hectares	Scenario SC1: No Constraints 1994–2010 loss (ha)	Scenario SC1: No Constraints 1994–2010 % change	Scenario SC2: Farmland Protection 1994–2010 loss (ha)	Scenario SC2: Farmland Protection 1994–2010 % change	Scenario SC3: Environmental Protection 1994–2010 loss (ha)	Scenario SC3: Environmental Protection 1994–2010 % change
Upland Redwood Forest	45,353	−405	0.8%	−620	−1.3%	−1,232	−2.5%
Agriculture	20,296	−902	4.4%	−447	−2.2%	−367	−1.8%
Mixed Evergreen Forest	7,723	−41	0.5%	−81	−1.0%	−282	−3.7%
Coastal Prairie	5,282	−4	0.1%	−12	−0.2%	−1	0.0%
Central Maritime Chaparral	4,079	0	0.0%	0	0.0%	0	0.0%
Upper Sonoran Manzanita	3,318	0	0.0%	0	0.0%	0	0.0%
Urban or Built-up	3,313	−1070	32.3%	−1,251	−37.8%	−850	−25.7%
Chamise Chaparral	2,517	0	0.0%	0	0.0%	0	0.0%
Tan Oak Forest	2,041	0	0.0%	0	0.0%	0	0.0%
Blue Brush Chaparral	1,955	0	0.0%	0	0.0%	0	0.0%
Coast Live Oak Forest	949	0	0.0%	0	0.0%	0	0.0%
Nonnative Grassland	670	−2	0.3%	−4	-0.6%	−145	−21.6%
Knobcone Pine Forest	633	0	0.0%	0	0.0%	0	0.0%
Central Coastal Scrub	607	0	0.0%	0	0.0%	0	0.0%
Mesic North Slope Chaparral	426	0	0.0%	0	0.0%	0	0.0%
Monterey Pine Forest	409	0	0.0%	0	0.0%	0	0.0%
Northern Coastal Scrub	399	0	0.0%	0	0.0%	0	0.0%
Orchard or Vineyard	356	0	0.0%	0	0.0%	0	0.0%
Coast Range Ponderosa Pine Forest	224	0	0.0%	0	0.0%	0	0.0%
Strip Mine	168	0	0.0%	0	0.0%	0	0.0%
Central Coast Arroyo Riparian	158	−14	8.9%	−19	−12.0%	0	0.0%
Central Coast Cottonwood Sycamore	96	0	0.0%	0	0.0%	0	0.0%

More significant than the issue of loss is that of fragmentation. Table 5 presents multiple measures of fragmentation change for two types of land cover—Agricultural and Upland Redwood Forest—for each of the three scenarios. With respect to Agricultural land cover, it is *Scenario SC2: Farmland Protection* which, surprisingly, results in the most additional fragmentation: compared to their initial 1994 level, the number of vegetation patches increases the most, while average patch size declines the most. Scenario SC2 also produces the highest patch density. Across the board, *Scenario SC3: Environmental Protection* results in a somewhat lower level of agricultural land-cover fragmentation than Scenario SC2. The reason for this surprising result is that agricultural land cover is more extensive than are cultivated agricultural lands. Thus, the preservation of agricultural lands under Scenario SC2 does not result in a comparable conservation of agricultural habitat quality.[27]

TABLE 5. HABITAT FRAGMENTATION, AGRICULTURAL LAND AND UPLAND REDWOOD FOREST, ALTERNATIVE YEAR 2010 DEVELOPMENT SCENARIOS, SANTA CRUZ COUNTY

Patch Measure	Land Cover: Agricultural Land				Land Cover: Upland Redwood Forest			
	Initial (1994)	SC1	SC2	SC3	Initial (1994)	SC1	SC2	SC3
Total Area (hectares)	20,296	19,394	19,849	19,929	48,353	47,948	47,732	47,121
Percent of Landscape (%)	17.6	16.8	17.2	17.3	41.9	41.5	41.3	40.8
Largest Patch Index (%)	13.5	12.8	13.2	13.3	38.7	36.5	36.4	36.2
Number of Patches	31	44	46	34	54	61	64	72
Mean Patch Size (hectares)	654.7	440.7	431.5	586.2	895.4	786.0	745.8	654.5
Maximum Patch Size (hectares)	15,583	14,779	15,267	15,319	44,676	42,218	42,100.1	41,767
Minimum Patch Size (hectares)	1.0	1.0	1.0	1.0	1.0	1.0	1.0	1.0
Patch Density	0.027	0.038	0.040	0.029	0.047	0.053	0.055	0.062
Patch Size Variance	7,867,201	5,024,516	5,125,581	6,940,817	36,892,930	29,185,897	27,661,359	24,203,030
Patch Size Standard Deviation	2,804.5	2,241.5	2,263.9	2,634.5	6,073.9	5,402.4	5,259.4	4,919.7
Total Edge (km)	559.0	552.8	562.6	587.4	1,008.0	1,006.0	1,005.0	1,045.2
Edge/Area Ratio (m/hectare)	27.5	28.5	28.3	29.5	20.8	21.0	21.1	22.2
Edge Density (m/hectare)	4.8	4.8	4.9	5.1	8.7	8.7	8.7	9.0

The results for Upland Redwood Forest land cover are also surprising. Of the three scenarios, it is *Scenario SC1: No Constraints* that consumes the least additional land and results in the least additional fragmentation. The most injurious scenario, ironically, is *Scenario SC3: Environmental Protection*. *Scenario SC3* shifts growth inland from coastal hillsides, thereby resulting in greater Upland Redwood Forest land loss and fragmentation. *Scenario SC1*, conversely, preserves redwood land cover at the expense of agricultural land.

TABLE 6. RED FOX AND YUMA MYOTIS HABITAT FRAGMENTATION, ALTERNATIVE YEAR 2010
DEVELOPMENT SCENARIOS, SANTA CRUZ COUNTY

Habitat Patch Measure	Habitat: Red Fox				Habitat: Yuma Myotis			
	Initial (1994)	SC1	SC2	SC3	Initial (1994)	SC1	SC2	SC3
Total Area (hectares)	14,356	13,555	14,045	14,092	2,811	1,835	1,664	2,040
Percent of Landscape (%)	12.4	11.7	12.2	12.2	2.4	1.6	1.4	1.8
Largest Patch Index (%)	11.55	10.8	11.2	11.3	0.7	0.5	0.5	0.5
Number of Patches	29	39	33	29	102	89	96	115
Mean Patch Size (hectares)	495.0	347.6	425.6	485.9	27.6	20.6	17.3	17.7
Maximum Patch Size (hectares)	13,290	12,486	12,975	13,026	859	605	576	577
Minimum Patch Size (hectares)	1	1	1	1	1	1	1	1
Patch Density	0.025	0.034	0.029	0.025	0.088	0.077	0.083	0.100
Patch Size Variance	6,074,182	3,993,370	5,091,642	5,835,308	9,281	5,040	4,027	3,398
Patch Size Standard Deviation	2,464.6	1,998.3	2,256.5	2,415.6	96.3	71.0	63.5	58.3
Total Edge (km)	352.6	347.6	358.6	375.4	262.4	171.8	167.0	223.8
Edge/Area Ratio (m/hectare)	24.6	25.6	25.5	26.6	93.3	93.6	100.4	100.4
Edge Density (m/hectare)	3.1	3.0	3.1	3.2	2.3	1.5	1.4	1.9

Many species occupy multiple vegetative land-cover types. As a result, the effects of urban growth on the viability of particular species will ultimately depend on how it impacts multiple land covers. For each species identified by the user, the CURBA Model can calculate total habitat loss across multiple vegetative land coverages, as well as changes in species-based habitat fragmentation. One example is shown in table 6.

SUMMARY AND CHALLENGES

SUMMARY

The California Urban Futures family of urban simulation models—CUF, CUF II, and CURBA—break new modeling ground in several ways. They are the first set of operational urban simulation models to reference sites, not zones. They are the first set of operational urban growth models to incorporate, and indeed, depend on GIS for key functions. The original CUF Model was the first operational urban growth simulation model to incorporate land developers and homebuilders as central actors in determining the pattern, location, and density of new development. Its successor, CUF II, is the first operational urban growth simulation model to incorporate competitive site bidding between land uses, and to incorporate redevelopment activities. The CURBA Model is the first, and so far, only operational urban growth simulation model to deal with issues of habitat consumption and quality.

These "firsts" aside, are these models truly useful? As much as they extend technique, do they also extend the practicality and art of urban land-use modeling? And are they truly useful for real-world visioning and alternatives analysis? In his landmark 1973 article, "Requiem for Large-Scale Models," Douglas Lee, Jr. suggested seven criteria against which large-scale urban models should be measured. They include: hypercomprehensiveness, grossness, hungriness, wrong-headedness, complicatedness, mechanicalness, and expensiveness. How do the CUF family of models stand up against Lee's criteria?

Hypercomprehensiveness refers to the possibility that a model's structure is too complicated to understand, or that a model is expected to serve too many competing purposes, and must therefore sacrifice transparency and robustness. The original CUF model suffered from a degree of hypercomprehensiveness. Conceptually, at least, CUF II and CURBA are more straightforward.

Grossness refers to a model's inability to provide relevant and reliable results at a less-than-regional level. Because they were designed from the start to be spatially explicit, none of the CUF Model family suffers from grossness. Indeed, their ability to reconcile multiple layers of fine-scale data is one of the CUF Model family's greatest achievements.

Hungriness refers to a model's need for data, for calibration purposes as well as for running simulations. Because it is spatially explicit, the CUF family of models is voracious in its appetite for data, at least by historical standards. A typical county CUF Model data set will include a half million separate locations, and two dozen attributes or variables. Yet because most of this data is now available digitally, often in map form, and because it can be managed using desktop GIS and statistical packages, many of the difficulties of data collection, integration, and management that plagued the modelers of Lee's day have been significantly reduced. The greatly improved availability of fine-grained, correctly projected, digital map data, particularly over the Internet, is a recent phenomena. As recently as 1990, the cost and difficulty of collecting the variety and quality of data required by CUF-type models would have been prohibitive.

Wrongheadedness refers to existence of discrepancies between the way that the world works in reality, and the way the world works as represented in a model. The larger the discrepancies, the more wrongheaded the model. Wrongheadedness results from having the wrong unit of analysis, from mismeasurement, from model misspecification, and from biased or incomplete model structures. One symptom of wrongheadedness is lack of transparency. The original CUF Model was wrongheaded in its use of artificially generated developable land units (DLUs), but rightheaded in its attempt to incorporate the decision calculus of large-scale residential developers. Because the CUF II and CURBA Models are reduced-form models, their dynamics are less transparent than those of the original CUF model. Yet because they are calibrated from historical experience, they are more likely to be reliable.

Complicatedness refers to the potential for unanticipated interactions between model variables and components. Interactions can occur spatially—as when the development of one site encourages the development of its neighbor—or through market, political, or social linkages. As Lee notes, complicatedness is a particular problem for urban models when there is the potential for measurement and modeling errors to compound. The original CUF Model suffered from complicatedness, particularly in its Bottom–up Population Growth Submodel component. The original CUF Model was also incapable of incorporating spatial interactions between neighboring sites. The CUF II and CURBA models can and do incorporate spatial interactions, and attempt to control for variable interactions through careful specification. The original CUF Model was designed to be run recursively—something Lee highlights as promoting error—but was subsequently implemented using a single, fixed, 20-year simulation horizon. The CUF II and CURBA models are run using a single simulation period.[28]

Mechanicalness refers to the inability to replicate real urban processes using computer algorithms. A major issue in 1973, this problem has been substantially reduced thanks to the advent of improved statistical, stochastic, optimization, and neural-net modeling procedures, and the expanding ability to incorporate spatial dimensions in those models. The CUF family of models are all deterministic, but they are not mechanical.

Expensiveness refers to the high acquisition, data processing, and staff costs of developing and using urban models. Today, thanks to the advent of cheap yet powerful PCs, most of the costs associated with developing urban models involve data acquisition and staff time, not hardware and computing. For modelers working in digitally data-rich environments, the costs of developing and using urban models are quite reasonable. For example, the incremental cost of adapting the CURBA Model to an additional California county is probably on the order of only $10,000 to $15,000. On the other hand, for researchers working in data-poor environments who must acquire and code their own data, the costs of model development can easily exceed $100,000.

CHALLENGES

Like all models, the CUF Model family still has plenty of room for improvements. Factors like local zoning designations and codes need to be tested and added to the models, as do measures of local public service quality and availability. Other limitations are more fundamental. Because they represent space as small grid cells, the CUF II and CURBA models are both plagued by problems of spatial autocorrelation. Spatial autocorrelation refers to the fact that adjacent or nearby objects tend to influence each other. For example, a farmer who observes his next-door neighbor selling to a developer may be influenced to do the same. Some types of spatial autocorrelation are legitimate, as in this example. Other types are generated by the choice of spatial unit. When using small grid cells as we have to represent land-use change, single larger-scale land-use changes are mistakenly measured as multiple events. The resulting over-counting of land-use changes will tend to bias the results of any statistical models as well as any forecasts based on those results. For most counties, these biases show up through the unrealistic over-generation of small, independent growth centers. Cell-based urban growth models that are not corrected for spatial autocorrelation tend to over-forecast leapfrog development.

There are a number of ways to account for issues of spatial autocorrelation. The easiest way to avoid the problem of over-counting land-use change is to reset the spatial unit of analysis from grid cells to parcels. Unfortunately, this requires having reliable parcel maps for two points in time. Measuring neighborhood effects around irregularly shaped parcels rather than square grid cells is also difficult. Alternately, one can increase grid-cell size until it approximates the average parcel size. This reduces the problems of spatial autocorrelation for the "average" land-use change, but results in a corresponding under-counting of small land-use changes. Randomly sampling grid cells could also reduce the problem, but in the wrong way, by minimizing the possibility that adjacent parcel changes really do influence each other. One can also take a purely statistical approach to the problem by rewriting the procedures used to estimate the model parameters to account for given levels of spatial autocorrelation. This is difficult to do and would required making *ex ante* guesses regarding the extent of spatial autocorrelation in a given sample. And while it might reduce the extent of bias for typical values, it could actually increase bias for atypical values. Still another approach—and the one being used in our most recent models—is to incorporate additional independent variables which explicitly measure neighborhood effects.

Another problem with the CUF family of models is in their lack of actual or imputed real estate prices. Prices serve three essential functions in urban real estate markets. They provide independent signals to both buyers and producers regarding appropriate land uses and land-use intensities. Second, and of greater importance, prices function to "clear" real estate markets. Market clearing is the process whereby individual transactions between willing buyers and sellers lead to marketwide outcomes that are fully reflective of supplier costs, and of demander preferences and incomes. Third, prices are the mechanisms through which markets adjust to short-term imbalances between supply and demand.

The CUF and CURBA models' lack of prices is especially problematic when simulating spillovers. As currently structured, activities which can not be accommodated in one location (usually for reasons of insufficient land or because of policy constraints) costlessly spillover to the next best location. Within a particular radius (as determined by the user), there is no particular penalty associated with spillover. Real life does not work that way. Confronted with the possibility that their preferred sites may be unavailable, many activities will not consider alternative sites. They will instead raise their bid prices for their preferred sites. The result will be an increase in site prices (in the form of economic rents) together with some degree of spillover (by those activities which *will* consider alternative sites). Because the CUF Model family does not include explicit prices, it can not deal with different price elasticities of demand, or, for that matter, of supply. Its sole response to unaccommodated demand is through the spillover mechanism.

A final and related limitation of the CUF II Model is that it lacks agents. The multi- and binomial logit models that form the heart of CUF II and CURBA are all reduced-form models. That is, they focus on the characteristics of transactions (land-use change in this case) but give short shrift to the characteristics and motivations of buyers (e.g., households and businesses) or sellers (e.g., landowners and developers). To the extent that the timing and nature of actual land-use changes reflect the economic characteristics and personal motivations of real people and real businesses, and not just the locational characteristics of sites, the CUF II model may be regarded as seriously incomplete, or potentially biased, or both.

If history is any guide, these problems will all be solved, and perhaps sooner rather than later. With issues of smart growth and sustainability unlikely to fade, policy makers, local officials, and interested citizens will continue to look for workable approaches to understanding and directing urban growth. Simulation models such as those in the CUF family make it possible to better understand the dynamics of urban growth, to constructively manipulate those dynamics, and most important, to set forth better and practical urban futures.

FOOTNOTES

[1] Or its urban service area.

[2] The impacts of public infrastructure investments can be simulated in the CUF II Model but not in the original CUF Model.

[3] For modeling purposes, the greater Bay Area Region includes Alameda, Contra Costa, Marin, Napa, Sacramento, San Francisco, San Joaquin, San Mateo, Santa Clara, Santa Cruz, Solano, Sonoma, Stanislaus, and Yolo counties.

[4] Hectares are squares with 100-meter sides. One hectare equals 10,000 square meters, or 2.47 acres.

[5] The presence of many different and distinct land uses in a small area may make it difficult to discern broader land-use patterns. This is the problem of noise.

[6] Statistical models with discrete or categorical dependent variables have been classified by Fisher and Nijkamp (1985) as being of two types: discrete-choice models, and discrete-data models. Though they may be estimated using similar techniques (e.g., logit), the two model types are fundamentally different. Whereas the former has a clearly defined behavioral interpretation based on random utility theory, the latter does not.

[7] Multinomial logit models are harder to calibrate because the number of computations increases as a power function of the number of categories. They are harder to interpret because each additional category adds an additional coefficient estimate per independent variable.

[8] Urban economists sometimes assume that commercial land uses are superior to industrial land uses, which are in turn superior to residential land uses. Superior is used in this context to mean that one land use generates consistently higher land rents or profits than another. Another term used to identify superior land uses is "highest-and-best use."

[9] From a modeling perspective, the question is not whether land buyers and sellers engage in such behavior—we assume they do—it is whether that behavior is likely to succeed. To the extent that land development has been shown to be no more profitable over the long run than other businesses, the answer to this second question is probably *no*. Competition, we assume, levels the playing field and makes the expected return associated with strategic behavior close to zero.

[10] Consider the situations of commuters comparing alternative work-trip modes, or of households trying to decide where to live. In the commuter case, each traveler faces a series of mode choices (e.g., driving, walking, or taking the bus), all of which can be decomposed into a comparable set of attributes (e.g., travel time, wait time, travel cost). In the household location case, each household faces a series of residential choices, all of which can also be decomposed into comparable attributes (house size, neighborhood, distance to work, school quality, and so on). Each traveler chooses the work mode, which, based on its attributes, maximizes his or her utility. Similarly, each household chooses a house and location, which, based on their joint attributes, maximizes its utility. In both examples, an identifiable agent confronts and makes real choices.

[11] In a similar vein, we assume that parcel lines can be adjusted. Landowners can subdivide existing parcels, merge small parcels into larger ones, and petition for use changes and rezoning. Indeed, one way many successful developers become successful is by assembling and upzoning disjointed or "underzoned" sites. This allows them to "buy low" and "sell high."

[12] For reasons that are not exactly clear, population growth in the Bay Area during the 1980s favored newer and smaller cities over older, larger cities. All else being equal, we would thus expect sites in larger cities to be less likely to either change land use or be developed than sites in smaller cities. This suggests that the estimated coefficient associated with the number of households in each city should be negative.

The size-effect of a city's employment base may be either positive or negative. On the positive-effect side, there may be agglomeration economies associated with larger employment centers. This would tend to make nearby undeveloped sites more attractive, thereby increasing their probability of being developed. Moreover, recent employment growth in the Bay Area, unlike recent population growth, has been focused in a few large job centers. This would also suggest that the relationship between the size of a particular city's employment base, and the probability of a site within that city being developed or changing use, is likely to be positive.

On the negative-effect side, land and commercial space prices are likely to be higher in cities with larger economies than in cities with smaller economies. To the extent that employers are drawn to less expensive land, the effect of employment size on land-use change may be negative.

[13] We also measured the distances from each site to downtown Oakland and 20 other regional subcenters. The resulting (generalized) distance measures were highly correlated with the measured distances to San Francisco and San Jose. Accordingly, we excluded them from the model.

[14] Unlike BART, Caltrain, the San Francisco MUNI, and the San Jose light rail system do not provide regional transportation service. Moreover, these latter systems all offer much lower levels of service (in terms of train frequency and/or travel speed) than BART. Accordingly, we did not include distance to non-BART transit stations in the analysis.

[15] In some cases, where the view and exclusivity premiums associated with hillside development exceed the higher costs, it is conceivable that the relationship between site slope and the probability of residential development might actually turn from negative to positive.

[16] The dummy variable indicating a 0-percent slope was purposely omitted in order to guarantee a unique solution.

[17] Spheres of influence are established by Local Agency Formation Commissions, and, in theory, are supposed to define those areas planned for urban development, and for which essential urban services are committed. In practice, and depending on the county, intensive new development commonly occurs outside sphere boundaries. Also questionable is the assumption that urban service costs are a function of the linear distance to available capacity. In actuality, there are significant economies of scale in the construction of water and sewer trunk lines and major arterials.

[18] Because we were unable to assemble a complete and reliable schedule of impact fees for different uses in all Bay Area communities, we did not include variables measuring local impact fees for exactions.

[19] Indeed, California law stipulates that every city and county must prepare a General Plan, and that the jurisdiction's zoning map and ordinances be consistent with the General Plan.

[20] Current sphere-of-influence maps were obtained from each county's Local Agency Formation Commission (LAFCO) and digitized.

[21] We computed these variables in two steps. First, for every site, we used GIS to identify the (initial) land uses of each adjacent site. (As noted above, sites are represented by 100-by-100-meter grid cells. Thus, every grid cell is surrounded by eight other grid cells.) Next, we computed the initial percentage of surrounding grid cells in residential use, commercial use, industrial use, public use, or use for transportation facilities. The resulting percentages vary between 1 and 0: a value of 1 indicates that a site is completely surrounded by a particular use, a value of 0 indicates no level of adjacency.

22 As above, we exclude Marin County from these comparisons because of a lack of observed land-use changes.

23 The Land-Use Change Model consists of a series of reduced-form equations. This means that they model market outcomes, and not the demand functions of supplier cost functions that determine those outcomes. The fact that individual supply-and-demand curves can not be inferred from reduced-form equations does not mean that we lack all information regarding the preferences of buyers and sellers. To the extent that the local land market is truly competitive, one may infer that an observed land-use change, or transaction, would only take place if the seller's reservation price were met by the buyer's bid price.

24 The CURBA Model allocates urban development based on projected population growth and average population density. The model does not differentiate between different land-use types. Commercial, industrial, and other urban land uses are all subsumed in the average population density estimate.

25 Capitola, Santa Cruz, Watsonville, and Scotts Valley.

26 Two other land cover-types, Non-native Grassland and Mixed Evergreen Forest, would be substantially diminished under *Scenario SC3: Environmental Protection*. Non-native Grasslands would decline by 145 hectares, or 21.6 percent, while Mixed Evergreen Forest land cover would decline by 282 hectares, or 3.7 percent.

27 This result may also be the result of discrepancies between the GAP and CFMMP layers.

28 Ideally, the CUF II and CURBA models should be run in such a way so that remaining site development probabilities are updated after each site allocation. This would allow any spatial interactions to be fully accounted for.

REFERENCES

Association of Bay Area Governments (ABAG). 1995. *Bay Area Land Use Inventory*. Oakland: Association of Bay Area Governments.

Batty, Michael. 1992. Urban Modeling in Computer-Graphic and Geographic Information System Environments. *Environment and Planning B* 19:689–708.

Batty, Michael and Y Xie. 1994. From Cells to Cities. *Environment and Planning B: Planning and Design* 21:531–48.

Ben–Akiva M. and S. R. Lerman. 1985. *Discrete Choice Analysis: Theory and Application to Travel Demand*. Cambridge: MIT Press.

Clarke, Keith, S. Hoppen, and L. Gaydos. 1997. A Self-modifying Cellular Automaton Model of Historical Urbanization in the San Francisco Bay Area. *Environment and Planning B-Planning and Design* 24(2):247–61.

Domenich, Thomas A. and Daniel McFadden. 1975. *Urban Travel Demand: A Behavioral Analysis*. Amsterdam: North–Holland.

Fisher, M. Manfred and P. Nijkamp. 1985. Developments in Explanatory Discrete Spatial Data and Choice Analysis. *Progress in Human Geography* 9:515–51. California Department of Resources. 1986. Farmland Mapping Project.

Hickman, J. C., ed. 1993. *The Jepson Manual of Higher Plants of California.* Berkeley: University of California Press.

Landis, John. 1994a. The California Urban Futures Model: A New Generation of Metropolitan Simulation Models. *Environment and Planning B: Planning and Design* 21:399–420.

Landis, John D., and Ming Zhao. 1994b. Pilot Study of Solano and Sonoma Land Use and Development Policy Alternatives. Working Paper 618. Berkeley, CA: Institute of Urban and Regional Development.

Landis, John. 1995. Imagining Land Use Futures: Applying the California Urban Futures Model. *Journal of the American Planning Association* 61(1):438–57.

Landis, John and Ming Zhang. 1998a. The Next Generation of the California Urban Futures Model: Part II. *Environment and Planning B* 25:657–66, 795–824.

Landis, John, and J. P. Monzon, M. Reilly, and C. Cogan. 1998b. Development and Pilot Application of the California Urban and Biodiversity Analysis Model. Berkeley: Institute for Urban and Regional Development.

Landis, John. 1998c. Simulating Highway and Transit Effects. *Access* 12 (Spring).

Lee, Douglas B. 1973. Requiem for Large-scale Models. *Journal of the American Institute of Planners* 39:163–78.

McFadden, Daniel. 1973. Conditional Logit Analysis of Quantitative Choice Behavior. In *Frontiers in Econometrics,* ed. P. Zarembka. New York: Academic Press.

Scott, J. M., F. Davis, B. Csuti, R. Noss, B. Butterfield, C. Groves, H. Anderson, S. Caicco, F. D'erchia, T. C. Edwards Jr., U. Ulliman, and R. G. Wright. 1993. *Gap Analysis: A Geographic Approach to Protection of Biologica.*

U.S. Census Bureau. 1995. 1994 (Post-Census) California TIGER Files.

Waddell, Paul and V. Shukla. 1993. Manufacturing Location in a Polycentric Urban Area: A Study in the Composition and Attractiveness of Employment Subcenters. *Urban Geography* 14:277–96.

Wegener, Michael. 1994. Operational Urban Models: State of the Art. *Journal of the American Planning Association* 60(1):17–30.

———. 1995. Current and Future Land Use Models. In *Proceedings of the Travel Model Improvement Program,* Land Use Modeling Conference, February 19–21, 1995. Washington, D.C.: U.S. Departments of Transportation and Energy, and the Environmental Protection Agency.

Paper 8

Between Politics and Planning: UrbanSim as a Decision-Support System for Metropolitan Planning

PAUL WADDELL

ASSOCIATE PROFESSOR, DANIEL J. EVANS SCHOOL OF PUBLIC AFFAIRS,

AND DEPARTMENT OF URBAN DESIGN AND PLANNING

UNIVERSITY OF WASHINGTON, SEATTLE

ABSTRACT

UrbanSim is a land-use model being developed in a variety of localities to systematically address deficiencies in currently available alternatives to projecting urban futures. The UrbanSim model is designed to assist metropolitan planning agencies in making mutually consistent transportation, land-use, and air quality plans. The model differs from others in that it is based on a behavioral approach and simulates the land development process. UrbanSim is also unique in that it is object oriented, designed for Web distribution, and has been placed in the public domain. The model is being implemented in four states—Hawaii, Oregon, Utah, and Washington. Work is continuing on the model, focusing on the development of flexible software architecture and extension into environmental issues.

OVERVIEW

There has often been an uneasy relationship between politics and planning in the selection of policies and investments that shape urban areas. Competing interests vie to shape these decisions through the political process, while planning attempts to rationalize the process through analytical methods. Experience has shown that politics all too often trumps analysis, leaving both sides frustrated and the outcome poorly informed. The quest to elevate the political process through informed and objective analysis is a central objective of the development of decision-support systems. This paper describes the recent development of UrbanSim, an urban simulation system, and its application as a decision-support system for metropolitan land use and transportation planning.

The need to address consistency between land-use, transportation, and air quality planning has motivated a substantially different approach to planning than characterized these efforts in previous decades. Transportation planning, perhaps through the 1970s, was preoccupied with reducing congestion through capacity increases. The secondary effects of transportation on land use, and the resulting induced congestion and consequent increase in emissions from a new expansion of capacity, were concepts that had been well and widely documented (e.g., Downs 1992). But these ideas did not fully impact the planning practice in most metropolitan areas until the passage of federal legislation mandating that these interactions be considered in transportation planning. In the early 1990s, the Sierra Club and Environmental Defense Fund lawsuit in the Bay Area took on the metropolitan transportation-planning process and sent a wake-up call to metropolitan planning organizations (MPOs) across the nation (Garrett and Wachs 1996).

What has ensued in the years after the Bay Area lawsuit might be described as a frenzy of activity by MPOs, consultants, researchers, and activists to focus on the weaknesses in the current transportation and land-use models, and to begin making improvements in them to respond to a new generation of requirements. The Federal Highway Administration, through its Travel Model Improvement Program (TMIP), has invested millions of dollars in developing TRANSIMS, a long-term project to improve travel models using extremely disaggregate microsimulation techniques. On the other hand, there has to date been only token federal support for any research on land-use model improvement. In the face of federal legislation requiring more sophisticated treatment of land-use and transportation interactions, on the one hand, and a dearth of support for the development of new tools to do so, MPOs have been scrambling to develop their own approaches or to stretch their existing tools as far as possible, all under the shadow of potential legal challenge.

This paper describes a land-use model that is being developed by several states and the federal government as part of an effort to more systematically address the shortcomings of existing tools currently in use in the pressing planning and policy questions of the day. The UrbanSim model represents a work in progress, now being implemented for the first time in four states, and with further federal funding to extend the model and software implementation in an ongoing research program. It is being developed entirely within the public domain, so as to minimize the impediments to improving these new tools through collaborative research and development efforts.

The organization of this paper begins with an overview of the design of the model and its software implementation. Due to space constraints, the design is only summarized here, though a more complete treatment is available elsewhere (Waddell 1998a, 1998b, 1998c). Following the overview of the design, the user interface of the model is discussed, as a basis for describing the use of the model as a decision-support system for metropolitan land-use and transportation planning. The third section then reviews the status of the model and its application in several states, and the fourth section concludes with an agenda for further development.

DESIGN OF URBANSIM

The motivation for developing the UrbanSim land-use simulation model was based on the increasingly complex questions facing metropolitan planning agencies attempting to make mutually consistent, long-term plans for transportation, land use, and air quality. The Oahu Metropolitan Planning Organization was the first to take a new direction in land-use modeling, acknowledging a need for new integrated land-use and travel models, and supporting the initial design of UrbanSim and the development of a tour-based travel model system. The Oregon Department of Transportation subsequently funded the full implementation of the UrbanSim model and its application to Eugene–Springfield as a prototype metropolitan land-use model to be linked to existing MPO travel models in Oregon. The state of Utah has also begun adapting the UrbanSim model to the Greater Wasatch Front area, in combination with a public visioning process organized by a public–private collaboration known as Envision Utah. These applications will be discussed in some detail in a subsequent section, after a more complete description in this section of the model and its use for strategic metropolitan planning.

The basic features of the UrbanSim model and software implementation are highlighted in table 1. The model is relatively unique in that virtually all existing operational land-use models are cross-sectional, equilibrated, and fairly aggregate in nature (see Miller and Hunt, 1998, for a review of operational models, including UrbanSim). While simpler, these approaches require very strong assumptions about human behavior and the nature of metropolitan regions. The UrbanSim model is based on a behavioral approach that focuses on the key actions taken by the principal urban actors, namely, households, businesses, developers, and governments. Moreover, the model is very explicit in its treatment of land, being the only model to date to actually simulate the land-development process at the level on which it actually occurs, the land parcel. In modeling household and business location choices, the model also treats explicitly the choice of whether to move or not, a key aspect of more accurately reflecting the dynamics of change over time. Location choices are currently expressed in terms of both the housing or commercial building type and the traffic analysis zone for location. This degree of spatial detail is consistent with the travel models used at the metropolitan scale, another aspect that makes this model unique and more useful for interactive land-use and transportation modeling.

The software design was developed to make the system as portable and modular as possible, with a long-term intent of implementing the model and its user interface over the Internet for distributed use and review. Most existing software for land-use and travel modeling is based on software development approaches that do not take advantage of the fundamental advances in object-oriented software engineering that have taken place over the past two decades. We expect that there will be substantial gains in the reusability and flexibility of a completely object-oriented approach to model development. As will be noted in the final section of the paper, we are now in the process of developing a completely new software implementation to support substantially greater flexibility in the definition of model components than can currently be accommodated, and will be refining each of the model components in this effort.

TABLE 1. KEY FEATURES OF URBANSIM

Key Features of the UrbanSim Model	The model simulates the decision makers and choices impacting urban development; in particular, the mobility and location choices of households and businesses, and the development choices of developers;
	The model explicitly accounts for land, structures (houses and commercial buildings), and occupants (households and businesses);
	The model simulates urban development as a dynamic process over time and space, as opposed to a cross-sectional or equilibrium approach;
	The model simulates the land market as the interaction of demand (locational preferences of businesses and households) and supply (existing vacant space, new construction, and redevelopment), with prices adjusting to clear market;
	The model incorporates governmental policy assumptions explicitly, and evaluates policy impacts by modeling market responses;
	The model is based on random utility theory and uses logit models for implementation of key demand components;
	The model is designed for high levels of spatial and activity disaggregation, with a zonal system identical to travel model zones;
	The model presently addresses both new development and redevelopment, using parcel-level detail.
Key Features of the UrbanSim Software Implementation	The model and user interface are currently compatible with Windows 95, Windows NT®, UNIX®, Macintosh®, and other platforms supporting Java™ JDK 1.2; reporting tools are currently implemented in Microsoft Excel;
	The user interface focuses on policy assumptions and the creation and evaluation of scenarios;
	The model is implemented using object-oriented programming to maximize software flexibility;
	The model inputs and results can be displayed using ArcView GIS, Arc/Info, or other GIS software;
	Model results are written as ASCII tab-delimited files for external use.

The components of the model can be described with reference to the object diagram in figure 1. The model represents the processes by which developers construct new buildings or redevelop existing ones. Buildings are located on land parcels that have particular locational features and characteristics such as value, land use, slope, and other environmental characteristics. Governments set policies that regulate the use of land, such as land-use plans, urban growth boundaries, environmental regulations, or pricing policies such as development impact fees. Governments also build infrastructure, including transportation infrastructure, which interacts with the distribution of activities to generate patterns of accessibility at different locations that in turn influence the attractiveness of these sites for different consumers. Households have particular characteristics that may influence their preferences and demands for housing of different types at different locations. Businesses also have preferences that vary by industry and size of business (employees) for alternative building types and locations.

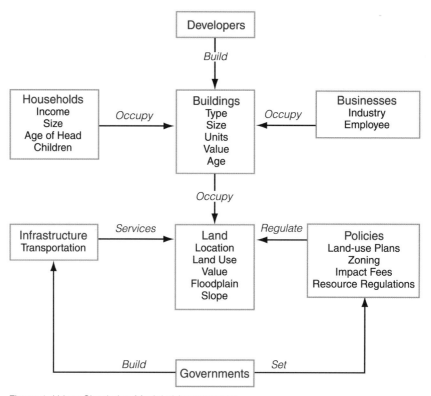

Figure 1. Urban Simulation Model object structure.

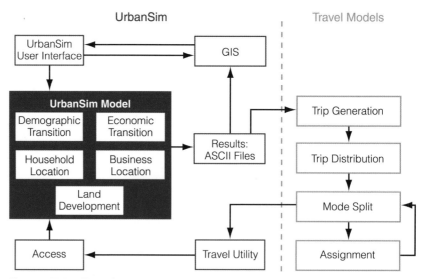

Figure 2. UrbanSim software implementation.

These urban actors and processes are implemented in model components and connected together through a software implementation as shown in figure 2. The diagram reflects the interaction between the land-use and travel model systems, and between the land-use model and a GIS for data preparation and visualization.

The model predicts the evolution of these objects and their characteristics over time, using annual steps to predict the movement and location choices of businesses and households, the development activities of developers, and the impacts of governmental policies and infrastructure choices. The land-use model is interfaced with a metropolitan travel model system to deal with the interactions of land use and transportation. Access to opportunities such as employment or shopping is treated as a composite utility using all available modes of travel, with consideration of the time involved and other costs of access included.

TABLE 2. FACTORS CONSIDERED IN LOCATION DEMAND COMPONENTS

Household Demand for Housing Types and Locations	Housing Type: Single-family, Residential with 2–4 Units, or Multifamily
	Accessibility to total employment
	Accessibility to retail employment
	Net density in units per acre of a particular housing type in a zone
	Number of housing units of a particular type in a zone
	Average age of the buildings of a type in a zone
	Percent of households in a zone in the lowest income group
	Percent of households in a zone in the second-lowest income group
	Percent of households in a zone in the highest income group
	Percent of households in a zone that have one or more children
	Percent of developed land in the zone that is in industrial use
	Percent of developed land in a zone that is in residential use
	Travel time to Central Business District, in minutes
Business Demand for Building Types and Locations	Building Type: Industrial, Warehouse, Retail, Office, or Special-purpose
	Accessibility to total population, total employment, and high-income households
	Basic employment in a zone per square mile
	Retail employment in a zone per square mile
	Service employment in a zone per square mile
	Accessibility to Basic, Retail, and Service employment
	Total square feet of commercial space of a particular type
	Building age
	Net density of the building type in a zone
	Percent of developed land in a zone in industrial use
	Percent of developed land in a zone in retail use
	Travel time to Central Business District, in minutes
	Presence of a highway in a zone

The key factors considered in the household and business location demand functions are shown in table 2. The influence of these factors on household and business location and building type choices are estimated through a calibration process, with different parameters estimated for significantly different subgroups of household types or business types. Some common elements considered in both are accessibilities to population or employment at each location, the density of development, and the age of the development. Prices that each subgroup would be willing to pay for each alternative are estimated and form the basis for predicting which consumer type will outbid others for a particular site. The probability of choosing a particular site, and being the highest bidder on it, is resolved using consumer surplus theory. The consumer having the highest consumer surplus for a particular alternative is most likely to be the highest bidder on it. Consumer surplus is defined as the willingness to pay for a good less the actual cost incurred.

The factors considered in determining development and redevelopment of land parcels are shown in table 3. These factors are combined to estimate the profitability of land development on each parcel of land, for all allowed development types. The assumption that drives the development component of the model is that the most profitable sites and uses will have the highest probabilities of development. Although the development component of the model actually operates at the level of the individual land parcel, this level of detail is used for behavioral realism and the ability to incorporate and test spatially explicit policies. It is not intended to reflect an expectation that one could anticipate the precise timing and nature of development on specific parcels two decades into the future. This is why results are currently aggregated to the level of the Traffic Analysis Zone, to provide a reasonable level of aggregation for use of the model results. Nonetheless, the model provides useful information about the type of development patterns that are likely to occur as a result of policy interventions. The quantity of greenfield development, infill, and redevelopment that occurs in different scenarios can be compared, as well as the distribution of densities and property values in new development.

The revenue component of the profit calculation is straightforward. This involves using the current estimated market price for each development type within a zone, and multiplying it by the anticipated size of the new development. The costs are more complex, and involve the land cost, structure construction (hard) cost, site preparation, and policy-based costs such as impact fees (soft costs). In addition, in order to consider redevelopment, the developed parcels with relatively low improvement-to-land-value ratios are sampled and compared to greenfield development. In order to equalize these and make them comparable, the costs of acquiring any existing buildings on a parcel and demolishing them are included in the case of redevelopment.

TABLE 3. FACTORS CONSIDERED IN LAND DEVELOPMENT AND REDEVELOPMENT COMPONENT

Expected Revenue	Current market price for type of development at zonal location Quantity and type of development feasible under development rules
Expected Costs for New Development	Land cost Hard construction (replacement cost of structure) Soft construction (development impact fees, infrastructure costs, taxes, or subsidies)
Density of Development	Regulatory constraints (land-use plan, urban growth boundary, environmental constraints) Land value Land use
Filter for Considering Developed Parcels for Redevelopment	Improvement to land-value ratio of parcel
Additional Costs for Redevelopment	Current building improvements Demolition costs

In order to reconcile these demand and supply components of the local real estate markets, the model implements a market-clearing and price adjustment mechanism. This is similar to the stock-adjustment model (DiPasquale and Wheaton 1996), and is based on the use of structural or normal vacancy rates as market signals that trigger new construction and also price adjustments. Movers and new migrants are assigned into the available vacant space in each year on the basis of their consumer surplus for each alternative, and subsequently, new construction decisions set development in progress for addition to the stock of space in the following year. Vacancy rates at the end of the year are used to make price adjustments that influence location choices in the beginning of the following year. This model sequencing, over short time periods of one year, reflects the tendency of real estate development to respond to market signals, and typically to seek a balance between supply and demand, but rarely to find one.

URBANSIM AS A PLANNING DECISION-SUPPORT SYSTEM

A DETAILED DESCRIPTION

We now turn to a more in-depth description of the use of the UrbanSim model for analyzing transportation and land-use alternatives. The discussion is organized around the description of the current (beta) version of the UrbanSim user interface, as a way to convey the use of the model for strategic metropolitan planning. The core of this user interface is designed to create and test policy scenarios. Since the term "scenario" has been appropriated by many to mean different things, we will elaborate on the intended meaning and use within the UrbanSim application.

The public and community leaders are occasionally invited to participate in a community visioning process as a way to begin a community planning process. This visioning process may evoke from its participants general values they hold, overall community goals and objectives, or benchmarks they would like to achieve. Often this kind of an exercise involves having participants articulate a vision of the community as they would like to see it at some time in the future, as a way to develop consensus about the direction in which participants wish to head. Sometimes these visions are labeled as "scenarios" for the future. They are characterized by describing the world (or community) in some future state, as a set of desired outcomes. This process and use of the term "scenarios" is distinct, though perhaps complementary, to our intended use.

While a community visioning process is an excellent means to elicit from community residents and stakeholders their values and general goals, it generally does not provide much in the way of concrete and specific direction on how to achieve these goals and objectives. Before any vision of the future can be realized, or approximated, those stakeholders that have the power to make decisions and take actions that can potentially affect certain outcomes of interest must choose courses of action, and anticipate the eventual consequences of these actions. These stakeholders certainly include local governments and metropolitan planning agencies, among others. The tools or instruments of action they possess to influence the outcomes of interest are varied, but include at least three broad categories of tools: regulatory, infrastructure, and pricing. In order to move beyond a community visioning process, a community needs to be able to assess the costs and benefits of different combinations of these policy instruments, and estimate their potential for achieving the desired outcomes. In short, imagining a particular future is only a small step in the long-term process of achieving it.

What the UrbanSim model attempts to provide is a systematic vehicle for developing and testing the potential effectiveness of combinations of these policy instruments in achieving desired outcomes. We use the term scenario, then, to indicate the packages of infrastructure, regulations, and pricing on which one intends to test the consequences of a variety of outcomes. The simulation model incorporates these scenarios as external interventions that influence the operation of real estate markets through both demand and supply of real estate of each type at each location within the metropolitan area. The model predicts outcomes that can be used to assess the degree to which different objectives are potentially achieved using this scenario, and the trade-offs between objectives that may result.

TABLE 4. DATA INPUTS AND OUTPUTS FROM URBANSIM

UrbanSim Inputs	Employment data, in the form of geocoded business establishments
	Household data, merged from multiple census sources
	Parcel database, with acreage, land use, housing units, nonresidential square footage, year built, land value, improvement value, city, and county
	Land-use plan
	GIS overlays for environmental features such as wetlands, floodways, steep slopes, or other sensitive or regulated lands
	Traffic Analysis Zones
	GIS overlays for any other planning boundaries
	Travel model outputs
	Development costs
UrbanSim Outputs (by Traffic Analysis Zone)	Households by income, size, age, and presence of children
	Businesses and employment by industry
	Acreage by land use
	Dwelling units by type
	Square feet of nonresidential space by type
	Land values per acre by land use
	Improvement values per unit or square foot by land use
Travel Model Outputs (Zone-to-Zone)	Travel time by mode
	Composite utility of travel using all modes

The data inputs and outputs for operating the UrbanSim model are shown in table 4. Developing the input database is a difficult challenge, owing to its detailed data requirements. A geographic information system is required to manage and combine this data into a form usable by the model, and may also be used to visualize the results of the model. Once the database is compiled, the model equations must be calibrated and input to the model. A final step before actual use is a validation process to test its operation over time and make adjustments in dynamic components to improve the realism. Ideally, this latter process will be undertaken with historical data over a fairly long period of time, such as was done in the Eugene–Springfield area from 1980 to 1994.

TABLE 5. POLICY INSTRUMENTS INCORPORATED IN URBANSIM SCENARIOS

Transportation (From Travel Models)	Transportation Capacity: Highway, Arterial, Bus, Rail, and HOV Transit Level of Service Pricing: tolls, gasoline tax, etc.
Land Use	Land Use Plan: restrictions on conversion of land to alternative urban land uses Density Constraints: minimum as well as maximum density by land use Soft Construction Costs: development impact fees, infrastructure costs, taxes, or subsidies
Policy Overlays (can affect land uses allowed, density, soft development costs)	Urban Growth Boundary Environmental Restrictions Other Policy Overlays (special planning areas designated for exceptional policies)

The policy instruments that can be incorporated into an UrbanSim scenario are summarized in table 5. In addition to the transportation system assumptions regarding capacity, level of service, and pricing, there are several land-use policy instruments available to the user to modify as part of a scenario. These policy instruments include the comprehensive land-use plan, land-use conversions to be allowed in new development or redevelopment, minimum and maximum density constraints, and pricing instruments such as development impact fees and infrastructure costs. In addition, instruments can include regulatory overlays such as the rules regarding development outside an urban growth or urban service boundary, within each type of environmentally sensitive land, and within any special planning overlays designated by the user. Several of these rules, including the allowed land-use conversions, soft-development costs, and density constraints, can be varied by the user between counties, cities, and even specific overlays. That is, different regulatory and pricing policies can be applied to each county, city, and overlay area if needed. This affords an extremely high degree of flexibility in articulating the character of local government land policies, which are controlled, after all, by municipalities and counties.

The process of entering these land-use policies is straightforward. The user interface of UrbanSim facilitates the creation and editing of the policy scenarios, and the operation of the model using these scenarios. We present below several components of the user interface of the Beta version of UrbanSim in order to describe how scenarios may be created and modified. The process of interacting with the model, once the database and calibration steps are completed, is as follows:

1 Create a new scenario or open an existing one

2 Set the metropolitan control totals and the reporting years for output

3 Set the land-use conversion rules based on the land-use plan designations in the parcel database

4 Set density constraints

5 Set development costs

6 Set normal vacancy rates

7 Save scenario

8 Run the model on the scenario

9 Visualize and interpret results

10 Repeat process on other scenarios and compare results

EDITING SCENARIOS

To edit a scenario, a user clicks on the "edit scenario" button to reveal the screen shown in figure 3. This screen has five tabs corresponding to the major variable types that the user specifies for a particular scenario: regional control totals, land use conversion, density constraints, development costs, and vacancy rates.

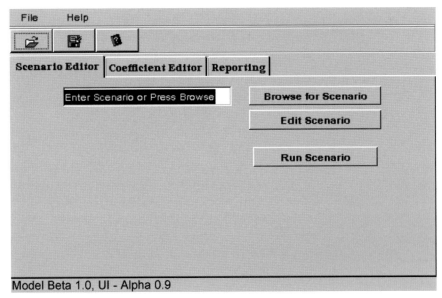

Figure 3. Initial UrbanSim Menu: Edit Scenarios and Execute Model.

CONTROL TOTALS

The first tab, representing control totals, is shown in figure 4. It allows the user to input the years and data for which there are available population and employment forecasts. The user first enters the base year and the ending year. While UrbanSim will interpolate projections for years in which there is no forecast, the model requires, at a minimum, both population and employment forecasts for the ending year. Since the model operates on a yearly timetable, the data produced by the forecasts can be written out as ASCII files for any or all years of the model run for use in future analysis. The selection of reporting years is made by checking years for which the user wishes outputs reported.

| Control Totals | Land Use Conversion | Density Constraints | Development Costs | Vacancy Rates |

Project Base Year is: 1995   Ending Year for Scenario: 2010

Year	Population	Employment	ReportYear	Travel
1995	172559	96217	✔	☐
1996	175148	97660	✔	☐
1997	177775	99125	✔	☐
1998	180441	100612	✔	☐
1999	183148	102121	✔	☐
2000	185895	103653	✔	☐
2001	188684	105208	✔	☐
2002	191514	106786	✔	☐
2003	194387	108388	✔	☐
2004	197302	110013	✔	☐
2005	200262	111664	✔	☐
2006	203266	113339	✔	☐
2007	206315	115039	✔	☐
2008	209410	116764	✔	☐
2009	212551	118516	✔	☐
2010	215739	120293	✔	☐

Figure 4. Control Totals.

When the model reaches a year that the user has selected as a travel model year, it writes results for that year into external data files in ASCII format, and suspends operation until the travel model sequence is executed using the current land-use data. Once new travel time matrices are created from the travel model run, the urban model simulation is resumed by the user and proceeds to run until the next travel model year, at which point this process is repeated. The years for which a user plans to run a travel model may be checked here.

LAND USE CONVERSION

The Land Use Conversion screen, figure 5, allows a user to specify those actual land uses (ALU) permitted in each planned land use (PLU), and whether or not conversion to such use is permitted within each county, city, or overlay. If an overlay constraint is specified, it overrides the conversions allowed for the given city or county. While the model is not currently designed to handle multiple uses on one parcel of land, it can reflect mixed-use policies by allowing different parcels within a cluster to be developed into each of the allowed uses in a plan designation.

Control Totals	Land Use Conversion	Density Constraints	Development Costs	Vacancy Rates

		Planned to Actual Land Use Conversion		
County	City	Overlay	PLU	ALU
-1	-1	-1	1	0
-1	-1	-1	2	3
-1	-1	-1	2	6
-1	-1	-1	2	7
-1	-1	-1	3	2
-1	-1	-1	3	3
-1	-1	-1	3	6
-1	-1	-1	3	7
-1	-1	-1	3	8
-1	-1	-1	4	6
-1	-1	-1	4	7
-1	-1	-1	5	8
-1	-1	-1	6	0
-1	-1	-1	7	4
-1	-1	-1	7	8
-1	-1	-1	8	3
-1	-1	-1	9	5
-1	-1	-1	10	4
-1	-1	-1	11	2

Figure 5. Land Use Conversion.

Control Totals	Land Use Conversion	Density Constraints	Development Costs	Vacancy Rates

Constraints - Land Use Density

County	City	Overlay	ALU	Min Density	Max Density
-1	-1	-1	1	2.0	8.0
-1	-1	-1	2	10.0	15.0
-1	-1	-1	3	15.0	30.0
-1	-1	-1	4	0.1	1.3
-1	-1	-1	5	0.2	1.3
-1	-1	-1	6	0.25	6.0
-1	-1	-1	7	0.3	6.0
-1	-1	-1	8	0.05	4.0
-1	-1	-1	9	0.0	0.0
-1	-1	-1	10	0.0	0.0
-1	-1	-1	11	0.0	0.0
-1	-1	-1	12	0.0	0.0
-1	-1	-1	13	0.0	0.0
-1	-1	-1	14	0.0	0.0

Figure 6. Land Use Density Constraints.

DENSITY CONSTRAINTS

Figure 6 shows a tab containing density constraints that may be set by the user. The user may specify the minimum and maximum density permitted by land-use policy in any county, city, or overlay area. It is also in this screen that a user may specify land-use policies that may pertain to critical environmental areas. UrbanSim allows modification of the allowable development densities (in a protected area) as a percentage of the normal densities allowed. For example, if a user wishes to totally exclude an environmentally sensitive type of land use, such as wetlands, from any development, then the density adjustment of zero would eliminate all wetlands from development. If the constraint were to reduce densities by 50 percent in selected areas such as those with high slope, then the applicable density adjustment input by the user would be 0.5. Densities for residential uses are entered in units per acre whereas all others are entered as a floor area ratio. If an overlay density/constraint is specified, it overrides the general density constraints for the city or unincorporated county.

The use of these density constraints in the model is to provide upper and lower bounds on the feasible densities for developing specific land parcels affected by a combination of land-use plan designations, environmental regulations, and policy overlays such as urban growth boundaries or enterprise communities. The land development component of the model estimates the density of development for any feasible development types and predicts the profit-maximizing density at which to develop a parcel. This estimate is compared to the applicable policy constraints on density, and if it falls below or above the policy guidelines, the density is adjusted to the density that conforms to the applicable regulations.

| Control Totals | Land Use Conversion | Density Constraints | Development Costs | Vacancy Rates |

Hard Costs of Development

ALU	Hard Cost	Demolitio...
1	74000.0	4000.0
2	40000.0	4000.0
3	24000.0	4000.0
4	55.0	4.0
5	20.0	4.0
6	27.0	4.0
7	41.0	4.0
8	46.0	4.0
9	0.0	0.0
10	0.0	0.0
11	0.0	0.0
12	0.0	0.0
13	0.0	0.0
14	0.0	0.0

Soft Costs of Development

County	City	Overlay	ALU	SoftCost
1	1	1	1	2000.0
1	1	1	2	2000.0
1	1	1	3	2000.0
1	1	1	4	3.0
1	1	1	5	3.0
1	1	1	6	3.0
1	1	1	7	3.0
1	1	2	1	2000.0
1	1	2	2	2000.0
1	1	2	3	2000.0
1	1	2	4	3.0
1	1	2	5	3.0
1	1	2	6	3.0
1	1	2	7	3.0
1	1	3	1	2000.0
1	1	3	2	2000.0
1	1	3	3	2000.0
1	1	3	4	3.0
1	1	3	5	3.0

Figure 7. Hard and Soft Development Costs.

DEVELOPMENT COSTS

Figure 7 depicts a tab containing development costs that may be set by the user. Hard development costs represent the labor and material costs of construction, not including costs of urban service extensions. Commonly referred to as replacement costs for a building structure, hard development costs are assumed to be the same across the metropolitan area, but to vary across different building types. They may be estimated for each building type from assessed improvement values, local construction industry information, or other sources.

Soft construction costs include a variety of fees set by local governments, which are assumed by the developer. Depending on the site, these costs could play a significant role in determining the profitability of a development. While specific fees vary greatly across municipalities, they can be classified into three common categories: development and impact fees, service extension charges, and building permit fees. However, because of the tremendous variability in the way such fees are implemented, the model adopts a simplification that collapses them into an average "soft cost" applicable to each building type, and a soft cost "adjustment factor" that allows this cost to be adjusted up or down by location based on such factors as project-specific service extension levels and costs. Again, if an overlay value is provided for this factor, it overrides the soft development costs for the given City, County, and Actual Land Use.

NORMAL VACANCY RATES

The final tab, shown in figure 8, allows a user to enter estimates for normal vacancy rates for each actual land use. These should be interpreted as structural vacancy rates that signal price adjustments and new construction when actual vacancy rates fall below them.

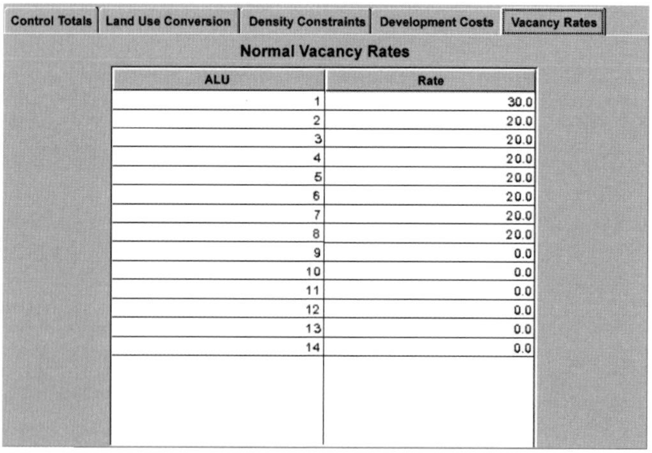

Control Totals	Land Use Conversion	Density Constraints	Development Costs	Vacancy Rates

Normal Vacancy Rates

ALU	Rate
1	30.0
2	20.0
3	20.0
4	20.0
5	20.0
6	20.0
7	20.0
8	20.0
9	0.0
10	0.0
11	0.0
12	0.0
13	0.0
14	0.0

Figure 8. Normal Vacancy Rates.

VISUALIZING SIMULATION RESULTS

Because the model produces voluminous results, a GIS is used to visualize these outputs in map form, in addition to any other data visualization and reporting that the user may wish to use. Figure 9 portrays the cumulative single-family housing production generated by a particular diagnostic scenario for the Eugene–Springfield metropolitan area. The results of the model are summarized by Traffic Analysis Zone, and may be linked to boundary files in a GIS for display. This particular display used ArcView GIS 3.1, though other systems could be used as well.

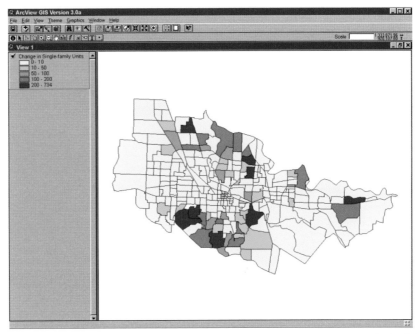

Figure 9. Visualizing Simulation Results: Single-Family Construction in Eugene–Springfield.

TESTING SCENARIOS

As is evident from the foregoing discussion, there is currently substantial flexibility in the ability to define scenarios of policy instruments that affect transportation and land use, through infrastructure, regulation, and pricing. The use of the model then focuses on the creation of multiple scenarios and the execution of the model with each scenario. Results of the model are stored for evaluation in a scenario directory, with results for each reporting year specified by the user. Typically, a series of benchmarks or measures of particular interest to the model users would be derived from these results and compared across scenarios. These measures might include, for example, the quantity of agricultural land consumed, the average density of new residential development, average housing values, total infrastructure costs, and total vehicle miles traveled per capita.

It is entirely to be expected that the analysis of these results will expose underlying trade-offs between different policy objectives. An example might be housing affordability and preserving open space. The real utility of the model as a decision-support system for metropolitan planning is in the assistance it can provide in exploring the nature of these trade-offs. Use of analytical tools such as UrbanSim to explore the effects of policies on the outcomes of interest and the nature of the trade-offs involved in achieving the desired objectives, may help achieve greater mutual understanding and reasonable compromise among the many constituencies affected by metropolitan plans and policies. While it is unlikely that analysis will ever trump politics, perhaps there is some ground on which the two could be more constructively engaged. It is this hope on which the research agenda described in this paper is based.

APPLICATIONS OF URBANSIM

UrbanSim is presently being applied in four states: Hawaii, Oregon, Utah, and Washington. It will be further distributed as an open, nonproprietary software application via the Internet. It remains, however, a new analytical tool, and is undergoing rapid evolution and further development. This section reviews briefly the development and application of the model to date. The closing section describes its further development as a decision-support system as planned under currently funded research grants.

HAWAII

The initial design of the UrbanSim model was funded by the Oahu Metropolitan Land-Use Model as part of a larger effort to undertake the development of new travel models. Oahu presents a highly unusual location for development of land-use and transportation models, for several reasons. First, it more closely approximates a closed system than any metropolitan area in the mainland United States, eliminating some of the boundary conditions that plague analysis of many mainland metropolitan areas. Second, the use of land is highly constrained by water, mountains, and policy. Approximately 4 percent of the land area is designated for urban uses, with the vast majority of land on the island assigned to agricultural and watershed preservation areas. Development is highly regulated, and the City and County are consolidated, eliminating the jurisdictional fragmentation that characterizes most mainland metropolitan regions. These factors, coupled with high density, extremely high housing prices, and high transit ridership make Honolulu an interesting application of these modeling tools.

Several policy concerns have guided the land use and transportation model development effort in Honolulu. Recent proposals for light rail systems have been turned down by voters, though variations on bus-alternative transit continue to be brought up for discussion, and linkages between transportation investments and land development are key to these analyses. Of particular concern in Honolulu are issues regarding housing affordability, and the degree to which policies to steer development toward certain areas such as Ewa can be realized. The high degree of state and local regulation of land development also motivates questions regarding how to make these development decisions in ways that are responsive to market conditions. The use of UrbanSim to assist in these analyses will be guided by the adaptation of the land development component to incorporate anticipated development events directly into the model. The ability to incorporate anticipated events of development projects in the pipeline, major business relocations, or major policy changes, are some of the extensions of the model that are planned for near-term implementation.

The project also involves the development by Parsons Brinckerhoff of a travel model system based on modeling activities of tours rather than trips. The linkage of the land use modeling with this new generation of travel models will open new venues for more accurately representing the nature of land-use and transportation interactions. For example, the choice of households to locate in a dense, transit-oriented neighborhood is likely to be interdependent with their choice of auto-ownership and travel modes. These kinds of linkages are not easily explored within a traditional four-step travel modeling system, but are open research avenues with activity-based travel models.

OREGON

In 1996 the Oregon Department of Transportation (ODOT) launched an ambitious project to support growth management policies within the state. The Transportation and Land Use Model Integration Project (TLUMIP) sought to develop analytical tools to support both statewide and metropolitan scale land-use and transportation planning. The development of the prototype metropolitan land-use model was based on the UrbanSim design developed in Honolulu, and was extended and fully implemented as an operational prototype software system within the TLUMIP project. The model was calibrated for a case study in Eugene–Springfield, principally using cross-sectional data. In a second TLUMIP project, a longitudinal calibration and validation process, to examine the dynamic behavior of the model over the period from 1980 to 1994, has been completed, and has proved to be a valuable aid in refining the model's dynamic properties. A broader agenda of the second TLUMIP project is to develop more integration between analytical tools for statewide land-use and transportation planning with those for the Willamette Valley substate area and the metropolitan scale models. Given the diversity of the state and the variation in the issues, theoretical concerns, and data availability at these three scales, the design of the second-generation models will be breaking substantially new ground.

The key policy concerns motivating the Oregon project relate to the effects of different growth management policies on a series of outcomes of interest, and the interaction between land-use and transportation initiatives. For example, what might the effect of an overly restrictive urban growth boundary in Portland be on the potential relocation of businesses and households into other metropolitan areas in the Willamette Valley, such as Salem? If this were substantial, it might seriously undermine the original objectives of growth management, promoting long-distance commuting on an already congested Interstate 5. Other questions concern the effects of the urban growth boundary on housing densities and housing costs. Critics of the urban growth boundary complain about its effects on housing prices, but there is little compelling evidence in either direction on these questions.

Oregon is a mature growth-management state, perhaps even the national leader in this arena. Yet the ongoing evaluation and refinement of growth management strategies remain problematic, owing to an absence of systematic monitoring and evaluation tools. UrbanSim was developed to assist in this process, by providing a way to simulate the various changes of these elaborate growth management strategies and their potential effects. If coupled with a consistent monitoring program, this approach may offer a valuable prototype for not only developing and testing growth management strategies, but also maintaining and refining them over time.

UTAH

In Utah, the Governor's Office of Planning and Budget has been coordinating a technical process in close cooperation with a community visioning process titled Envision Utah. The Envision Utah process has engaged community leaders from the public and private sectors to assess alternative visions of how the community might wish to evolve over the next several decades, in the face of unrelenting population growth that threatens the region's environmental amenities and quality of life. Peter Calthorpe and John Fregonese have been engaged to lead this public visioning process, and have raised community awareness of more transit-oriented, dense, and walkable urban neighborhoods as an alternative to continued sprawl.

Utah provides a fascinating political testing ground for the growth-management debate. Environmental groups are very active and concerned about the potential environmental damage not only from continued sprawl, but also from large-scale infrastructure such as the proposed Legacy Highway that is being considered through some of the region's prime wetlands. Yet Utah is also a state where private property rights are held in high regard, and intervention by state and local government on the rights of landowners to develop property is viewed with skepticism. In many ways, Utah provides a microcosm of the political debate likely to be played out across much of this country, as citizens grapple with congestion and environmental concerns on the one hand, and on strongly held sentiments about individual property rights and limited governmental intervention on the other.

The Utah Governor's Office has chosen to use UrbanSim as a way to facilitate the public visioning process of Envision Utah. The product of many public workshops conducted by the Envision Utah process will be a preferred scenario for the future of the Greater Wasatch Front area. This will be a broad vision of the desired future of the region, along with some broad policies to be endorsed as the means to achieve this vision. UrbanSim will be used to facilitate the testing of packages of policy instruments, and to assess their ability to achieve the desired vision of the future. This will involve examining the costs of alternative scenarios, the mediating role of real estate markets, and the trade-offs between objectives that result from alternative policy packages. The final selection of a preferred scenario, then, will be based on an iterative process of community workshops and technical analysis. This process provides an outstanding opportunity to seek constructively engaged public participation and technical analysis. The coming year will provide substantial insights into the issues involved in making such a linkage productive.

WASHINGTON

The State of Washington is also a growth-management state, though with perhaps less stringent application than in Oregon. Much of the control for implementing the Growth Management Act remains in the control of local governments, and there has been relatively little evaluation of compliance to date. Recent concerns over the imminent listing of the Chinook salmon as an endangered species in several watersheds in the greater Puget Sound region have generated substantial interest in better understanding the linkages between urban development, agricultural and forestry practices, and the quality of the salmon habitat in these watersheds. A University of Washington research project, dubbed PRISM (Puget Sound Regional Synthesis Model) has taken on the ambitious challenge of engaging researchers from many scientific disciplines ranging from hydrology to atmospheric science to landscape ecology to urban planning, in order to begin linking models of urban development and natural ecosystems.

UrbanSim was selected as the basis for the modeling of urbanization, and will be extended by the development of complementary model components for predicting land cover, water demand, and the emissions of nutrients. The target area for this application is the core Puget Sound region, encompassing the four central counties in the Seattle–Tacoma metropolitan area. This direction of development begins to emphasize the potential for more integrated modeling of land use, transportation, and environmental interdependencies. Not only do land-use and transportation choices create environmental consequences, but these environmental consequences may also impact land uses and location choices. Air quality and open space may influence the attractiveness of locations for residential location, for example, and habitat preservation may restrict areas from further development.

FUTURE RESEARCH AND DISTRIBUTION This section concludes the paper with a review of the current commitments to extend and distribute the UrbanSim model, and to engage in ongoing research to improve the analytical components and their usability as a decision-support system for metropolitan planning. Two specific projects are described briefly, followed by general conclusions.

INTERNET DISTRIBUTION

The National Cooperative Highway Research Program recently funded a research project (8–32(3)) entitled "Integration of Land Use Planning and Multimodal Transportation Planning," coordinated by Parsons Brinckerhoff, which now has been completed. A component of this project was the development of new analytical tools for integrated land-use and transportation planning. For this component, the UrbanSim model prototype developed in Oregon was used as a foundation. Three products were completed from this project that are now available. The first is a guidance document for land-use and transportation planning, which reviews the nature of land-use and transportation interactions, and the existing tools used by Metropolitan Planning Agencies to undertake such analyses. The second is a beta version of the UrbanSim software implementation, and supporting reference and user guides, developed at the University of Washington. The software, as mentioned previously, is entirely in the public domain, and is covered by a GNU General Public License, otherwise known as "Copyleft." This licensing approach guarantees that the source code, and any extensions of it, will remain nonproprietary in the future. The adoption of this open approach was a reaction to high-priced and proprietary approaches to land-use and transportation modeling software that inhibits innovation or even correction of deficiencies, and also restricts access to large organizations that can afford the license fees.

Considering the ongoing evolution of the software and model system, a Web site (urbansim.org) was implemented to provide ongoing access to system improvements as well as documentation and news regarding the project. The beta version of the model described in this paper has been substantially updated since the time of this draft. Details of the new version are available on the project Web page and in other forthcoming papers. Version 0.9 was released in mid-August 2000, and within the first two weeks had been downloaded by almost 300 planners, policy analysts, researchers, and consultants in

North America, South America, Europe, and Asia. We plan to develop collaborative relationships with others interested in further extension of these tools.

The following sections summarize current development activity on the model and future research.

REUSABLE SOFTWARE ARCHITECTURE

The National Science Foundation launched an Urban Research Initiative in 1998, signaling new attention to the need for basic research and model development dealing with the interactions between built, social, and natural environments. The University of Washington was awarded a grant entitled "Reusable Model Components for Simulating Land Use, Transportation and Land Cover." This project has developed a flexible software architecture to support modular development and evaluation of model components related to land use, transportation, and land cover. The basic research that the project seeks to undertake concerns the effects of scale and resolution in space, time, and behavior on the utility and realism of urban models. This project is exploring implementation of the various model components dealing with demand and supply of land development at a microsimulation level, using a grid locational reference underlying the parcel and zonal features now forming the basis of location in the models. By developing more aggregate models and evaluating the trade-offs between scale and resolution among these model implementations, we hope to learn more about the nature of the compromises involved in selecting the scale and resolution of models. We anticipate that higher resolution in each dimension will achieve greater realism, but will come at increasing cost. Reasonable compromises may be found where the marginal costs match the marginal improvements in the model capacity to represent behavior and policy responsiveness.

DATA PREPARATION TOOLS AND USER INTERFACE

The process of assembling parcel, employment, environmental, and other data inputs and preparing them for use in the model system is currently the subject of a significant focus of activity. Calibration tools to support the estimation of the coefficients for the model components also are under development, and a user interface that will likely include Web-based access. A prototype visualization system that includes two- and three-dimensional mapping, charting, and graphing has been developed and is being tested. And finally, development of flexible user-evaluation measures to facilitate the evaluation of multiple scenarios is beginning, and may provide a foundation to move the tools increasingly from the technical black box into the open, to support a participatory and deliberative policy process for evaluating land-use, transportation, and environmental policies.

IN THE LONG RUN

The long-term objectives of the research and development agenda described in this paper are to improve the ability of planning agencies and the general public to understand the complex interactions between land use, transportation, and the environment and the potential effects of alternative policy choices on these outcomes. Our hope is that there is some middle ground between politics and planning, and that well-designed analytical tools can help explore this territory. We also hold out some expectation that there is a way to constructively engage public participation and objective technical analysis, and to this end we are developing a strategy to deploy these tools over the Internet, in the form of a distributed decision-support system.

The objectives laid out in this paper are clearly ambitious. The echoes of Lee's 1973 paper "Requiem for Large Scale Models" (Lee 1994) still resonate today, providing a valuable caution against unguarded optimism for the potential for such models. It is indeed far too early to tell the degree to which these objectives are achievable, but the options of not attempting to achieve them seem a far more daunting prospect.

ACKNOWLEDGMENTS

This research has been funded in part by National Science Foundation Grant No. CMS–9818378, and in part by the University of Washington PRISM project.

REFERENCES

Downs, Anthony. 1992. *Stuck in Traffic: Coping with Peak-hour Traffic Congestion*. Washington, D.C.: The Brookings Institution.

Garrett and Wachs. 1996. *Transportation Planning on Trial: The Clean Air Act and Travel Forecasting*. Thousand Oaks, CA: Sage Publications.

Lee, D. B. 1994. Retrospective on Large-scale Urban Models. *Journal of the American Planning Association 60* (1):35–40.

Miller, Eric, David Kriger, and J. D. Hunt. 1998. *Integrated Urban Models for Simulation of Transit and Land-Use Policies, Final Report,* Transit Cooperative Highway Research Project H-12.

Waddell, Paul. 1998a. *UrbanSim Reference Guide, Beta Version,* National Cooperative Highway Research Project 8–32(3).

Waddell, Paul. 1998b. An Urban Simulation Model for Integrated Policy Analysis and Planning: Residential Location and Housing Market Components of UrbanSim. *Proceedings of the 8th World Conference on Transport Research,* Antwerp, Belgium.

Waddell, Paul. 1998b. UrbanSim: The Oregon Prototype Metropolitan Land Use Model. *Proceedings of the 1998 ASCE Conference on Land Use, Transportation and Air Quality: Making the Connection,* Portland, OR.

Paper 9

INDEX: Software for Community Indicators

ELIOT ALLEN, AICP, PRINCIPAL

CRITERION PLANNERS/ENGINEERS, INC.

PORTLAND, OREGON

ABSTRACT

INDEX is a planning support system based on a GIS that estimates the potential impacts of community land-use and design decisions. Widely used, INDEX is centered around a set of indicators that are used to assess current community conditions, evaluate alternative courses of actions, and monitor changes over time. INDEX was developed in response to central themes in contemporary planning—collaborative decision making by citizens and public officials, the new urbanism movement, and sustainable development initiatives. One important feature of INDEX is its capacity to estimate the transportation impacts of land-use decisions, including the exploration of how travel behavior is influenced by design decisions.

INTRODUCTION

INDEX is a GIS-based planning support system (PSS) that uses indicators to measure the attributes and performance of community plans and urban designs. Introduced in 1994, it is one of the most widely distributed PSS in the United States, with over 70 local governments and other organizations in 25 states licensed to use the software. It was developed for practitioners as a productivity tool to facilitate stakeholder participation in community alternatives analysis and goal-setting; improve the consistency of incremental development decisions with plan goals; and periodically measure cumulative progress toward goals.

At its heart is a set of indicators that are used to benchmark existing conditions, evaluate alternative courses of action, and monitor change over time. Figure 1 illustrates the integration of these support functions into the community planning process. The premise is that policy choices and plan implementation can be valuably informed by a standardized set of indicators that are derived from community goals and used regularly to gauge planning actions.

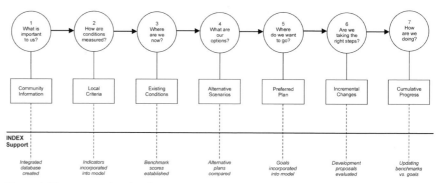

Figure 1. The community planning process.

Indicators are scored in tabular form, and more importantly, the explanatory power of GIS is used to map indicator results. In this way, users obtain both quantitative and spatially explicit evaluations of a situation. For example, the transit-orientation indicator "employees per acre within a one-quarter mile walk of transit stops" is tabulated as an average value for a neighborhood, and a map of the spatial pattern of parcel-based walking distances that produced the score is also generated. Indicator maps are key to the software's effectiveness as a PSS in that they relate directly to a jurisdiction's spatial scheme of land-use and development regulations. For each policy topic being measured by an indicator, the maps delineate geographic areas of strength and weakness relative to that policy. Areas that meet or exceed policy goals can be designated for preservation and protection of those values, while deficient areas can be targeted for corrective actions. A representative list of indicators is given in table 1 for Dane County, Wisconsin, where the county Planning Department is using INDEX for development impact analysis. Figure 2 presents an indicator mapping example of transportation circulation efficiency as measured by street connectivity in Leon County, Florida, with favorably rated areas in shades of green and unfavorable areas in shades of red. In this case, street connectivity is used to characterize a neighborhood's suitability for multimodal travel, which is a principal transportation goal of the county's.

TABLE 1. SELECTED DANE COUNTY, WISCONSIN, INDICATORS

	Definition	Area-Based	Parcel-Based
Demographics			
Population	Total number of residents	Y	Y
Employment	Total number of employees	Y	Y
Land Use and Community Form			
Block size	Average size of blocks in acres		Y
Use mix	Proportion of mixed or dissimilar land uses among a grid of 1-acre cells, expressed on a scale of 0 to 1.	Y	Y
Use balance	Proportional balance of land uses, by land area, expressed on a scale of 0 to 1.	Y	Y
Developed acres per capita	Total developed acres divided by total number of residents.	Y	Y
Housing			
Population density	Total residents per acre.	Y	Y
Residential acres per capita	Total residential-designated acres divided by total residents.	Y	Y
Single-family dwelling density	Single-family dwelling units per net acre of land designated for single-family use.	Y	Y
Multifamily dwelling density	Multifamily dwelling units per net acre of land designated for multi-family use.	Y	Y
Single-family/Multifamily mix	Percent of dwelling units that are single-family and multifamily.	Y	Y
Amenities proximity	Average travel distance from all dwellings to closest designated amenity (school, park, shopping, etc.).	Y	Y
Transit proximity	Average walk distance from all dwellings to closest transit stop in feet.	Y	Y
Water consumption	Total residential water use in gallons per day per capita.		Y
Employment			
Jobs/Housing balance	Total number of jobs divided by number of dwelling units.	Y	Y
Employment density	Number of employees per net acre of land designated for employment uses.	Y	Y
Transit proximity	Average walk distance from businesses to closest transit stop in feet.	Y	Y
Recreation			
Park space supply	Acres of park and school yards per 1,000 residents.	Y	Y
Park proximity	Average walk distance from dwellings to closest park or school yard in feet.		Y
Environment			
Oxides of nitrogen (NOx) emissions	NOx emitted from light vehicles in lbs/capita/year.	Y	Y
Carbon monoxide (CO) emissions	CO emitted from light vehicles in lbs./capita/year.	Y	Y
Greenhouse gas (CO_2) emissions	CO_2 emitted from light vehicles in lbs./capita/year.	Y	Y
Open space	Percent of land area dedicated to open space.	Y	Y
Imperviousness	Amount of impervious surface in acres per capita.	Y	Y

TABLE 1 (CONTINUED). SELECTED DANE COUNTY, WISCONSIN, INDICATORS

	Definition	Area-Based	Parcel-Based
Travel			
Street connectivity	Ratio of street intersections versus intersections and cul-de-sacs expressed on a scale of 0 to 1.	Y	Y
Street network density	Density of streets in centerline miles per square mile.	Y	Y
Street miles per capita	Total street centerline distance divided by total residents.	Y	Y
Transit-oriented residential density	Average number of dwelling units per net residential acre within 1/4-mile walk of transit stops.	Y	Y
Transit-oriented employment density	Average number of employees per net nonresidential acre within 1/4-mile walk of transit stops.	Y	Y
Transit service density	Miles of transit routes multiplied by number of transit vehicles traveling those routes each day, divided by total acres.		Y
Sidewalk network coverage	Percent of total street frontage with improved sidewalks on both sides.		Y
Pedestrian route directness	Ratio of shortest walkable route distance from outlying origin points to central node destination versus straight-line distance between the same points.		Y
Bicycle network coverage	Percent of total street centerline distance with designated bike route.	Y	Y
Source: Criterion Planners/Engineers			

CENTRAL CORE INSET

Street Connectivity
0.9 - 1.00
0.8 - 0.9
0.7 - 0.8
0.6 - 0.7
0.5 - 0.6
0.4 - 0.5

Units = ratio of street intersections to intersections and cul-de-sacs

Map Note: internal street connectivity was classified by equal interval.

Criterion Planners/Engineers Inc.

Figure 2

In addition to indicators, INDEX is distinguished by its:

- Capacity for customization, with each community using a framework of modules and components that are tailored to local policy interests and institutional settings.

- Capability to address a full range of typical community planning decisions, from parcel-level site design up to areawide land-use planning.

- Time scale, which can be configured for either static (single point in time) or dynamic (change over time) applications.

- Specialized capability for integrated land-use/transportation planning with sketch-level transportation impacts estimated from land-use changes.

- Use of visualization tools and multimedia features to engage stakeholders and help visualize scenarios and outcomes.

As with any PSS, INDEX has definite limitations that need to be recognized. It is not a highly sophisticated integrated urban model (Wegener 1994). Those systems, such as UrbanSim and TRANUS, are powerful predictive tools for dynamic analysis of complex urban systems (Waddell 1998; de la Barra 1989). In contrast, INDEX is primarily intended for static time scale applications focused on built environment measurements from the regional level down to the neighborhood level. It does have an optional capability for modeling dynamic urban change over time, but that function uses a simplified gravity method of spatial growth allocation that does not consider land economics, and is therefore only suitable for "what if" sketch planning. The balance of this paper focuses on static time scale applications of INDEX because those account for a large majority of its use to date. Moreover, it is suggested that static time scale PSS tools may have as much or more relevance to day-to-day community planning as dynamic predictive tools.

BACKGROUND

INDEX was developed by Criterion Planners/Engineers in 1994 when desktop GIS, such as ESRI's ArcView GIS, first began to be widely used by local governments. It was conceived as a productivity tool to automate planning calculations typically performed by planning staff working on alternatives analyses for long-range plans or evaluating current development proposals.

The design of INDEX was generally informed by impact assessment and master planning methodologies that have been in common use in the U.S. over the past 30 years (McHarg 1969; DeChiara 1975; Lynch 1984; Burchell 1994). More specifically, creation of the software was influenced by the following forces in contemporary planning:

- *Citizen participation and PSS.* Public involvement is now a standard component of virtually all community planning processes. As information technology becomes more accessible to nontechnical users, the opportunity arises for greater emphasis on informal decision making using PSS interactively among citizens (Batty 1996). Increasingly, tools like GIS are successfully enhancing public participation at the neighborhood level (Elwood 1998; Craig 1998; Shiffer 1999; Al–Kodmany 2000).

- *Traditional town planning and new urbanism.* The 1990s saw the emergence of a major urban design movement advocating a return to traditional town planning where the neighborhood is the fundamental planning unit. Known as the "new urbanism," this design philosophy emphasizes a carefully orchestrated mix of uses and circulation features that increases amenities, reduces travel needs, and improves livability in general. PSS tools can play an important role in evaluating and substantiating the claims of new urbanist proposals and their performance once built (Moudon 2000; Allen 2000).

- *Ecological/sustainable planning.* The need to consider ecological consequences of urbanization is being increasingly recognized by communities, and responded to with sustainable development practices. Local governments such as the city of Austin, Texas, and national organizations such as the U.S. Green Building Council, are implementing "green certification" programs that take land-use and transportation factors into consideration. The Center for Neighborhood Technology in Chicago has successfully implemented a "location-efficient" mortgage program that relates housing affordability to transit proximity. Again, PSS tools can play an important role in advancing and evaluating such policy initiatives (Allen 1999).

In addition to these larger considerations, the design of INDEX was purposely directed to the routine, day-to-day planning decisions made by communities. Issues such as zone changes, conditional use permits, and residential subdivisions constitute the greatest number of local planning decisions, and are arguably the least supported decisions communities make, due both to the large volume of requests that must be handled, and the limited time available for their evaluation. However, such incremental decisions have significant cumulative effects on whether plans are actually achieved or not. Regrettably, many long-range community visions formulated through elaborate PSS modeling are slowly undermined or "nibbled to death" at monthly zoning hearings that do not have the same kind of PSS support. INDEX was conceived to fill this need through a software system that satisfies the following objectives:

- *Relevancy.* Provide meaningful answers to commonly asked questions.

- *Comprehensiveness.* Encompass the elements typically found in community plans (e.g., housing, employment, transportation, infrastructure, environment).

- *Resolution.* Provide the versatility to operate at multiple levels of geographic scale (e.g., as fine-grained as building footprints or as coarse as traffic analysis zones).

- *Precision.* Provide results within acceptable ranges of accuracy for planning-level estimates.

- *Portability.* Provide ease of use in multiple venues (e.g., staff offices, neighborhood meetings, and official hearings).

- *Feedback speed.* Generate results quickly enough to support interactive use at public meetings.

- *Transparency.* Completely document all data, assumptions, and calculations.

- *Temporal capability.* Evaluate a single point in time or dynamic change out to a typical planning horizon (e.g., 20 years).

- *Linkage potential.* Provide linkage potential to other models and databases to leverage their utility and investments.

- *Resource/expertise requirements.* Keep the software usable by planning practitioners with nominal modeling skills.

- *Data requirements/maintainability.* Use existing community data to the greatest extent possible.

Based on the software's first six years of development and use, most of these objectives have been satisfactorily achieved. It has performed all of its functions acceptably in several dozen locations, including the examples given in table 2. Refinements continue to be made in the software's relevancy, comprehensiveness, precision, speed, and expertise requirements. The two most problematic aspects of using the software in local government settings have been limitations on staff resources and data. Community planning staff are almost always fully committed to their regular work duties, making it difficult to set aside the incremental time needed to implement and sustain PSS operations. Similarly, many community databases have not received sufficient development to support a full range of data-hungry PSS calculations. However, both of these conditions should improve over time as the labor intensiveness of the tool declines, and as the general availability of community data continues to grow exponentially through public and private sources.

TABLE 2. SELECTED INDEX APPLICATIONS

Location	Application	User
Tallahassee, Florida	Land-use/transportation comprehensive planning	City of Tallahassee/Leon County
Madison, Wisconsin	Community impact analysis	Dane County
Tampa, Florida	Inner city neighborhood revitalization	City of Tampa
Sacramento, California	Neighborhood land-use planning	City and County of Sacramento
Beaverton, Oregon	Transit station area master planning	Oregon Department of Transportation
San Diego, California	Low-income neighborhood revitalization	San Diego Association of Governments
Vancouver, British Columbia	Land-use-based energy planning	BC Hydroelectric Authority
Queens, New York	Property value impact assessment	Federal Transit Administration
Palm Beach, Florida	Comprehensive land-use planning	Palm Beach County

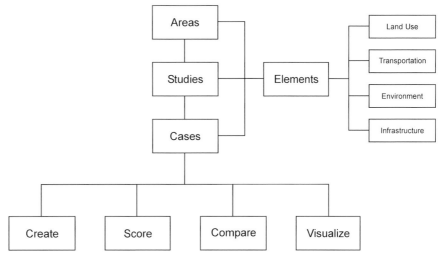

Figure 3

INDEX is structured as a framework, shown in figure 3, containing the following modules and features:

- *Areas and studies.* This module provides a geographic and topical hierarchy for organizing and accessing software runs. Studies are classified by geographic area (e.g., neighborhood or district), and by topical focus (e.g., housing infill, or transit stations).

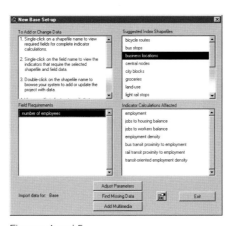
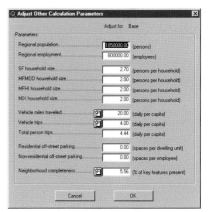

Figures 4 and 5

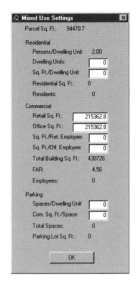

Figure 6

- *Cases.* This module is used to create planning scenarios or cases. Cases may describe real or proposed conditions in a study area. A "base case" could describe existing conditions in a neighborhood and "alternative cases" would be created to describe different concepts for infilling vacant land in the neighborhood. Similarly, a "base case" could represent a developer's initial proposal for a project, and "alternative cases" would represent modifications negotiated by neighboring residents and planning officials. Figures 4 and 5 illustrate the portions of the case set-up procedure devoted to data importation and parameter setting, respectively. To facilitate interactive case preparation with public audiences, "scenario builder" wizards are used as shown in figure 6.

- *Elements.* This module contains the database used to support indicator calculations. It is organized according to elements typically found in community plans, including land use, housing, employment, recreation, environment, transportation, and infrastructure.

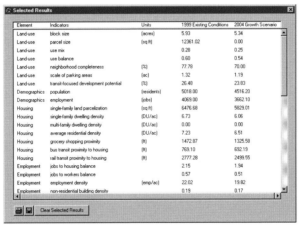

Figures 7 and 8

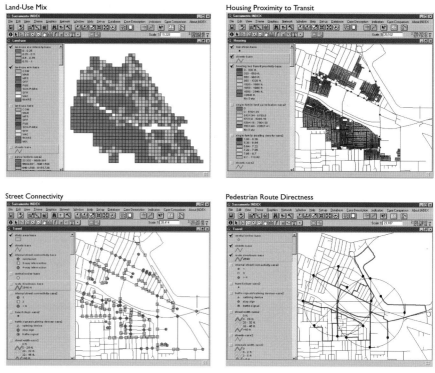

Figure 9

- *Indicators.* This module scores cases with indicators selected by the user, as shown in figure 7. Cases can be evaluated with all indicators, or the user may select a subset focused on a particular issue (e.g., a subset of "housing" indicators when the application is a residential subdivision evaluation). Indicator results are tabulated and mapped, providing both an absolute value result and a diagrammatic outcome. Figure 8 illustrates the tabular results and figure 9 presents a sampling of indicator mapping from Sacramento, California's 65th Street and Folsom Boulevard neighborhood.

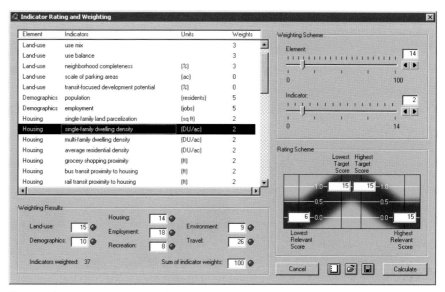

Figure 10

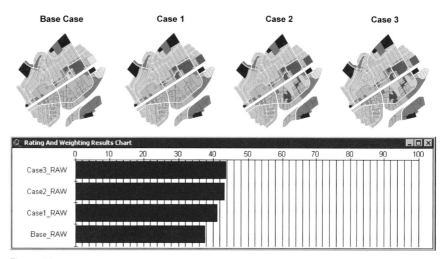

Figure 11

- *Rating and Weighting.* This feature provides an option for stake-holders to weight the importance of indicators relative to one another, and to establish acceptability ratings for indicator scores. Figure 10 presents the software's rating and weighting dialogue, and figure 11 shows the results of a multi-alternative evaluation of plans for the Zinfandel neighborhood of Sacramento.

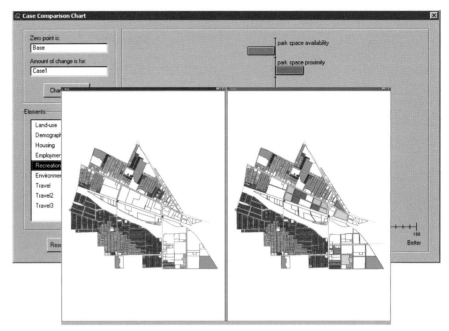

Figure 12

- *Case Comparison.* This module compares cases using charting and mapping to communicate differences between cases. The user selects cases to be compared and is then able to review changes in indicator scores between the cases by topical category. Another example from Sacramento's 65th Street neighborhood is illustrated in figure 12, where the effect of a proposed infill on the proximity of park and housing is evaluated against existing conditions.

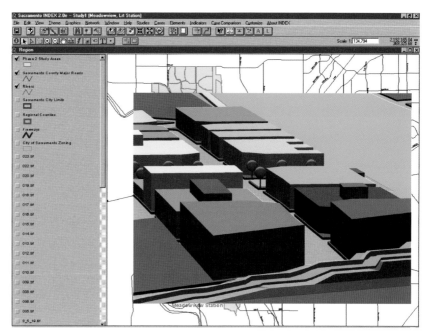

Figure 13

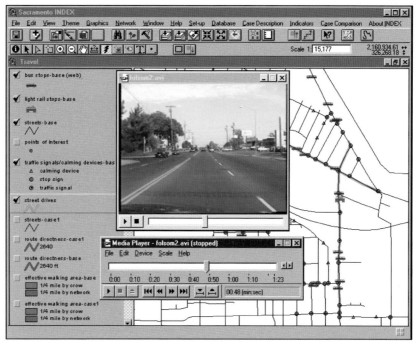

Figure 14

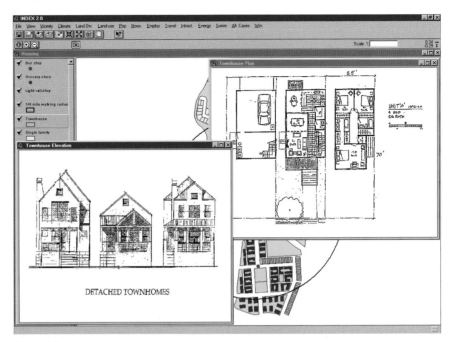

Figure 15

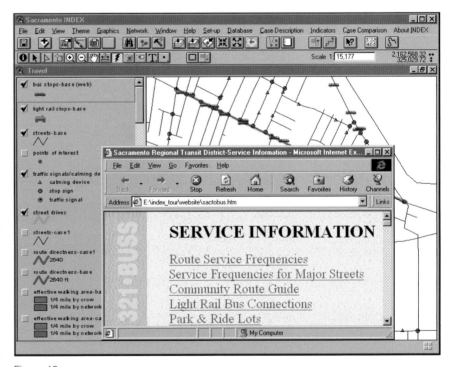

Figure 16

- *Visualization Tools and Internet Links.* This group of features is used to visually communicate proposals and outcomes to stakeholders. As shown in figures 13 through 16, they include use of ArcView 3D Analyst, attachment of video and other imagery to area features, and Internet links to other relevant resources. Experience has shown these features to be very helpful in working with citizen groups at public meetings.

- *Customize.* To accommodate changing community conditions and stakeholder interests, this module allows users to add new indicators and other functions as needed. The intent is twofold: to electronically enable quick software changes without having to alter its source code; and to encourage a sense of "ownership" of a system where users help to build and strengthen it over time.

- *Online Help.* This module provides online access to the software's user guide.

INDEX is built as an ArcView GIS extension or a MapObjects® application. ArcView GIS-based versions require ArcVIew® Network Analyst for certain land-use/transportation indicators. Windows NT is the recommended operating system because of its superior stability. The suggested minimum hardware configuration is a 300-MHz PC with at least 128 MB of RAM, a monitor capable of 800×600 resolution and 32-bit color, and at least 1.5 GB of available hard disk space.

MODELING PROCESS

The INDEX modeling process varies from community to community according to local circumstances and the functionality specified by users during customization. In general, three application methods have emerged consistent with the software's original objectives: long-range alternatives analysis; current development proposal evaluation; and periodic progress reporting.

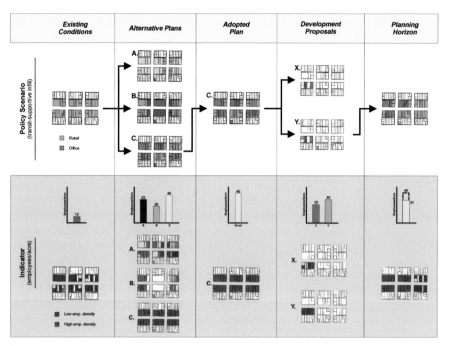

Figure 17

The first application process is based on the classic planning sequence of issue identification, alternatives analysis, and goal setting. This method is distinguished by citizen participation throughout the process. It is shown in generalized fashion in figure 17 and detailed as follows:

- *Select study area.* The user is able to define a geographic area over which indicators will be calculated using established boundaries (e.g., neighborhoods, traffic analysis zones, census tracts, ZIP Codes, or any user-created unique boundary).

- *Select applicable indicators.* The user selects those indicators that are relevant to the issues being studied.

- *Create existing conditions case.* Data is imported to describe existing conditions for the given issues in the study area.

- *Score base case with indicators.* The area's existing conditions are scored with indicators to define benchmark conditions against which future change can be measured.

- *Public review.* The results of the existing conditions analysis are shared with stakeholders in order to identify issues, opportunities, and constraints that bear on future options.

- *Stakeholder weighting of indicators and rating of indicator scores.* Stakeholders are allowed to weight the relative importance of indicators and assign acceptability ratings to ranges of indicator scores.

- *Create alternative scenarios.* Alternative cases are created to represent concepts or modified proposals. Using a "scenario builder" tool, the user may alter features of the study area to simulate different concepts.

- *Score alternative cases with indicators.* Alternative scenarios can be evaluated with both unweighted and weighted indicator scores and maps. Unweighted scores can provide valuable diagnostic feedback for design professionals, and weighted scores can help nontechnical groups quickly summarize a scenario's overall acceptability.

- *Continued iterations of scenario refinement and public review.* One of the major advantages of GIS-based PSS comes into play at this stage when spatial scenario "tweaking" can be accomplished easily, quickly, and most importantly to build consensus for a preferred alternative.

- *Save adopted scenario scores for implementation monitoring.* Once a scenario has been iterated to the point of adoption as an official plan, its indicator scores become quantitative "goal posts" against which incremental development proposals can be measured during plan implementation.

The second method of applying INDEX is an adjunct to traditional staff reports on current development actions. In this instance, the software produces a supplemental "score card" that tabulates and maps the effects a site-specific proposal would have on its surrounding vicinity if approved (similar to the sequence shown in figure 17). This type of modeling generally has the following steps:

1 *Acquire base case proposal in GIS form.* An increasing number of jurisdictions across the U.S. are encouraging electronic submittals of development proposals, often in CAD or GIS form.

2 *Score base case indicators and prepare staff report.* A staff planner uses INDEX to calculate the proposal's on-site and neighborhood vicinity scores, and prepare an indicator report accordingly.

3 *Present to decision maker and iterate to final action.* INDEX results are presented to appointed or elected officials with decision-making authority. Ideally, the deliberation process will allow the software to be used interactively among the participants in order to iterate to a final acceptable proposal, if needed.

The third application method is periodic reporting of community conditions and change over time (again see figure 17). Such PSS reporting is sometimes contained in annual progress reports or in periodic evaluation of local planning compliance with state land-use standards, such as that required in Oregon, Washington, and Florida. Periodic implementation monitoring can include the following steps:

1 *Retrieve benchmark indicator scores.* Indicator scores from previous benchmark years are used as the starting point.

2 *Incorporate changes in the built and natural environments.* The INDEX database is updated with approved or constructed changes in the built environment, and resulting changes in the natural environment.

3 *Update indicator scores.* The updated "existing condition" case is scored to establish new benchmarks for the reporting date.

4 *Produce change report.* INDEX describes the changes in its standard tabular, chart, and map forms.

ESTIMATION OF TRANSPORTATION IMPACTS FROM LAND-USE CHANGES

A unique feature of INDEX is its ability to provide sketch-level estimates of transportation impacts from land-use changes. Relationships between land use and transportation are increasingly recognized by communities as key forces in their growth and quality of life. There is emerging agreement that the land-use/transportation connection is significant and must be analyzed and accounted for to ensure that land-use and transportation plans can succeed (Moore 1994; Miller 1999). Consequently, one of the most common applications of INDEX has been integrated land-use/transportation planning. To facilitate such work, the software has been equipped with a set of elasticity factors that relate a neighborhood's built environment characteristics to the amount of vehicular travel generated in the neighborhood. These influential elements of urban form are known as the three Ds: density, diversity, and design, and they can be used to compute the percentage change in vehicle trips (VT) and vehicle miles traveled (VMT) resulting from different land-use plans and urban designs (Cervero and Kockelman 1997).

The elasticity methodology is based on recent research on the relationship between land-use and travel behavior (Cambridge 1994; Frank 1994; Dunphy 1996; Handy 1996; Rutherford 1996; Kockelman 1997; McNally 1997; Sun 1998; Hess 1999; and Buch, 1999). Taken as a group, these studies reveal how changes in land-use characteristics, such as residential density, relate to changes in travel generation, as measured by motorized trips and vehicle miles of travel. By synthesizing the results of these studies, it was possible to produce transferable formulae that predict proportional changes in travel relative to key land-use variables. The independent variables found in the research to most reliably predict changes to VT and VMT include:

Density = Percent change in [(Population + Employment) per Square Mile]

Diversity = Percent change in {1 − [ABS(b * population - employment) / (b * population + employment)]}

where:

b = regional employment / regional population

Design = Percent change in design index

Design index = 0.0195 * street network density + 1.18 * sidewalk completeness + 3.63 * route directness where:

street network density = length of street in miles/area of neighborhood in square miles

sidewalk completeness = length of sidewalk/length of public street frontage

route directness = average airline distance to the neighborhood center/average road distance to the neighborhood center

The resulting individual elasticities are relatively small, but meaningful. For the individual urban design factors, the VT elasticities range from -0.02 to -0.06. This implies that a 100 percent improvement in an area's density or diversity or design would result in a 2 to 6 percent reduction in VT generation per capita. A 100 percent change in all factors could result in roughly a 15 percent reduction in VT per capita. For VMT, individual density, diversity and design elasticities are less than about B0.05. A 100 percent increase in all three AD's can produce a 10 to 15 percent reduction in VMT per capita.

As a sketch-planning tool, the primary benefits of the three-D methodology are simplicity and efficiency, requiring considerably less data, time, and effort than conventional four-step transportation demand modeling. It should be stressed, however, that the three-D method is not intended to supplant standard four-step modeling, but rather precede it in situations where quick, sketch-level responses are needed.

INDEX APPLICATIONS

Since its introduction in 1994, more than 70 copies of INDEX have been licensed to organizations in 25states. Approximately half of these users are city and county planning departments; 25 percent are regional planning agencies; and the remaining 25 percent are divided among state and federal agencies, advocacy organizations, and academic institutions.

Experience to date shows the software is being used most frequently in urban and suburban rather than rural settings. The most common topical focus is integrated land-use/transportation planning, and the most frequently analyzed geographic unit is the neighborhood, followed by metropolitan regions. Examples are summarized below for a series of neighborhood-scale applications in Sacramento, California that have emphasized public participation; and a regional-scale application in Atlanta, Georgia that was prepared as a staff technical analysis.

SACRAMENTO, CALIFORNIA: A NEIGHBORHOOD EXAMPLE

In 1998, the Sacramento Metropolitan Air Quality Management District sponsored the development of Sacramento INDEX as a neighborhood design tool for encouraging multimodal travel. Creating neighborhoods where walking, biking, and transit are viable mode choices is seen as an important step toward achieving Sacramento's air quality improvement goals. A neighborhood-level version of INDEX was configured with 50 indicators to measure built environment and circulation features. Copies were widely distributed to stakeholder organizations. Within its first two years of availability, 20 users were trained and the following applications put underway:

- *Neighborhood redevelopment planning.* The City of Sacramento Planning Department is using the software to identify inner city redevelopment opportunities and work with affected property owners to refine alternative revitalization plans.

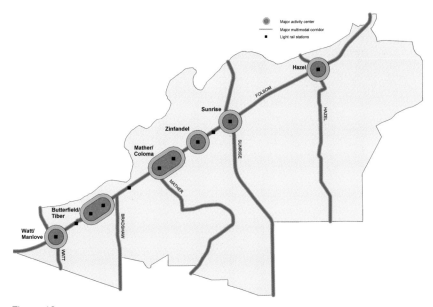

Figure 18

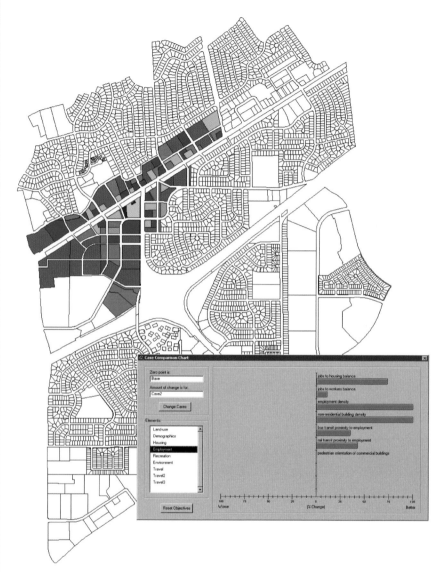

Figure 19

- *Business corridor reorientation.* The Sacramento County Planning Department is using the software in the suburban Rancho Cordova area to evaluate multimodal activity centers that will anchor the reorientation of a previously auto-oriented corridor, as shown in figure 18. An infill design formulated by the project's citizen advisory committee for the Mills-Coloma area is shown in figure 19 along with its indicator results. Approximately 25 citizens have used the software over five months to assess four neighborhoods, and to conceptualize and evaluate multiple development scenarios for each site.

- *Transit station area planning.* For its light rail system expansion, the Sacramento Regional Transit District is using INDEX to catalog existing conditions around new station areas and identify opportunities for joint real estate development. Fifteen station areas have been evaluated to date for the North, East, South, and West Lines of light rail.

- *Plan implementation monitoring.* For the 9,000-acre mixed-use North Natomas area, the City of Sacramento is using the software to measure the conformity of incremental development proposals with the adopted community plan.

- *Comparison of infill versus sprawl.* The Natural Resources Defense Council and Environmental Protection Agency used the software to measure the environmental performance of the Metro Square residential infill project in midtown Sacramento compared to conventional subdivisions in the region.

- *Air quality benefits of land-use changes.* The Metropolitan Air Quality Management District is using the software to estimate countywide air quality improvements from neighborhoods experiencing reduced auto use and air pollution as a result of increased density, use diversity, and pedestrian orientation.

- *Student research and field experience.* Environmental planning students at the University of California are applying the software as part of a federal research project on urban village benefits in Sacramento, and in the process gaining valuable practical experience using the tool to also assist city planning staff on some of the projects cited above.

To date, the software has been applied to 20 neighborhoods and similar sites in the greater Sacramento region. Benchmark indicator scores have been established in all of these locations, and stakeholders are regularly using the software to assess neighborhood proposals and decisions. Examples of specific accomplishments that have been attributed to INDEX include: prevention of a right-of-way closure that would have seriously diminished pedestrian and bicycle circulation efficiency near a neighborhood center; reconfiguration of a pedestrian network to shorten walk distances between employment sites and transit stops; reorientation of a commercial office proposal for better multimodal access to the project; and proposed construction of a pedestrian/bicycle overcrossing to link a major employment site with neighborhood amenities. Sacramento INDEX is in its second release and refinements continue to be made in cooperation with the local user group.

ATLANTA, GEORGIA: A REGIONAL EXAMPLE

In contrast to Sacramento, where neighborhood details are the focus, INDEX has served as a sketch pad for broad regional concepts in Atlanta, Georgia. The Georgia Regional Transportation Authority (GRTA) is responsible for transportation-related growth coordination in the Atlanta region through its oversight of transportation facilities development. As part of its long-range planning, the authority was interested in the potential travel impacts of a set of "smart growth" community centers and transit corridors throughout the greater Atlanta 13-county region. To accomplish this, INDEX was used to rapidly create and analyze a regional concept land-use plan that focused growth in existing communities and along new transit-oriented travel corridors. This plan, shown in figure 20, was conceptualized as follows:

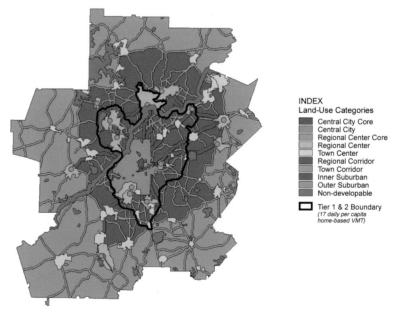

INDEX
Land-Use Categories

Central City Core
Central City
Regional Center Core
Regional Center
Town Center
Regional Corridor
Town Corridor
Inner Suburban
Outer Suburban
Non-developable

Tier 1 & 2 Boundary
(17 daily per capita home-based VMT)

Figure 20

- *Town-centered/transit-first growth.* The heart of the plan was a growth focus in existing communities and along established non-freeway travel corridors. These centers and corridors are already well served by existing infrastructure; they contain most of the region's employment and community services and amenities; and they are suitable for expanded transit service if supportive land-use policies are implemented within them. The town centers also have the established "sense of place" that is critical to successful urban development. The strategy was to concentrate growth in these areas through a combination of compact infill and redevelopment, with transit integrated into land-use design within the centers and serving as the primary link between centers.

- *Hierarchy of centers and corridors.* The plan was organized around a hierarchy of activity centers and corridors, beginning with the central core of Atlanta and descending through regional centers (15,000–60,000 persons) to town centers (2,000–15,000 persons). The central city was linked to fourteen regional centers by eighteen regional corridors aligned on noninterstate highways and light rail routes. In turn, the regional centers were linked to thirty-eight town centers by eighty town corridors aligned on arterials and major suburban roads. Table 3 presents land-use and transit service goals for the centers and corridors based on a national synthesis of selected regional planning frameworks. The remaining developable lands between the central city and regional centers were designated inner suburban, and all remaining developable land was designated as outer suburban.

- *Tiered centers and corridors.* The community centers and transit corridors were further divided into Tier 1 and 2 groups using a boundary aligned on the approximate mean VMT for the region's households. Tier 1 includes those centers and corridors where daily per capita home-based VMT averages 17 or less, and Tier 2 includes all other centers and corridors where VMT exceeds 17.

- *Protection of nondevelopable lands.* Parks, open space, and other sensitive environmental lands were set aside as nondevelopable.

TABLE 3. GOALS FOR ATLANTA COMMUNITY CENTERS AND TRANSIT CORRIDORS

	General Size (acres or width)	Residential Density (DU/ac)	Employment Density (Emp/ac)	Jobs to Housing Ratio	Population Density (residents + workers)		Transit Service Level
					Persons/ acre	Persons/ sq.mi.	
Community Centers							
Central City Core	13,000	60	200	2.0	200	100,000	# Commuter and light rail # Express bus # Local bus
Regional Center Cores	1,000	50	100	1.5	100	50,000	# Commuter and light rail # Express bus # Local bus
Regional Centers	5,000	30	80	1.0	75	40,000	# Light rail # Express bus # Local bus
Town Centers	500	25	40	0.9	50	25,000	# Express bus # Local bus
Transit Corridors							
Regional Corridors	1 mi.	30	30	1.0	35	20,000	# Commuter and light rail # Express bus # Local bus
Town Corridors	2 mi.	20	20	0.9	20	16,000	# Express bus # Local bus
Source: Criterion Planners/Engineers							

The next step in modeling the smart growth concept was an estimation of population that could be attracted to the community centers and transit corridors. INDEX distributed an assumed 25 percent of the region's 1998–2010 population growth, or 130,000 persons, among the community centers and transit corridors. Two-thirds of this group, or 87,000 persons, were allocated to Tier 1 centers and corridors.

TABLE 4. LAND-USE CHANGE: SMART GROWTH VS. TREND

Community Centers and Transit Corridors	Density (a)		Diversity (b)		Design (c)	
	Trend	Smart Growth	Trend	Smart Growth	Trend	Smart Growth
Tier 1						
Central City Core	69	100	0.20	1.00	21	30
Central City	11	38	0.95	1.00	12	30
Regional Center Cores	11	50	0.79	1.00	14	30
Regional Centers	6	38	0.91	1.00	9	30
Town Centers	4	25	0.92	1.00	8	30
Regional Corridors	7	18	0.75	1.00	8	30
Town Corridors	3	10	0.98	1.00	5	30
Tier 2						
Regional Center Cores	11	50	0.79	1.00	14	30
Regional Centers	6	38	0.91	1.00	9	30
Town Centers	4	25	0.92	1.00	8	30
Regional Corridors	7	18	0.75	1.00	8	30
Town Corridors	3	10	0.98	1.00	5	30

(a) Population and employment / acre
(b) Percent of avg. regional jobs / workers ratio
(c) Miles of street centerline / square mile

The smart-growth results are shown in tables 4 through 6. Table 4 compares land-use characteristics (density, diversity, design) between the current trend and the smart-growth scenario. Density, measured in residents and employees per acre, was substantially increased in all areas consistent with the region's long-range goals. On average, density was increased 312 percent. Diversity, measured as an area's mix of jobs and housed workers relative to the regional average mix, has been modestly increased in most areas, except for a major increase in housing in the central city core. The average diversity increase, across all areas, was 15 percent. Design, expressed in pedestrian and transit terms of street network density, has been substantially increased in all areas. On average, street network density was increased 249 percent. It is important to note that these increases are not for the entire land area of the centers and corridors, but rather represent values for the growth increment of individual infill and redevelopment projects.

TABLE 5. TRAVEL AND EMISSION CHANGES FROM SMART GROWTH IN 2010
(DAILY PER CAPITA)

Community Centers & Transit Corridors	VMT			VT			Nox (lbs)		
	Trend (a)	Smart Growth (b)	% Change	Trend (a)	Smart Growth (b)	% Change	Trend (a)	Smart Growth (b)	% Change
Tier 1									
Central City Core	15	12	-22	1.5	1.1	-24	0.05	0.04	-22
Central City	20	18	-10	2.0	1.8	-12	0.07	0.06	-10
Regional Center Cores	26	22	-15	2.6	2.2	-17	0.09	0.07	-15
Regional Centers	27	21	-20	2.7	2.0	-24	0.09	0.07	-20
Town Centers	28	23	-19	2.8	2.2	-23	0.09	0.07	-19
Regional Corridors	27	25	-8	2.7	2.5	-9	0.09	0.08	-8
Town Corridors	29	26	-11	2.9	2.5	-12	0.10	0.09	-11
Tier 2									
Regional Center Cores	32	27	-15	3.2	2.6	-17	0.11	0.09	-15
Regional Centers	35	28	-20	3.5	2.6	-24	0.12	0.09	-20
Town Centers	39	32	-19	3.9	3.0	-23	0.13	0.10	-19
Regional Corridors	37	34	-8	3.7	3.4	-9	0.12	0.11	-8
Town Corridors	40	36	-11	4.0	3.5	-12	0.13	0.12	-11

(a) Derived from TRANPLAN
(b) INDEX "3-D" estimate

Table 5 presents daily travel and emission changes for a typical resident living in such a infill or redevelopment project, in comparison to that resident's travel and emissions at trend levels in 2010. All of the community centers and transit corridors, in both tiers, produce notable reductions in travel and emissions when compared to trend estimates. These are totaled in table 6 for the entire 130,000-person market segment assumed for smart growth infill and redevelopment projects. On average, the smart growth scenario produces an approximate 15 percent reduction in per capita VMT for the targeted population segment.

TABLE 6. TOTAL TRAVEL AND EMISSION SAVINGS
FROM SMART GROWTH IN 2010

Community Centers and Transit Corridors	Savings for 130,000 Smart Growth Residents	
	Daily VMT (thousands)	Daily NOx (lbs)
Tier 1		
Central City Core	60	197
Central City	33	109
Regional Center Cores	57	187
Regional Centers	72	237
Town Centers	54	178
Regional Corridors	8	61
Town Corridors	8	61
Subtotal	311	1,030
Tier 2		
Regional Center Cores	60	200
Regional Centers	79	260
Town Centers	60	198
Regional Corridors	20	65
Town Corridors	17	56
Subtotal	236	779
TOTAL	547	1,809

The INDEX results showed considerably larger per capita travel and emission savings than previous regional studies because the former used much larger increases in density and multimodal design factors. Whereas previous scenarios had 22 percent and 25 percent increases in density and design, respectively, the INDEX smart growth cases had 312 percent and 249 percent increases, respectively. Land use clearly does matter when encouraging multimodal travel behavior, and if properly focused at the strongest locations, it can make a major difference in a region's livability.

ACKNOWLEDGMENTS

The author gratefully acknowledges the significant contributions of Alan Cowan, Nick Seigal, Eric Main, and Karen Conner, all with Criterion Planners/Engineers. The three-D method of estimating land-use/transportation change was developed jointly by Criterion Planners/Engineers and Fehr & Peers Associates.

REFERENCES

Al–Kodmany, Kheir. 2000. Extending Geographic Information Systems to Meet Neighborhood Planning Needs. *URISA Journal*, Volume 12, No. 3.

Allen, Eliot. 1999. Measuring the Environmental Footprint of New Urbanism. *New Urban News*, Volume 4, No. 3.

———. 2000. Environmental Characteristics of Smart Growth Neighborhoods. National Resources Defense Council, Washington, DC.

Batty, Michael, and Paul Denshan. 1996. Decision Support, GIS, and Urban Planning. Center for Advanced Spatial Analysis, University College, London.

Buch, M., and M. Hackman. 1999. The Link Between Land Use and Transit: Recent Experience in Dallas. Paper presented at the 78th Annual Meeting, Transportation Research Board, Washington, D.C.

Burchell, Robert, et.al. 1994. Development Impact Assessment Handbook, Urban Land Institute, Washington, D.C.

Cambridge Systematics, Inc. 1994. The Effects of Land Use and Travel Demand. In *Management Strategies on Commuting Behavior*. Technology Sharing Program. Washington, D.C.: Department of Transportation: (3)1–25.

Cervero, R. and K. Kockelman. 1997. Travel Demand and the 3Ds: Density, Diversity, and Design. *Transportation Research D*, Vol. 2: 199–219.

Craig, W., and S. Elwood. 1998. How and Why Community Groups Use Maps and Geographic Information. *Cartography and Geographic Information Systems*, Volume 25, No. 2.

DeChiara, Joseph. 1975. Urban Planning and Design Criteria. New York: Van Nostrand Reinhold.

de la Barra, Tomas. 1989. *Integrated Land-Use and Transport Modeling*, Cambridge, UK: Cambridge University Press.

Dunphy, R. T., and K. Fisher. 1996. Transportation, Congestion, and Density: New Insights. *Transportation Research Record*, 1552:89–96.

Elwood, S., and H. Leitner. 1998. GIS and Community-Based Planning, *Cartography and Geographic Information Systems*, Volume 25, No. 2.

Frank, L. D., and G. Pivo. 1994. Relationships Between Land Use and Travel Behavior in the Puget Sound Region. Washington State Department of Transportation, Seattle: 9–37.

Handy, S. 1996. Urban Form and Pedestrian Choices: Study of Austin Neighborhoods. *Transportation Research Record*, 1552:135–44.

Hess, P. M. et al. 1999. Neighborhood Site Design and Pedestrian Travel. Paper presented at the Annual Meeting of the Association of Collegiate Schools of Planning, American Planning Association, Chicago.

Kockelman, K. M. 1997. Travel Behavior as a Function of Accessibility, Land Use Mixing, and Land Use Balance: Evidence from the San Francisco Bay Area. Paper presented at the 76th Annual Meeting, Transportation Research Board, Washington, D.C.

Lynch, Kevin. 1984. *Site Planning*. Cambridge, MA: MIT Press.

McHarg, Ian. 1969. *Design With Nature*. New York: Doubleday.

McNally, M. G. and A. Kulkarni. 1997. An Assessment of the Land Use–Transportation System and Travel Behavior. Paper presented at the 76th Annual Meeting, Transportation Research Board, Washington, D.C.

Miller, Eric et al. 1999. Integrated Urban Models for Simulation of Transit and Land-Use Policies. Report 48, Transportation Research Board, Washington, D.C.

Moore, Terry. 1994. The Transportation/Land-Use Connection, American Planning Association, Chicago, IL.

Moudon, Anne. 2000. Proof of Goodness: A Substantive Bases for New Urbanism. *PLACES*, Volume 13, No. 2, New York.

Rutherford, G. S., E. McCormack, and M. Wilkinson. 1996. Travel Impacts of Urban Form: Implications From an Analysis of Two Seattle Area Travel Diaries. TMIP Conference on Urban Design, Telecommuting, and Travel Behavior, Federal Highway Administration, Washington, D.C.

Shiffer, M. 1999. Managing Public Discourse: Towards the Augmentation of GIS with Multimedia. *Geographical Information Systems*. New York: John Wiley & Sons.

Sun, X., C. G. Wilmot, and T. Kasturi. 1998. Household Travel, Household Characteristics, and Land Use: An Empirical Study from the 1994 Portland Travel Survey. Paper presented at the 77th Annual Meeting, Transportation Research Board, Washington, D.C.

Waddell, Paul. 1998. UrbanSim Reference Guide, University of Washington, Seattle, WA.

Wegner, Michael. 1994. Operational Urban Models: State-of-the-Art, *American Planning Association Journal*, Winter 1994.

The What If? Planning Support System

RICHARD E. KLOSTERMAN

UNIVERSITY OF AKRON

AKRON, OHIO

ABSTRACT

This paper describes *What if?*, a scenario-based, policy-oriented planning support system (PSS) that uses increasingly available geographic information system (GIS) data to support community-based processes of collaborative planning and collective decision making. It incorporates procedures for conducting land suitability analysis, projecting future land use demands, and allocating the projected demands to the most suitable locations. The system allows users to create alternative development scenarios and determine the likely impacts of alternate public policy choices on future land-use patterns and associated population and employment trends. It is easy to use, can be customized to the user's database and policy issues, and provides outputs in easy-to-understand maps and reports.

INTRODUCTION

The field of urban and regional planning is experiencing two fundamental changes that are having a profound impact on the use of computer-based models in planning practice and education. On the one hand, the dramatically increased availability of powerful, low-cost, and easy-to-use GIS software, and more extensive spatially referenced data, are making GIS an essential tool for planning tasks such as land use monitoring, code enforcement, and permit tracking. However, with this increased use has come an increased realization that GIS alone cannot serve all of the needs of planning (see, e.g., Couclelis 1991; Harris 1989; Harris and Batty 1993). This realization has renewed planners' interest in computer modeling and stimulated the development of planning support systems that combine GIS (and non-GIS) data, computer-based models, and advanced visualization techniques into integrated systems to support core planning functions such as plan preparation and evaluation (see, e.g., Finaly and Marples 1992; Holmberg 1994; Klosterman 1997).

On the other hand, planners are increasingly abandoning the attempt to "plan for" the public in favor of more collaborative efforts to "plan with" the public. These attempts take a variety of forms, such as strategic visioning conferences, design charettes, and other community-based collaborative planning and consensus building efforts (see, e.g., Godschalk et al. 1994; Lowry et al. 1997). These efforts attempt to involve private citizens and other stakeholders directly in the planning process to help identify and prioritize the public's needs and desires, explore alternative development scenarios, and establish benchmarks for evaluating ongoing development efforts. These carefully structured consensus building processes can help achieve the ideals of communicative rationality and traditional comprehensive land-use planning (Healey 1992; Innes 1992; Innes 1996).

What if? is an interactive GIS-based planning support system that responds directly to both of these trends. It uses the GIS data sets that communities have already developed to support community-based efforts to evaluate the likely implications of alternative public policy choices. It provides a single integrated package that allows planning tasks that now require weeks or even months to do to be completed quickly and easily. The package can be customized to a community's existing GIS data, concerns, and desires, and provides outputs in easy-to-understand maps and reports which can be used to support community-based collaborative planning efforts.[1]

Reflecting the movement from "planning for the public" to "planning with the public," *What if?* assumes that planning and policymaking should not be based on closed and unsupervised "objective" analysis of technical experts. Instead, it provides a set of computer-based tools which facilitate open and ongoing processes of community learning, debate, and compromise. By providing information, techniques, and evaluation criteria which can be used to support particular public policy perspectives and critique others, it supports explicitly political processes of "adversary" or "counter" modeling similar to Davidoff's (1965) advocacy planning model. By involving the public directly in the planning process, it constrains the discretion of professionals and political insiders, reduces the knowledge differential between professionals and laymen, and gives the public a sense of ownership in the plans and proposals that are developed.

Acknowledging the limitations of planners' knowledge, information, and resources, the model abandons the unrealistic goal of producing a single "exact" prediction of the future for the preparation of a range of alternative scenario-based forecasts which in turn reveal a range of potential futures. Recognizing that models are only useful in a policy context if they are understood by policy makers, *What if?*'s underlying structure, relationships, and assumptions are made as explicit and clear as possible.

Most importantly, as its name suggests, the model adopts the "what if" metaphor popularized by electronic spreadsheets by acknowledging that the model's results identify only *what* would happen *if* a scenario's underlying assumptions are correct. It does this by explicitly identifying alternative policy choices, allowing users to choose between these alternatives and determine their likely effects on the area being studied. Similarly, the model's underlying assumptions concerning the "state of nature" are explicitly stated and easily modified, allowing users to determine the effect that these assumptions have on the model results (Klosterman 1987: 444–448).

This remainder of the paper is divided into four sections. The next section provides an overview of the modeling process and the application areas for which *What if?* is most appropriate. The following section describes the three analysis steps that are incorporated in the model, the procedures for conducting each step, and the associated model outputs. The third section identifies the information and procedures that are required to adapt the system for use in a particular study area. The paper concludes with an evaluation of the model's strengths and weaknesses.

SYSTEM OVERVIEW

As its name suggests, *What if?* does not attempt to predict future conditions exactly. Instead, it is an explicitly policy-oriented planning tool that can be used to determine *what* would happen *if* clearly defined policy choices are made and assumptions concerning the future prove to be correct. Policy choices that can be considered in the model include the staged expansion of public infrastructure, the implementation of alternative land use plans or zoning ordinances, and the establishment of farmland or open space protection programs.

Assumptions for the future that can be considered in the model include future population and employment trends, assumed household characteristics, and anticipated development densities.

What if? is a "bottom-up" model which begins with homogeneous land units or uniform analysis zones (UAZs), applies alternative policy choices to these units, allocates projected land-use demands to them, and then derives regional conditions (e.g., population and employment growth trends) by aggregating the values for these land units.[2] UAZs are GIS-generated polygons which are homogeneous in all respects considered in the model. Thus, for instance, all points within a UAZ have the same slope, are located in the same municipality, have the same zoning designation, are within the same distance of an existing or proposed highway, and so on.

UAZs are created by using GIS overlay functions to combine all of the relevant layers of information on natural and man-made features to define the UAZs that are used in a study area. The map layers can contain information on natural conditions (e.g., slopes, soils, and scenic vistas), existing and proposed infrastructure (e.g., the proximity to intersections or major roads and the availability of sewer and water service), and land-use controls such as zoning districts and planned land uses. The UAZs contain information that was provided in each of the constituent layers (i.e., each UAZ contains information on the slope, the availability of sewer and water service, planned land use, and so on for all points lying inside of it).

As will be described in detail below, *What if?* projects future land-use patterns by balancing the supply of, and demand for, land suitable for different uses at different locations. Alternative visions for an area's future can be explored by defining alternative suitability, growth, and allocation scenarios. For example, a "Trend" scenario could determine the effects of continuing current development policies. An "Environmental Protection" scenario might consider the impact of policies that severely limit growth in scenic areas and on land that is most suitable for agricultural uses. A "Build out" scenario would reveal the implications of allowing growth to continue until it reached permitted density levels for all developable parcels in the study area. The assumptions underlying these and other scenarios can be easily modified to incorporate the full range of alternative visions for an area's future.

The results generated by considering these alternative scenarios provide concrete and understandable expressions of the likely results of a scenario's underlying policy choices and assumptions. For instance, the model might demonstrate that there is insufficient land simultaneously to accommodate high growth, low residential densities, and strict agricultural protection policies, forcing the community to choose between highly desirable, but inconsistent, policy goals.

What if? is most appropriate for areas that are experiencing, or anticipating, rapid urbanization and the associated problems of traffic congestion, inadequate public infrastructure, and the loss of agricultural and open land. Areas that are currently undeveloped and will remain so in the future have few impacts and policy options to consider. Currently developed areas face complex issues of redevelopment and reuse that are extremely difficult to capture in a computer model. Areas on the urban fringe experiencing rapid and uncontrolled urbanization and industrialization face difficult and complex issues of managing growth and maintaining a sound fiscal base. As a result, *What if?* is particularly useful in promoting public dialogue and collective decision making in these rapidly changing areas.

What if? was developed with Microsoft's Visual Basic and ESRI's MapObjects software. It incorporates many of the design concepts in the first California Urban Futures (CUF) model (Landis 1994; Landis 1995) and similar models such as the San Diego Association of Governments Sophisticated Allocation Process (SOAP) model (San Diego Association of Governments 1994). However, it is unique in providing a portable system which can be adapted to any community's GIS data and policy issues.

MODELING PROCEDURES

What if? provides three major components—Suitability, Growth, and Allocation—which include the three aspects of the land-use planning and development process. The first component, Suitability, considers the supply of land (i.e., the characteristics and location of land that is available for accommodating future land use demand). The second component, Growth, considers the demand for land (i.e., the amount of land that will be required to accommodate future population and business growth). The final component, Allocation, jointly considers supply and demand by allocating the projected demand (as determined by the Allocation component) to the most suitable locations (as determined by the Suitability component) to project future land-use patterns. These three aspects of the modeling process are described briefly below.

ANALYZING THE SUPPLY OF LAND

The first stage in the *What if?* analysis process, determining land-use suitability, incorporates standard "weighting and rating" procedures (McHarg 1969; Hopkins 1977) into a quick and easy computer-based process. The suitability analysis process begins by modifying a previously defined suitability scenario or by creating a new one. The user is then presented with the Suitability Scenario Assumptions form shown in figure 1. As its name suggests, this form is used to specify the assumptions which underlie a particular suitability scenario. The label in the upper left corner of the form identifies the scenario for which a set of suitability assumptions is to be specified. The drop-down list box in the upper right corner allows the user to select the land use for which a set of particular suitability assumptions is to be specified. Thus, for example, in figure 1 the user is specifying the assumptions for the Regional Office land use for the Farm Preservation suitability scenario.

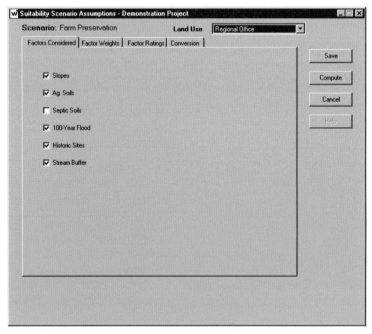

Figure 1. Specifying Suitability Scenario Assumptions.

As shown in figure 1, the Suitability Assumptions Screen contains four tabbed sheets. These sheets correspond to the four steps of the suitability analysis process: (1) identifying the suitability factors, (2) specifying the suitability factor weights, (3) specifying the suitability factor ratings, and (4) specifying the permissible land-use conversions. These four steps are described briefly below.

Identifying Suitability Factors

The first sheet, labeled "Factors Considered" and shown in figure 1, contains a series of check boxes that are used to specify the factors which the user feels should be considered in determining the suitability of different locations for a particular land use. Thus, for example, in figure 1 the user has specified that all of the suitability factors, except for Septic Soils, should be considered in determining the most suitable locations for low-density residential development. The suitability factors included on the list are determined by the available data for the study area and can include the full range of natural features (e.g., slopes, soils, and hazardous areas). Suitability factors must be identified for each land use considered in the study. Different factors may be selected for different land uses; for instance, good septic soils may be assumed to be important for locating residential land uses but not important for locating retail and office uses.

Specifying Factor Weights

The second sheet, labeled "Factor Weights," contains a series of text boxes that are used to specify the suitability factor weights (i.e., the numerical scores indicating the relative importance of different factors for determining the relative suitability of different locations for a particular land use). Thus, for example, the Slope factor could be given a factor weight of 2 and the Septic Soils factor could be given a factor weight of 1 to indicate that slope is considered to be twice as important as septic soils in determining a site's suitability for a particular land use. Factor weights are assigned on a three-point scale from 1 (low) to 3 (high).

Specifying Factor Ratings

The third sheet, labeled "Factor Ratings," contains a series of text boxes that are used to specify ratings for the different types within a particular suitability factor (e.g., the different slope types: <5%, 5%–10%, and so on). "Factor ratings" are numerical values which indicate the relative suitability of locations with a particular factor type for locating a specified land use (e.g., the suitability of locations with different slopes for locating low-residential development). The factor types are rated on an six-point scale from 5 (High) to 1 (Low) and 0 (Excluded). The "Excluded" category identifies areas from which development is to be excluded, regardless of its suitability with respect to other factors. Thus, for example, the user might specify that residential development should be excluded from all locations with slopes that exceed 20 percent.

Specifying Land Use Conversions

The fourth suitability assumption sheet, labeled "Conversion," contains a series of check boxes that are used to specify land uses that may be converted from their current use (e.g., agriculture) to another use (e.g., low-density residential) as a result of the projection process. If no land uses are identified as conversion candidates, only currently undeveloped land will be available for satisfying the projected land-use demands.

Suitability factors, factor scores, factor weights, and permitted land-use conversions must be specified for all of the land uses considered in the analysis. After providing this information, the user can click on the "Compute" button on the Suitability Scenario Assumptions form shown in figure 1. The model then computes the factor scores for each UAZ by multiplying the user-specified factor weights by the corresponding user-defined factor rating and summing these values. The resulting suitability scores indicate the relative suitability of each UAZ for each land use when all of the suitability factors have been considered.

The model then generates a series of maps showing the relative suitability of different locations for each land use, as shown in figure 2. The system also generates two reports that can be read on the screen or sent to a printer. The first report identifies the number of acres within each suitability class for all land uses. The second report lists the assumptions that underlie a specified suitability scenario (i.e., the factors which were considered in the analysis, the user-specified factor weights and rates, and the permissible land-use conversions).

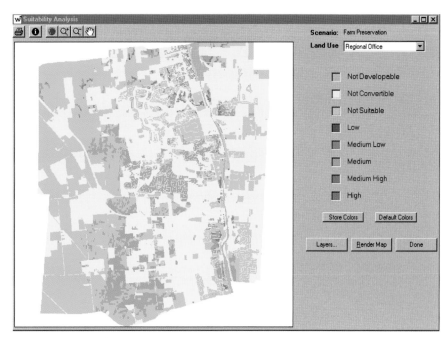

Figure 2. Suitability Scenario Map

PROJECTING LAND-USE DEMANDS

What if? considers the demand for land by converting the five main categories of land-use demand—residential, industrial, commercial, preservation, and locally oriented uses—into the equivalent future land-use demands. The demands are computed for three projection periods and for buildout, allowing the system to incorporate a staged development process in which future development patterns are based on the previously existing development patterns and anticipated infrastructure improvements.

The process of projecting land-use demands begins by selecting a growth scenario to create, view, or revise. The user is then presented with the Growth Assumptions form shown in figure 3. The form has five subsidiary sheets that are used to specify the assumptions which define the demand for different types of land use. The procedures for specifying these assumptions and the growth analysis outputs are described briefly below.

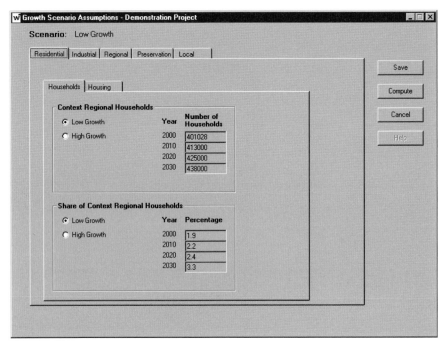

Figure 3. Specifying Residential Demand Assumptions.

Computing Residential Demand

As shown in figure 3, the Residential sheet contains two tabbed sheets. The first sheet allows the user to select up to five independently prepared projections for the total number of households in the context region (e.g., county) and the study area's share of the region's households. These two values are multiplied to compute the projected number of households in the study area in each projection period.

The second sheet is used to specify the assumptions about new residential units, including: (1) the breakdown by housing type for new residential construction; (2) the housing density for each housing type; (3) the average household size for each housing type; (4) the residential vacancy rates; and (5) the proportion of existing housing units that will be lost to demolition, fire, and so on during each projection period. The model uses the values specified on the two residential sheets to compute the projected demand for residential land in each projection period.

Computing Regional Business Demand

The next two sheets, labeled "Industrial" and "Regional," are used to specify the assumptions that determine the projected demand for regionally oriented land uses. As shown in figure 4, the Industrial sheet allows the user to select between previously developed projections for the total regional employment in each projection year. It also allows the user to specify: (1) the average square footage of floor space per employee, (2) the industrial floor area ratio (FAR), and (3) the vacancy rate for each industrial land use. The Regional sheet provides similar options for up to five different types of regional commercial development (e.g., regional retail, office, and mixed-use areas). These values specified on these two sheets are used to compute the projected demand for industrial and commercial land uses in each projection year.

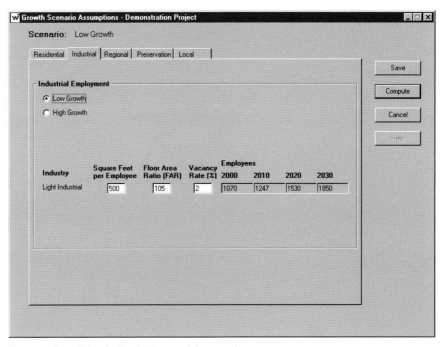

Figure 4. Specifying Industrial Demand Assumptions.

Computing Preservation Demand

The Preservation sheet allows the user to specify the amount of land that should be preserved for environmentally oriented uses such as agriculture, forestry, and open space/environmental protection. These values are treated as land-use demands along with the other land-use demands.

Computing Local Demands

The Local sheet allows the user to specify the quantity of land that will be required per thousand new community residents to satisfy locally oriented land uses whose location and size are dependent on the local (e.g., municipal) population. These uses include local parks and recreational areas, local retail (e.g., strip malls), and public and semipublic uses. The specified land-use standards for each local land use are applied to the projected population in each political jurisdiction to compute the amount of land in each jurisdiction which must be devoted to each use.

After providing all of the required information on the Growth Scenario Assumptions form, the user can click on the "Compute" button shown in figures 3 and 4 to calculate the projected demand in each projection year for each land-use type. The system generates a report which identifies the projected demand for each land use in each projection year and a report listing the assumed values that were used to compute these demands.

ALLOCATING PROJECTED LAND-USE DEMANDS

What if? projects future land-use patterns by allocating the projected land-use demands derived as specified by the assumptions of a growth scenario to different locations on the basis of their relative suitability as defined by the assumptions of a user-selected suitability scenario. For instance, the demand for low-density residential land is assigned first to the most suitable sites, then to the second most suitable sites, and so on until all of the projected residential demand in a projection year has been satisfied. If desired, the growth allocation can be controlled by user-selected land-use controls (land-use plans and zoning restrictions) and infrastructure plans. The user is notified if not enough land is available to satisfy the projected demand. If this occurs, the user must modify the suitability, growth, or allocation scenario assumptions (e.g., relax the land suitability requirements, allow more land uses to be converted to other uses, or increase development densities) to make them consistent.

The growth allocation process begins by selecting the suitability and growth scenarios that will be used for a given allocation scenario. The user is then presented with the Allocation Assumptions form shown in figure 5. The form contains five tabbed sheets which are used to specify the assumptions that underlie a growth allocation scenario, as described briefly below.

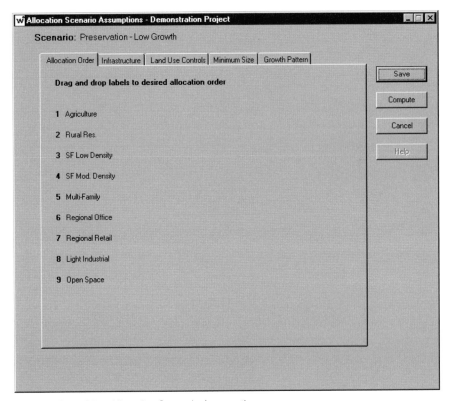

Figure 5. Specifying Allocation Scenario Assumptions.

The first sheet, labeled "Allocation Priority," is used to specify the order in which projected land-use demands are to be allocated in each projection year (i.e., the land-use demand to be satisfied first, the demand to be satisfied second, and so on). The allocation priority list can be revised by selecting a land-use label and dragging it to its preferred location in the list. Thus, for example, in figure 5, the user has specified that the Agriculture demand should be satisfied first; the Rural Residential demand should be satisfied second; and so on.

Infrastructure Sheet

The Infrastructure sheet contains two tabs. The "Infrastructure Plans" sheet is used to select previously defined infrastructure plans that will be used to guide the allocation process. If no infrastructure plans are selected, all of the land uses will be located in their most suitable locations, regardless of the availability of sewer and water service or their proximity to major roads or expressway interchanges.

The Infrastructure Required sheet is used to specify the assumed relationship between infrastructure provision (or proximity) and land-use development patterns. The first option, "Not Affected," can be used for land uses such as those whose location is assumed to not be affected by the availability of (or proximity to) a given type of infrastructure. Thus, for instance, one might assume that the location of large-lot residential units is not affected by the availability of sewers because these units could be served by septic systems. In these cases, the projected land-use demands will be located in the most desirable locations, regardless of the presence of this infrastructure.

The second option, "Required," can be used to identify land uses which are assumed to require (or be near to) a particular type of infrastructure. Thus, for example, one could assume that Neighborhood Retail uses require water and sewer service and Regional Retail uses must be located near expressway interchanges. In these cases, the specified land-use demand will only be allocated to areas that are served by (or near to) the specified infrastructure.

The third option, "Excluded," is used to identify land uses that are assumed to be excluded from areas that are served by (or near to) a particular type of infrastructure. Thus, for example, one could assume that agriculture would be excluded from areas that are served by water and sewer or are near expressway interchanges because these locations will be too expensive for agricultural uses. In these cases, future land-use demands will be excluded from areas that are served by, or near to, a particular type of infrastructure.

Land-use Control Sheet

The Land-use Control sheet allows the user to select a previously defined land-use plan or zoning ordinance that will be assumed to control the location of future growth. If a land-use control ordinance or plan is selected, projected land-use demands will only be allocated to areas in which the land use is permitted or planned. If no land-use control plan is selected, land-use demands will be located to their most suitable location, without any restrictions.

Minimum Size Sheet

The Minimum Size sheet is used to specify the minimum UAZ size into which a given land use can be allocated. Thus, for example, it might be assumed that regional commercial land uses cannot be located in areas that are smaller than five acres.

Growth Pattern Sheet

The final Growth Pattern sheet may be used to specify the general pattern in which future development will take place. Thus, for instance, the user may specify that growth will occur in a concentric ring pattern from a neighboring central city or radially along major transportation corridors.

When the user clicks on the "Compute" button the system projects future land-use patterns by allocating the projected land-use demands to the most suitable sites, subject to any land-use controls or infra-structure plans selected by the user. The resulting land-use projections for each projection year can then be viewed in map or report form.

For example, figure 6 shows the projected land-use patterns for a "Farm Preservation" scenario in which growth is prohibited from areas that have prime agricultural soils. Figure 7 shows the projected land -use patterns for a "No Farm Preservation" scenario that incor-porates the same land-use demand assumptions but does not impose any restrictions on where growth can occur. These two examples illustrate the power of tools such as *What if?* for graphically portray-ing the implications of alternative policy choices. The system also generates reports which record the projected land-use quantities for the study area and each political subdivision in each projection year and the assumptions that underlie a scenario.

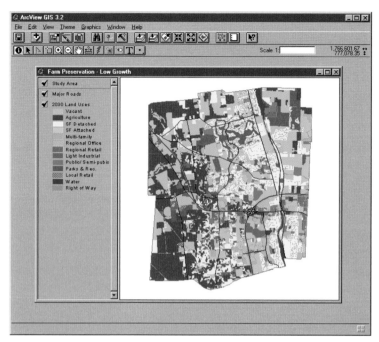

Figure 6. Farm Preservation Scenario Map for 2030.

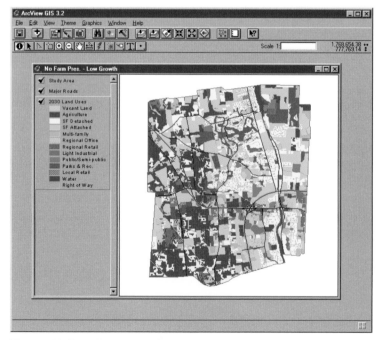

Figure 7. No Farm Preservation Scenario Map for 2030.

While incorporating many of the concepts of other GIS-based models such as the first California Urban Futures model (Landis 1994; Landis 1995), *What if?* is unique in its ability to be adapted to the GIS data sets and policy concerns for one or more study areas. These capabilities are provided by the software's GIS-created UAZ files, Setup, and Manager programs which are described briefly below.

CREATING UAZ FILES

Before using *What if?*, standard GIS overlay functions must be used to create the UAZs for a particular study area. The UAZs are created by combining GIS layers containing information on, among other things, natural conditions, existing and proposed infrastructure, land-use controls, and the boundaries for political and administrative subdivisions of the study area. The GIS user then combines these layers into a single layer made up of UAZs containing information from each of the constituent layers. That is, each UAZ contains information on the natural features, available infrastructure, planned land use, and so on for all points lying inside of it. The UAZs are stored in ESRI's shapefile format and incorporated directly into the *What if?* program.

The only GIS layer that is absolutely essential for using *What if?* is the existing land uses. A variety of additional layers can be added, depending on the available GIS data, the user's analysis and policy needs, and the requirements of any secondary applications that will utilize the *What if?* outputs. In most cases it is desirable to have at least three natural features layers for the suitability analysis, two or three land-use control and infrastructure layers, and some basic boundary display layers.

SETUP PROGRAM

The *What if?* Setup program creates the system files that customize the software for a particular collections of GIS (and non-GIS) data. It does this by allowing the user to define the land-use categories, suitability factors, and factor types that will be used in the analysis and the labels that appear on the suitability, growth, and allocation scenario assumption forms.

For example, the form shown in figure 8 can be used to specify labels for the suitability factors that will be used in a particular analysis.

Thus, six suitability factors will be used in this application. The first factor will be slopes; the second will be agricultural soils; and so on. Similar forms are used to define the land uses that will be used in the study and all of the labels that appear on the suitability, growth, and allocation forms. After entering all of the required data, the Setup program can be used to create customized scenario assumption forms containing the labels defined by the user. The user then can use these forms to create the suitability, growth, and allocation scenarios as described previously.

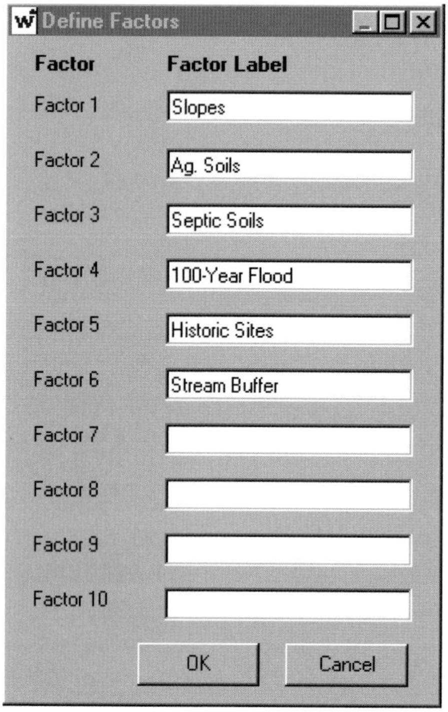

Figure 8. Specifying Labels for Suitability Factors.

MANAGER PROGRAM

The *What if?* Manager program can be used to revise or delete a set of scenario assumption forms once they have been created. It allows the user to modify the labels that appear on the scenario assumptions forms (to, for instance, correct any spelling errors), modify the names used to identify different land use categories, or change system-defined variables such as the household and employment projections.

EVALUATION *What if?* has many obvious strengths, many of which are equally obvious weaknesses. Its biggest advantage is that it is a fully operational model that can be adapted to the particular data sets and policy concerns in any area which satisfies the model's rather modest data requirements. These requirements include: (1) a required GIS layer containing current land uses; (2) optional layers describing natural features, administrative boundaries, and land-use and infrastructure plans; and (3) projected, or assumed, values for the region's projected population and employment, household and employment densities, and the like. These data requirements are particularly modest in comparison to those of other operational urban models such as DRAM/EMPAL (Putman 1983; Putman 1992), MEPLAN (Echenique et al. 1990), the California Urban Futures models (Landis 1994; Landis and Zhang 1998), and UrbanSim (Waddell 1998).

A second obvious advantage is the model's simple and intuitive modeling structure. The general concepts of balancing the supply of, and demand for, land by determining the relative suitability of different locations, projecting the various demands for land, and allocating the projected demands to the most suitable locations, can readily be understood by elected officials and the public. The detailed computations required to carry out these three stages are, of course, too complex for most users to understand fully. However, the model's underlying structure is much easier to understand than the other, much more complex urban models listed above.

What if? shares many of the advantages (and disadvantages) of the first California Urban Futures (CUF) model to which it is similar in many ways (Landis 1994: 400–402, 418–419; Landis 1995: 444). Like the CUF I model—and unlike other operational urban models—*What if?* is GIS-based. This allows the model to take advantage of the diversity of spatially referenced data available in a particular study area and to improve as more data becomes available. The use of spatially disaggregated GIS data also allows the model to project land-use demands to particular sites and not to spatial aggregates such as census tracts or traffic analysis zones. Again, like the CUF model, *What if?* is a policy oriented simulation model that simulates alternative development patterns as determined by local land development policies. Unlike traditional urban models, the critical variables that determine different model outcomes are local land development policies, not abstract "second hand" effects of these policies such as changes in travel times or accessibility.

What if?'s simple structure and minimal data requirements are directly associated with the model's most glaring weakness, its lack of a rigorous theoretical basis. The model does not include measures of spatial interaction which are widely recognized to be an important—if not the most important—determinant of long-term urban growth patterns and the key component of most urban models. Unlike the acknowledged "state of the art" in urban models (Wegener 1995:22), it does not rely on random utility or discrete choice theory to explain and predict the behavior of urban actors such as households, investors, and firms. It also does not represent the interlinked markets for land, housing, nonresidential uses, labor, and infrastructure or provide any procedures for "market clearing" and price adjustment in the face of changes in demand and supply. In addition, *What if?* does not explicitly model the behavior of actors such as households, businesses, and developers like "object-oriented" models such as UrbanSim (Waddell 1998).

Instead of incorporating any of these theoretically appealing, but complex, concepts, *What if?* has been designed to provide a plausible, intuitive, adaptable, and fully operational model of the urban development process. The behavior of urban markets and actors are represented implicitly in the assumption that land uses will be allocated to their most suitable location, as determined by a set of user-specified suitability assumptions. Similarly, the impact of alternative growth management policies is incorporated into the model as an assumption that development will only occur in places where it is permitted under a zoning ordinance or land-use plan. Neither assumption begins to capture the complexities of actual urban development processes. However, they do provide a readily understandable and plausible basis for considering the implications of alternative public policies. The overarching goal, after all, is not projecting the future exactly, but providing a meaningful foundation for community dialog and debate.

The ideal planning support system will provide an "intelligent digital toolbox" that helps users select the most appropriate software tools from a range of alternative analysis and forecasting models, applies these tools to data which have been accessed locally or via the Internet, and allows them to quickly view the implications of alternative policy choices in intuitive graphic, map, and interactive video/sound displays (Klosterman 1997:52). *What if?* is only one of a number of systems being developed to help achieve this ideal. However, it is unique in providing a readily available package that is easy to use and understand, fully customizable to a community's existing GIS data set, and incorporates the suitability, growth, and allocation portions of the planning process. As a result, it may become a useful component in a more comprehensive PSS which considers a wide range of issues related to land use, such as the fiscal, transportation, and environmental impacts of alternative growth scenarios.

NOTES

[1] *What if?* has been developed by Community Analysis and Planning Systems, Inc. The model is fully operational and available for both professional and academic uses. A fully functional demonstration version of the model is available at no cost. For further information, consult the *What if?* Web site, www.what-if-PSS.com, or contact the author.

[2] The term "uniform analysis zone" (UAZ) is used instead of Landis's (1994) comparable concept of "developable land unit" (DLU) because these spatial units may, or may not, be "developable," depending on a particular set of scenario assumptions.

REFERENCES

Couclelis H. 1991. Geographically Informed Planning: Requirements for Planning-relevant GIS. *Papers in Regional Science*, 70:9–20.

Davidoff P. 1965. Advocacy and Pluralism in Planning. *Journal of the American Institute of Planners*, 32:331–37.

Echenique M. H., A. D. Flowerdew, J. D. Hunt, T. R. Mayo, I. J. Skidmore, and D. C. Simmonds. 1990. The MEPLAN Models of Bilbao, Leeds, and Dortmund. *Transport Reviews*, 10:309–22.

Finaly P. N., and C. Marples. 1992. Strategic Group Decision Support Systems— A Guide for the Unwary. *Long Range Planning*, 25:98–107.

Godschalk D. R., D. Parham, D. Porter, W. R. Potapchuk, and S. Schulkraft, 1994, *Pulling Together: A Land Use and Development Consensus Manual.* (Program for Community Problem Solving, Washington, D.C.)

Harris B. 1989. Beyond Geographic Information Systems: Computers and the Planning Professional. *Journal of the American Planning Association*, 55:85–92.

Harris B., and M. Batty. 1993. Locational Models, Geographical Information, and Planning Support Systems. *Journal of Planning Education and Research*, 12:184–98.

Healey P. 1992. Planning through Debate: The Communicative Turn in Planning Theory. *Town Planning Review*, 63:143–62.

Holmberg S. C. 1994. Geoinformatics for Urban and Regional Planning. *Environment and Planning B: Planning and Design*, 21:5–19.

Hopkins L. D. 1977. Methods of Land Suitability Analysis. *Journal of the American Institute of Planners*, 43:386–400.

Innes J. E. 1992. Group Processes and the Social Construction of Growth Management: Florida, Vermont and New Jersey. *Journal of the American Planning Association*, 58:440–53.

———. 1996. Planning through Consensus Building: A New View of the Comprehensive Planning Ideal. *Journal of the American Planning Association*, 62:460–72.

Klosterman, R. E. 1987. Politics of Computer-aided Planning. *Town Planning Review*, 58:441–52.

———. 1997. Planning Support Systems: A New Perspective on Computer-aided Planning. *Journal of Planning Education and Research*, 17:45–54.

Landis, J. D. 1994. The California Urban Futures Model: A New Generation of Metropolitan Simulation Models. *Environment and Planning B: Planning and Design*, 21:399–420.

———. 1995. Imagining Land Use Futures: Applying the California Urban Futures Model. *Journal of the American Planning Association*, 61:438–57.

Landis J., and M. Zhang. 1998. The Second Generation of the California Urban Futures Model: Part I: Model Logic and Theory. *Environment and Planning B: Planning and Design*, 25:657–66.

Lowry K., P. Adler, and N. Milner. 1997. Participating the Public: Group Processes, Politics, and the Public. *Journal of Planning Education and Research*, 16:177–87.

McHarg I. 1969. *Design with Nature*. Garden City, New Jersey: Natural History Press.

Putman S. H. 1983. *Integrated Urban Models: Analysis of Transportation and Land Use*. London: Pion.

———. 1992. *Integrated Urban Models 2: New Research and Applications of Optimization and Dynamics*. London: Pion.

San Diego Association of Governments. 1994. *Technical Description. Series 8: Regional Growth Forecasts—Subregional Allocation*. San Diego, CA: San Diego Association of Governments.

Wegener M. 1995. Current and Future Land Use Models. In *Travel Model Improvement Program, Land Use Modeling Conference Proceedings*: 15-40. Washington, D.C., Travel Model Improvement Program.

Paper 11

CommunityViz: An Integrated Planning Support System

MICHAEL KWARTLER

ENVIRONMENTAL SIMULATION CENTER

NEW YORK, NEW YORK

ROBERT N. BERNARD

PRICEWATERHOUSECOOPERS

ITHACA, NEW YORK

ABSTRACT CommunityViz™ is an ArcView GIS-based decision support system for community planning and design applications. The software is unique in that it fully integrates the words, numbers, maps, and images that planners and designers traditionally use for planning purposes into one, real-time, multidimensional environment. This is achieved by enabling ArcView GIS to modify data on the fly, linking it to real-time photo-realistic 3-D visualizations, and adding the fourth dimension (time) through the use of agent-based predictive modeling. In doing so, all types of data become mutually accountable to each other and the impacts of alternative planning scenarios and designs can be evaluated on the fly. This article outlines the development and general structure of CommunityViz, each of its three components (Scenario Constructor™, TownBuilder 3D, and Policy Simulator™), and how the software could be used in a real-world planning context.

COMMUNITYVIZ: DECISION SUPPORT SOFTWARE

CommunityViz software is a set of planning and decision support tools that integrates 2-D mapping information, 3-D visualization, and policy simulation technologies that can be applied to the planning and design issues of specific communities. CommunityViz creates an interactive, 3-D, real-time environment in which citizens and professionals alike can come to clear understandings of plans for the community. Users can propose policies and suggest design alternatives. They can visualize immediately how these changes might affect their environment—physically, economically, and socially. This interactive process enables citizens, planners, designers, and public officials to make better informed decisions and facilitate the building of consensus when controversial or complicated proposals are negotiated. CommunityViz is unique in its integration of GIS, 2-D and 3-D visualization, and multiagent simulation modeling. Figure 1 shows CommunityViz in action.

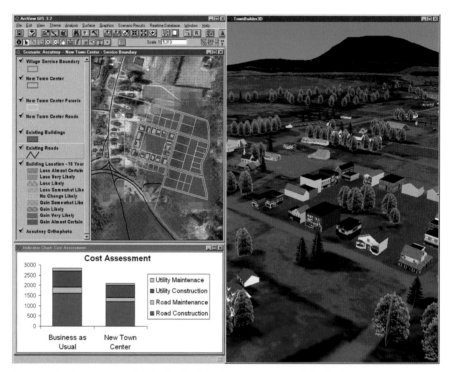

Figure 1. Typical CommunityViz. An illustration of the three modules that comprise CommunityViz, displaying a proposed policy in GIS and 3-D.

BACKGROUND

The Orton Family Foundation, a nonprofit organization based in Rutland, Vermont, contacted Coopers and Lybrand in 1996 about building computer software that would help satisfy the Foundation's mission to "help citizens of rural America define the future, shape the growth and preserve the heritage of their communities" (Orton Family Foundation, 2000). Rural areas throughout the country were slowly eroding, working landscapes were being transformed into subdivisions and "starter castles," while traditional towns and villages were being rendered obsolete as new forms of retailing emerged in the changing economy. In Vermont, a grassroots coalition consisting of government officials, planners, consultants, architects, preservationists, conservationists, and, most importantly, Vermont citizens themselves, formed to stop this erosion. Not coincidentally, it is citizen volunteers who do most of the local town planning in Vermont in the first place, without much—if any—formal training in land use planning, demography, or economics. In effect, these citizen planners are the embodiment of the Jeffersonian model of government run by an informed and engaged citizenry (Peterson 1975).

Vermont citizen planners were nevertheless at a disadvantage. Without the information and tools to (literally) envision what the future might look like, it would continue to be extremely difficult for them—no matter how committed—to grasp the inexorable land-use patterns and changes that might emerge from the simplest decisions or nonactions. These citizen planners needed new tools that would support and add new vitality to the Jeffersonian model of collaborative decision making. The planning tools required would assist citizens in learning about the potential resources in their communities, understanding the complex interrelationships between land use, the environment, and the economy, visualizing possible futures, and evaluating them against a set of policies and ordinances, as well as personal values.

THE DESIGN OF THE SYSTEM

CommunityViz represents the Orton Family Foundation's contribution to, and support and development of, work pioneered by the Environmental Simulation Center (ESC) and Coopers and Lybrand's Emergent Solutions Group (now PricewaterhouseCoopers Washington Consulting Practice, "PwC"). The Environmental Simulation Center and the Orton Family Foundation gathered together other partners to develop the software that eventually became CommunityViz. Coopers and Lybrand's experience in simulation modeling (Koselka 1997; Byrne 1998; Farrell 1998) dovetailed well with the Environmental Simulation Center's work with urban, suburban, and rural communities employing visualization and simulation in the analysis and design of plans, regulations, and policy scenarios (Bressi 1995; Dunlap 1992; Teicholz 1999). These entities were well-suited to help the Foundation realize its vision of building a software suite that would assist rural communities in planning their futures.

Under the direction of the ESC, and with the assistance of Green-Mountain Geographics (the project's GIS consultant), the remaining members of the development team were assembled. These included MultiGen-Paradigm, Inc. (MP) (now a part of Computer Associates), a leader in real time three-dimensional visualization (Chan and Zucker 1999; Delaney 2000) and Fore Site Consulting, Inc., a leader in the creation of GIS-based "spatial spreadsheets" and impact analysis tools (Faber 1997). After the team was assembled, the ESC assumed the role as project director and one of the lead designers of the Orton Family Foundation's CommunityViz planning and decision support system.

COMPONENTS

CommunityViz is a series of modules built on ESRI's ArcView GIS, which was chosen because of its widespread use by the planning agencies in small cities, towns, and rural communities. The system runs on a standalone PC, running Windows NT®, and works with ArcView GIS 3.2 and ArcView® Spatial Analyst 1.1. CommunityViz consists of three modules:

- Scenario Constructor
- TownBuilder 3D
- Policy Simulator

While each module was conceived to be able to function as a standalone extension to ArcView GIS, it was clear from the beginning that the whole was significantly more than the sum of the parts. The vision was always of a fully integrated decision support software that functioned interchangeably in two, three, and four dimensions. The software itself was conceived as a shell that had to be filled with data and information unique to the community and adaptable to the countless ways in which communities might use it. In the following sections, we describe the three major components of CommunityViz, and then explain how they work together as a complete planning support system.

**MODULE 1: SCENARIO
CONSTRUCTOR**

AN OVERVIEW

The Scenario Constructor mediates the integration of ArcView GIS and its extensions, and TownBuilder 3D and Policy Simulator. It permits nontechnical users to interactively create land use scenarios, and evaluate those scenarios against community objectives and constraints. It measures effects, evaluates performance, and performs sensitivity analyses. It is intended to assist small cities, towns, and rural communities in assessing the immediate consequences of alternative land-use proposals in an interactive and visual context. The Scenario Builder also serves as the spatial (two-dimensional GIS) component of CommunityViz. Figure 2 depicts the spatial data exchange and dependencies between Scenario Constructor and the other CommunityViz modules.

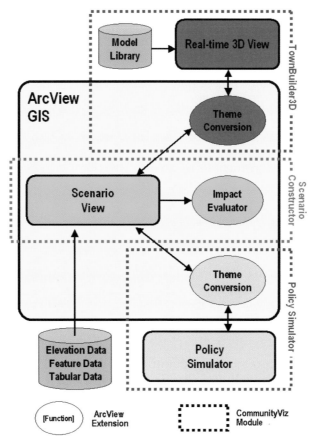

Figure 2. The Structure of CommunityViz. Three modules comprise the structure of CommunityViz. The Scenario Constructor moderates the interaction to ArcView GIS and interacts with both TownBuilder 3D and Policy Simulator.

Scenario Constructor manipulates data and tags contained in a specialized ArcView GIS document referred to as a "Scenario View." In the overall design of CommunityViz, the primary communication mechanism between program modules is spatial data. Scenario Views serve as the clearinghouse and translation center for this data. The Scenario View contains both vector and raster themes. A subset of these themes is designated as "Scenario Themes," which are vector shape themes that can be modified by the user. The Scenario Constructor ArcView GIS extension enables the user to interactively create copy, paste, drag, resize, and edit features or zones within any Scenario Theme.

The impact evaluation component of Scenario Constructor supports defining, evaluating, and tracking the performance of multiple planning alternatives. When other CommunityViz modules, such as the Policy Simulator, simulate alternative future scenarios, a new Scenario View is generated. This allows the impact analysis on any alternative generated within the overall software suite.

The Scenario Constructor evaluates impacts in real time by constantly checking user-defined indicators and benchmarks with the current state of a scenario, as it is edited. A user would set up an indicator by defining a formula that looks for and performs operations on data in the GIS. The results of these formulas are displayed as customizable indicator charts. Each time a feature in the Scenario is added, deleted, or moved, the GIS is updated, the formula is automatically rerun, and the indicator chart updated accordingly. In this manner, the user has constant feedback about actions. Scenario Constructor also allows the user to challenge or change assumptions (i.e., "variables," such as a property tax rate, cost of new construction, etc.) and perform sensitivity analyses at any point. Therefore, very sophisticated "what-if" scenarios can be quickly generated and evaluated on the fly.

FUNCTIONALITY

The Scenario Constructor's functionality also includes interactive exploration of present and proposed landscape scenarios, on-screen feature editing, and automatic calculation of attributes for each new or edited feature. The module dynamically tracks and displays indicator results as land-use proposals are modified, permitting the rapid comparison of alternative scenarios. Figure 3 presents three different indicators—open space, local employment, and school impacts—for a proposed development and as forecast by the Policy Simulator in ten years. The results are displayed in the form of easily understood bar charts. The user sees both the two-dimensional map and the indicators at the same time, permitting the visualization of planning choices on the landscape.

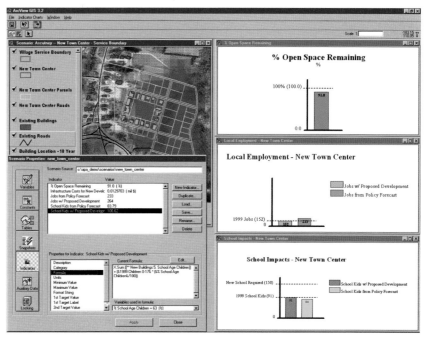

Figure 3. Scenario Constructor Indicators. Using the Scenario Constructor, users can generate easily understandable indicators, benchmarks, and thresholds that are used to evaluate the performance of a policy, plan, or design.

MODULE 2: TOWNBUILDER 3D

AN OVERVIEW

Displaying 2-D data in a 3-D virtual world has become increasingly important as a means to better understand the experience of "place" as information. Since we experience the world dynamically, 3-D data should be viewed in real time, where the user can explore policies, plans, and designs by moving through the world and receiving instantaneous visual feedback.

MultiGen-Paradigm (MP) designed TownBuilder 3D to explore the 3rd dimension, with real-time movement and object manipulation in a photo-realistic model. Using software originally designed for visual simulation for the gaming and defense industries, MP built on the 3-D/GIS concepts developed by the ESC (Dunlap 1995). Town-Builder 3D is capable of representing real places as photo-realistic models. The photorealistic models are created by mapping perspective corrected photographs of the building to a digital wireframe or massing model of the building. Of equal importance, it synchronizes the experiential world and the GIS world, allowing the user to seamlessly and simultaneously shift between the world of numbers and words and the 3-D experiential world; the user is thus able to move anywhere in the 3-D model's virtual world without restraint.

In addition, the landscape can be altered on the fly. Change in the 3-D world will change the GIS database for the scenario. Similarly, any change in the scenario database would be synchronously reflected in the 3-D world. Planning decisions will no longer be abstractions, but rather translatable into actions on objects in the virtual world.

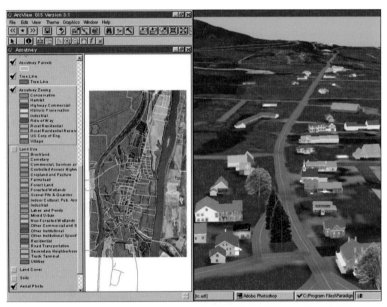

Figure 4. TownBuilder 3D View. TownBuilder 3D allows users both to seamlessly interact with and easily manipulate ArcView GIS and the 3-D view. The red avatar "view cone" locates the position of the viewer.

TownBuilder 3D has two interrelated elements. The first component builds a photo-realistic real-time database (the 3-D model), using the GIS database managed by Scenario Constructor and actual photos from the site. The second component is the runtime system that allows the user to interact with the 3-D real-time model, the GIS database, and Scenario Constructor simultaneously. By coupling TownBuilder 3D with ArcView GIS, the user can visualize proposed changes to a planning area in both 2-D and 3-D. As shown in figure 4, TownBuilder 3D is displayed side by side with Scenario Constructor on the monitor. The user can query both the ArcView GIS database and Scenario Constructor as well as locate herself on the ArcView GIS map with a "view cone" that synchronously moves as the viewer navigates through the 3-D model.

If the user manipulates the 3-D model, the Scenario Constructor module is notified, updates the GIS database, and provides the citizen planner with real-time feedback about consequences and constraints. For example, if an area were zoned for residential use, the system would notify the user that a rule-based constraint has been violated when the user tried to place a commercial building in the zone. The system can draw on the GIS knowledge that exists, enabling a user to receive a real-world visualization of proposed changes, as well as real-world constraints, via a user-determined GIS rule base.

FUNCTIONALITY

TownBuilder 3D has a broad range of automated functions, including creation of the terrain models, texture mapping of orthophotographs, and creation of 3-D models representing buildings, tree canopies, roads, rivers, fences, hedgerows, and other natural and man-made features. These photo-realistic 3-D models of buildings, roads, structures, and landscape elements are stored in and retrieved from the TownBuilder 3D Model Library. This library also stores physical information about each model, such as footprint square footage, total square footage, number of stories, tree types, etc. Cultural attributes, which are not inherent to physical objects, are assigned in the Scenario Constructor Module. For instance, a detached house could either be a residence, a residence with a shop, or professional offices. The power of TownBuilder 3D is its capacity to assemble scenarios using pre-built structures, roads, and landscape features, and its synchronicity with the other modules in CommunityViz.

AN OVERVIEW

The Policy Simulator module forecasts the probable land use, and demographic and economic changes in a community given alternative governmental and community choices. The Policy Simulator takes input from a user about a course of action (or nonaction) and returns a general prediction of what the future might bring. For example, the user might be interested in predicting what might happen if the town adopted an "Urban Service Boundary." The user would add this policy to the town's existing Policy Set, and the Policy Simulator would provide its prediction of demographic, economic, and land use change over a selected period as part of an ArcView GIS feature theme or table.

The Policy Simulator differs from many other small area demographic and economic forecasting tools in that it utilizes a technique in simulation called "adaptive agent-based modeling" (Holland 1995). The "agents" in this model are not what is now referred to as Web agents, pieces of software code that perform tasks for a computer user. Instead, we are dealing with an "economic agent," an autonomous decision-making entity that has individual goals and preferences, and which interacts with and creates—through its actions—the environment in which it resides. Traditionally, computer models of urban systems have dealt with aggregate data and have been characterized as "top down." National forecasts are allocated to the states, state forecasts to regions, etc. Using equations and statistical analysis, these aggregate projections for a region are then allocated to subregions using an urban allocation model. For example, if the region were a metropolitan area, the allocation model might project population into the future for census tracts within the area (see Putman and Chan or de la Barra in this volume). These allocation models forecast demographic, economic, and land use change for aggregate areas. This kind of modeling leaves little room for interaction. If users wanted to learn how they might change their fate, these models usually cannot provide options. Figure 5 displays some of the differences between an agent based simulation model in planning and a more traditional model (based on a table in Bernard 1999).

TRADITIONAL MODELS	AGENT MODELS
Units of analysis are groups	Units of analysis are individuals
Equation-based formulas	Adaptive agents
Allocative (top-down)	Aggregative (bottom-up)
Deterministic (one future)	Stochastic (multiple futures)
Few parameters	Many parameters
Do not give explanations	Explanatory power
Spatially coarse	Spatially specific
Environment given	Environment created
You can REACT to them	You can LEARN from them

Figure 5. Traditional and Agent-Based Simulation Modeling. Traditional predictive modeling and adaptive agent-based modeling are different in several ways.

In agent-based models, however, the units of analysis (i.e., those units being modeled directly) are the specific individuals or households living in the environment. These agents are the people who live and work in the community being simulated, including residents, business owners, and employers. Policy Simulator models the specific behaviors and interactions of these individual households and persons (e.g., where Mr. Jones shops, where Mrs. Smith works) in the study area. Agents are programmed to make decisions regarding their life autonomously, based upon their own individual characteristics. Each agent has different motivations and values.

Policy Simulator is a stochastic simulation model. The decisions that the agents make are not based on a deterministic model structure. Instead, each possible alternative of a particular decision is weighted in a probability distribution, with a random number generator used to select one of the alternatives in the decision set. There is considerable variability in the behavior of agents from one simulation to the next, even if the agents are in the same perceived situation. This kind of stochastic modeling can lead to situations wherein one small change in one agent's behavior can lead to very large changes in the resulting system. For instance, in one simulation run an agent may decide to purchase a tract of land, while in another simulation run the agent may decide not to purchase the land, even if the exact same choices in exactly the same circumstances confronted the agent. Such a small decision may lead to big changes in the short- and long-term futures of the two simulations. This type of stochastic, agent-based simulation modeling is a main experimental method in the field of complexity theory (Cowan, Pines, and Meltzer 1994).

Policy Simulator's adaptive agent-based modeling incorporates cultural as well as economic values. Each policy simulation is inherently different, reflecting the contingent or existential nature of the world. Contradictions are built into the agent's belief system reinforcing the ability of the agents to learn—that is, to shift their beliefs and the decisions that come out of them. This last point is particularly important. Planning to an agreed degree is based on perceptions (e.g., the point at which an individual believes a loft is not only an industrial workplace, but also a place to live and work). Unlike many traditional equation-based simulation models, agent-based models allow the user to trace back the causes of the decisions and diagnose the decision-making process as well as understand how the agents are modeled. It takes policy forecasting out of the "black box" and makes the process more transparent.

Policy Simulator consists of several interacting submodules that assist in generating input data, calibrating and running the model, displaying the results, and developing policies in the community.

GENERATING INPUT DATA

Policy Simulator requires a great deal of data that may be difficult for communities to acquire. As it is an agent-based model and requires data about specific individuals and households in the community, it is impossible (at least in the U.S.) to acquire this information from the federal census; thus, we developed tools that deal with the issue. Information is also required about the buildings, parcels, and economic entities (businesses) in the community. Such information is available from various sources (assessor's office, Dun and Bradstreet) but again, we attempt to compensate for those communities that do not have complete data sets.

Required spatial data includes zoning, land use, parcels, and building locations. We convert these GIS layers for the user into Policy Simulator-recognized formats. Other required data includes federal, state, and local taxes (income, sales, and property). Finally, we require consumer expenditures by good type, derived from the Consumer Expenditure Survey (Division of Consumer Expenditure Surveys 1994).

Finally, Policy Simulator, and the philosophy behind CommunityViz in general, is to focus on information at a very fine-grained spatial level. Policy Simulator predicts land-use changes at a grid cell size level of anywhere from 1,000 to 25,000 square meters. Forecasting on such a small scale guarantees that the model will not be entirely accurate much of the time. However, our calibration techniques (see below) and our method of displaying results make it possible to present correct general patterns most of the time.

POLICY SIMULATOR COMPONENTS

SIMPREP AND DATA INTEGRITY

SimPrep is a submodule in Policy Simulator that permits users to create a complete set of data for use in a simulation run. One of the major difficulties we anticipated with the Policy Simulator was the fact that communities would not have the requisite data to run the program successfully. In SimPrep, a community enters general information about the demographics and economics of the area from generally available federal census data. SimPrep then generates an appropriate data set. For instance, agent-based models require specific data on individuals in the community (namely, variables such as the age, race, and beliefs). Through surveys conducted by various communities, we analyzed individual responses and gathered data on demographic, economic, and psychographic variables. From these responses, we then constructed an "agent pool" from which SimPrep creates an artificial population for a community; this population matches well with the actual residents who live there. Finally, we have a facility for users to check the integrity and viability of their data sets to see if their data preparation adequately works with the simulation.

CALIBRATION

The calibration program uses a proprietary combination of a genetic algorithm (Mitchell 1996) and simulated annealing (Kirkpatric, Gelatt Jr., and Vecchi 1983) to calibrate the approximately 30 free parameters in the Policy Simulator simulation model. The calibration program tries different combinations of the values of the free parameters, keeps track of those that work well, and gradually moves toward a solution. To work well, the number of forecasted households and jobs (for example) in the community must match with linearly extrapolated historical patterns or predetermined future numbers. In addition, the land-use changes over time can also be calibrated. Since there are many combinations of free parameters, there are many solutions as well. The calibration program notes this, and presents these results to the user.

SIMULATION

The simulation engine itself is the core component of the Policy Simulator. The simulation engine does the actual forecasting of the demographic, economic, and land-use data. To do so, the simulation engine either uses the data the user has prepared manually or has generated with SimPrep. The engine then runs. In a run, agents in the community can do a variety of activities—working, shopping, moving, buying and selling land and buildings, visiting the community, and so on. Businesses can open and close, raise and lower prices in their stores, hire and fire employees, and so forth.

Agent activities are guided by individual characteristics. An agent with minimal education is unlikely to work at a white-collar job making a large salary. Businesses hire agents who have skills that match the jobs that they need done. When a business closes, agents are fired and must seek employment elsewhere. When agents shop, they use a function that balances distance, price sensitivity, and need for particular goods (as determined by typical expenditures). They spend their available income to satisfy the needs they have.

Agents also have the ability to move into, out of, and within the community. Agents typically only move within the community if their household gets too large for their current dwelling. Agents move into or out of the community based on several factors, the most salient being whether they get a job or lose a job. In addition, agents constantly assess the quality of life in the community, and if they believe it has gone down, they have a greater chance of moving out. Conversely, if an agent living outside of the simulated community assesses the quality of life to be improving, that agent might consider moving into the town.

A simulation consists of specifying the number of months in the run, the data sets to be used, the current best set of calibrated parameters, a set of policies, and a random number seed. The simulation engine runs iteratively, with each iteration simulating one month. The user can view the output in ArcView GIS at the conclusion of the simulation.

DISPLAYING THE OUTPUT

Policy Simulator exports its output to ArcView GIS. Much of the information consists of tables of information (new buildings, population changes, etc.). In addition, several types of spatial information are also available (maps of new buildings, land value, etc.). Policy Simulator can also create "splat" themes, thematic probability distribution maps where the variable mapped (new development, for instance) is represented by different color intensities. These splat maps convey the uncertainty behind the Policy Simulator's forecasts, while still presenting useful information. Figure 6 shows an example of splat themes.

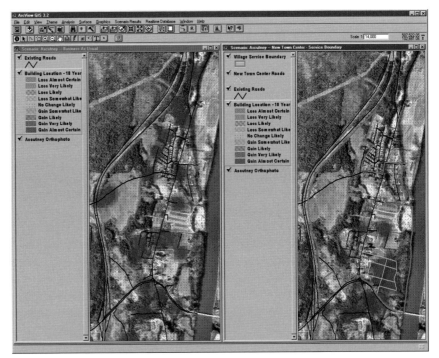

Figure 6. Policy Simulator Splat Themes: Policy Simulator produces themes that display spatial probabilities of change through its splat themes.

Early users of Policy Simulator indicated that they wanted greater access to the decisions and motivations of agents in the simulation, spurring development of the Agent Viewer and Polling Module. In this module, users have the ability to look at the timelines of major decisions and events in each agent's life. Users can also group agents by a variety of characteristics to better understand the simulation process and results.

DEVELOPING POLICIES

The Policy Construction Template (PCT) submodule is used for creating the policy sets used in the simulation runs. Policy sets are groups of various local policies that the user may want to "try out" as alternatives to the "no change" policy set (i.e., business as usual). A user can explore a range of public policy options designed to capture, as closely as possible, the type of planning alternatives available to local decision makers. The PCT Module provides templates for approximately sixteen policy options through which users can create customized local alternatives. These sixteen types of policies were organized into three major categories:

- Tax incentive ordinances

- Site alteration and land-use ordinances

- Municipal budgeting options for construction, leasing, and demolition

The policy templates assist users in readily identifying relevant information requirements and in understanding the data interactions driving the simulation. In addition, the structure of the templates gives decision makers flexibility in designing and implementing the various policy options. Figure 7 shows the specific policy options for tax-related policies.

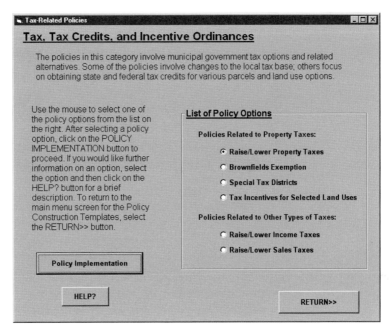

Figure 7. Policy Simulator Tax Policies: Users can try out various land-use and economic policies in Policy Simulator and see how those changes might affect the results of simulation runs.

Many of the policy options represented in the PCT Module include a distinct spatial component. For example, several of the tax-related policy options require the user to specify certain buildings or parcels of land within the municipal landscape to which to apply the tax credit or rate change. Other policy options, such as constructing new roads or determining a service boundary area, require the user to modify the local landscape by drawing or choosing new feature elements for the relevant data layers. Once the spatial extent of the policy option has been decided, the PCT Module allows the user to customize the details of how the policy should be applied. For instance, if the policy option involves a tax credit or rate reduction, the user would be asked to enter the dollar amount or percentage calculation of the credit. The PCT Module takes all the information generated by the user and integrates it with the larger simulation process of the Policy Simulator simulation engine.

POTENTIAL CONCERNS IN USING THE POLICY SIMULATOR

There are several concerns that might be raised regarding the Policy Simulator. Of foremost concern is the "hypercomprehensiveness" argument (Lee 1973). With all the data sets required, the Policy Simulator is a comprehensive model. Yet, it does not succumb to some of the issues that surrounded other comprehensive models, such as the one developed by Forrester (1969). First, Policy Simulator is spatially disaggregated. Furthermore, users can calibrate it so that aggregate data from their community matches Policy Simulator's predictions.

Another concern is the openness of the system that we are modeling. Forrester (1969) modeled a completely closed system. The city was self-contained and had no interactions with the outside world. The Policy Simulator, on the other hand, does model the outside world. In one community using the model there were 700 residents and workers inside the simulated area and 1,900 outside. Policy Simulator modeled the lifecycles of all 2,600 agents in the model. When agents live outside the town, however, we do not explore many individual behavioral patterns. Instead, we assume that agents outside of the simulated area will not change too much (except for their life cycle changes—aging, marriage, childbirth, death, educational changes, and some shopping inside the simulated area). We are trying to maintain a balance between a completely closed system, which is unrealistic but easier to model, and a completely open system where we would have to model everything.

The third major concern is the plethora of free parameters in the Policy Simulator. This is a general problem with many agent-based models. Our calibration routines better match the results of the simulations with broader aggregate measures, but we do realize that you can get from A to B on many different paths.

The fourth major concern is the wealth of data required for the Policy Simulator to function. We have partially addressed this problem by providing intelligently generated data using SimPrep, but we heed the old adage—garbage in, garbage out. Nevertheless, we are confident that with the increase of enterprise GIS systems, better remote sensing data for building identification, and other advances, these data problems will eventually be overcome.

THE PROCESS OF USING COMMUNITYVIZ

The process of using CommunityViz is neither linear nor hierarchical. The system does not require either a specific entry point or a pre-determined order in which its component modules are used. For example, the user is not required to enter at the macro-scale of public policy choices and work toward the micro-scale of the design of a neighborhood block. Instead, the system has been designed to encourage the user to simultaneously test and evaluate the implications of a proposal at different scales.

CommunityViz allows users to analyze a proposed development from its policy effects on land use to its impact on neighborhood infrastructure or potential obstruction of view corridors. For example, CommunityViz could be used at a series of community planning and design workshops that would be programmed to address the development pressures that may irrevocably change the character of that community. The objectives of such workshops would be described, and the participants asked questions such as the following: What are the social, economic, cultural, man-made, and natural characteristics that make their community special? What are the issues confronting them? What are their choices? How might they begin to implement those that they agree upon? CommunityViz is designed to help define these considerations and inform the planning and design decision-making process. Like any tool, it depends upon the craftsmen who use it. CommunityViz does not present answers. It helps the users frame the important questions, then provides a comprehensive environment in which users can propose responses, policies, plans, and designs, and see possible future results of decisions made today.

In a community meeting the 3-D digital model and ArcView GIS map are projected side by side on the screen, introducing the participants to the tools and information (see figure 4). A moving view cone, outlined in red, locates the viewer on the map while a meeting facilitator navigates through the 3-D model. The 3-D model and GIS contain specific information on the town, its people, and its environment. Census data, infrastructure use and location, zoning, soils, parcels, roads, land use, among others, are all organized and available for use. By visualizing policy alternatives in both two and three dimensions, the workshop participants can better understand how various policies would affect the land and the town and what the impacts of alternative development patterns might be on schools and local infrastructure. The workshop process is open-ended and permits widespread participation.

The implications of a community's existing zoning, land-use, and environmental regulations can be evaluated in CommunityViz. The program translates the words, numbers, maps, and diagrams in these regulations into a 3-D model. Prebuilt buildings from the Community-Viz Model Library can be used to illustrate the type of places that would typically result from the application of a community's existing regulations. Participants can then locate themselves interactively in the 3-D model to better understand both the overall patterns of development and the specific impacts on places.

CommunityViz can also be used to demonstrate the effects of a build-out if current policies, practices, and regulations remained in place for ten to fifteen years, the life span of most regulations. Using the policy construction templates in the Policy Simulator, current tax, land-related, and capital budgeting policies can be combined into a "business as usual" policy set and then simulated. Some communities may find that this may irrevocably change their community in ways that are unacceptable. Simulations of the same policy set can be run repeatedly. Because of the stochastic nature of agent-based forecasting, each simulation will yield different results, showing a range of possible futures (see figure 6 as an example).

Alternative land development policies can also be explored in CommunityViz through different scenarios. The first scenario might be the extension of existing built-up areas. The second might be the creation of a series of discrete interconnected hamlets set among the community's forested areas, working farms, and ranches. The common goal for both growth area scenarios would be to accommodate the anticipated population growth. The boundaries of each growth area scenario would be delineated and checked against the rule-based constraints checking feature of Scenario Constructor. For example, growth areas that reduced habitat areas to unworkable sizes would be highlighted simultaneously in the model and on the map.

The next step would be to evaluate the capacity of the newly developed areas outlined in the two scenarios to accommodate the anticipated growth. Working simultaneously in the 3-D model and map, the workshop participants select parcelization grids (e.g., acre, 1 acre, etc.) that roughly estimate the land areas developed in the two scenarios. In 2-D the participants see a map that delineates the proposed growth areas with the parcelization grid and building footprints. More impressively, participants see the parcels and buildings in 3-D on the landscape. Almost instantaneously, virgin land is populated with buildings, vacant lots in town are infilled, underdeveloped areas filled with new development, and impacts assessed. See figure 8.

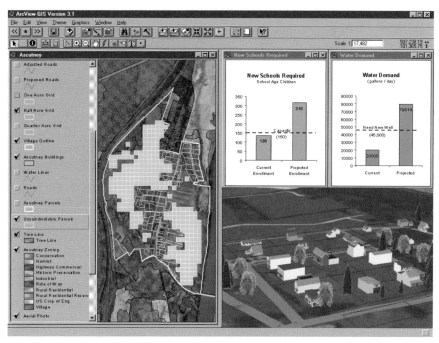

Figure 8. Half-Acre Scenario. Users have created a half-acre scenario and new town center that is displayed in both the 2-D and 3-D environments, as well as having its impacts assessed.

This example demonstrates that CommunityViz can be used to both visualize and quantify abstract policy and planning issues. Citizen planners can see that the form development takes is as important as the aggregate numbers. These digital tools open new possibilities for the fostering of community consensus and decision making, and the design of innovative-use regulations and other regulatory structures. The CommunityViz planning support system represents an opportunity to move from static regulation to management, creating a participatory structure that learns and adjusts regulations over time in response to events and experience (Kwartler 1993; Kwartler 1998).

FUTURE DEVELOPMENTS OF COMMUNITYVIZ

In the first release of TownBuilder 3D, the Model Library consists only of completed buildings. It is envisioned that subsequent versions of TownBuilder 3D will come with a "Kit-of-Parts" that communities could use to create a hypothetical set of buildings that are place-based (Moed 1994; Carlton, Kwartler, and Morgan 1996). The Kit-of-Parts would be like smart LEGO® bricks, architectonic geometric solids and planes that could be fashioned into buildings that reflect the patterns and conventions unique to the community. As a 3-D model of a building is assembled from component parts, the Model Library would update the physical attributes of the model on the fly. For instance, if an addition were added to a house, the Model Library would calculate the total square footage of the house and the result would be instantaneously passed to the corresponding record in the appropriate Scenario Theme. Cultural attributes could also be assigned to the component parts of a model, allowing sophisticated planning and design analyses in support of techniques such as mixed-use and "vertical" zoning.

In later versions of CommunityViz we expect that the Policy Simulator will be better able to deal with issues more typically found in urban communities. For instance, in the current version, the handling of zoning is rather basic. We anticipate that more comprehensive and complicated land-use regulations (density, complex mixed uses, etc.) will be available to the user. In addition, we anticipate that we will have many more policies from which the user can choose, policies that deal with crime, homelessness, storm water, and so on. Finally, the Policy Simulator will incorporate a more complete transportation model, perhaps including integration with other agent-based models such as TRANSIMS (Nagel, Beckman, and Barrett 1998).

We anticipate that CommunityViz will be updated to ArcView 8, to take full advantage of its object-oriented architecture. To make it easier for citizen planners to use CommunityViz, future releases will likely incorporate wizards that will walk the use through setup and integrated application of CommunityViz's three modules.

ACKNOWLEDGEMENTS

This paper was completed with the generous help of Paul H. Patnode of the Environmental Simulation Center. CommunityViz represents the work of many people and many organizations, including the Orton Family Foundation (Bill Shouldice, Noel Fritzinger, Lyman Orton, Andy Bush, Helen Whyte, Towny Anderson), the Environmental

Simulation Center (Paul Patnode, Roy Chan, Elke Solomon), Green Mountain GeoGraphics (Gary Smith), PricewaterhouseCoopers and its subcontractors (George Janes (PwC), Win Farrell (PwC), John Rannenberg (PwC), Holly Morehouse, Joe Oh, Nick Taylor, Paul Carmouche, Peter Duval), Fore Site Consulting (Brenda Faber, Jim Faber), MultiGen-Paradigm, (Jon Zucker, Steve Hanning, Dan Brockway, Gordon Tomlinson, Jay Kidd), Nina Seaman, as well as many other developers, beta testers, coordinators, trainers, and support staff, without whom this project would not be complete.

CURRENT STATUS

At the time this article was written, CommunityViz had been tested with eight communities, and it will be by at least another 20 in the first six months of 2001. For more information, please see the following Web sites:

- CommunityViz (www.CommunityViz.com)

- Orton Family Foundation (www.orton.org)

- Environmental Simulation Center (www.simcenter.org)

- PricewaterhouseCoopers (www.policysimulator.com and www.pwcglobal.com)

- MultiGen-Paradigm (www.multigen.com)

Note: Articles may refer to the working names for CommunityViz, Community Works, and Community Planning Simulation Project.

REFERENCES

Bernard, Robert N. 1999. Using Adaptive Agent-based Simulation Models to Assist Planners in Policy Development: The Case of Rent Control. Working paper 99-07-052E. Santa Fe, NM: Santa Fe Institute.

Bressi, Todd. 1995. The Real Thing: We're Getting There. *Planning* (July):16–20.

Byrne, John A. 1998. Virtual Management. *Business Week*, September 21:80–82.

Carlton, John, M. Kwartler, and L. Morgan. 1996. New York, New Jersey Highlands Demonstration Planning Project: Balancing Economic Development and Environmental Conservation Priorities in Rural and Exurban Communities. New York, NY: Regional Plan Association.

Chan, Roy, and J. Zucker. 1999. Urban Planning Simulation. *The Military Engineer*, 92:603.

Cowan, George A., D. Pines, and D. Meltzer, eds. 1994. *Complexity: Metaphors, Models, and Reality*. Reading, MA: Addison–Wesley.

de la Barra, Tomas. 2001. Integrated Land Use and Transport Modeling: The Tranus Experience. *Planning Support Systems: Integrating Geographic Information Systems, Models, and Visualization Tools,* ed. Richard Brail and Richard Klosterman. Redlands, CA: ESRI Press.

Division of Consumer Expenditure Surveys. 1994. Consumer Expenditure Survey. Washington, D.C.: Bureau of Labor Statistics.

Delaney, Ben. 2000. Visualization in Urban Planning: They Didn't Build LA in a Day. *IEEE Computer Graphics and Applications* (May/June).

Dunlap, David. 1995. Bringing Downtown Back Up. *New York Times* (October 15):1.

Dunlap, David. 1992. Impact of Zoning is Pretested on Computers. *New York Times* (June 14):1, 11.

Faber, Brenda. 1997. Active Response GIS: An Architecture for Interactive Resource Modeling. *Proceedings of the GIS '97 Annual Symposium on Geographic Information Systems.* Vancouver.

Farrell, Winslow. 1998. *How Hits Happen.* New York: Harper Collins.

Forrester, Jay. 1969. *Urban Dynamics.* Cambridge, MA: MIT Press.

Holland, John H. 1995. *Hidden Order.* Reading, MA: Addison–Wesley.

Kirkpatric, S., C. D. Gelatt Jr., and M. P. Vecchi. 1983. Optimization by Simulated Annealing. *Science,* 20:671–80.

Koselka, Rita. 1997. Playing the Game of Life. *Forbes* 159 (7):100–7.

Kwartler, Michael. 1993. Planning and Zoning for a Mature City. *Planning and Zoning New York City: Yesterday, Today and Tomorrow,* ed. Todd Bressi. New Brunswick, NJ: Center for Urban Policy Research.

Kwartler, Michael. 1998. Regulating the Good You Can't Think of. *Urban Design International 3* (vol. 1 and 2).

Lee, Douglass B., Jr. 1973. Requiem for Large-scale Models. *Journal of the American Institute of Planners,* 39:163–78.

Moed, Andrea. 1994. Mapping the Neighborhood. *Metropolis* (Jan/Feb):60–65.

Mitchell, Melanie. 1996. *An Introduction to Genetic Algorithms.* Cambridge, MA: MIT Press.

Nagel, K., R. J. Beckman, and C. L. Barrett. 1998. TRANSIMS for Transportation Planning. Unclassified Report LA-UR 98–4389. Los Alamos, NM: Los Alamos National Laboratory.

Orton Family Foundation. 2000. www.orton.org

Peterson, Merril, D., ed. 1975. *The Portable Thomas Jefferson,* New York: Viking.

Putman, Stephen H., and S. Chan. 2001. The METROPILUS Planning Support System: Urban Models and GIS. *Planning Support Systems: Integrating Geographic Information Systems, Models, and Visualization Tools,* ed. Richard Brail and Richard Klosterman. Redlands, CA: ESRI Press.

Teicholz, Nina. 1999. Shaping Cities: Pixels to Bricks. *New York Times* (December 16):G1.

Paper 12

Computer-aided Visualization: Possibilities for Urban Design, Planning, and Management

RICHARD LANGENDORF

UNIVERSITY OF MIAMI

CORAL GABLES, FLORIDA

ABSTRACT

This paper explores possibilities for computer aided visualization. This journey is premised upon four assumptions: (1) in our complex world, to understand nearly any subject of consequence it is necessary to consider it from multiple viewpoints, using a variety of information; (2) we are rapidly moving from an information-poor to an information-rich society; (3) the understanding of complex information may be greatly extended if visualized; and (4) problem solving and commitment to action in a complex world requires communication and collaboration among many participants, and visualization aids this interaction. The paper begins with a description of a wide diversity of visualization software and continues by describing visualization environments—information landscapes and information workspaces. These descriptions set the stage for considering visualization as much more than creating realistic images of what is or what might be, and much more than creating attractive charts and maps. Visualization is concerned with foraging for data in a data-rich environment made much more accessible by the World Wide Web. It is involved with transforming data—to information, to knowledge, and into action. It can include recreating a sense of history and place; supporting collaborations that alter the way we work; and creating compelling experiences that alter people's view of the world about them, moving individuals, organizations, and communities to change that world, or perhaps some small place in the world. Computer visualization is about all these things.

INTRODUCTION

Neighborhoods, cities, and regions are complex phenomena. They are difficult to understand today, and it is even more difficult to foresee how they may be. When planners examine existing conditions or plan for the future, they are likely to incorporate a diversity of information in their analyses and solutions. Census data, printed reports, newspaper articles, minutes of meetings, aerial and eye-level photographs, satellite images, drawings and maps, and remembered conversations all aid in forming a sense of the planning area or the problem at hand, and in envisioning alternative futures.

This brings us to the *first premise—that in our complex world, to understand any subject of consequence it is necessary to consider it from multiple viewpoints, using a variety of information sources.* This, of course, is a less poetic restatement of the well-known Indian parable about six blind men who were asked to describe an elephant. Each described the part of the animal with which he was familiar, convinced that he perceived its true nature. Perceiving only a part, each had a laughable idea of the whole.

The second premise is that we are rapidly moving from an information-poor to an information-rich society. The amount of data readily available is increasing exponentially, and access to this data is increasing even more rapidly. The high-resolution satellite imagery now available is but one example and it will accelerate this change and provide new opportunities, especially for those concerned with urban areas. Such changes present new challenges. They require the careful construction of an information architecture; the development of new tools for data selection, reduction, and synthesis; and better means for understanding complex patterns through visualization.

The third premise is that the understanding of complex information may be greatly extended if visualized. Visualization aids in conceptualization—that is, in developing understanding and creative problem solving. Our language embodies the association of vision and thinking. Consider insight, foresight, hindsight, oversight. The word "idea" comes from the Greek "idein," to see. We say we "see" to mean we "understand." We examine the big picture, seek perspective, foster imagination. Imagination and image have common roots: imagination can be thought of as images in the mind. We try to make our ideas clear, bring them into focus. Visual thinking is an important mode of thought (McKim 1980). This position is strongly defined by Gyorgy Kepes: "Vision can no longer be employed simply to support verbal and conceptual meaning; its potential as a cognitive power in its own right must be exploited" (Kepes 1965, *v*). The extent to which computing may support this process is suggested in a report to the National Science Foundation that described scientific visualization and its objectives as follows.

> ". . . Visualization is a method of computing. It transforms the symbolic into the geometric, enabling researchers to observe their simulations and computations. Visualization offers a method for seeing the unseen. It enriches the process of scientific discovery and fosters profound and unexpected insights. In many fields it is already revolutionizing the way scientists do science." (McCormick, DeFanti, and Brown 1987, 2)

The fourth premise is that problem solving and commitment to action in a complex world require communication and collaboration among many participants, and that visualization aids this interaction. Collaboration is often required because complex problems typically require the efforts of many. These efforts typically require interdisciplinary teams and communication across disciplines. Complex problems are also likely to involve many diverse stakeholders who demand participation and whose participation may well contribute to more effective and equitable proposals. Visualization aids in such communication because it provides a more understandable representation, and because images more easily than words can cross disciplinary, cultural, and language divides. Also, visual representations, in contrast to verbal ones, tend to be more memorable and more trustworthy. Perhaps it is because most of us learn that "seeing is believing" that people often have a distrust of words and a confidence in the truthfulness of pictures.

**VISUALIZATION
APPLICATIONS
SOFTWARE**

Before describing the various visualization tools, it is appropriate to remind ourselves that the way we represent a city, or any topic, will influence how we think about it. The following two quotes express this insight.

"The architects, engineers, and city planners trained in the design of cities acquire the skills necessary to represent what exists and what might become reality. But because the richness and complexity of the real world cannot be completely represented, they must, out of necessity, select from reality an abstraction of actual conditions. For them the process of representation is a complex form of reasoning. *What they choose to represent influences their view of reality and very significantly defines the outcomes of designs and plans, and thus the future form of cities*" (Bosselman 1998, *xiii*, emphasis added).

Similar notions have been expressed with respect to architecture, and are equally applicable to planning.

"The media used to investigate and analyze architecture has a profound effect upon the kind and character of the ideas explored. To the extent that we can become aware of the potential and limitation of different modes of description and proposition, we can expand the horizons of our design and research" (Robinson 1990).

This review is broad and eclectic regarding forms of representation. It will focus upon those types of software that may be useful to urban planners and designers, including software that is not yet commonly used. It will include commercially available software and software evolving in research and development labs that may point the way toward future possibilities.

As the capabilities of software broaden, the distinction between software for particular applications and software environments that support multiple uses becomes blurred. Consequently, the classification used below is, of necessity, imprecise. Nevertheless, it distinguishes between different types of application programs and graphic environments—information landscapes and information workspaces. Application programs, environments and their relationships are briefly described below and illustrated in figure 1. The relationships among applications, information workspaces, and information landscapes are summarized, after the fuller discussion, in figure 7.

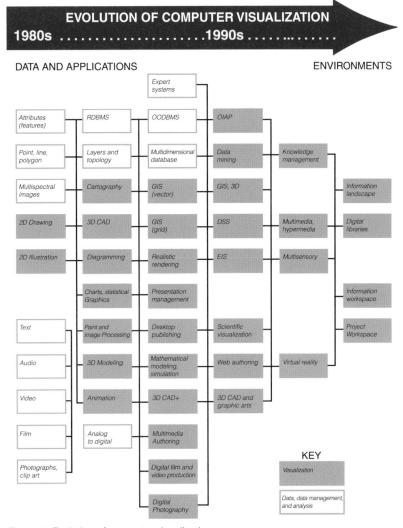

Figure 1. Evolution of computer visualization.

MAPPING AND GEOGRAPHIC INFORMATION SYSTEMS

Cartography

Mapmaking has served humankind for many centuries. Among the earliest maps are those from Mesopotamia on clay tables dating from 1500 B.C. Today, planners regularly use thematic maps offering visual displays relating various types of data to geographic areas, and they conveniently generate maps with desktop mapping programs.

From the standpoint of this article, mapmaking took a significant step forward in the 1950s when Arthur Robinson (1952) and others urged that cartographers shift their focus from the efficient production of maps to the design of "functional" maps. They urged that the characteristics of perception be analyzed and applied to maps so that symbolization and design decisions could be based on objective rules. In the late 1960s and the 1970s the approach was broadened to consider cartography as graphic communication. In 1981 Jacques Bertin, a cartographer, shifted the focus of maps and graphics beyond communication to emphasize their role in processing and analyzing information (Bertin 1981). Cartography has been reconceptualized "as a process of communicating spatial information that had inputs, transmission, and reception of information, and that therefore could be analyzed as a system" (MacEachren 1995).

Interactive Maps and Geographic Information Systems (GIS)

As the use of computers increased, the interests of cartographers and map users extended to new types of data, new forms of representation, and interactive maps (MacEachren and the ICA Commission on Visualization 1998). The possibility of digital maps set the stage for the development of geographic information systems and georeferenced scientific visualization.

GIS provides more sophisticated capabilities than mapping. With GIS, the map represents linked and spatially encoded data. Spatial information is topologically coded to permit spatial query and analysis, and large and complex sets of diverse data types can be efficiently managed (Scholten and Stillwell 1990). Today, most GIS systems are capable of handling both vector and raster data. A growing number of GIS vendors provide readers or translators for popular CAD programs. As GIS vendors continue to add capabilities to their systems, more are providing 3-D and VRML (virtual reality modeling language) representations, and the ability to integrate such multimedia data such as still images, audio, and video clips (Rhyne 1997; E. Verbree, G. van Maren, R. Germs, F. Jansen, and M. J. Kraak 1999).

With the added scope and complexity of spatial data and methods of representation, and the possibility of interactivity, the interest of cartographers and spatial data users shifted from static maps to multiple views into the data, both concurrently and sequentially. Work has explored the possibilities of computer-based dynamic representations. These include the incorporation of spatial-temporal representations and animation (DiBiase, MacEachren, Krygier, and Reeves 1992; MacEachren 1995; Peterson 1995). Dorling (1991) provides an example of visualizing small area population change through animation. Acevedo and Masuoka (1997) and Batty and Howes (1996) use animation to depict urban change. Others have sought to extend the idea of representation to reinforce and supplement the visual by including sound (Krygier 1994) and tactile sensations (Vasconcellos 1993). One interesting example is shown in figure 2. This figure shows a multimedia tool developed by Sara Fabrikant at the Department of Geography, University of Zurich. It allows interactive visualization of passenger flows on the Swiss train network.

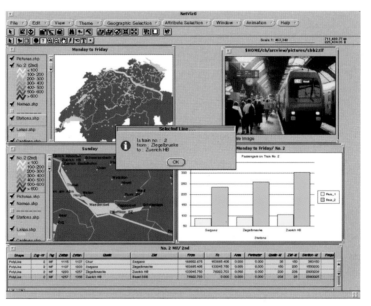

Figure 2. Interactive visualization of passenger flows, featuring maps, chart, table, and real-time video.

The map view may become an interface for retrieving multimedia representations. This linking capability can extend beyond a particular GIS data set to provide access to associated data through the World Wide Web (Kraak and van Dreil 1997; Cartwright 1997). Recent evolutions in enterprise databases now permit the integration of geospatial and nonspatial data within a single enterprise database—most notably with Oracle, but also with IBM, Informix, and Sybase databases (Limp 1999).

The graphical user interface, through direct manipulation, becomes a vehicle for univariate and multivariate exploratory spatial data analysis (ESDA) (Kraak and MacEachren 1999). Here, developments in scientific visualization have compelled GIS to incorporate multivariate data representations and direct manipulation into the graphical user interface. Gennady and Natalia Andrienko (1999) offer an example of software for the automated presentation of data on maps and interactive facilities for direct manipulation of the linked data, in the form of Java applets, enabling exploratory spatial data analysis on the World Wide Web. Commercial vendors also are developing software components for spatial data visualization and manipulation over the Web (Limp 1999). A later discussion in this chapter on digital libraries and visual databases provides additional examples of the possibilities for increased access to spatial information and the "spatialization" of nonspatial data to facilitate query and navigation in very large text, video, Web, and other data sets.

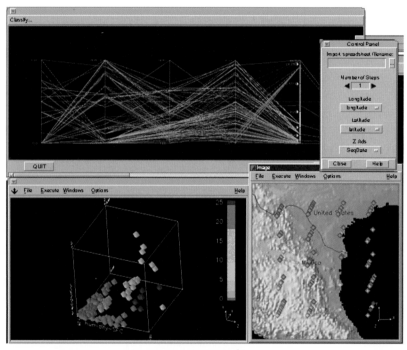

Figure 3. This shows a parallel coordinates plot, 3-D scatter plot, and 3-D map images, with selected variables colored consistently across representations. The vertical elements on the map view represent different time slices. Attribute, spatial, and time characteristics for each variable are expressed.

The increased availability of geospatial data, the growing capabilities for direct manipulation, and the access provided by the Web—all are contributing to the growing interest and ability in data sharing, professional interdisciplinary collaboration, and broadened participation in the use of these data and tools. For urban planners, GIS may be viewed as one increasingly popular strategy for both integrating and sharing information from many sources within a single information management system, as well as for exploring, analyzing, and visualizing that data through various two- and three-dimensional representations.

COMPUTER AIDED DESIGN (CAD)

Early CAD programs were essentially 2-D drawing programs. Modern CAD programs provide the added benefits of maintaining 3-D data for analysis and three-dimensional viewing (Sheppard 1989). The visualization capabilities of these programs have been rapidly improving.

Two important changes have been occurring in CAD programs. First, most have become object oriented. The user now works with objects, like doors and windows, or buildings and trees, rather than points, lines, and planes. These objects may be defined by the user or selected from libraries, parametrically altered, and endowed with properties. Second, CAD programs now are likely to provide database tools that allow the association of external data with CAD objects. Such integration is significant for both analysis and visualization.

More and more development projects use digital models for design development, construction drawings, marketing and sales, citizen participation, and regulatory review. Digital models of proposed projects can be inserted and viewed in context. Such models can be used to evaluate design and planning alternatives, examine views, and solicit citizen input. In some communities this is now required for regulatory review.

Computer models have also been used to reconstruct buildings and cities that no longer exist, serving both as a method of scholarly research and as a way of preserving history (Novitski 1998; Emmett 1998; Forte and Siliotti 1997).

CAD PLUS

Though much of the early work in 3-D modeling occurred within the context of the development of CAD programs for the aerospace, automobile, and atomic energy industries, it has also evolved in other environments, including GIS, the entertainment industry, and in scientific visualization. These distinct developments have interacted and enriched the possibilities of 3-D.

Three-dimensional (3-D) modeling and realistic rendering

Much of the recent drive for improvement in 3-D modeling, rendering, and animation comes from the entertainment industries. These developments reflect a different emphasis than traditional CAD— that is, less precise dimensional control, greater typographic choice, more freedom in creating 2-D and 3-D curved and irregular shapes, more special effects, shape and color transformations, and complex animation scripting.

Relatively simple modeling of complex man-made objects and natural phenomena calls for advanced techniques. Many of these techniques have been developed for scientific computing and in special effects studios. They include procedural models, fractal models, particle systems, grammar-based models, volume rendering, flow models, physically based modeling, and special models for natural and synthetic objects. Many of these developments have found their way back into CAD programs.

CAD and GIS

Traditionally, CAD programs have been better for modeling of 3-D physical objects, and GIS programs have been better for representing the underlying, spatially coded data. However, there now appears to be a convergence between CAD and GIS, with GIS programs getting better at modeling 3-D physical reality and CAD improving in storing, analyzing, and viewing of underlying data. Nevertheless, some of the most interesting progress in integrating the 3-D models with underlying data involves linking CAD and GIS programs rather than relying upon one or the other.

Generally speaking, GIS provides more abstract representations, and CAD, greater realism. Indeed, cartography has evolved increasingly abstract representations for making the world easier to understand. In contrast, advances in computer graphics have resulted in CAD representations approaching near photo-realism. Determining the appropriate level of abstraction or realism for specific contexts—defined by intended uses, users, types of data, and data representations—remains an insufficiently examined and important issue. Providing the user with a continuum of choices on the abstraction—realism axis in CAD, GIS, and integrated systems—is likely to be a desirable goal in any case.

Modeling urban areas or more complex structures is time-consuming and labor-intensive. CAD programs have been making more progress than GIS regarding rapid model development, especially for sketch planning. However, the restructuring of much CAD and GIS software so that it is object oriented prepares a foundation that should facilitate rapid model development. The work of Erik Kjerns, Michael Batty, Lewis Hopkins and his colleagues, and others, suggests that planners are now recognizing the need for useful sketch planning support, and are developing prototypes of such systems (Hopkins, Johnston, and Varkki 1999; Kjerns 1999; Batty, Dodge, Jiang, and Smith 1998; Singh 1996). Another foundation technology that should contribute to sketch planning in the future is image recognition—that is, software that can interpret visual structure and relationships from sketches. Researchers at Xerox PARC have developed a prototype (Saund and Moran 1994). Other approaches are described below.

CAD and GIS, 2-D to 3-D

Moving from 2-D to 3-D, as with CAD and GIS, is labor intensive, requiring significant effort, time, and cost. This is a problem if simple building masses are used, and it is even more of a problem if near photo-realistic imagery is desired. It is a problem that is confronted somewhat differently if one is attempting to visualize what is, or if one is recreating what was, or generating images of what might be.

In portraying existing reality there is a physical environment that can be "captured" in digital form. Several technologies may be very helpful in capturing existing urban detail for computer models. The first is laser scanning. Cyra Technologies, Inc., for example, has a 3-D laser mapping system for rapid modeling and visualization of large structures and sites. For creating 3-D models of large areas, radar inferometry, a rapidly improving technology, processes two or more radar images of the same location. Using multiple space-based sensors, it is often possible to recognize changes as small as a centimeter.

Radar inferometry may make possible the rapid mapping of 3-D detail, including roof outlines, and automatically classify surfaces as forests, paving, buildings, or croplands. LIDAR (light defection and ranging) offers the promise of similar benefits. With current systems it is possible to survey thousands of square kilometers in less than 12 hours and have a highly detailed digital terrain model with vertical accuracy of 15 centimeters available within 24 hours (Limp 1999; also, www.airbornelasermapping.com).

Other methods are image-based. Draping satellite imagery over digital terrain models is a well-established technique in GIS. When digitized aerial photographs or satellite images are draped over 2-D digital elevation maps, realistic 3-D images result. The viewpoint and angle can be changed, and some systems can animate the image, providing realistic flyovers (MacEachren and Taylor 1994; MacEachren 1995).

Programs that use algorithms for edge detection and which measure parallax to derive 3-D data from two or more photographs shot at different angles have been automating 2-D to 3-D conversions for a few years. Such programs are now entering the mainstream of commercial products. These programs also extract the surfaces from the photographs, creating texture maps that are applied to the generated 3-D massing models. The texture maps provide much of the realistic detail that otherwise would need to be laboriously modeled. More recent examples use digital orthophotos to build mass models and to texture map building façade detail. Such a model of downtown New York City is presently under construction. The same principles have been used for creating 3-D models from video, then creating 3-D texture mapped models (www.ise.imagica.co.jp). Other software now extracts camera motion, pan, tilt, and zoom from live-action footage and exports it to such modeling and animation programs as 3D Studio MAX™ (Autodesk), SOFTIMAGE™ (Avid Technology, Inc.), and LightWave™.

Bringing together a number of technologies, Evans and Sutherland's RAPIDsite™ is focused upon providing fast model creation for photorealistic, interactive 3-D visualization at the scale of urban and suburban development. Rapidsite is actually a collection of programs that accept data and models from GIS and CAD programs and use photographic imagery as source materials for creating models of existing terrain complete with site elements such as buildings, vegetation and the background panorama (www.es.com).

Three-dimensional (3-D) modeling, realistic rendering, and paint and image processing: 2-D or 3-D?

For those confronted with 3-D imagery today, there is the practical reality of deciding what to do in 2-D and what with 3-D. Consider a 3-D image that includes a proposed building complex, an urban setting, landscape, cars, and people. Any or all of these component parts of the image may be generated by 3-D modeling and rendering software, created in paint programs, or adjusted and added from digital photographs. It is often easier, and more realistic, to create a proposed urban intervention in a 3-D program but then insert it in a 2-D photograph of the site. Landscape elements, cars, and people may be easier to digitize from photographs. Even generating alternatives, such as exploring the consequences of adding a story to a parking garage, may be easier to manage with 2-D image manipulation than 3-D modeling. The optimum mix of 2-D and 3-D tools in image creation is likely to be determined by the particular requirement, and may require trade-offs regarding ease in creating and modifying, the degree of realism needed, cost, and time available.

Animation

Animation creates the illusion of incremental change through the presentation of still images at the rate of 24 to 30 frames per second. While people often think of animation as synonymous with motion, it includes all changes that have a visual effect—changing shape, color, transparency, structure, and texture of objects (update dynamics); changes in lighting and light source position; camera position, orientation, and focus; and even rendering technique.

Animation is helpful in understanding time-varying data of all types. Examples of animations that simulate physical reality are walkthroughs and flyovers, examinations of changing shadow patterns at different times of day throughout the year, and evaluations of views and safety along roadways. Data-driven animations may portray the flow of pollutants in the air, underground, or along waterways; or changes in population density over time (Dorling 1991). Animation has always been at the core of film industry graphics. It has been more an "add-on," though an increasingly important add-on, for advertising, CAD, GIS, and scientific visualization.

Animating natural phenomena is quite difficult and has received much special attention. Computer simulations of human movement, dinosaurs, trees blowing in the wind, fire, and explosions are only some of the problems faced by computer animators.

Modeling and rendering programs intended for the motion picture and television industries have had extensive animation capabilities from the outset. CAD programs developed for architecture, engineering, and construction industries were likely to add animation capabilities later. The addition of animation to GIS is relatively new, and typically lacks many of the refinements available in other animation systems (Peterson 1995).

Animation and Film and Video

As animation systems become more capable, they begin to approach the level of compelling experience that films have traditionally provided. While cartoons and the early animated films made no effort to simulate reality, computer animation entered the modern film business by creating special effects that provided the illusion of physical reality. The extent to which special effects are used in contemporary filmmaking has increased steadily. By the late 1990s, *Toy Story,* the first feature-length 3-D animated film, had reached theaters and became an instant box office success. While the movie did not truly provide a realistic simulation of actual physical environments and people, it did clearly demonstrate the ability of animations to capture the human imagination, to express human-like emotions in digital characters, and to provide a compelling experience for the audience.

In time the distinctions between film and animation are likely to blur and perhaps even disappear. The potential for animation should not be underestimated.

LINKING WHAT WE SEE AND WHAT WE DON'T

Architects and urban designers can benefit by visualizing their physical design ideas within a broader context. Those who prepare zoning codes and urban plans and policies could benefit by visualizing the 3-D implications. Both the physical form of a building or city, and associated characteristics are important. It is desirable to visualize the relationships between the physical and other attributes.

ESRI's ArcView® 3D Analyst extension provides 3-D visualization and access to associated attribute data within a GIS system. While the visualization capabilities are somewhat limited (lacking, for example, many features of photorealistic rendering), this nevertheless provides an important start.

Other programs do a better job of visualization, but these are research, not commercial, efforts that show the possibilities. A program developed at the University of Toronto links geometric models with attributes. One can query the model visualization and see the underlying attributes. The original model was developed for the city of Ottawa and used for a variety of purposes, including the evaluation of proposed development upon views of the capital. The program has been extended to support linked attribute knowledge and synchronous and asynchronous model exchange for distributed-collaborative work (Dave and Danahy 1998).

The UCLA School of Architecture has built a system that utilizes cameras, 3-D modeling, and GIS features. The photographs provide texture maps that are applied to surfaces in the 3-D model. Model features are linked to underlying data, as in GIS systems. One can fly over or walk through areas of Los Angeles, interactively controlling the path, and querying physical features to obtain linked data (Liggett and Jepson 1995). The system can be programmed to quickly flip through alternatives—substituting, for example, one type of tree for another, or one building for another. The UCLA system has recently been integrated with GPS, providing real-time input or view control (Jepson and Friedman 1998). Both Toronto and UCLA provide thought-provoking paradigms for what planners should be demanding from software providers.

The representation of physical forms usually omits much relevant information regarding design standards and intent, decision criteria and controversies, and the like. Linking such information with the representation of the resulting physical forms is discussed later under the heading of information and project workspaces.

SCIENTIFIC VISUALIZATION

Scientific visualization is directed at seeing the unseen. ". . . Visualization . . . transforms the symbolic into the geometric, enabling researchers to observe their simulations and computations. Visualization offers a method for seeing the unseen" (McCormick and DeFanti 1987). It is this National Science Foundation (NSF) initiative on scientific visualization that generally defines the field today.

All the NSF examples of scientific visualization are directed at displaying information about physical phenomena, always with spatial dimension, and often with temporal. Though some of this has been used in natural resource and environmental work, it has not impacted most other areas of planning. Here lies a body of literature and a set of tools that provide a rich, largely untapped, resource for planners.

Mathematical modeling and simulation

Special purpose modeling and simulation techniques have been widely used in the sciences, engineering, and planning. Population and economic forecasting, land-use, transportation, housing, and other models have had a checkered history, though transportation models are now well established. Graphical representations of the numerical simulations are now often considered a necessity in understanding simulation results (Friedhoff 1989; Thalman 1990).

General purpose simulation modeling languages have existed for many years and been applied to a wide variety of problems, including simulations of transportation flows; the movement of people along urban sidewalks and within shopping centers; the operations of health systems, hospitals and other building types, and emergency dispatch systems, and a manufacturing plants. Several of these general-purpose modeling systems allow model specification with graphic tools, are now highly interactive in operation, and are capable of displaying model behavior and results in a variety of formats, including tables, charts, and animated graphics. Indeed, "Easy-to-use animation is one of the main reasons for the increased popularity of simulation modeling" (Law and Kelton 1991, 241).

CAD, GIS, and mathematical models

Geometric modeling and GIS programs associate attributes with objects, providing a foundation for scientific visualization regarding physical objects. This data may also be exported to other mathematical models for further processing, perhaps projecting population or land-use changes, simulating traffic flow or rain runoff, calculating temperature and wind speed on urban streets or between buildings, and the like. Many mathematical models, of course, can also run alone, but the entry of spatial data and the graphic display of analytic results facilitated by CAD and GIS makes model creation and interpretation easier, and at times, provides understanding that might otherwise not be possible (DiBiase, MacEachren, Krygier, and Reeves. 1992; Batty and Howes 1996; MacEachren and Taylor 1995). There is an unmet need and considerable opportunity for the integration of modeling capabilities with CAD and GIS programs.

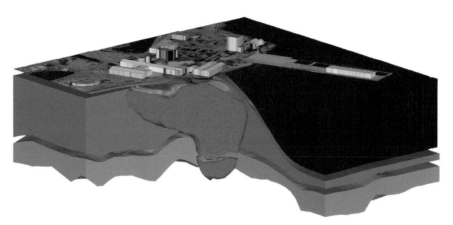

Figure 4. This 3-D image, created with an environmental visualization system (EVS), shows a chlorinated hydrocarbon contaminant plume at an industrial facility on the coast, computed using scientific modeling. Sand and rock geological layers are shown below the ocean. A color aerial photograph of the actual site was used to texture map a 3-D AutoCAD model of the facility building and the ocean layer. This is a still image captured from an animation.

THE PHOTOGRAPHIC IMAGE: STILL PHOTOGRAPHY, FILM, AND VIDEO

From the first half of the 19th century photographers have documented their times. Photographs not only document the present and contribute to a shared understanding of the present, but also foster an understanding of the past. Consider, for a moment, how you would remember what you looked like as a child without early childhood photographs. Photographs can fulfill the same function in reconstructing and sharing a sense of history of place—of our neighborhoods, civic events, and cities. For the past 150 years, in fact, photographs have provided a visual inventory of places, people, and events (Bamberger 1996; Hockings 1995; Stilgoe 1998).

Architecture and cities have been represented in still images, film, and video for many years. These representations, particularly film images, have had an impact on the public's perception of architecture and cities and on their design (Albrecht 1986; Penz and Thomas 1997).

An understanding of the power of the photographic image has been unfolding for most of the 20th century. Today, image-driven celebrity status and "image politics" provide clear evidence of the power of the mediated image—still photographs, film, and video.

Photographic images may also change the way we see and understand the world, in more profound ways than shaping tastes (Guimond 1991; Wakin 1993). It was the first photographs from outer space that showed the world as a whole, undivided by political boundaries. It is not coincidence that the first photographs were returned to earth in 1969, the first Earth Day was celebrated in 1970, the concept of Spaceship Earth emerged, and the environmental movement gained significant momentum in the early 1970s. We had come to see the earth as a fragile, interdependent environmental whole.

At MIT's Media Lab, the News of the Future project is approaching the opportunities existing in photographic images from a different perspective. The general approach is to consider news and information not as end products, but as models to think with. One part of this research looks at photographs and video as primary data sources for observational inquiry. They have experimented with students collaborating around photographs and video, activities leading to deeper inquiry, and to the development of explanatory models. One of the experiments looked specifically toward explaining community change through photographs. Students photograph their communities and annotate the images with features that appear to be changing. They compare their images with historical photographs. Based on such comparisons they build causal models of patterns in the community. A software interface that facilitates search, retrieval, comparison, and model building supports these efforts (Smith and Blankinship 1999; also cf. Nardi, Whittaker, and Schwarz 1996; Tsui 1998).

Today, an increasing number of photographic images are captured digitally. Existing analog collections of photographic images are being converted to digital. The traditional still photo camera is being replaced by the digital camera, and the darkroom is being replaced by the digital darkroom—2-D paint and image processing programs. Moving picture and video cameras are becoming digital also, and the editing rooms of film and television studios are rapidly becoming nonlinear digital video editing rooms. New forms of distribution for digital still images, film, and video are also evolving.

The photographic image provides a vast, largely untapped, resource for planners to document and recreate a sense of place; to enrich the understanding of the past and the processes of change, and to offer images of alternative futures that can capture the imagination, alter taste, shape public opinion, and mobilize support. As the photographic image goes digital, it becomes vastly more accessible and useful for all.

2-D PAINT, IMAGE PROCESSING, AND ILLUSTRATION

Paint and image processing capabilities are typically found in the same programs. These programs can "post process" digital photographs or computer models. Digital paint brushes, pens, and airbrushes can retouch and manipulate selected areas or whole images, altering color, providing special effects, or simulating pencil, charcoal, watercolor, or other media. These programs provide all the tools available in the photographic darkroom and many that are not.

These programs can be used to correct or otherwise manipulate not only digital photographs but also images created in other programs; to create original images; and to compose images created from any number of sources. Paint programs are also used to create texture maps for computer rendering. The figures on the following page illustrate the application of digital filters to alter an image. These illustrate only a few of the possible effects that can be created.

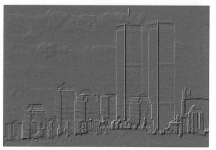

Though paint programs are frequently used to provide near photo-realistic presentations, they may also be used for sketch planning (Van Asperdt and Diamond 1999). Most paint programs now provide layers, so that one can simulate the advantages of sketching, working with several layers of tracing paper.

Illustration and 2-D CAD programs are similar in that both are vector based, but the CAD programs tend to provide the more precise controls required for drafting, while illustration programs provide better freehand and typographic tools needed by graphic artists. Illustration programs are typically superior for general illustration and diagramming. Each is adding capabilities provided by the other, but each remains targeted at a distinct market.

These programs may also be used for enhancing images prepared in other programs, as CAD and GIS. They typically allow much more refinement in color control, composition, rendering, annotation, and presentation.

COMPUTER-BASED REALITY

Virtual Reality

Virtual Reality is a broad and ill-defined concept that has many forms of implementation and involves both special hardware and software (Heim 1998). In its most common form, a user, rather than looking at a computer screen, puts on headgear and gloves to be immersed in a computer-created 3-D simulation. The model views respond to the user's behavior and to programmed model behavior, such as the laws of gravity. Depending upon the implementation, sensors may input to the model such aspects of user behavior as gesture (via the glove); eye, head, or body movement; or voice commands. The reality may be perceived by the user as a wide screen view inside the helmet or projected on a screen, and may include other sensory input and output such as sound, touch, taste, and smell.

A more careful examination of VR may distinguish among the types as follows:

- Immersive VR, with head-mounted display, body and head tracking, glove control, and possibly other sensory inputs as audio, tactile, and olfactory

- Semi-immersive VR, with special glasses to see on-screen stereo display, handheld 3-D navigation device or large-screen projections on one or more walls

- Desktop 3-D for 3-D worlds, with 3-D objects on a 2-D display, handheld 3-D navigation device.

These various methods differ in many respects, particularly in the degree of immersion and the potential for collaboration or group work. All are characterized by users becoming relatively highly immersed in the computer-synthesized environment, experiencing a strong sense of presence there, and, by responding, influencing what happens in the virtual world (Durlach and Mavor 1995, 22).

Mixed reality

Mixed reality environments blend computer-generated and real (as captured in photographs, video, or film) images. One could imagine, for example, planners at a construction site who put on head-mounted displays and look at life-size 3-D models of proposed buildings integrated into the real setting. The Mixed Reality Systems Laboratory (MSRL) in Tokyo was created to explore such possibilities (Robinson 1999). At the University of Washington's Human Interface Technology Lab, research has an emphasis upon applicability to collaborative work (Billinghurst and Kato 1999; also see Klaus et al. 1995 and Li-Shu 1994).

Similar explorations are being pursued in North Carolina under the description of "spatially augmented reality." In both "mixed" and "augmented" environments, the illusion of virtual objects coexisting with the real world is achieved. However, in the former, HMD-based techniques supplement the user's view with images of virtual objects. In spatially augmented reality, the user's physical environment is augmented with images that are projected onto real objects or embedded in the environment with flat panel displays (Raskar, Welch, and Fuchs 1998).

Multisensory

Truly immersive virtual reality environments may need to engage more than vision. Conjure up memories of your favorite architectural or urban space, and you have a visual image. But you may also recollect the sound and feel of walking on a soft carpet or a cobblestone street or rubbing against a handrail or wall. There may be other sounds of people talking, music, or traffic. You may remember smells of flowers, or food, or fresh brewed coffee. The experience of place may involve many senses. Many possibilities exist to incorporate such experiences in the representation of place. (For a general discussion and interesting perspective of our sensorial experiences, cf. Ackerman 1990.)

- Auditory: Animation, multimedia, and hypermedia frequently add audio—as voice, music, or sound effects. Audio systems continue to provide increasingly realistic renditions of the simulated sound. Aureal Semiconductor, Inc., now a part of Creative Technology Ltd, has built a 3-D audio simulator that models the physics of sound, tracking the surfaces it bounces off, the surface properties, and a number of other variables, providing a realistic, three-dimensional, immersive audio experience (Carlile 1996).

- Tactile: As 3-D computer modeling and especially immersive 3-D environments become more common, the desire to "touch" virtual objects becomes stronger, leading to a renaissance for haptics, the study of how people sense the world through touch. Force-feedback systems sense and analyze the forces applied by the user, and in real time simulate the physical sensations of consequent responses. The major types of haptic interface include joysticks and hand controllers, exoskeletal devices (flexible gloves and suits worn by the user), and tactile displays (shape changers, vibrotactile, and electrotactile) (Durlach and Mavor 1995, 175).

- Olfactory: Work is also progressing on simulating smells. Artificial Reality Corp., a VR company, is developing the nasal equivalent of the head-mounted VR display. The device, which looks a little like a gas mask, dispenses scents from bottles of liquid odorants, carrying the vapors to the nose (*Technology Review*, January/February 1999).

  DigiScents, Inc., is developing an odor synthesizer. There are about 1,000 odors the human being can detect. Digiscents is hoping that 100 to 200 "scent primaries" will be sufficient to simulate most smells on demand. They now have a tiny box that, for example, in a recent demo released 26 scents sequenced with an eight-minute video clip. The company's hope is not just for smell-enabled computers in virtual reality applications, but to extend this capability to general computing and Web surfing (Platt 1999).

- Multisensory: The world that we experience engages all our senses. Our responses to that world are both intellectual and emotional. The meaning that we derive from our experiences, and certainly the value we place upon those experiences, may well depend upon our full range of sensory input and our cognitive and emotional responses (Bragdon, Juppé, and Georgiopoulos 1995). All are relevant.

REPRESENTING WHAT WE SEE AND EXPERIENCE: FURTHER THOUGHTS ON WHAT IS, WHAT WAS, AND WHAT MAY BE

It is often desirable to simulate a physical likeness of the environment as it is, was, or may be (Bosselmann 1998). Our perceptions, however, of physical environments are mediated by our minds. Each person creates a mental representation that is personal. The new representation media allow one to create not only a likeness, but also to construct a mental representation and an architectural or urban identity (Lynch 1960; Portugali 1996). That identity may be endowed with meaning, personal or cultural (Gottdiener and Lagopoulos 1986; King 1996; Westwood and Williams 1997; Hall 1998). Real estate developers and city promoters recognize this as they market to the general public, tourists, and prospective employers (Jackson 1995; Neill, Fitzsimons, and Murtagh 1995; Sorkin 1992). The new media provide new possibilities. In computer-visualized worlds the distinction between imaging the city and imagining the city may blur (Benedikt 1991; Boyer 1996; Lévy 1998). Planners also could benefit by creating more compelling images of urban possibilities that capture the attention and build commitment for urban change.

CHARTING AND STATISTICAL GRAPHICS

Charting started about the time of Playfair (Playfair 1786; Tufte 1983). Charting includes text charts and data driven charts—the representation of numeric values by bar, pie, line, area, or other chart types. Many computer programs convert numeric data into charts that can enhance publications and presentations. Some programs add illustration capabilities for enhancing charts and diagrams. Several are evolving into full presentation management systems (Langendorf 1995).

Statistical graphics builds upon the original foundation established by data-driven charting. At first it added a few statistical niceties, logarithmic axis, error bars, new graph types, and the like. John Tukey began a more radical departure with his work on exploratory data analysis (Tukey 1977). His interest was not on presentation graphics, but upon the use of graphic images that could provide rapid statistical insight into the data. Cleveland and McGill extended this work by using the computer's capabilities to provide direct manipulation of graphic elements on screen to facilitate and enhance exploratory data analysis (Cleveland and McGill 1988). There has also been a growing interest in visualizing data sets with many variables (Inselberg and Dimsdale 1990). Dorling has added animation to portray complex patterns of change over time (Dorling 1991). Exploratory data analysis tools are now commonplace in statistical programs, but few yet allow for the simultaneous consideration of more than two or three variables.

DIAGRAMMING

Diagrams are one of the oldest, simplest, most useful, and underused forms of graphics representation. Diagrams can convey simple relationships, depict how to get from here to there, or reveal complex stories as they unfold in space and time (Bertin 1983; Herausgegeben 1988; Pederson 1993; Stovall 1997). As the variety of diagrams is virtually limitless, only an illustrative sampling is provided below.

Decision trees, decision matrices, and organization charts are some of the more common diagrams used in business (Witzling and Greenstreet 1989; Mintzberg and Van der Heyden 1999). Diagrams often take the form of a bubble, area, matrix, hierarchy, or network, but the possibilities are limitless (Lasseau 1986). The pages of *Scientific American* and *National Geographic* are typically filled with diagrams that help explain complex scientific ideas.

Diagrams can be connected to underlying data and be automatically generated by stacking and layout, statistical, database modeling, project management, process modeling and simulation, and other programs. Diagrams, if data driven, may be interactively manipulated (Ahlberg, Williamson, and Shneiderman 1992). Diagrams may also be animated.

Some programs allow the user to construct a diagram that then directs actions taken on the data. Some statistical programs (AMOS, for example), support the definition of structural equations models and report model analysis graphically, facilitating the communication of results (figure 5). For GIS, ModelBuilder™ for the ArcView Spatial Analyst extension provides a graphic means for creating, running, and documenting spatial models. Data mining programs also may provide visual tools for building, editing, and running process flow diagrams. Such diagrams are executed based on graphically defined model specifications.

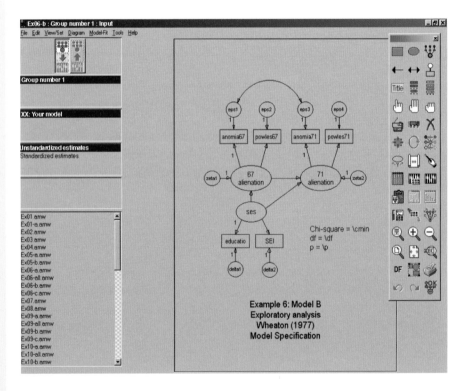

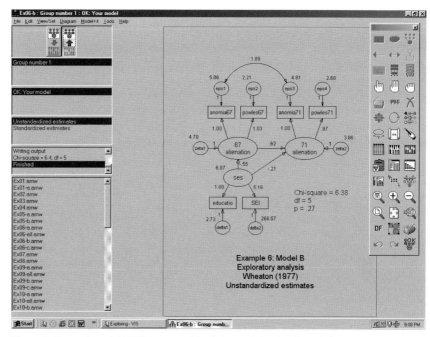

Figure 5. Examples of AMOS 4, a graphically based structural modeling program.

Complex, collaborative projects require coordination. Here, also, visualization aids—particularly diagrams—have helped. The varieties of graphics that support project management are well known—bar charts, Pert charts, and various forms of matrices (Witzling and Greenstreet 1989; Kerzner 1984). A virtual design studio coordinating student work in Hong Kong, Zurich, and Washington State provides a less traditional example. In addition to video conferencing and other methods, specific graphics tools were developed that captured the evolution of each design, the "parent" and "children" of each design idea, and attributed the contribution of each team member. This data was stored in a central database that could be viewed graphically from a diversity of perspectives (Kolarevic, Schmitt, Hirschberg, Kurmann, and Johnson 1998).

DECISION SUPPORT SYSTEMS AND BEYOND

With the growth in computing there has been a rapid increase in the amount of data accumulated, a recognition that much useful knowledge may be hidden in this data, and an interest in developing methods to uncover, understand, and use this knowledge. One of the first methods was decision support systems (DSS), followed by executive information systems (EIS), data mining (DM), and online analytic processing (OLAP) (Langendorf 1985; Paller and Laski 1990; Berson and Smith 1997; Brodley, Lane, and Stough 1999).

Common to all of these developments is the use of visualization to find and communicate patterns in large and multiple data sets. Visualization tools may support the various distinct modeling techniques. In addition to specific visualization aids for select analytic methods, visualization has more generally facilitated knowledge discovery and communication through the design of the graphical user interface; in data selection; building, editing, and running process flow diagrams; and the display of results. Such visualization aids have flattened the learning curve, making such analytic capability available to more people, as well as contributing to more efficient and effective analysis and better communication of results.

INFORMATION GRAPHICS

In recent years there has been growing interest and use of visualization to improve communication in business, in design and other professions, and in newspapers and magazines. This is resulting in earlier work being integrated into the newly evolving field of information graphics (Meyer 1997; Tufte 1983, Tufte 1990; Tufte 1997; Wurman 1996; Wildbur 1998). Information graphics encompasses a broad interest in graphic communication, including charts, maps, diagrams, pictographs, plans, sections, and a variety of other forms of visual representation. It is more concerned with how people perceive and understand information and how design principles and graphic expression can contribute to more efficient and effective communication of information. The fruits of these interests are likely to be seen not only in the design of a particular graphic suited to a particular audience and message, but also in the page layouts and relationships between text and graphics. The results are found in well-designed books, newspapers, presentations, and now Web sites.

Once one acknowledges that visual communication includes not only individual graphic images, but the organization of text and images, then word processing, desktop publishing, presentation management, multimedia and Web authoring all become potential categories of visualization software. Not only the design of a particular graphic, but also the decision regarding what to express in text and what in graphic images, the spatial relationships of text and images, the sequencing and navigation on screen or page or book—all effect the viewer's attention, understanding, and retention of the information presented. To realize this potential requires a different approach and broader set of skills than is traditional in the use of such software for design and document production.

Strictly speaking, information graphics is not so much an application as an attitude that is intended to increase effectiveness in using application programs. It has also defined design methodologies for the creation of information environments.

VISUALIZATION ENVIRONMENTS

The visualization applications software described above typically perform designated tasks on specified sets of data. Visualization can also greatly aid in providing environments that facilitate task management and integration, the search for additional relevant data, and collaboration. It is with the rapid evolution of the World Wide Web that an appreciation of the potential of visualization environments can be achieved. In the discussion below we distinguish between two broad, sometimes overlapping, environments: information visualization and workspace visualization. Workspace visualization reaches beyond a particular visualization application to include associated tools, data, and support for collaboration. Information visualization reaches yet further, into the infosphere—the world of information that may be accessible anywhere

INFORMATION VISUALIZATION: WAYFINDING IN REAL AND CYBERSPACE

People get lost in buildings, in parks and highways, in urban places. In recent decades there has been a growing interest and understanding regarding how people picture and navigate physical environments (Passini 1992; Golledge 1999). Architects, environmental designers, and others have sought to apply this knowledge as they design and build spaces. Kevin Lynch has made operable such concepts to aid in evaluating and creating good city form (Lynch 1960). The problems of navigating in a more abstract infosphere or cyberspace may be similar, and undoubtedly even more challenging.

Most of the above-described visualization tools use spatially associated data and specific data sets. Here we consider especially visualization for aspatial data and for data that may be widely distributed and not necessarily assembled into data sets.

As the magnitude of such data increases exponentially, the difficulty of finding useful data becomes ever more challenging. The World Wide Web was created as a response to this problem. By succeeding in providing access to a rapidly expanding universe of information, paradoxically, the Web has generated a demand for ever more powerful means for browsing, searching, linking, retrieving, and relating such information. Visualization tools have proved invaluable aids in these endeavors. Here we will look at recent work described under such topics as information landscapes, cyberspace, information, and project workspaces. Such environments have been used for a variety of purposes including Web navigation and Web site design, large scale data monitoring, managing large text databases, mapping cyberspace, and as a front end for knowledge management. These visualization environments also provide a context for the more effective use of the applications programs previously described.

INFORMATION LANDSCAPES

The late Muriel Cooper, founder of the Visible Language Workshop at the MIT Media Lab, coined the phrase "information landscape" to express the idea of visually navigating a world of information where

> information 'hangs' like constellations and the reader 'flies' from place to place, exploring yet maintaining context while moving so that the journey itself can be as meaningful as the final destination.

> A landscape, whether real or virtual, provides an experience in which context is continuous and meaningful. It is through context that we can understand new information and can relate it to what is already known . . . . (Small 1996, 516)

The early work at the Media Lab laid a foundation for what would follow. A method was developed for displaying typography at any size, position, and orientation in 3-D space, and for moving a virtual camera through the space, exploring the information, both text and images, that inhabit the space. This foundation work was then extended for specific experimental applications.

Financial Viewpoints is an experimental information landscape that uses three dimensions to visualize a sample portfolio of seven mutual funds (Cooper and Small 1996, 204). News Views uses visualization techniques to navigate current news stories (Ibid., 208; Rennison 1994). The plays of William Shakespeare were also used to explore the design of a virtual information space that maintains the qualities of a meaningful landscape. The typography is designed to handle text at a variety of scales, from about one hundred words to several hundred thousand words, allowing the viewer to move smoothly between detailed views and overviews of as many as one million words.

> In making information accessible to people, it is necessary for designers to rethink current design paradigms. The computer screen is not a piece of paper and should not be treated as such. By taking advantage of the ability of the computer to display dynamic, flexible, and adaptive typography, we can invent new ways for people to read, interact with, and assimilate the written word. Like a garden, well designed information should be legible, inviting, and comfortable, and its exploration should and can be a true delight (Small 1996, 524f.).

Most of the Media Lab experiments described above populate the landscape with full text renditions, though higher levels of abstraction are also used. Other work at MIT and elsewhere places more emphasis upon the higher levels of abstraction for organizing and accessing large document collections. These may typically involve some forms of document content analysis, themes extraction, and the spatial clustering of documents around the themes. Such visualizations may facilitate finding documents on a particular topic, and tracing related documents. They support as well the navigation of theme-based landscapes, again providing an understanding of context for individual documents or document collections.

Cyberspace

Cyberspace is a particular information landscape of interest in its own right. The science fiction writer William Gibson coined the word "cyberspace," defining it as "a consensual hallucination experienced daily by billions of legitimate operators, in every nation, by children being taught mathematical concept . . . a graphical representation of data abstracted from the banks of every computer in the human system. Unthinkable complexity. Lines of light ranged in the non-space of the mind, clusters and constellations of data. Like city lights, receding . . . ." (Gibson 1984). The World Wide Web as cyberspace is not far different. A tally of the Web in 1998 found that the Web contained about 10 terabytes of information in about

200 million documents, and that amount is doubling every 12 months. Finding some order and sense in this cyberworld has brought forth a variety of visualization efforts.

Some of the resulting visualizations map the information landscape of the Web. Martin Dodge, a geographer at the Centre for Advanced Spatial Analysis at University College, London, has compiled an online atlas of many of these efforts to visualize virtual space (www.cybergeography.org/atlas).

Digital libraries and visual databases

For centuries museums have collected art work and photographs. Libraries have collected not only books, but also photographs and maps. Advertising agencies, architecture and planning offices, and academic institutions have slide collections. Film institutes collect movies. News agencies and television broadcasters assemble vast libraries of still and video images. Stock photo houses have tens of millions of still images, video and film clips. Many of these collections are being digitized.

In this digital age everything is changing. The boldest and largest scale efforts however are national and international digital library initiatives in Australia, Japan, Singapore, Korea, United Kingdom, European Community, and the United States. This discussion will mostly focus upon the Digital Library initiatives in the United States. These efforts typically include digitized versions of traditional library materials as well as visual resources. They are broadly defined to not merely enhance digitized collections with cataloging, search, and retrieval tools. Rather, digital library efforts seek to support the full life cycle of creation, dissemination, use, and preservation of data, information, and knowledge (Duguid 1997). There is an emphasis upon supporting distributed knowledge work environments for individuals, teams, organizations, and communities.

In the United States, IBM, Xerox, the Library of Congress, and NASA, among others, have significant digital library efforts underway. From among the many projects that are part of the American initiative, efforts at Carnegie Mellon and the University of California at Santa Barbara are singled out here as particularly relevant.

The Infomedia Project at Carnegie Mellon University is primarily directed at enabling full content, knowledge-based search and segment retrieval from digital video libraries. It addresses the challenge to catalog and find a short video clip in 1,000 hours or 100,000 hours of video. This project uses both the images and speech on video to integrate image analysis, speech recognition, and natural language processing to segment the video into small consistent pieces, to analyze and derive additional metadata for creating alternative representations of the video, and to augment it with indices for fast searching and retrieval. To complement this automated populating of the video library, visualization techniques are being developed for the user interface (Christel and Martin 1998).

The researchers at Carnegie Mellon realized that much of the video information was associated with locations. They developed automated techniques for recognizing geographic references, associating spatial coordinates with referenced names, and finally converting this information into shapefiles from which map representations were constructed. The resulting map displays can be used for viewing and for searching. Thus the capabilities of the system have been extended to include word, image, and spatial query (Christel and Olligschlaeger 1999).

The central goal of the Alexandria project at the University of California at Santa Barbara was to allow users to access and manipulate geospatially referenced information from distributed collections, in a variety of forms including maps, images, text, and multimedia items. In 1998 the Alexandria project extended its scope and coordinated, as part of the InterLib project, with digital library efforts at Stanford University and the University of California at Berkeley. The InterLib agenda is defined as follows:

> InterLib will allow individuals from various groups, such as business people, government employees, scientists, and students, to act individually or collectively in performing a wide array of information creation and processing activities. They will, for example, be able to use services that enable them to access and synthesize information from a wide variety of distributed collections, to evaluate the quality and importance of the accessed information, to perform relevant manipulations of the information, and to disseminate the results of their activities. Perhaps most important, users will be able to use services that help them find each other, explore and visualize each other's data and documents, and annotate each other's data and documents so that individuals can benefit from their insights and

expertise. In effect, users will be able to organize themselves into informal or formal distributed collaborative groups, as their needs require, making efficient use of a broad spectrum of distributed collections and services (Acharya et al. 1998, 1f).

The Alexandria project's extension, ADEPT, is intended to allow people to access and process distributed georeferenced information resources through sets of digital library, analysis, and modeling services. ADEPT is further described here by reference to a scenario included in the proposal.

> The *instructor* uses the services of ADEPT to discover and use information resources for class presentations, laboratory sessions, and interactions with students. For presentations on flood management, for example, the instructor uses services for (1) discovering information resources for display during class presentations that include images, videos, tables, data sets, and even simulation models; (2) constructing additional meta-information describing semantic relationships and compatibilities between resources that facilitate their joint use; and (3) constructing an appropriate Iscape (Information landscape). An example of the additional meta-information constructed describes whether a rainfall dataset is compatible with the input requirements of a hydrograph simulation model. The instructor uses the visual presentation services of ADEPT to examine maps on which icons indicate the availability of different information resources characterizing rivers in prescribed counties, as well as the availability of flood simulation procedures. During class presentations, the instructor accesses services enabling the visualization and flexible, joint use of these information resources in interacting with students. In response to questions about different flood hydrograph simulations, the instructor displays an ADEPT visualization showing which rivers are characterized by data sets compatible with the input requirements of a simulation model, and runs the model by dragging and dropping data sets onto its icon.

> The *students,* in collaborative study groups, use ADEPT to reach informed decisions about managing environmental resources. In evaluating a flood control policy that allows rivers to assume their natural course, for example, groups of students use the services of ADEPT to (1) discover and integrate into Iscapes (Information landscapes) information resources about

the nature, effects, and management of rivers that flood in the assigned area; (2) access, visualize, and evaluate relevant information resources for understanding the social costs of flooding; (3) simulate and evaluate alternative management strategies in terms of their net social benefits. Students access a range of presentation services when visualizing their results, including desktop, projected, and immersive displays, as well as an array of services supporting the *information life cycle* including, for example, the publication of the results of their learning experiences" (Ibid., 6, parenthesis added).

Consider substituting planner for instructor and participants in the planning process for students. Such research and development work regarding digital libraries points toward substantially richer and more useful information environments for planning, environments where visualization has important and diverse roles to play. Such environments may significantly alter the way planners work and the environments planners may create for their collaborators and citizenry.

INFORMATION WORKSPACES

Information workspace refers to the collection and organization of data and information, often from multiple sources, for a particular person or task. The desktop metaphor for graphical user interfaces performs a similar function—that is, it organizes an individual's computing workspace so that information that is needed is at hand and locatable. It is no accident that some of the most interesting work on information workspace is occurring at Xerox PARC, the birthplace of the graphical user interface. The researchers at Xerox PARC draw parallels with scientific visualization.

Recent work in scientific visualization shows how the computer can serve as an intermediary in the process of rapid assimilation of information. Large sets of data are reduced to graphic form in such a way that human perception can detect patterns revealing underlying structure in the data more readily than by a direct analysis of the numbers. Information in the form of documents also has structure. *Information visualization* attempts to display structural relationships and context that would be more difficult to detect by individual retrieval requests. (Robertson, Card, and Mackinlay 1993, 523).

In the Information Visualizer, Xerox scientists explore 3-D visualizations for some of the classical data organizations: hierarchical, linear, spatial, continuous data, and unstructured. These visualizations are interactive and animated, permitting easy movement between focus and context. They are quite sophisticated in their ability to detect user patterns, and in their employment of color, lighting, shadow, transparency, hidden surface occlusion, continuous transformations, and motion cues to induce object constancy and 3-D perspective (Ibid., also see Card, Robertson, and York 1996).

Project workspaces and collaborative environments

A project workspace is a particular type of information workspace—one that is geared to serve a team of individuals collaborating on a project. It serves two purposes: (1) it is a virtual workplace for people, providing services to enhance communication and collaboration; and (2) it is also a container for the data shared by the group and the work they produce. As a virtual workspace for people, the services it may provide—e-mail, scheduling, video-conferencing, and the like—are described in any number of books and articles on groupware or computer supported collaborative work (CSCW). White boards, white walls, immersive environments and other tools supporting collaborative graphic communication are also particularly relevant to planning and design, and have been described to a limited extent above (Moran, et. al. 1999). Following are a few examples suggestive of the ways visualization may contribute to collaborative environments, particularly regarding the augmentation of the visual record of physical planning and design development.

Projects that involve planning and design usually produce graphic displays of physical plans, building complexes—or more generally, representations of the proposed physical environments. However, it may also be important to capture information about design intent; the rationale for a particular decision; alternatives that were considered and debated regarding the choice; decision criteria and the process of decision making; codes, requirements, design guidelines and specifications; and the like. Several approaches have been developed to address this situation (Wong and Kvan 1999; McCall et al. 1988).

Maia Engeli and her collaborators at the ETH in Zurich, Switzerland, have developed and explored a variety of workspace environments to support learning and creative collaboration. These virtual environments have been tested in individual courses and collaborative design experiments involving collaboration among students in Zurich, Hong Kong, University of Washington, and elsewhere. Projects are supported by centralized databases that may capture information about when a contribution is made, by whom, based on what knowledge and design intent, related to what other data and previous work. Tracking these provides a recording of process, a process that invites reflection and open examination. The workspace environment provides highly interactive access to the database and supports multiple views of the data (Engeli and Mueller 1999).

Craig and Zimring, at the Georgia Institute of Technology, have developed a prototype system that supports design by allowing collaborators to mark up 3-D models over the Internet using a variety of tools, including diagrammatic marks, dynamic simulations, and text annotations, including threaded discussions. The system relies on VRML to view the models, and, through the models, to provide access to the supplementary information that explains the results (Craig and Zimring 1999).

John Danahy and Bharat Dave describe a very different model of collaboration. Students in different cities do not collaborate in design. Rather, students in each city design in the others' cities, and collaborate by providing the distant students with information about their city. Also, using custom software, the students discuss, analyze, and critique using synchronous and asynchronous three-dimensional model exchange and linked attribute data. The models are downloaded and investigated in advance of the reviews. As the model resides at each site, only instructions for model manipulation need be transmitted, facilitating low bandwidth interactive model manipulation of highly complex models during review. Whiteboards were also used, but were slow and less satisfactory than the 3-D model manipulations. As a consequence of the nature of the collaboration, this exercise served to enhance the interest and knowledge about context during the design (Dave and Danahy 1998).

Röscheisen, Mogensen, and Winograd have taken a more general approach to annotation, as part of Stanford University's digital library initiative. They are developing a general mechanism for shared annotations that allows people to annotate various document types (e.g., text and image, at any position in-place). Annotations may be used to add personal notes; to share comments and hyperlinks publicly, with a designated group, or privately; to denote "landmarks" and connect landmarks providing "tours" and "trails" through information landscapes; and to provide "seals of approval," a rating of other documents. The annotations are metadata, held in a central repository with links to the distributed documents (Röscheisen, Mogensen, and Winograd 1995).

Knowledge Management, an Enterprise Workspace

As extensive as the Web is, it is estimated that it accesses a fraction, about 3 percent, of online information. Most online information (e.g., databases, digitized and digitally created documents) is not on the Web, at least not yet. There is a growing recognition of the benefits that may be realized by capturing the knowledge stored in these online resources. Perhaps more importantly, there is the realization that much knowledge never is documented, but is retained in the minds of individuals within an organization.

Knowledge management is critically dependent upon capturing and classifying an organization's knowledge, no matter where it is located, and providing access to it for the individual or workgroup that could benefit in a timely fashion. Knowledge management is evolving in the direction of a virtual environment for collaboration. One could think of this as analogous to creating an information workspace for individuals, work groups, and organizations.

Though the emerging field of knowledge management has given little consideration to developing its own visualization methods, many practitioners have adapted an existing approach.

"Knowledge management has found its killer app. The enterprise information portal—simple in concept but previously elusive in practice—is suddenly front and center on the IT agenda. Bringing together in one embodiment the notions of business intelligence, document classification, text analysis, group collaboration, executive information and the company intranet, it promises to provide what we've been looking for from computers since the days of Norbert Weiner and Vannevar Bush." (Roberts–Witt 1999, 37. The July issue of *Knowledge Management* focuses upon portals, providing substantial coverage, case studies, and reviews of 50 products; also see Shroeder 1999.)

Knowledge management and supporting visualization could hold much promise for public planning—both for planners and their constituents.

PLANNING AND INFORMATION ENVIRONMENTS

As planning and design become more participatory and the quantity and accessibility of information rapidly increases, the role of planners may shift toward their becoming creators of information environments that empower themselves and other participants. This may mean greater time and effort will be devoted to the structuring of information architecture and interaction design, so that all participants are supported in their explorations, knowledge building, decisions, and actions.

Planners have long considered the role of the various participants in the planning process. Much of that consideration in the 1960s and 1970s revolved around debates regarding the role of citizen participation. Interactivity design can be thought of as participation design in the virtual world. In this virtual world the design of information landscapes and workspaces may determine, for example, what degree of control the user has, the data that is available, definitions of problems and objectives, the ability to independently analyze problems, the shaping of plans and designs, the evaluation of plans and designs, and implementation. Interactivity design can determine whether viewers review, comment, recommend, propose alternatives, vote, decide, and the extent to which they act individually or collaboratively.

The design of information landscapes and workspaces is not an issue that planners have typically considered. Nevertheless, there is likely to be an increasing need for planners to become such designers. The experience of participation may contribute significantly to the creation of a knowledgeable constituency and the preparation for purposeful action. Thus the traditional consumers of plans now become co-producers. Planners will be increasingly structuring information for a broader range of individuals and organizations to access and use as stakeholders and participants in the planning process. The digital world facilitates access and participation; it remains for planners to construct the environment in which this can happen. We can see how these many pieces of landscapes, workspaces, and applications fit together in figure 7.

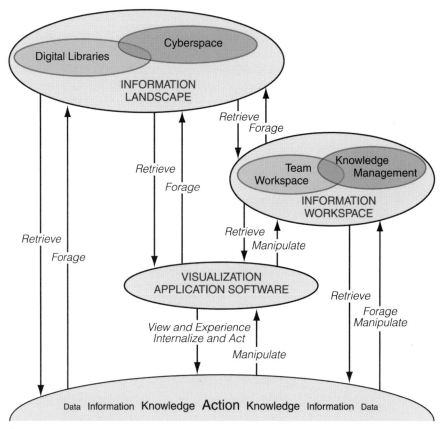

Figure 7. Relationships among information landscapes, workspaces, and applications.

SUMMARY AND CONCLUSIONS

Because we so easily take what is available today for granted, it is easy to forget how rapidly the field of visualization has changed. There is, of course, the continuing evolution in applications software. However, this evolution is being swamped by changes surrounding the applications. Personal computers have been networked, supporting collaborative work. Graphical user interfaces have become the norm, making possible several simultaneous workspaces that support multiple-application programs, to and from which data can move freely. Finally, the individual can reach out to the world of data beyond, directly, through applications programs or information workspaces. All this provides a much more open and dynamic environment, one that invites exploration and collaboration, one that is likely to engage active participants.

Returning to the original premises may help place this journey in context.

In our complex world, to understand nearly any subject of consequence it is necessary to consider it from multiple viewpoints, using a variety of information.

Structured and unstructured, primarily text, data; data representing what we see and what we don't; spatial, temporal, and multisensory data; statistics, reports, photographic and satellite images, 3-D models, audio, video, and animation—the quantity of all these types of data is exploding, and visualization applications and environments are providing increasing access and integration. They are also providing considerable viewing flexibility—the ability to zoom in and out between overview and detail, to achieve a focus without losing context, to simultaneously display multiple views. A map or near photorealistic view may serve as an end in itself, or it may provide an interface between the user and the underlying data, helping to link and integrate the views of what we see with what we don't.

The second premise is that we are rapidly moving from a data-poor to an information-rich society.

Visual applications software is adapting but in particular, information environments—information landscapes and information workspaces—are evolving as a direct response. They are enabling wayfinding—providing navigation aids and a historic record. The navigation aids are indispensable to finding what is relevant.

The third premise is that the understanding of complex information may be greatly extended if visualized.

Highly interactive visual applications and environments are providing the editing flexibility that facilitates the exploration of many options. They are providing flexible tools for structuring, organizing, integrating—transforming data into information, and information into knowledge.

Visualizations, whether an architect's renderings or a scientist's charts, represent facts and possibilities. But visualization may accomplish much more. The movies have always recognized the importance of visualization in telling compelling stories. Modern computing technology is extending that storytelling capability to the desktop of the average computer user. Finally, hyperrealism, multimedia, and virtual reality are providing the possibility for providing compelling experiences—the fuller experiences that architecture, the city, and life entail.

The fourth premise is that problem solving and commitment to action in a complex world require communication and collaboration among many participants, and that visualization aids this interaction.

Nowhere can the case for visualization be made in a more compelling way than regarding the Internet. For 20 years the Internet remained the plaything of a relatively small elite, the computer literate who were comfortable with command language interfaces. Then, with the introduction of the graphical user interface, the Internet, in the form of the World Wide Web, experienced explosive growth and opened up to more than one hundred-million users in the United States and many more worldwide. The visualization and collaboration possibilities of the Web change everything. Visualization applications software and their products are greatly enriched by being placed within the environments—information landscapes and workspaces—now available. The products transform static, often paper, products into dynamic documents with which individuals interact and around which individuals may collaborate.

In the interactive computing environment, everything is changeable, and the distinctions between author and reader dissolve. Traditionally, the producers—the professional planners, architects, and others—would be responsible for selecting data, transforming data into information, knowledge, plans, and designs. The consumers would be responsible for action, for implementing the plans and designs. The boundary between producer and consumer now overlap. In this new environment, consumers can reach back to original data and participate actively in its transformation to information and knowledge. The consumer is now a much more active player, potentially at all stages of the process. The relationship between producer and consumer, professional and stakeholder, has changed.

In such an environment can planning remain the same? May visualization have a transforming ability? Perhaps after this brief tour of visualization upon which we have ventured, the opening statement or premises about visualization will have gained additional context and meaning.

These four premises are the underlying assumptions that frame the approach that is taken here. They set the stage for considering visualization as much more than creating realistic images of what is or what might be, and much more than creating attractive charts and maps. Visualization is concerned with foraging for data in a data-rich environment made much more accessible by the World Wide Web. It is involved with transforming data to information to knowledge and into action. It can include recreating a sense of history and place; supporting collaborations that alter the way we work; and creating compelling experiences that alter people's view of the world about them and move individuals, organizations, and communities to change that world, or perhaps some small place in the world. Computer visualization is about all these things.

BIBLIOGRAPHY

Acharya, Anurag et al. 1998. *The Alexandria Digital Earth Modeling System (ADEPT). Towards a distributed digital model of the earth in support of learning.* Unpublished proposal. Santa Barbara, CA.: University of California, Santa Barbara.

Ackerman, Diane. 1990. *A Natural History of the Senses.* New York: Random House.

Ahlberg, C., C. Williamson, and B. Shneiderman. An Information Visualization and Exploration Environment. *Proceedings of CHI'92, ACM Conference on Human Factors in Computing Systems,* 619–26.

Albrecht, Donald. 1986. *Designing Dreams: Modern Architecture in the Movies.* New York: Harper & Row.

Andrienko, Gennady L. and Natalia V. Andrienko. 1999. Interactive Maps for Visual Data Exploration. *International Journal Geographic Information Science.* June, 13:4, 355–74.

Acevedo, W. and P. Masuoka. 1997. Time-series Animation Techniques for Visualizing Urban Growth. *Computers and Geosciences.* 23:4, 423–36.

Bamberger, Tom. 1996. *City Stories: 150 years of Photography of Milwaukee.* Milwaukee, WI: Milwaukee Art Museum.

Batty, Michael, Martin Dodge, Bin Jiang, and Andy Smith. 1998. *GIS and Urban Design.* Paper 3. London, UK: Centre for Advanced Spatial Analysis, University College London, June.

Batty, Michael and David Howes. 1996. Exploring Urban Development Dynamics through Visualization and Animation. *Innovations in GIS.* ed. David Parker, Vol. 3. London: Taylor & Francis, 149–61.

Batty, Michael and Paul Longley. 1994. *Fractal Cities: A Geometry of Form and Function.* London, San Diego: Academic Press. 1994.

Benedikt, Michael, ed. 1991. *Cyberspace: First Steps.* Cambridge, MA: MIT Press.

Berson, Alex and Stephen J Smith. 1997. *Data Warehousing, Data Mining, and OLAP*. McGraw–Hill Series on Data Warehousing and Data Management. New York: McGraw–Hill.

Bertin, Jacques. 1981. *Graphics and Graphic Information Processing*. Berlin: Walter de Gruyter.

———. 1983. *Semiology of Graphics: Diagrams, Networks, Maps*. Madison, WI: University of Wisconsin Press. Translated to English by Walter de Gruyter. Originally published 1967, as La Graphique et le Traittment Graphique de l'Information. Paris: Flammarion.

Billinghurst, Mark and Hirokazu Kato. 1999. *Collaborative Mixed Reality. Proceedings of the First International Symposium on Mixed Reality (ISMR '99). Mixed Reality—Merging Real and Virtual Worlds*. Berlin: Springer–Verlag.

Bosselmann, Peter. 1998. *Representation of Places. Reality and Realism in City Design*. Berkeley, CA: University of California Press.

Boyer, M. Christine. 1996. *CyberCities: Visual perception in the age of electronic communication*. New York: Princeton Architectural Press.

Bragdon, C. R., J. M. Juppé and A. X. Georgiopoulos. 1995. Sensory Spatial Systems Simulation (S^4) Applied to the Master Planning Process: East Coast and West Coast Studies. *Environment and Planning B 22*, no. 3:303-14.

Brand, Stuart. 1988. *The Media Lab. Inventing the Future at M.I.T.* New York: Penguin Books.

Brodley, Carla E., Terran Lane, and Timothy M. Stough. Knowledge Discovery and Data Mining. *American Scientist.*, January–February 1999.

Burden, Ernest E. 1985. *Design simulation: Use of Photographic and Electronic Media in Design and Presentation*. New York: Wiley.

Card, Stuart K., Jock D. Mackinlay, and Ben Shneiderman. 1999. *Readings in Information Visualization: Using Vision to Think*. The Morgan Kaufmann Series in Interactive Technologies. San Francisco: Morgan Kaufmann Publishers.

Card, S. K., G. G. Robertson, and W. York. 1996. The Web-Book and the Web Forager: An Information Workspace for the World-Wide Web. *Proceedings of CHI'96, ACM Conference on Human Factors in Computer Systems*. New York: ACM, 111–17.

Carlile, Simon. 1996. *Virtual Auditory Space: Generation and Applications*. Neuroscience Intelligence Unit. New York: R.G. Landes.

Cartwright, W. 1997. New Media and their Application to the Production of Map Products. *Computers and Geosciences*. 23:4, 447–56.

Charney, Leo and Vanessa R. Schwartz, eds. 1995. *Cinema and the Invention of Modern Life*. Berkeley: University of California Press.

Christel, Michael and David Martin. Information Visualization within a Digital Video Library. *Journal of Intelligent Information*. Special issue on information visualization. June 1998.

Christel, Michael and Andraes M. Olligschlaeger. Interactive Maps for a Digital Video Library. *IEEE International Conference on Multimedia Computing and Systems.* Florence, Italy, June 7–11, 1999.

Cleveland, William S. and Marylyn E. McGill. 1988. *Dynamic Graphics for Statistics.* Pacific, CA.: Wadsworth & Brooks/Cole Advanced Books & Software.

Cooper, Muriel and David Small. Visible Language Workshop. In Wurman, Richard Saul. 1996. *Information Architects.* Zurich: Graphis, 202–11.

Craig, David Latch and Craig Zimring. 1999. Support for Collaborative Design Reasoning in Shared Virtual Spaces. Ataman, Osman and Bermúdez, Julio, eds. *Media and Design Process.* Conference Proceedings. October 29–31, 1999.

Dave, Bharat and John Danahy. 1998. Virtual Study Abroad and Exchange Studio. *Digital Design Studios: Do Computers Make a Difference? Acadia '98.* ed. Thomas Seebohm and Skip Van Wyk. Albuquerque, NM: The Association for Computer-Aided Design in Architecture (ACADIA), 100–15.

DiBiase, David, Alan M. MacEachren, J. Krygier, and C. Reeves. 1992. Animation and the role of map design in scientific visualization. *Cartography and Geographic Information Systems 19,* no. 4:201–14.

Dorling, Daniel. 1991. Visualizing People in Space and Time. In *Second International Conference on Computers in Urban Planning and Management,* ed. Richard E. Klosterman. Akron, OH: Institute for Computer-Aided Planning: 305–36.

Dorling, Daniel. 1992. Stretching Space and Splicing Time: From Cartographic Animation to Interactive Visualization. *Cartography and Geographic Information Systems 19,* no. 4:215–27.

Dorling, Daniel and Stan Openshaw. 1991. Some Experiments Using Computer Movies to Visualize Space-Time Patterns. In *Second International Conference on Computers in Urban Planning and Management.* ed. Richard E. Klosterman. Akron, OH: Institute for Computer-Aided Planning: 391–406.

Duguid, Paul. 1997. *Report of the Santa Fe Planning Workshop on Distributed Knowledge Work Environments: Digital Libraries.* Ann Arbor, MI: University of Michigan School of Information, Report Version September 20.

Durlach, Nathaniel I., Anne S. Mavor, and National Research Council Committee on Virtual Reality Research and Development. 1995. *Virtual reality : Scientific and Technological Challenges.* Washington, D.C.: National Academy Press.

Earnshaw, Rae A. and John Vince. 1997. *The Internet in 3D: Information, Images, and Interaction.* San Diego: Academic Press.

Emmett, Arielle. 1998. Virtual Journeys: Computer-generated Museum Displays Let Visitors Travel Great Distances through Space and Time without Stepping out of the Building. *Computer Graphics World,* May 1998:34–49

Engeli, Maia and Andre Mueller. 1999. Digital Environments for Learning and Collaboration. Architecture, Communication, Creativity. In Ataman, Osman and Bermúdez, Julio. 1999. *Media and Design Process.* Conference Proceedings. October 29–31, 1999.

Forte, Maurizio, and Alberto Siliotti. 1997. *Virtual Archaeology: Re-creating Ancient Worlds.* New York: Harry N. Abrams, Inc.

Friedhoff, Richard Mark. 1989. *Visualization: The Second Computer Revolution.* New York: Harry N. Abrams, Inc.

Gallagher, Richard S. 1995. *Computer Visualization : Graphics Techniques for Scientific and Engineering Analysis.* Boca Raton, FL: CRC Press.

Gibson, William. 1984. *Neuromancer.* New York: Ace.

Giffin, A.L. 1999. Feeling It Out: The Use of Haptic Visualization for Exploratory Geographic Analysis. Paper presented at *NACIS XIX.* NACIS, Williamsburg, Virginia, October 20–23.

Golledge, Reginald G. 1999. *Wayfinding Behavior: Cognitive Mapping and Other Spatial Processes.* Baltimore, MD: Johns Hopkins University Press.

Gottdiener, Mark and Alexandros Lagopoulos. 1986. *The City and the Sign: an Introduction to Urban Semiotics.* New York: Columbia University Press.

Greenwald, Ted. 1999. Worth the Wait. *3D. Advanced Graphics & Animation.* 5:11, November 7.

Guimond, James. 1991. *American Photography and the American Dream.* Chapel Hill, NC: University of North Carolina Press.

Hagen, Hans, Heinrich Müller, and Gregory M. Nielson. 1993. *Focus on Scientific Visualization.* Berlin, NY: Springer–Verlag.

Hall, Tim. 1998. Transforming the Image of the City. *Urban Geography.* Routledge Contemporary Human Geography Series. London; New York: Routledge, 110–32.

Heim, Michael. 1998. *Virtual Realism.* New York: Oxford University Press.

Hearnshaw, H. and D. Unwin, eds. 1994. *Visualization in GIS.* New York: John Wiley & Sons.

Hockings, Paul, ed. 1995. *Principles of Visual Anthropology.* New York: Mouton de Gruyter.

Hodges, Mark. 1998. It Just Feels Right: Tools that Add the Sense of Touch to the Computer Desktop are Providing Users with a Sense of Reality. *Computer Graphics World.* 48ff.

Hoffnagle, Gene F., ed. 1996. MIT Media Lab. *IBM Systems Journal.* 35:3, 4.

Hopkins, Lewis D., Douglas M. Johnston, and R. Varkki George. 1999. Computer Support for Sketch Planning. In *Computers in Urban Planning and Urban Management on the Edge of the Millennium,* ed. Paola Rizzi. *Proceedings of the 6th International Conference.* September 8–11, 1999, Venice, Italy.

Inselberg, A. and B. Dimsdale. 1991. Parallel Coordinates: A Tool for Visualizing Multivariate Geometry. *Proceedings of IEEE Visualization '90 Conference.* Los Alamitos, CA, 361–375.

Jacobson, Robert, ed. 1999. *Information Design.* Cambridge, MA: MIT Press.

Jackson, E. 1995. *Marketing an image for main street: How to develop a compelling message and identity for downtown.* Washington, D.C.: National Main Street Center, National Trust for Historic Preservation.

Jepson, William and Scott Friedman. 1998. *A Real-Time Visualization System for Large Scale Urban Environments*. Unpublished paper. Los Angeles: Urban Simulation Team, University of California, Los Angeles.

Kepes, Gyorgy, ed. 1965. *Education of Vision*. New York: George Braziller.

Kerzner, Harold. 1984. *Project Management: A Systems Approach to Planning, Scheduling and Controlling*. Second Edition. New York: Van Nostrand Reinhold Company.

King, Anthony D. 1996. *Re-presenting the City: Ethnicity, Capital and Culture in the 21st-Century Metropolis*. New York: New York University Press.

Kjems, E. 1999. Creating 3D-Models for the Purpose of Planning. *6th International Conference. Computers in urban planning & urban management*. September 8–11, 1999, Venice, Italy.

Klaus, A., et. al. 1995. Distributed Augmented Reality for Collaborative Design Applications. *Proceedings of Eurographics '95*. September, C–3 to C–14.

Kolarevic, Branko, Gerhard Schmitt, Urs Hirschberg, David Kurmann, and Brian Johnson. 1998. An Experiment in Design Collaboration. In *Digital Design Studios: Do Computers Make a Difference?* ed. Thomas Seebohm and Skip Van Wyk. ACADIA 98: 90–99.

Kraak, Menno–Jan and Alan MacEachren, guest eds. 1999. *International Journal Geographic Information Science*. Special issue on Visualization for Exploration of Spatial Data. June, 13:4

Kraak, Menno–Jan and R. van Driel. 1997. Principles of Hypermaps. *Computers and Geosciences*. 23:4, 457–64.

Krygier, J. 1994. Sound and Geographic Visualization. In *Visualization in Modern Cartography*, ed. Alan M. MacEachren and D. R. F. Taylor. 1st ed. Oxford, U.K.; New York: Pergamon, 149–66.

Langendorf, Richard. 1985. Computers and Decision Making. *Journal of the American Planning Association*. 51:4, August, 422–33.

———. 1991. 1990s: Information Systems and Computer Visualization for Urban Design, Planning, and Management. *Second International Conference on Computers in Urban Planning and Management*, ed. Richard E. Klosterman, Akron, OH.: Institute for Computer-Aided Planning, 415–38.

———. 1995a. *Presentation Graphics*. Planning Advisory Service Report Number 453. Chicago, IL: American Planning Association.

———. Guest ed. 1995b. Special Issue on Visualization in Urban Analysis and Design. *Environment and Planning B*. Vol. 22.

Laseau, Paul. 1986. *Graphic Problem Solving for Architects and Designers*. 2nd ed. New York: Van Nostrand Reinhold.

Lévy, Pierre. 1998. *Becoming Virtual: Reality in the Digital Age*. New York: Plenum Trade.

Law, Averill M. and W. David Kelton. 1991. *Simulation Modeling and Analysis*. 2nd Edition. New York: McGraw–Hill, Inc.

Liggett, Robin S., and William H. Jepson. 1995. An Integrated Environment for Urban Simulation. *Environment and Planning B 22*, 3:291–302.

Li-Shu and W. Flowers. 1994. Teledesign: Groupware User Experiments in Three-Dimensional Computer Aided Design. *Collaborative Computing.* 1:1, 1–14.

Limp, W. Frederick. 1999. Ride the Waves of Innovation: New Technologies and Products Swell into the Next Millennium. *GEO World.* December, 12:12, 54–58.

Lynch, Kevin. 1960. *The Image of the City.* Cambridge, MA: Technology Press and Harvard University Press.

MacEachren, Alan M. 1995. *How Maps Work: Representation, Visualization, and Design.* New York: Guilford Press.

———. 2001. An Evolving Cognitive-Semiotic Approach to Geographic Visualization and Knowledge Construction. *Information Design Journal* 10(1):26–36.

MacEachren, Alan M., and D. R. F. Taylor. 1994. *Visualization in Modern Cartography.* 1st ed. Oxford, U.K.; New York: Pergamon.

MacEachren, Alan M. and the ICA Commission on Visualization. 1998. VISUAL-IZATION—Cartography for the 21st century. *Proceedings of the 7th Annual Conference of Polish Spatial Information Association.*

MacEachren, Alan M., M. Wachowicz, D. Haug, R. Edsall, and R. Masters. 1999. Constructing Knowledge from Multivariate Spatiotemporal Data: Integrating Geographic Visualization with Knowledge Discovery in Database Methods. *International Journal of Geographic Information Science.* 13:311–34.

McCall, Ray, Sonja Holmes, Josh Voeller, and Erik Johnson. 1998. World Wide Web Presentation and Critique of Design Proposals with Web-PHIDIAS. In *Digital Design Studios: Do Computers Make a Difference?* ed. Thomas Seebohm and Skip Van Wyk. 1998. Conference Proceedings.

McCormick, Bruce H., Thomas A. DeFanti, and Maxine D. Brown. 1987. Visualization in Scientific Computing. *Computer Graphics* 21.

McKim, Robert H. 1980. *Thinking Visually: a Strategy Manual for Problem Solving.* Belmont, CA: Lifetime Learning Publications.

Meyer, Eric K. 1997. *Designing Infographics.* Indianapolis, IN: Hayden Books.

Mintzberg, Henry, and Ludo van der Heyden. 1999. Organigraphs: Drawing How Companies Really Work. *Harvard Business Review.* September–October, 87–94.

Moran, Thomas P., Eric Saund, William van Melle, Anuj Gujar, Ken Fishkin, and Beverly Harrison. 1999. Design and Technology for Collaborage: Collaborative Collages of Information on Physical Walls. *ACM Symposium on User Interface Software and Technology.*

Morgan, Conway Lloyd and Giuliano Zampi. 1995. *Virtual Architecture.* New York: McGraw–Hill.

Nardi, B. A., A. Kuchinsky, S. Whittaker, R. Leichner, and H. Schwarz. 1996. Video-as-data: Technical and Social Aspects of a Collaborative Multimedia Application. *Computer Supported Collaborative Work.* 4:73–100.

Neill, William J. V., Diana S. Fitzsimons, and Brendan Murtagh. 1995. *Reimaging the Pariah City Urban Development in Belfast & Detroit.* Urban and Regional Planning and Development. Aldershot, U.K.; Burlington, VT: Ashgate Publishing.

Nielson, Gregory M., H. Hagen, and Heinrich Müller. 1997. *Scientific Visualization: Overviews, Methodologies, and Techniques.* Los Alamitos, CA: IEEE Computer Society Press.

Novitski, B. J. 1998. *Rendering Real and Imagined Buildings.* Gloucester, MA: Rockport Publishers.

Paller, Alan, and Richard Laska. 1990. *The EIS Book Information Systems for Top Managers.* Homewood, IL: Dow Jones–Irwin.

Passini, Romedi. 1992. *Wayfinding in Architecture.* Paperback. ed. New York: Van Nostrand Reinhold.

Pederson, B., ed. 1988. *Graphis Diagram 1.* Zurich: Graphis Press.

Pedersen, B., ed. 1993. *Graphis Diagram 2.* Zurich: Graphis Press.

Penz, Francois, and Maureen Thomas. 1997. *Cinema and Architecture.* London: British Film Institute.

Peterson, Michael P. 1995. *Interactive and Animated Cartography.* Englewood Cliffs, NJ: Prentice Hall.

Platt, Charles. 1999. You've Got Smell: DigiScent Is Here. If This Technology Takes Off, It's Gonna Launch the Next Web Revolution. *Wired.* November, 256–63.

Playfair, William. 1786. *The Commercial & Political Atlas.* London: Debrett.

Portugali, Juval. 1996. *The Construction of Cognitive Maps.* Dordrecht, Netherlands; Boston: Kluwer Academic Publishers.

Raper, Jonathan, ed. 1989. *GIS: Three Dimensional Applications in Geographic Information Systems.* New York: Taylor & Francis.

Raskar, Ramesh, Greg Welch, and Henry Fuchs. 1998. Spatially Augmented Reality. *First IEEE International Workshop on Augmented Reality.* San Francisco.

Rennison, Earl. 1994. Galaxy of News: An Approach to Visualizing and Understanding Expansive News Landscapes. *Proceedings of UIST'94,* 3–12.

Rhyne, T. M. 1997. Going Virtual with Geographic Information and Scientific Visualization. *Computers and Geosciences.* 23:4, 489–92.

Riera Ojeda, Oscar, and Lucas H. Guerra. 1996. *Hyper-realistic Computer Generated Architectural Renderings.* New York: McGraw–Hill.

Robertson, G. G., S. K. Card, and J. D. Mackinlay. Information Visualization Using 3D Interactive Animation. *Communications of the ACM.* 36:4, 57–71.

Roberts–Witt, Sarah L. 1999. Making Sense of Portal Pandemonium. *Knowledge Management.* July.

Roncarelli, Robi. 1988. *The Computer Animation Dictionary.* New York: Springer–Verlag.

Röscheisen, Martin, Christian Mogensen, and Terry Winograd. 1995. *Beyond Browsing: Shared Comments, SOAPs, Trails, and On-line Communities.* Palo Alto, CA: Computer Science Department, Stanford University.

Robinson, Arthur H. 1952. *The Look of Maps.* Madison, WI: University of Wisconsin Press.

Robinson, Laura. 1999. "Mixed Reality" R&D: Fusing 3-D Graphics and Imaging for Real Commercial Applications. *Advanced Imaging.* July, 28–30.

Robinson, Julia W. et al. 1990. *Representation and Simulation in Architectural Research and Design.* Report on the ARCC Conference.

Sanoff, Henry. 1991. *Visual Research Methods in Design.* New York: Van Nostrand Reinhold.

Saund, Eric and Thomas P. Moran. 1994. A Perceptually Supported Sketch Editor. *Proceedings of the ACM Symposium on User Interface Software and Technology.*

Scholten, Henk J. and John C. H. Stillwell, eds. 1990. *Geographic Information Systems for Urban and Regional Planning.* Boston: Kluwer Academic Publishers.

Schroeder, John. 1999. Enterprise Portals: A New Business Intelligence Paradigm. *DM Review.* September.

Seebohm, Thomas and Skip Van Wyk, eds. 1998. *Digital Design Studios: Do Computers Make a Difference?* Conference Proceedings.

Sheppard, Stephen R. J. 1989. *Visual Simulation: A User's Guide for Architects, Engineers, and Planners.* New York: Van Nostrand Reinhold.

Singh, R. R. 1996. *Adapting Geographic Information Systems to Sketch Planning Needs.* Unpublished Masters thesis, Cambridge, MA: Department of Urban Studies and Planning, MIT.

Small, David. 1996. Navigating Large Bodies of Text. In *IBM Systems Journal.* ed. Gene F. Hoffnagle. 35:3, 4: 514–25.

Smith, Brian K. and Erik Blankinship. Imagery as Data: Structures for Visual Model Building. At http://www.media.mit.edu/explain/papers/imagery_as_data.pdf, November 23, 1999. *Proceedings of Computer Supported Collaborative Learning 99.*

Sorkin, Michael. 1992. *Variations on a Theme Park: the New American City and the End of Public Space.* 1st ed. New York: Hill and Wang.

Stilgoe, J. R. 1998. *Outside Lies Magic: Regaining History and Awareness in Everyday Places.* New York: Walker and Company.

Stovall, James Glen. 1997. *Infographics: a Journalist's Guide.* Boston: Allyn and Bacon.

Thalman, Daniel, ed. 1990. *Scientific Visualization and Graphics Simulation.* New York: John Wiley & Sons.

Tsui, C. 1998. *Multimedia Data Integration and Retrieval in Planning Support Systems.* Unpublished M.S. thesis. Massachusetts Institute of Technology, Cambridge, MA.

Tufte, Edward R. 1983. *The Visual Display of Quantitative Information.* Cheshire, CT: Graphics Press.

———. 1990. *Envisioning Information.* Cheshire, CT.: Graphics Press.

———. 1997. *Visual Explanations: Images and Quantities, Evidence and Narrative.* Cheshire, CT: Graphics Press.

Tukey, John W. 1977. *Exploratory Data Analysis.* Reading, MA: Addison–Wesley.

Van Asperdt, Anita and Beth Diamond. 1999. Integrating Digital Media in the Landscape Architecture Studio: Overlaying Media and Process. In *Digital Design Studios: Do Computers Make a Difference?* ed. Thomas Seebohm and Skip Van Wyk. Conference Proceedings.

Vasconcellos, R. 1993. Representing the Geographical Space for Visually Handicapped Students: A Case Study on Map Use. *Proceedings, 16th International Cartographic Conference:* 993–1004.

Verbree, E., G. van Maren, R. Germs, F. Jansen, and M. J. Kraak. 1999. Interaction in Virtual World Views—Linking 3D GIS with VR. *International Journal of Geographical Information Systems.* 13: 85–396.

Wakin, Edward. 1993. *Photos that Made U.S. History.* New York: Walker.

Warniers, Randall. 1998. Every Picture Tells a Story: Image-based Modeling and Rendering Introduces New Methods for Creating Photorealistic Imagery. *Computer Graphics World.* October, 25ff.

Westwood, Sallie and John Williams. 1997. *Imagining Cities: Scripts, Signs, Memory.* London; New York: Routledge.

Wildbur, Peter. 1998. *Information Graphics: Innovative Solutions in Contemporary Design.* New York: Thames and Hudson.

Witzling, Lawrence and Robert Greenstreet. 1989. *Presenting Statistics. A Manager's Guide to the Persuasive Use of Statistics.* New York: John Wiley and Sons.

Wong, Wilson and Thomas Kvan. 1999. Textual Support of Collaborative Design. In *Media and Design Process,* ed. Osman Ataman and Julio Bermúdez. Conference Proceedings: 168–77.

Wurman, Richard Saul. 1996. *Information Architects.* Zurich: Graphis.

Paper 13

Spatial Multimedia for Planning Support

MICHAEL J. SHIFFER

ASSOCIATE PROFESSOR OF URBAN PLANNING AND POLICY

UNIVERSITY OF ILLINOIS AT CHICAGO

ABSTRACT ▶ Collaborative community planning, with extensive involvement, has emerged as a central component of public policy. There are a variety of ways in which the public can share knowledge about their communities, and there are advantages and limitations to each of these approaches. Spatial multimedia refers to the integration of video, sound, and text within a distributed environment. Within this general approach we discuss spatial annotation, visual navigation aids, and devices for scenario construction. Implementing spatial multimedia can be done at different levels—face-to-face and in both centralized and distributed contexts.

INTRODUCTION

CHALLENGES TO KNOWLEDGE SHARING

Sharing knowledge has become an increasingly important part of the planning process, especially in light of federal, state, and local initiatives that mandate a certain degree of public participation. For example, the Intermodal Surface Transportation Act of 1990 requires that there be public input at the early stages of any project. This is not necessarily new. The participation of the public has been an important element of planning processes for years (Steger 1972). There are, however, a variety of political, institutional, and administrative limitations to sharing knowledge in public and semipublic forums. Rather than highlighting these, this work sets out to address functional limitations that may exist where all parties are indeed willing to communicate, but where the participation of stakeholders with a wide range of skills and knowledge makes communication difficult.

To better understand these functional limitations, it is first useful to understand how people share knowledge about the future of their communities. Knowledge in the planning context is frequently shared by means of communicating recollections of the past, descriptions of the present, and speculation about the future. We will now briefly explore these three activities and identify some of the challenges associated with each. The following section will explore how spatial multimedia is positioned to address these challenges.

Conversations involving recollection may incorporate what was said, what was done, or what a place was like. For example, members of a group may try to recall the consequences of past projects in order to improve their understanding of what may lie ahead in similar circumstances. Structured recollection can incorporate records and systematic documentation of past interactions. Access to this information, however, can be dependent on having a specialized information recording and retrieval "system," such as the official minutes of previous meetings. Such methods of recollection rarely incorporate any degree of spatial referencing. Where systematic documentation is lacking, the high level of dependence on individual recollection can lead to problems of inconsistency inherent in human memory. This can result in arguments that dominate a discussion and shift the focus of a meeting from the matters at hand.

Descriptions of present conditions generally involve getting everyone in a collaborative situation "on the same page" with respect to an area being discussed, so that everyone can work from a common base of spatial knowledge. Verbal spatial references, such as "near the transit station," can be inappropriate where some participants lack familiarity with a site. This problem can be addressed through the use of an up-to-date map as a central reference point. The map's use can be further enhanced using photos or video. This juxtaposition can strengthen a group's understanding of the various characteristics of a given site. Until recently, however, such juxtapositions have been limited by their dependence on the integration of various physical objects (such as paper maps and photos), and electronic media, which could be either analog or digital.

Speculation about the future of an area can be either informal and heuristic (based on "rules of thumb"), or it can be systematic and formalized. Informal speculation may involve people applying their memories of past experience (such as perceptions of how traffic changed after a new development opened). More formalized speculation will typically draw upon systematically collected data that indicates a relationship that can be expressed quantitatively (such as with travel demand modeling). Regardless of which form speculation takes, it typically involves learning from past experience and applying those lessons to the future. Real-time augmentation of public discourse using speculative aids (such as computers) has traditionally been limited by a lack of human–computer interactivity and somewhat abstract output. In public situations, this could result in the inadvertent exclusion of various stakeholders from the technical points of a conversation. For example, technical output such as noise or automobile traffic levels can be impenetrable to nonspecialists.

Sharing knowledge in a planning-related setting thus involves difficulties stemming from inconsistencies in recollection of past experience, descriptions of areas of interest that relevant parties may be unfamiliar with, and abstractions resulting from technical explanations that are derived from speculative models. This work will now explore how information technology, and spatial multimedia in particular, is positioned to address these impediments to the sharing of knowledge.

Many of the challenges described above have been addressed through various implementations of multimedia information technologies (see, for example Câmara et al. 1991; Fonseca et al. 1993; Jones et al. 1994; Laurini and Milleret–Raffort 1990; Polyorides 1993; Shiffer 1992). Spatial multimedia (as discussed in this context) capitalizes on the integration of video, sound, text, and distributed communication. We will discuss a variety of concepts and tools useful to both professionals and the community, including spatial annotation, visual navigation aids, and aids that create concrete scenarios and options.

SPATIAL ANNOTATION

ANNOTATION MECHANISMS SUPPORTING RECOLLECTION

Spatial annotation mechanisms allow users of an information system to relate their comments to a geographic (or spatial) area. These have essentially been with us since ancient times when humans would draw in sand to illustrate spatial relationships while telling stories. They can be as simple as pens, pins, or other devices that might be used to mark up a shared map or diagram. In fact, 3M's Post-It Note® is probably one of the most significant and accessible spatial annotation technologies to be developed in recent times.

Spatial multimedia gives us the capacity to link ideas and comments to simple marks that we make on shared electronic maps either before, during, or after a meeting. It goes further by allowing us to link external resources, such as text, sound, or imagery that may be either centrally located or distributed across a network, to maps. Planners can take advantage of various types of digital annotation. For instance, at the simplest level such annotations might be simple graphical marks (such as lines, circles, dots, etc.) that are intended to convey spatial flow, physical alterations, or a multitude of related concepts. Such graphical marks would likely be tied to a variety of more descriptive annotations. The remainder of this section will describe three types of annotation (text, audio, and video), and some of the benefits and drawbacks associated with each.

TEXTUAL ANNOTATION

Spatially linked textual annotation typically takes the form of an "Internet-like" discussion thread that is linked to a location on a map shared over a network. In essence, a user could click on a map location to access an "Internet-like" discussion thread that relates to that spatial area. As opposed to the other forms of annotation described below, textual annotation offers the benefits of exceptionally low storage overhead (and subsequently low demands on network resources) and a quality of commentary limited only by the descriptive talents of the contributors.

AUDIO ANNOTATION

Audio annotation allows one to link verbal comments to a location on a map. This is accomplished by simply speaking into a microphone that is linked to a computer-based digitizer. This can theoretically work more rapidly than other forms of annotation. However, early experiences have demonstrated a reluctance to annotate a map with one's voice due to the awkwardness of stopping a meeting and concern about how one's comments might be viewed out of context.

VIDEO ANNOTATION

We have the capacity to link video images of contributors to maps in a manner similar to audio annotation. Such a system might be employed as part of a kiosk installation in a public place where voluntary comments could be solicited from the public using an embedded camera. This has the effect of enabling one to view "the face behind the name."

On the positive side, this method can elicit expressive and compelling opinions about various proposals. On the negative side, such images can lead to eliciting unintended bias on the part of the viewer (who can, for instance, make judgments based on appearance). Video annotation also requires significant storage overhead and can be exceptionally difficult to convey through a network using existing technologies. This last concern is being addressed with continual advances in compression technologies and network bandwidth.

Figure 1. An example of video annotation: Scenes from the Mission Main Web site.

EVALUATING ANNOTATION MECHANISMS

The archive that results from multiple annotations can augment recollections gathered in subsequent meetings. Access to this archive can be based on geographic, chronological, and associative relevance. Geographic relevance allows users of an information system to search for annotations that are related to a specific region or subregion using typical GIS spatial selection operations. Chronological relevance allows a user to add the capacity to search for annotations made before, after, or between two dates. Finally, associative relevance allows searching by keywords or related concepts that could be linked together in a Web-like associative structure.

While it is certainly conceivable that GIS-based archival mechanisms can be set up to aid future recollective efforts, this requires that a substantial spatial data infrastructure be already in place. As we are only beginning to realize the development of substantial spatial data infrastructures around the world, we will need to continue to rely on the (frequently paper-based) libraries of local historical societies for more specific spatial descriptions that can effectively convey the character of a local area. The issue becomes a question of what material is worth maintaining. The answer has profound implications for the scalability of such a system. For instance, is it reasonable to expect a planning council to archive a spatial representation of every proposal made, along with the corresponding minutes of every planning meeting? If so, what is a reasonable time frame for keeping the record in the archive? Five years? Fifty years? Forever? If not every proposal is archived, then how is the choice of what is relevant made? These questions aside, such annotations have the capacity to significantly enhance recollection by providing a means of encoding informal memories of a location. These can be juxtaposed with other forms of information, such as those described below.

VISUAL NAVIGATIONAL AIDS

VISUAL NAVIGATIONAL AIDS SUPPORTING DESCRIPTION

Another implementation of spatial multimedia for planning involves visual navigational aids. For many years now, these have had the capacity to support descriptions of existing, past, or proposed conditions of a place by offering a link between oblique imagery and orthographic maps. This section will begin by discussing technical developments and early experiences with computer-supported access to imagery. This discussion will briefly take us through analog video-disk, to digital still, and to digital motion video, along with some planning-related experiences encountered with each. We will conclude by discussing the various techniques that can be employed to support the development of "shared visions" of existing conditions in urban spaces with nodal, navigational, and fixed position imagery.

Figure 2. Panoramic photo of Park Street Station, showing Park Street Church and State House in distance, Boston, Mass. Copyright E. Chickering & Co., October 22, 1903. (From U.S. Library of Congress American Memory Collection).

THE EVOLUTION OF TECHNOLOGY

The whole point of visual navigational aids has been to support a shared vision of an urban area. Techniques have evolved from the panoramic photos of urban landscapes in the early 1900s (see figure 2) and vehicular mounted motion picture cameras from the early days of film in the same era (as illustrated in figure 3), to mid-century interpretation of aerial photos for military intelligence and later urban planning purposes (Branch 1948) and post-WWII time-lapse studies of public spaces (Whyte 1979).

Figure 3. Scenes from navigational film titled "Interior New York subway, Fourteenth Street to Forty-second Street", Copyright: American Mutoscope & Biograph Co.; June 05, 1905 (from U.S. Library of Congress American Memory Collection).

Random Access to Images via Computer-Controlled Analog Devices

One of the earliest practical applications of information technology to visual surveys of the built environment was the conventional[1] videodisk. Applications such as the BBC Domesday Disk (Rhind et. al 1988) and the "Aspen Disk" developed by the MIT Media Lab (Brand 1987) provided early examples of how computer control of a videodisk machine could provide virtually instant access (frequently under one second) to any one of 54,000 video frames on a single disk. Connecting more than one disk player to the same computer could provide still greater capacity. In some cases, such as with the St. Louis Riverfront project (Shiffer 1990), a relevant video frame on the disk would be accessed through a look-up table or database that would relate a selected coordinate on a map with the associated video frame(s).[2] Videodisk technology is particularly adept at allowing a user to access information through the navigational metaphor, due largely to the technology's capacity for the playback of motion pictures at variable speed.

This capacity was illustrated during several meetings held by the St. Louis Community Development Agency. In one such meeting, a computer, videodisk player, and large television monitor were situated at the front of the room. After a brief introduction to the technology (to prevent later digressions), the meeting proceeded with a proposed bicycle trail along the city's Mississippi riverfront as the topic of conversation.

In this situation, whoever had the floor (typically a planner) would direct a technical specialist to fly a conceptual helicopter up and down the river, stopping at various locations to examine them more closely. Further examination would consist of viewing a site from several different perspectives or zooming into a specific location for a closer look. The capacity to view from multiple perspectives was made possible by filming the riverfront from different perspectives and relating the different views with the map as the common reference point. Zooming was accomplished (rather crudely) by simply magnifying the image on the television screen.

Although it provided what was (and still is) one of the fastest mechanisms for access to images, videodisk technology was not without significant drawbacks. The primary drawback was the added cost of the hardware necessary to display the video images. In the simplest case this might be a videodisk player and a separate monitor. A more complex setup would involve the display of the video images on the same screen as the map (made possible through a video overlay board for the computer). Since most conventional videodisks were designed as a read-only medium (for example, Pioneer's Laserdisc system), still greater cost would be incurred if one were to purchase a recordable videodisk machine. These machines were typically 20 to 50 times the price of a conventional videodisk player and were thus out of the financial reach of many planning agencies.

Figure 4. Computer-controlled videodisk machine in use during a planning meeting in St. Louis.

Finally, a significant drawback of videodisk technology is the fact that the video images stored on the disks are nondigital and would require electronic transfer through a digitizing board if they were to be manipulated on a computer. All of the above drawbacks (and the resulting "customized" hardware setups required to electronically link images with maps) resulted in little adoption of this technology by planning agencies. In the case of the St. Louis example, the difficulty in adapting the technology for new areas of study (or to effectively update it for existing areas of study) caused the videodisk approach for visual surveys of the built environment to be abandoned after a very short period of time.

Digital Still Images

One technology that rapidly began to supplant the use of conventional videodisks was the capacity to store large quantities of images on computer-readable media. This was made possible by low-cost advancements in image compression, hard disk (and other high speed storage device) capacities, and effective mechanisms for the capture and subsequent transfer of high-quality images into standardized digital files. Thus it has become unnecessary to have a customized hardware configuration to display the images and maps that support visual surveys of the built environment.

In the simplest implementation, still images can be linked to points on a map. For example, an application for Crawford County, Illinois provided an example of how scanned maps at varying scales could be linked to digitized photos of specific areas. The implementation was designed to support a historic preservation workshop by students at the University of Illinois at Urbana–Champaign. The system focused on four small towns in the county where project participants were primarily concerned with the preservation of the centers of their towns.

Development of this system consisted of scanning existing topographic maps for each town along with an overview map of Crawford County. Transparent color polygons were overlaid on points of interest. Pointing a cursor at these areas yielded more detailed maps and site sketches that included arrows representing camera locations and angles of photographic images taken from a ground-level perspective. Selecting an arrow would highlight it and display the appropriate photographic image in a separate window (figure 5). The users could also search through the photographic images for specific visual criteria and see the corresponding locations highlighted on the map.

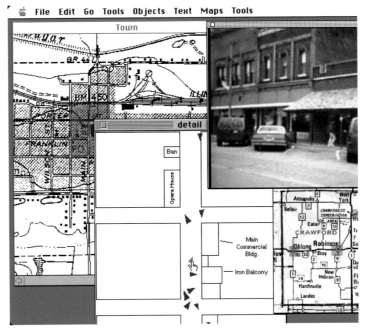

Figure 5. The interface of the Crawford County visualization tool as developed in 1988.

Another relatively early example of how a set of still video images could support visual surveys of a built environment was provided through an experimental collaborative planning system that was developed for Rantoul, Illinois in 1988. Among other things, the system (as described originally in Shiffer 1992) supported visual surveys of the built environment using a base map (consisting of aerial orthographic photos) linked to a digital video window that displayed oblique aerial views of a site looking north or south from a 1,000-foot altitude at 45 degrees. This navigator allowed one to fly around the community looking for specific visual criteria that may not have been apparent using orthographic aerial photos or ground level views. The user could fly north, south, east, or west while looking north or south. The relative location of the viewing area in relation to the rest of the site was automatically tracked on an overview map of the site during the flight. A particular viewing area could be accessed in the video window by selecting a location on the overview map with a pointing device. The illusion of forward (or backward) navigation was accomplished by dissolving sequentially through a set of still images. Navigation to the right or left was simulated using graphical visual effects that would "move" still images appropriately.

In addition to the aerial oblique images described above, the Rantoul implementation incorporated panoramic images taken from an eye-level perspective. This would allow users to select a location on a map that would display an image of same, and pan around to view the surrounding area. This was accomplished by rotating a video camera around 360 degrees at predetermined locations. Selected frames from the video would then be digitized and electronically pasted together (in much the same manner someone might tape together holiday snapshots of a sweeping vista) to create a 360-degree panoramic image. When viewed in a smaller window on a computer, the act of scrolling to the right or left would give the user a sense of "turning" to the right or left. The resulting video segments would be linked to their corresponding locations on a base map. The capacity of such panoramic images to illustrate the entire area around a selected location proved to be quite useful in the case of Rantoul, where specific attention was being paid to the evaluation of a former U.S. air force base for reuse alternatives.

Digital Motion Video

The Crawford County and Rantoul implementations of technology for visual surveys of the built environment offered significantly greater flexibility over videodisk-based methods due to their all-digital formats. The resulting animations (i.e., suggestions of motion from the user's point of view) were crude but effective. Nevertheless, they suffered from the fact that standards for digital video file formats had yet to be invented at the time of their use, and, because of the large size of the files, were cumbersome and slow as well.

In the early 1990s several standards for digital motion video files began to arise. These included (among others) the Motion Picture Expert's Group (MPEG) standard, Apple Computer, Inc.'s Quick-Time™, and Micro-soft's Video for Windows®. These file formats allowed significant space savings due to compression algorithms. They also had the capacity to allow for a variety of playback speeds and control mechanisms. This, combined with a capacity to rapidly access still frames from within a motion picture file, made it possible to effectively mimic the functionality of a laser disk machine entirely within software.

These digital motion video formats also allowed for the capture and subsequent playback of ambient sound. This, combined with moving images taken from a fixed location, would have the capacity of providing a rich, descriptive representation of an existing urban environment. By linking moving video clips of a site (taken from different angles) to a number of specific locations on a map, the planner could play the role of director by changing the point of view to support descriptions of that location.

The National Capital Planning Commission of Washington, D.C. (NCPC), experimented with such use of digital video representations in support of an ongoing (monthly) environmental design review process of major developments in the D.C. area. In this context, a multimedia database was made accessible to commission members and staff in a large meeting room used for monthly public meetings.

TECHNIQUES UNDERLYING VISUAL NAVIGATIONAL AIDS

Some of the earliest implementations of spatial multimedia technology involved visual surveys of the built environment. In concept, this activity can be accomplished by simply linking images to locations on a map. The relationship between image and map can support several methods of browsing. For example, a visual survey can be geographically driven—the user views an associated image by selecting a location on a map—or navigationally driven—the user moves through a sequence of images (that may or may not be animated to give one the illusion of actual travel). Stopping at a specific site could have the effect of displaying the relative location of the associated map. More sophisticated visual surveys could be created to be content-driven—the user queries a database (or does a hypertext search of the textual annotations described above) that yields both the appropriate images and their relative locations highlighted on an associated map.

To better understand an area under study (using visual navigation techniques), it may be necessary to view it from several different perspectives. Several types of video shots can be linked to a map in the service of such a visual survey. Three of the most common video modes are fixed position shots, nodal video (360-degree rotation), and navigational sequences.

Fixed Position

Fixed position shots allow the user to view a video clip of a particular site from a fixed camera angle. These can be symbolized on a map as arrows that match the direction of the camera's angle. Sites can be viewed from several different angles that allow the user to switch perspectives the same way a television director can switch cameras to show different angles of a sporting event. Fixed position imagery is useful for studies of movement such as with automobile traffic, pedestrian flow, time-lapse studies of public space usage, and so on.

Nodal Video

The nodal video image allows the user to look completely around from a fixed vantage point at a 360-degree axial view. These views are useful for illustrating the environment surrounding a particular location. They allow the user to zoom, pan to the left or right, and tilt up and down. This offers additional views of what is beyond the camera by allowing the user to look around at a surrounding area while standing at a single location. This is useful for analysis of relationships between elements of place. It has been popularized with QuickTime VR® and LivePicture® file formats.

Navigational Sequence

The navigational sequence approach shows users what it would be like to walk, drive, or fly through a study area. It is designed to aid visual navigation by enabling the user to view a geographic area from a moving perspective such as might be experienced when actually traveling through a region. Navigation images may be represented on a map as linear symbols that represent the routes available to the user.

EVALUATING VISUAL NAVIGATIONAL AIDS

Visual navigational aids to assist in surveys of the built environment are becoming increasingly distributed through advances in inter-application communication, object linking and embedding, and the World Wide Web. This is rapidly leading to the full integration of digital video representations with GIS, which has been played out in three predominant ways. First, digital video files are now accessible from within most GIS applications. Thus, by simply selecting a feature on a map, associated images can be displayed either from directly within the GIS application, or through external viewing software. Second, digital video files can now communicate the relative position of the viewer back to the GIS through inter-application communication protocols. This makes it possible to highlight one's relative location on a map as one navigates via the video. Third, GIS and digital video are becoming integrated in entirely new, Web-based hybrid applications that combine elements of spatial representation and digital imagery in the massive associative information infrastructure that is provided by the Web. This has been made possible largely by the rapidly growing object-based software development environments (such as Sun's Java).

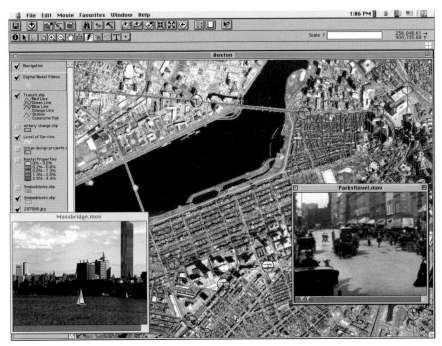

Figure 6. Visual analysis of Boston using navigational images that have been integrated with ArcView GIS software using "hotlinks."

Nevertheless, developers of these systems will continue to make tradeoffs in the production and delivery of such representation. For example, high quality images (for engineering applications, etc.) will remain largely dependent on local delivery mechanisms such as CD–ROM rather than the Internet, due to bandwidth constraints.

AIDS TO PROVIDE CONCRETE OPTIONS AND SCENARIOS

For many years planning professionals have had to face the challenge of describing technical information to non-technical audiences. For example, where abstractions have been used to convey concepts such as noise and traffic levels, more descriptive indicators have been somewhat elusive. Representational aids are designed to make the abstract more concrete by employing a richer set of descriptions. They have evolved from gestural and verbal tactics (such as waving of hands and copious use of adjectives), to artistic conceptualizations, and on to the employment of linked media. The intent has been to close the gap of understanding between technical specialists and key stakeholders. This has most recently been accomplished through the augmentation of typically abstract environmental representations with direct manipulation interfaces and multimedia representational aids, which have been made available in planning settings through recent increases in computing power. Unlike the cases of annotation mechanisms and visual navigational aids, it is difficult to easily classify the various types of representational aids. Therefore, the remainder of this section will discuss two implementations of representational aids: automobile traffic scenarios and urban transit visualization.

AUTOMOBILE TRAFFIC SCENARIOS

Many potential urban developments are evaluated in planning contexts for their impact on a community's existing transportation infrastructure. In particular, this impact is frequently represented as a projected change in traffic conditions. Several measures have been used to represent perceived changes in traffic conditions. Some of the more popular measures include average daily traffic (ADT) measures and standardized levels of service (LOS).

ADT is usually expressed as a numeric value that describes the average number of vehicles passing a fixed point over a 24-hour period. In the context of a planning meeting, a use of ADT might be to describe the impact of a new development on an existing traffic network. For example, a traffic specialist might convey this information to a planning commission meeting by saying, "If the new shopping center is built, the ADT at that location is projected to rise from 11,300 to 14,500." Unfortunately, this numeric value may have very little meaning for people unfamiliar with these types of measurements.

One approach to conveying traffic information, as described in the Highway Capacity Manual (Transportation Research Board 1985), has been to classify or grade traffic conditions using a measure known as Level of Service (LOS). In most cases, LOS is represented as a discrete scale from "A" to "F" where "A" represents very good traffic conditions and "F" represents very poor ones. While LOS measures are designed to simplify projected traffic levels through the assignment of a letter grade, this simplification continues to make for a level of abstraction that is frequently difficult for members of the general public and decision makers to find useful. This is not so much due to complexity as it is to a lack of satisfying descriptions of conditions.

An early attempt to make LOS measures more descriptive involved a juxtaposition of LOS representations as described in the Highway Capacity Manual with a library of generic indicative images. The images were taken as digital video clips that represented approximately ten seconds of traffic at a given LOS. The user (after selecting a traffic situation such as three lanes of continuous flow) could then explore how that traffic was likely to behave under various predicted LOS conditions. That yielded the associated digital video clips and a brief textual description of traffic and driver behaviors under those conditions (as is illustrated in figure 7). The user then selected other LOS scenarios for comparisons of varying traffic levels at the same type of location.

The electronic library of LOS descriptions can be effectively delivered to various planning organizations using the Web, provided that the representations are drawn from a fairly generic set of situations. This data can be provided and maintained in a distributed manner by these organizations using an overall structure such as that which is being developed in this research as a guideline. While this type of analysis can lead to a broadened understanding of how one LOS for a given set of physical conditions compares to another, it assumes that the user has some concept of existing or predicted LOS for their area. Where this is not the case, it may be desirable to predict future, or describe existing, LOS using the standard metrics published in the Highway Capacity Manual. Future implementations will likely include a mechanism for calculating and predicting LOS.

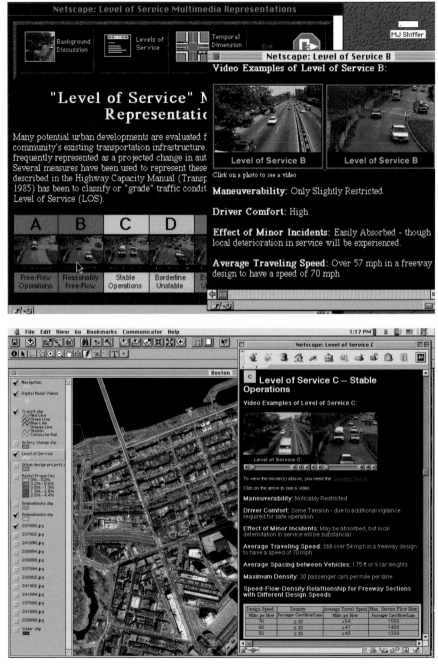

Figure 7. Multiple representations of LOS data for a continuous-flow highway as represented on the Web.

URBAN TRANSIT MODE REPRESENTATIONS

Multimedia representational aids also can convey the operating characteristics of mass transit vehicles in various environments. The intent of this approach is to provide a multimedia repository where the experiences of various localities with different transit configurations can be shared on a national scale. Like the automobile traffic representations, this implementation makes use of motion video clips and descriptive text. The tool is designed to augment standard quantitative measures of transit operations, with qualitative characteristics drawing upon a range of comparable examples from across the country. The hope is that this resource can lead conversations concerning proposed transit alternatives to rely less on hyperbole and more on the practical experiences of similar communities.

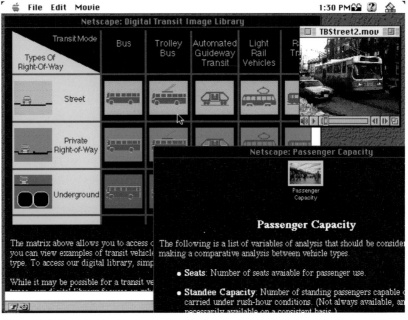

Figure 8. A Web site that illustrates the characteristics of urban transit vehicles and operating environments using digital motion video and sound.

As illustrated in figure 8, the transit visualization prototype grew out of situations where communities were contemplating new transit lines, and were uncertain of the various operating characteristics of a broad range of alternative vehicles. While several studies of quantitative performance measures exist, there is very little that describes the qualitative aspects of various transit modes (such as noise, visual impact, and so on), which often become a point of debate among decision makers (many of whom are not transit specialists). Thus, the purpose of the project is to: (1) provide qualitative descriptions (using text, video, and sound) of the operating characteristics of the various transit modes and operating environments; (2) provide a comprehensible structure to which further quantitative and qualitative descriptions of transit modes, best practices, etc. can be attached; and (3) to provide a central forum through which an informed discussion of the environmental characteristics of various transit modes can be organized.

The potential users of such a system are state and local government officials, transit and environmental professionals, academics, and others concerned with selecting transit services where levels of demand have already been estimated. The ability to widely distribute this information using the Internet can allow many smaller to medium-sized communities to benefit from a large information base constructed to reflect the experiences of other communities with similar challenges. Thus, many small planning agencies without the resources necessary to perform exhaustive analyses can learn from the experiences of others. This can result in a more effective public review of the potential effects of transportation planning-related projects.

The intended result of the examples of representational aids described above is to make analytic tools and their outputs more manipulable, understandable, and appealing, so that information that would normally be inaccessible to the layperson can be more effectively understood. Nevertheless, just as this technology has the capacity to deliver compelling and descriptive representations, it can deliver compelling and descriptive misrepresentations. It is therefore necessary for users to understand how to avoid making simple mistakes in representation. A good place to start is with the works of Mark Monmonier and Edward R. Tufte.

IMPLEMENTING SPATIAL MULTIMEDIA

There are several types of environments in which people are likely to access planning-related information. They include face-to-face meetings, centralized resources (such as libraries), or distributed resources (such as the news media). This section will explore some of the environments where the concepts of spatial multimedia have been implemented.

FACE-TO-FACE

This scenario represents situations (such as town meetings) where people meet face-to-face to discuss the future of their community. Recent advances have made it possible to augment this kind of environment with a Collaborative Planning System (CPS). Such tools have been implemented on an experimental basis as described in Shiffer (1993, 1995a, 1995b). A CPS makes significant use of the annotation mechanisms, navigational aids and representational aids (described above) projected on the wall of a meeting room. Participants interact with the system using cordless pointing devices or through a technical facilitator to elicit information about selected geographic areas through a graphical interface.

Some valuable lessons were learned from early experiences with CPS. For instance, early tests illustrated reluctance on the part of users to pick up a pointing device and directly interact with the system during a meeting. Most preferred to interact with the CPS through an "expert" who is familiar with the system's content. Such an individual could anticipate group needs and display relevant information when called upon. Thus, while it would be necessary for the expert to be familiar with a meeting's agenda, this person could also track a random conversation and display maps and images as they came up in conversation.

The prototype CPS implementations have led to the identification of a broad set of issues ranging from institutionalization to technical infrastructure (some of which are discussed in Shiffer 1995b). The benefits are that it is fast and self-contained. However, key participants may not be able to attend meetings due to place and time constraints, as described in the scenarios below.

CENTRALIZED RESOURCES

This scenario represents situations where physical media are left in a physical location for review by a broad group of individuals over a period of time. Interaction in this case is usually limited and has traditionally taken the form of written comments that could be entered into a notebook. Recent implementations have included access to GIS or other types of information systems through the employment of electronic information kiosks. Kiosks make it somewhat easier to control access to the information insofar as they are strategically placed in the communities they are designed to serve (libraries and municipal buildings, for example). They also have the capacity to deliver large amounts of information (such as video) more rapidly and reliably than the Web can. Some of the more sophisticated kiosks have actually been designed to allow public interaction with GIS through the employment of graphical user interface modifications made possible in some of the more recent GIS tool kits.

The likely users of kiosks tend to include individuals with a broad variety of skill levels. Therefore, specific attention needs to be paid to human–computer interaction issues related to the design of the software interface. The drawbacks are that kiosks can't be everywhere and a physical deployment infrastructure (such as computers with touch screens and protective cases) is needed, which can be costly.

DISTRIBUTED RESOURCES

In this type of situation, a person with time constraints or conflicts may be unable to attend the meeting of the planning review board in their home community. Participation is consequently often limited to physical forms of discourse, such as letter writing and reading news items in the local paper. A significant difficulty here is that local news editors often become filters through which the information must flow. Archiving or categorizing exchanges in this kind of situation can prove to be challenging as well, due to the physical limitations of the media.

The Internet, (most specifically the Web) makes it possible to conduct a more deliberative review of planning-related proposals. For example, the prototype depicted in figure 9 illustrates a Web-based implementation of a "virtual streetscape" for Washington, D.C. that allows the user to explore an area using either an orthographic photo and map overlay, or by using a nodal digital video. A text annotation capability allows the user to attach comments to specific nodes identified on the map. This last scenario for deployment of spatial multimedia appears to be the most rapidly growing due to the popularity of the Internet, although limited network bandwidth and ensured access to relevant parties continues to be a potential drawback of this approach to planning-related discourse.

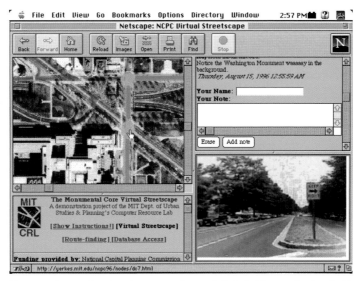

Figure 9. A test of a planning annotation and digital video navigational aid being tested in a "Different Place/ Different Time" environment using the Web to study the characteristics of various locations in Washington, D.C.

CONTINUING RESEARCH AREAS

These initial investigations into the potential roles of spatial multimedia in planning raise many questions. What follows is an attempt to organize them into three overlapping areas where further inquiry and research is needed.

INNOVATION

What IT models are most appropriate for delivery of this technology (GIS, Internet, kiosk)? How can we accommodate new media? How will Internet II enable us to leverage distributed information more effectively? Who will pay for development? What will be the implications of e-commerce and sponsorship for planning-related media implementations? How are public/private partnerships working?

IMPLEMENTATION

How can we effectively match an appropriate mix of technology to fit the resources of particular planning processes and environments? How can we "repurpose" existing IT? Who is responsible for the maintenance and the integrity of the information contained in these systems? What are the best means for delivering this technology to those who might benefit from its use? What economic (and institutional) limitations to implementation exist?

IMPACT

How can we evaluate the effects of these technologies in public environments? Is there something inherent in spatial multimedia that makes it more (or less) biased than other forms of media (such as traditional maps, television, or the printed word)? How does the use of this technology change the nature of community-related conversations?

This chapter may have raised more questions than it has answered. It will be the shared responsibility of practitioners, industry leaders, and academics to work together to begin to address these as we move ahead.

ACKNOWLEDGMENTS

Partial support for the projects described here was provided by the U.S. Department of Transportation, Federal Transit Administration, and Bureau of Transportation Statistics. Thanks are due to Sue Delaney for her valuable comments.

FOOTNOTES

[1] By "conventional" I refer to the analog videodisks that were popularized in the 1980s by Pioneer's Laserdisc system as opposed to the more recent Digital Video Disc (DVD) technologies that have been developed for home entertainment.

[2] Sometimes several frames would relate to a single location, such as where images would be available to allow the user to view a site from several different perspectives (or at different points in history).

REFERENCES

Branch, M. 1948. *City Planning and Aerial Information*. Cambridge, MA: Harvard University Press.

Brand, S. 1987. *The Media Lab: inventing the future at MIT*. New York: Viking.

Câmara, A., A. L. Gomes, A. Fonseca, and M. J. Lucena e Vale. 1991. Hypersnige—A navigation system for geographic information. *Proceedings of the European GIS Conference*. Brussels, Belgium. 1991: 175–79.

Fonseca, A., C. Gouveia, F. C. Ferreira, J. Raper, and A. Câmara. Adding Video and Sound into GIS. *Proceedings of the European GIS Conference*, Genoa, Italy. 1993: 176–87.

Jones, R. M., E. A. Edmonds, and N. E. Branki. 1994. An analysis of media integration for spatial planning environments. *Environment and Planning B: Planning and Design,* 21:121–33. London: Pion.

Laurini, R., and F. Milleret-Raffort. Principles of Geomatic Hypermaps. *Proceedings of the 4th International Symposium on Spatial Data Handling,* Zurich, 1990: 642–51.

Longley, P., M. Goodchild, D. Maguire, and D. Rhind, eds. 1999. *Geographical Information Systems.* New York: John Wiley & Sons.

Monmonier, M. 1991. *How to Lie with Maps.* Chicago: University of Chicago Press.

Polyorides, N. An Experiment in Multimedia GIS. *Proceedings of the European GIS Conference.* Genoa, Italy. 1993: 203–12.

Rhind, D. W., P. Armstrong, and S. Openshaw. 1988. The Domesday machine: a nationwide GIS. *Geographical Journal* 154, 56–68.

Shiffer, M. J. 1992. Towards a Collaborative Planning System. *Environment and Planning B: Planning and Design* 19:709–22.

———. 1993. Augmenting Geographic Information with Collaborative Multimedia Technologies. In *Proceedings of Auto Carto 11,* ed. R. B. McMaster and M. P. Armstrong, 367–76.

———. 1995(a) Environmental Review with Hypermedia Systems. *Environment and Planning B: Planning and Design* 22: 59–372.

———. 1995b Interactive Multimedia Planning Support: Moving from Stand-Alone Systems to the World Wide Web. *Environment and Planning B: Planning and Design* 22:649–64.

Steger, W. A. 1972. *Reflections on Citizen Involvement in Urban Transportation Planning.* Toronto: University of Toronto Press.

Transportation Research Board. 1985. National Research Council, *Highway Capacity Manual.* Washington, D.C.: Transportation Research Board, National Research Council.

Tufte, E. R. 1983. *The Visual Display of Quantitative Information.* Cheshire, CT: Graphics Press.

———. 1990. *Envisioning Information.* Cheshire, CT: Graphics Press.

——— 1997. *Visual Explanations: Images and Quantities, Evidence and Narrative.* Cheshire, CT: Graphics Press.

Whyte, W. H. 1979. *The Social Life of Small Urban Spaces* (motion picture). New York: Municipal Art Society of New York.

Paper 14 An Integrated Environment for Urban Simulation

WILLIAM H. JEPSON

ROBIN S. LIGGETT

SCOTT FRIEDMAN

URBAN SIMULATION TEAM, DEPARTMENT OF ARCHITECTURE AND URBAN DESIGN

UNIVERSITY OF CALIFORNIA, LOS ANGELES

ABSTRACT The genesis of the Urban Simulation Laboratory at the University of California at Los Angeles (UCLA) originated in the 1970s with ideas of visually creating urban simulations as an aid to better planning. The current manifestation of research is a three-dimensional real-time visualization system that produces realistic photo-quality simulations. This integrated simulation environment is built on work done at UCLA coupled to commercial software from MultiGen-Paradigm, Inc., Autodesk, Inc., and ESRI. The laboratory has developed a large-scale implementation of the environment, Virtual Los Angeles. Of particular concern in the building of such an extensive simulation is the design and implementation of the underlying database, which encompasses both GIS and three-dimensional object manipulation.

INTRODUCTION Within this decade we should see the wide-scale implementation of various graphics systems for urban researchers and decision-makers. More detailed mapping routines may be expected, permitting the rapid generation of color maps at a fraction of current costs. There is a pronounced trend in the direction of interactive computer graphics systems, which permit online planning, and design activities in a participatory decision environment. Such systems permit the juxtaposition of many different data displays to aid the decision-making process. Other computer graphics systems would permit the experiencing of alternative future environments in three dimensions and their immediate modification by user feedback (Kamnitzer 1972, 98).

In the early 1970s researchers at the Graduate School of Architecture and Urban Planning at the University of California at Los Angeles (UCLA), under the direction of Professor Peter Kamnitzer, proposed the creation of an Urban Laboratory. Using what was at that time very new computer graphics technology, this laboratory was to bring together researchers, decision makers, and representatives of the community to react to simulated alternative futures. The participants would be able to modify alternatives "in line with their needs and priorities in an interactive manner and thus become active participants in the planning process (Kamnitzer 1972, 311)."

Two pilot projects were developed to demonstrate the viability of such a process: INTU–VAL (Intuition and Evaluation), an online computer graphic program for iterative design and evaluation (Kamnitzer and Hoffman 1971); and CITYSCAPE, an urban "flight" simulator that was built by Kamnitzer in conjunction with the General Electric Corporation and implemented on the simulation facilities at the NASA Manned Space Flight Center in Houston. Because of the limits of the existing computer technology and enormous costs of the technology at that time, neither project became fully operational nor did the envisioned laboratory materialize. However, these projects demonstrated the feasibility of such a simulated environment. Kamnitzer's vision forms the basis for recent developments in this area at UCLA:

> This [simulator] will permit an observer–participant to insert himself into a dynamic, visual model of an urban environment by means of a visual simulation system employing on-line generation of color projections onto large screens with as much as 360 degrees of vision. By means of controls which direct his speed and the direction, as well as the movement of his eye, the viewer will be able to "walk," "drive" or "fly" through sequences of existing, modified or totally new urban environments. Such simulated environments would be initiated either by the researcher or by representatives of government and citizen groups participating jointly in urban planning and design activities. Simulations of sound and atmospheric conditions could be added to heighten the sensory experiences of the participants (Kamnitzer 1972, 315).

Although for many years these promises of what computers could bring to the fields of urban design and planning remained largely unfulfilled, recent innovations in computer hardware and software have produced systems which make the visions of the early 1970s possible. Much of this technology, originally developed for the military, is only now becoming available to the planning profession at a reasonable price. Researchers at the UCLA Urban Simulation Lab have adapted this advanced technology to create an integrated computing environment to meet the needs of the planning, architecture, and urban design professions.

The core of this integrated environment for urban simulation is a three-dimensional, real-time visualization system that provides high-quality photo-realistic simulations of selected communities and neighborhoods. The system can be used to combine aerial photographs with street-level video to create a realistic model (down to plants, street signs, and the graffiti on the walls) of the neighborhood, which can then be used for interactive fly-through and walk-through demonstrations. The system allows the decision maker to take a self-guided tour of a community either as it currently exists or as it might after a set of detailed urban revitalization measures have been implemented. Figure 1, for example, shows a computer-generated view of a model representing a proposed development around the new Staples Center adjacent to downtown Los Angeles. The system was recently used to present this project to the Los Angeles City Council.

Figure 1. Model of proposed development around Staples Center adjacent to downtown Los Angeles.

In this paper we describe the integration of this fully three-dimensional environmental simulation system with industry standard computer-aided design (CAD) systems, and the more traditional two-dimensional geographic information systems, and databases. Multiway links allow models (at varying levels of detail) to be efficiently generated using the CAD systems and translated into the form required for the visual simulation system. Links between the GIS and the visual simulation system provide the capability for dynamic query and display of information from the GIS database.

The integrated system makes it possible to model and explore alternatives in an easier and more sophisticated manner than any component system operating alone. It enhances the usefulness and capability of each individual system and makes feasible the type of urban simulation laboratory imagined more than twenty years ago.

SYSTEM COMPONENTS

The following four systems currently form the basis of the integrated simulation environment:

1 *UCLA Urban Simulation System.* This system, built upon Silicon Graphics, Inc.'s (Mountain View, California) IRIS Performer™ and OpenGL® graphic languages, provides an environment for developing real-time visual simulation applications.

2 *MultiGen/Creator* (MultiGen-Paradigm, Inc., San Jose, California). MultiGen-Paradigm makes three-dimensional modeling environments that allow the incorporation of photorealistic imagery. MulitGen Creator is a recent Microsoft Windows NT implementation of the system.

3 *AutoCAD®* (Autodesk Inc., San Rafael, California). AutoCAD is a general-purpose computer-aided design and drafting package which can be used for two- and three-dimensional modeling and representation.

4 *ArcView GIS* (ESRI, Redlands, California). ArcView GIS is a desktop GIS used for storing, organizing and displaying two-dimensional spatial information. ArcView GIS has a simple and intuitive interactive interface for display and query of spatial data.

These four systems provide the basic capabilities needed to perform the standard functions of dynamic simulation, modeling, and database management and retrieval. Linked they provide an integrated modeling and simulation environment (see figure 2).

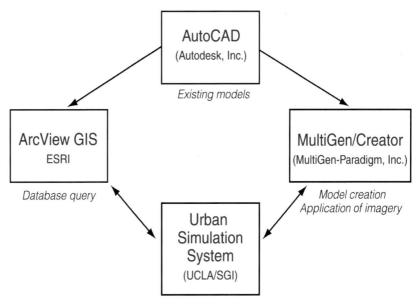

Figure 2. Integrated system components.

UCLA VISUAL SIMULATION SYSTEM

The focal point of the integrated system is a visual simulation engine that has been developed using the IRIS Performer application-development environment. Performer combines a C/C++ programming interface with a high-performance rendering library in a three-dimensional software toolkit that can be used for creating real-time visuals on SGI systems.

Using the toolkit, a programmer can create a user interface that allows a real-time drive-through or fly-through simulation of a three-dimensional model. The driver/pilot of the simulation can go anywhere and view any part of the model from a digitally accurate perspective. Objects in the model can be dynamic as well, allowing, for example, vehicles to move in the scene.

Building a special-purpose interface with the Performer package provides the flexibility to create a system that responds to individual needs (that is, it allows tailor-made solutions). Use of this supported tool set also permits easy adaptation to updated hardware environments. The system currently runs on the entire line of SGI equipment. The laboratory is also experimenting with a beta version of Microsoft Extensible Screen Graph (XSG) to port the simulation software to Windows NT running on personal computer platforms.

The Performer environment is structured to maximize the efficiency of frame display so that real-time dynamics are feasible. The run-time visual database, which is known as the scene, is organized into a hierarchical structure called a tree. The tree is composed of connected database units called nodes. The scene hierarchy supplies rules that describe how items in the database relate to one another. Performer can use the spatial organization of the database to efficiently cull unseen entities and thereby increase the performance of the renderer.

One particularly useful feature of this structure is the inclusion of "level of detail" nodes. Level of detail allows alternative geometric representations of an object to be specified and displayed based on the visual range between the object and the current viewpoint. This feature can be used to increase the efficiency of the renderer by limiting the amount of detail (number of polygons and resolution of imagery) displayed for objects that are a sufficient distance from the viewpoint. It also provides a method for displaying multilevel geographical information. For example, we might begin by looking down on a satellite image of a large urban area. As we move toward the image, the display can make the transition between different levels of aggregated data: from census tract information, to block data, to individual parcel representation, and finally down to the individual building forms. As we reach street level, a detailed model of the buildings can be displayed. Figures 3a through 3c show such a transition for UCLA's Virtual Los Angeles model. For this project, high-resolution street level models are inserted into a digital terrain model (DTM) which encompasses three hundred square miles of the Los Angeles basin.

Figures 3a, b, and c. Progression from aerial to street-level view of the
Virtual Los Angeles Model.

Another useful feature of the hierarchical data structure is the concept of "switching" nodes. A set of alternative objects can be described during the modeling process. These objects are attached to a switching node when the model is loaded. During execution of the simulation any individual member of the set of objects can be selected for display via a simple screen menu interface. This provides a mechanism for dynamically exchanging alternative objects during the simulation. Figures 4a and 4b, for example, shows *before* and *after* views of the proposed beautification project for the Los Angeles International Airport (LAX).

Figures 4a, b. Before and after views of the LAX Beautification Project.

The Urban Simulator interface uses a Motif®/X Windows™ standard and includes a well-defined set of functions that most users find sufficient for loading and viewing models without additional programming effort. If needed, the interface can be easily modified to implement unique features of an individual application. The interface currently includes the following functions:

Fly/Drive Interface—A mouse-controlled fly-through or drive-through interface allows the user to switch between drive and fly modes as well as to select from a menu of static points that can be returned to at any time.

Dynamic Objects—Dynamic objects that follow prespecified paths through the study area can be included in a model. Any of these objects can be added to an "attach" menu that allows the user to select a dynamic object and to attach himself or herself to the object for a ride through the study area. Dynamic objects can have realistic moving parts. For example, when a train stops at a station, its doors can open, allowing the viewer to enter and if desired, to ride along with the train.

Object Selection—In the three-dimensional simulation, objects can be selected by using the mouse (three-dimensional picking). Once selected, they can be highlighted by changing the underlying color, erased (as if a building were razed), or a simple text description of the object can be displayed in a pop-up window. It is also possible to query an associated database for object attributes. This option allows dynamic query and display of information from a GIS database in a real-time three-dimensional format. Additionally, Web URLs can be inserted into an attribute field for any object. On object selection, a Web browser is dynamically activated displaying the associated Web page.

Object Substitution—By means of the "switching" node concept, alternative representations for objects in the model can be stored, selected from menus, and switched into the model in real time. Alternatives can be discrete options (for example, alternative design options for a particular site) or can be a sequential set of options (for example, models that show development on a site over time or growth of a tree over time). Figures 5a thorough 5d illustrate the phasing of a proposed Los Angeles Metropolitan Transit Authority (MTA) development project that is intended to be built in four stages. By simply moving a "phase" slider on the simulator user interface, each phase of development can be added to the model.

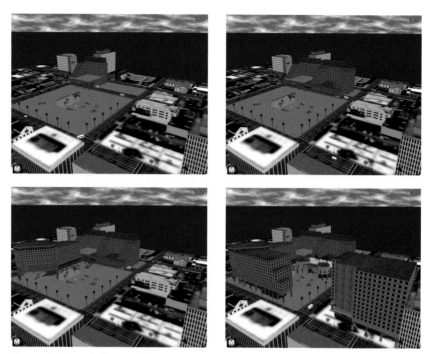

Figures 5a, b, c, d. Phases of proposed MTA development.

MULTIGEN

Performer defines a run-time-only database through its programming interface. It does not define an archival database or file format. A simulation application must input one or more predefined three-dimensional models and convert their data structures into Performer run-time structures.

The Urban Simulation Team uses MultiGen Creator as the primary three-dimensional modeler to link directly with Performer. MultiGen works closely with SGI to produce and maintain functions which convert MultiGen data files (.flt files) into the Performer runtime structure. MultiGen takes a hierarchical view of data organization that is consistent with the runtime tree structure. This consistency is necessary to optimize real-time simulation performance in the Performer environment. MultiGen also facilitates the specification of alternative levels of detail for objects.

MultiGen is a three-dimensional modeler that has the ability to model an urban scene quickly. A unique capability of MultiGen allows the application of photographic or video images ("textures") to highly simplified geometric models of objects (building, tree, street, light, car, etc.). Figure 6 displays a partial model for the proposed redesign of the UCLA Santa Monica Hospital. Here, textures have been applied to some of the simple three-dimensional forms shown. With very little modeling effort a photo-realistic three-dimensional scene can be created which can then be viewed dynamically with the UCLA simulator.

Figure 6. UCLA Santa Monica Hospital Model: images applied to simple geometric objects.

The procedure employed to create these models begins with plan-view aerial photographs. The aerial photographs are a quick, easy and accurate way to obtain up-to-date information on street widths, building footprints, foliage, etc. The photographs are scanned into the computer and appropriately scaled and rotated to fit into a global coordinate system (GCS). These photographs are then used as the base upon which the geometric model is built. Streets and blocks are quickly identified, outlined, and inserted into the database using MultiGen. The UCLA database/modeling methodology combined with the use of a global coordinate system allows individual projects to seamlessly integrate with other contiguous project areas. In addition, the utilization of a GCS allows dynamic entities (vehicles, etc.) to be accurately located within the model using Global Positioning System (GPS) coordinates.

Once the basic street/block infrastructure is modeled, a street-level survey is conducted by digitally photographing each building facade in the primary study area. The photo information for each building is then fed directly into the computer, perspective and color corrected, and saved in a texture database. This phase of the project is the most time consuming as it involves visiting the site to collect the data. The team has investigated the feasibility of adapting techniques that utilize two or three high-resolution oblique angle aerial photos to define a 360-degree representation of an area several blocks square. In this way a large area could be mapped in one sitting. Typically such an approach would be useful for the in-fill areas adjacent to, but not directly included in, the study area. To date, however, the technology available has not proven to be efficient enough to compensate for the inevitable loss in quality.

Once all of the image data (textures) describing the study area has been collected, the MultiGen modeler is used to create the appropriate built-form geometry and apply the textures (see Jepson, Liggett, and Friedman 1996, for a more detailed discussion of the modeling methodology). This process is both fast and efficient as the aerial photos provide site-accurate locational information. Building height, if not known beforehand, can be deduced from the street-level images collected during the site survey. Likewise, information about the location and size of foliage, shrubbery, streetlights, signage, etc., can be ascertained and included. The UCLA Urban Simulation Team has developed a realistic library of trees, streetlights, road signs, and so on, which can be incorporated into the models. These models can be animated in the real-time simulation (e.g., the cars can be moving down the street and the pedestrians can be walking along the sidewalk).

An interface between MultiGen and Performer is provided by MultiGen-Paradigm, Inc. in the form of a Performer flight format database loader. The loader allows user-developed functions to be registered as callbacks. Such functions have allowed the team to include special features in the simulation model such as the identification of switching node alternatives for object selection, substitution, and phasing. The team currently provides a simple file input interface to allow the specification of animation paths for dynamic objects that can be created in any of the supported modelers (MultiGen or AutoCAD). A new feature under development allows the user to specify paths by interactively defining three-dimensional splines directly on the model in the simulator environment.

AUTOCAD

While MultiGen software provides a powerful and easy-to-use modeling environment for generating three-dimensional scenes, there are reasons for modeling using a more standard, general purpose CAD system, (i.e., AutoCAD).

The current widespread use of AutoCAD provides a major incentive for including it as a component in the integrated system. Many existing models are available in AutoCAD format (or are DXF compatible). The ability to incorporate AutoCAD models is important both at the front and back end of the modeling process. In many cases it is possible to obtain detailed street, parcel, and building plan data in DXF format from public agencies. The use of this information can significantly shorten early phases of the modeling process (for example, working from an existing DXF file can reduce the digital terrain modeling time by as much as 30 percent). At the other end of the modeling process, more detailed models of proposed building development can be inserted into the scene. When using the simulation environment for architectural context studies, design firms will typically be able to supply models of proposed buildings in DXF form for inclusion in a larger neighborhood model.

The organizational viewpoint of data structures is an important consideration in the building of a modeling environment. MultiGen facilitates a spatial approach to the organization of the database. This approach makes for the most efficient traversal of the database—a requirement for Performer's real-time rendering. Figure 7b illustrates an efficient scheme for database organization from a visual simulation system perspective. In this case the physical database is partitioned into regions, called tiles. Objects, such as those displayed in figure 7a, are organized on a tile-by-tile basis in the tree structure.

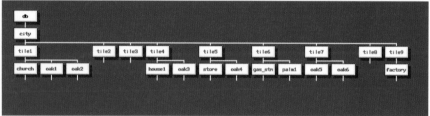

Figures 7a, b. Efficient scheme for database organization.

This can be contrasted with the data organization typically used for more detailed building design, where information is generally organized and displayed based on physical attributes rather than on spatial distribution. AutoCAD, for example, follows a logical layering paradigm for keeping track of the information in a project. Interesting work has been done on automatic spatial partitioning of models, which is particularly useful for navigating and viewing interior spaces (Teller and Sequin 1991; Airey, Rohlf, and Brooks 1990). When modeling at the urban scale, however, it is more efficient from both a modeling and a rendering perspective to construct models that conform to a spatial hierarchy.

To be used in the visual simulation environment, models built in AutoCAD must be transferred to MultiGen software for the addition of photo imagery. MultiGen software can also be used to reorganize the database into the hierarchical node structure required by Performer, and to facilitate the structuring of information for specifying alternative levels of detail for objects in the model.

There currently exists a DXF translation mechanism between AutoCAD and MultiGen. MultiGen translates the DXF file into tree-node form based on the AutoCAD layering structure. The user can then interactively modify the tree structure to make it more efficient with respect to visual traversal of the database tree.

There are some limitations to this approach. It is time consuming for the designer to restructure the tree interactively. More importantly, if any changes are made to the AutoCAD model, the user-driven tree-restructuring process must be repeated when the model is brought back into MultiGen. There are other limitations associated with the visualization process. For example, surfaces of objects must be specified with a particular orientation. The designer must, therefore, operate in a very exacting way to make the model coherent from the renderer's perspective. For these reasons, and because most of the models are built from fairly simple geometric forms, MultiGen is used as the modeler of preference when building new models.

ARCVIEW GIS

In the Urban Simulator's integrated environment, links have been established between the visual simulation module and ESRI's ArcView GIS. This provides the capability for dynamic query and display of information from a GIS database in a real-time three-dimensional format. A user can access a GIS database from the visual simulation window by selecting an object in the three-dimensional environment while navigating the urban neighborhood. This will highlight two-dimensional maps and tables in the GIS window. Alternatively, a query can originate in a traditional manner from the GIS side with results displayed by highlighting objects in the simulation window.

For example, one might wish to identify all sites with ten or more employees. The results of such a query are displayed by changing the underlying color of a building from natural to red. This highlights all buildings meeting the selection criteria by simulating the effect of shining several very powerful bright red spotlights on each facet of the building (roof included). Another example might involve calculating the traffic impact of different development alternatives. These impacts could be calculated by automatically adding the number of additional vehicle trips generated by each design alternative to existing traffic counts for streets and intersections. The results of this analysis could then be illustrated by changing the underlying color of impacted streets and intersections from their natural color to yellow and then to red as the magnitude of the result exceeds preset thresholds.

To make dynamic query feasible during the simulation process, links must exist between the physical objects and the attribute database. When the three-dimensional geometry of the model is constructed, geographic identifiers must be associated with objects in the scene. The MultiGen modeler allows the specification of a comment field with each object (node) of the geometric database. We use this comment field to assign a geographic descriptor (matching a spatial index in the GIS database) to nodes that represent a particular level of spatial aggregation in the three-dimensional database. These descriptors can be used in the Performer interface to key into GIS database records (see Liggett, Friedman, and Jepson 1995, for a more complete description of the linking process).

Figure 8 shows the system in operation on two side-by-side workstations (one displaying the visual simulation window and the other the ArcView GIS window). It is also possible for both processes to be run on the same machine (given sufficient resources), or run on two different machines with windows open on a single monitor. In this example, each window displays the results of a query at the census block level for a project in the Pico–Union district of Los Angeles. All blocks with less than two owner-occupied units are highlighted in both the two-dimensional GIS map format and the three-dimensional urban scene.

Figure 8. Side-by-side workstations display simulation window and ArcView GIS window.

CONCLUSION

The UCLA Urban Simulation Team has successfully implemented a system that combines custom simulation software and real-time database technologies with efficient modeling methodologies. This system is being used for a wide variety of "real world" projects including that of creating a virtual model of the entire Los Angeles basin.

Research at UCLA on client/server enhancements, which was funded by the National Science Foundation, has demonstrated that database systems can efficiently store and retrieve large amounts (more than one terabyte) of spatially distributed data. As network bandwidth increases this will dramatically increase the size of the problem that can be handled on a single workstation and will make possible the seamless interactive navigation of the entire Virtual Los Angeles Model (a model which is projected to reach terabyte size over the next several years). The client/server architecture will also enable the simultaneous support of hundreds of remote interactive users.

The Urban Simulator can be used both to identify existing problems and to quickly propose and evaluate alternative solutions to those problems. The technology described in this paper provides a framework for researchers and consultants wishing to build appropriate models, and provides a way to encourage and support the participation of the community in the planning and urban design process. Ideas thirty years old are now becoming a reality as the UCLA Urban Simulation Team continues to develop not only a system of computer hardware and software capable of graphically depicting the consequences of the planning process, but a methodology that allows all of the stakeholders of a community to participate in that process.

REFERENCES

Airey, J., J. Rohlf, and F. Brooks. 1990. Towards Image Realism with Interactive Update Rates in Complex Virtual Building Environments. *ACM SIGGRAPH Special Issue on 1990 Symposium on Interactive 3D Graphics*, 24 (2):41–50.

Jepson, W., R. Liggett, and S. Friedman. 1996. Virtual Modeling of Urban Environments. *Presence*, Vol. 5, No. 1:72–86.

Kamnitzer, P. 1972. Computers and Urban Problems. In *Computers and the Problems of Society*, ed. H. Sackman and H. Borko. Reston, VA: AFIPS Press, 263–338.

Kamnitzer, P. and S. Hoffman. 1971. INTU–VAL: An Interactive Computer Graphic Aid for Design and Decision Making in Urban Planning. *Proceedings of EDRA 2 Conference*: 383–90.

Liggett, R., S. Friedman, and W. Jepson. 1995. Interactive Design/Decision Making in a Virtual Urban World: Visual Simulation and GIS. *Proceedings of the Fifteenth Annual ESRI User Conference*.

Silicon Graphics, Inc. 1995. *IRIS Performer Programming Guide 2.0*. Mountain View, CA: Silicon Graphics, Inc.

Teller, S., and C. Sequin, 1991. Visibility Preprocessing for Interactive Walkthroughs. *Computer Graphics*, 25 (4):61–69

Visualizing the City: Communicating Urban Design to Planners and Decision Makers

MICHAEL BATTY, DAVID CHAPMAN, STEVE EVANS, MORDECHAI HAKLAY, STEFAN KUEPPERS,

NARU SHIODE, ANDY SMITH, AND PAUL M. TORRENS

CENTRE FOR ADVANCED SPATIAL ANALYSIS

UNIVERSITY COLLEGE LONDON

ABSTRACT New digital tools able to support the generic activity of planning and urban design involve rapid and effective methods for visualizing different aspects of the city from survey and analysis to design itself, as well as for communicating information and plans to various publics from design professionals to the affected community. In this paper, we present a worldwide review of these technologies, focusing specifically on developments in remotely sensed survey and the development of 3-D models integral to spatial databases based on GIS which contrast with more traditional methods based on computer–aided design (CAD). We illustrate these ideas with respect to developments in world cities, and then focus on two related but different ways of constructing such models for central London: first, in ad hoc fashion, linking various proprietary software based on Internet GIS, photo-realistic CAD, and panoramic imaging; and second, through a tighter coupling between 2-D and 3-D GIS, which is highly suited to incorporating digital data from remote sources.

Design begins with the definition of a problem context that is informed by data collection, and subsequently supported through analysis. This problem context is successively defined and redefined as the problem becomes better understood, and in highly intuitive design, these insights gradually merge the problem with its solution. In more self-conscious design, where solutions depend upon mobilizing the expertise of several diverse professionals and knowledge bases, the design process is usually constructed around a formal sequence of stages which are followed often in cyclic fashion. In urban design, the traditional sequence of survey—analysis—plan originally accredited to one of the founding fathers of town planning, Patrick Geddes, has been made explicit following models in systems engineering and decision theory. These begin with problem definition which involve the parallel activities of data collection and goal formulation, are followed by analysis, and then to the generation of alternative plans or solutions, their evaluation against criteria emanating from the initial set of goals, and finally the choice of one plan which is elaborated and then implemented. Such formal planning processes are nested within the more routine process of implementing and monitoring plans, which in turn may involve many such cycles of design and decision at different levels (Batty 1979). What makes these cycles converge is often some governmental mandate or in the case of commercially oriented decision making, the need to produce viable and profitable solutions or products.

These various stages need to be communicated to a wide variety of affected parties. Communicating urban design ideas to professionals themselves is required throughout the process where the knowledge involved is never the prerogative of any single expert. Communicating ideas to clients, whether they be political decision makers or the wider public, are key activities to the success or otherwise of the process. In urban design, the products or solutions—the plans—are ultimately visual in form, and the most effective way of communicating such ideas is inevitably visual too, notwithstanding the need to unpack such visualizations in functional, economic, and social as well as aesthetic terms. As visualization takes place at any and every stage of the design process, we must develop some rudimentary classification. A useful one is to distinguish between forward and backward visualization. *Backward visualization* involves developing visual tools and imagery which support experts and professionals, while *forward visualization* supports a less informed constituency, the public at large but more specifically particular interest groups. The same technologies might be used, but as we will see, these need to be closely adapted to their context (Batty, Dodge, Jiang, and Smith 1999).

Visualization is perhaps the most significant of all activities in the design process to have been affected by the development of digital technologies. The story of how digital computation moved through numbers to words, and then to pictures is well known, but as the dominant way we access computers and networks currently is visual, it is not surprising that there are a wide array of digital tools which support specific visualizations relevant to urban design. Information of course is central to all stages of design, and as most information is now digital, then software tools which add value to this information for the purpose of design, are key to all planning processes. Spatial information systems in the form of GIS are thus critical to the initial stages of design when an understanding is being built of the problem context. But tools for converting spatial information into mathematically related models which inform analysis, prediction, and optimization are also critical to good formal problem solving and to the generation and evaluation of alternative plans. Developing systems which query and extract subsets of information in routine fashion are often a part of these tools, as in GIS, but it is in visualization—in converting information into visual products—that these new digital tools have the widest appeal. Frequently such visualizations are through maps and models, and it is important to be clear about this usage. Discussions of models identify different types, from iconic to symbolic, with mathematical and computer models closely associated (Lowry 1965). In the digital age, however, this no longer suffices: computer models may be closer to iconic—as in 3-D visualizations of cityscapes—than to symbolic models built around urban processes that are simulated mathematically.

The models we refer to here are digital icons rather than simulations of urban processes and structures. In essence they are the digital form of the architect's block model, traditionally made of balsa wood. But they are more than this, in that, as their form is built on a digital geometry, this geometry can be tagged with attributes that comprise spatial databases that can be interrogated and analyzed. In short, these models can be fashioned as GIS equivalents which move them beyond iconic form (Teicholz 2000). Various functions can be embodied within them to the point of using their form and data as the geometric structure or skeleton on which the more symbolic models can be built. The way such visualizations are communicated, forward to the general public or backward to the professional, is equally varied. The desktop, laptop, and palmtop are the traditional media, but in the future, 2-D maps with some 3-D content will certainly appear on WAP (Wireless Applications Protocol) phones. At the high end, virtual reality (VR) displays such as those enabled through large-screen theatres as well as the more esoteric media of the headset, CAVE (Cave Automatic Virtual Environments), and holobench are all being used to engage decision makers (Batty and Smith 2001).

In this paper, we will begin our discussion of visualization with a review of 3-D iconic models of cities worldwide which will show the extent to which such models are being developed, but will also focus on the range of techniques that are now available. One of the theses that we will develop is based on the notion that 2-D digital maps and 3-D digital models are beginning to merge: that traditional CAD representations of cities are gradually being supplanted by spatial data models based on GIS and related technologies. We will present the diversity of techniques that now characterize the field, illustrating these ideas with various attempts at large-scale visualization in London. Most of these involve forward visualization—visualizations that have been produced for popular rather than professional audiences and which emphasize visual rather than functional attributes. We will then illustrate two somewhat different projects for developing backward visualization for professionals, the first based on ad hoc adaptations of existing software that we refer to as a loose coupling between CAD, GIS, and multimedia; the second based on a stronger coupling in which 3-D GIS, with all the functionality of 2-D GIS, is the main platform for development.

THE STATE OF THE ART: TECHNIQUES FOR CONSTRUCTING 3-D CITY MODELS

THE WORLDWIDE REVIEW

The GIS revolution has been intimately associated with our ability to visualize data in map and related statistical form and it might seem an obvious consequence that 3-D visualization, which is a little more complex, is developing in its wake. But the extension to 3-D is somewhat deeper, in that our ability to render complex geometries has now become routinely embedded in standard hardware, while techniques for rendering based on new methods of digital photography have added to the kinds of realism that are now possible. Added to this is the increasing supply of remotely sensed data concerning the 3-D environment, and 3-D visualizations of cities are thus becoming feasible and popular. Games have added to this spin just as developments in areas such as robotics are finding their way into electronic toys.

The increasing momentum in this field was confirmed by our comprehensive review of projects worldwide which we carried out in March 2000 for the City (Corporation) of London, the borough which includes the financial quarter of the city. Using e-mail targeted at the expert community, searches of the Web, and surveys of the literature, we identified 63 serious applications, 38 of these being developed in cities with greater than one million population, in contrast to 25 for cities of lesser population. The larger, more complex, and wealthier the city, the more likely that such visualizations were being developed, with the most elaborate being New York, Tokyo, and Los Angeles (Delaney 2000). For example, in Tokyo, we identified at least 15 different applications although we examined only eight in detail. We will review two of these in the next section, but a list of all the million-plus cities with Web sites which illustrate some these projects is reproduced in the Appendix.

These models were being developed for a very wide range of applications, much wider than we originally anticipated and very different from the original uses for design review where aesthetic impacts of new buildings are the main focus of interest (Teicholz 2000). We can define 12 different categories of use:

- Emergency services: applications to problems of policing, security, fire access, and ambulance access. These kinds of applications largely dwell on the intricate geometry of the urban fabric and the need to understand how different locations can be accessed quickly.

- Urban planning: problems of site location, community planning, and public participation all require and are informed by 3-D visualization, but detailed design reviews still form the main applications. The focus is on aesthetic considerations and daylighting as well as issues involving landscaping and line-of-sight.

- Telecommunications: in particular. the siting of towers for mobile and fixed communications is problematic in environments dominated by high buildings.

- Architecture: as in urban planning, site location and design review, in particular aesthetic issues and massing, are important factors, as are issues involving conservation and disruption to the urban environment.

- Facilities and utilities management: water, sewage, and electricity provision as well as road and rail infrastructure all require detailed 2-D and 3-D data for their maintenance and improvement.

- Marketing and economic development: 2-D and 3-D models provide extremely rapid ways of visualizing the environment of the city, the locations of cognate uses, and the availability of space for development.

- Property analysis: related to economic development but also to the general development of the city. Methods for visualizing cities enable detailed data to be computed concerning floor space and land availability as well as land values and costs of development.

- Tourism and entertainment: 3-D models provide methods for displaying the tourist attractions of cities as well as ways in which tourists and other newcomers might learn about the geography of the city.

- E-commerce: virtual city models in 2-D and 3-D provide portals to virtual commerce in that they provide the user with semi-realistic entries to new and remote trading and other commercial domains.

- Environment: 2-D and 3-D models enable various kinds of hazard to be visualized and planned for, in particular ways of visualizing the impact of local pollutants at a fine scale such as those associated with traffic.

- Education and learning: these kinds of visualization enable users at different levels of education to learn about the city as well as enabling other virtual experiences through the metaphor of the city.

- City portals: using 2-D and 3-D models as the entries to urban information hubs.

What we found was that the traditional methods of designing such models—based on computer aided architectural design, where detailed measurement of the geometry is the central activity and where geometric methods were employed to produce as detailed a rendering of the superficial structure as possible—are giving way to techniques based on spatial data analysis and GIS. The use of such models for analysis in the same way as GIS, for querying spatial data structures, and visualizing the results of such queries in 3-D, requires GIS-like functionality. At the same time, rendering techniques based on new methods of imaging involving, on the one hand, remotely sensed imagery, and on the other, photorealism, are being incorporated into such visualizations. These are emerging from developments in geomatic engineering (Fuchs 1996). All these approaches are now being supplemented by various ad hoc forms of multimedia which are developing as much in response to the dictates of visual content on the Web as to intrinsically different ways of representing such media.

We will quickly show the range of techniques being developed before we identify actual applications in world cities. In the past, CAD models of cities were built using full volumetric methods where the model was constructed using manual methods of measurement and detailing. These led to visualizations with high geometric content which were, and continue to be, expensive to produce. At the other end of the scale, new techniques of digital mapping with much less geometric content are being developed, with image-based rendering techniques and 2.5D image draping being quite widely used at present. There is a continuum of techniques now available which can be used to produce 2-D and 3-D computer models at different levels of detail. In turn, this is enabling different types of applications to be developed. Novel techniques of data capture are closely linked to these new methods of rendering. In particular, photorealistic imagery from digital photography is being widely used, while methods of remote sensing, in turn enabling automatic image creation and model construction, are being used at the city scale, for example, Light Detection And Ranging (LIDAR) methods from airborne devices used to create block models of cities (Morgan 2000). Many of the examples we found are making use of these technologies.

Finally, methods for delivering these visualizations are changing. Different types of desktop and workstation CAD and GIS are appearing which enable different scales of model to be displayed with much visualization shifting from the desktop to the Web, particularly in Web-based visualization technologies such as VRML (Virtual Reality Markup/Modeling Language). The Planet9 examples which have been developed for many cities, use such technologies (www.planet9.com/). Finally, there is multimedia visualization based on various kinds of animation and photorealistic display which again support different types of application. We can summarize the examples which we present below as involving

- Different proprietary software systems involving 2-D GIS, 3-D CAD, and multimedia methods

- Different levels of spatial abstraction from high to low geometric content

- Different types of data capture from detailed manual-based construction and rendering to fully automatic methods based on LIDAR

- Different methods for delivering visualization capability from the desktop to the Web

TECHNIQUES OF CONSTRUCTION: CAPTURING HEIGHTS AND FACADES

Against this background a spectrum of mapping solutions is appearing. These can be characterized in terms of their geometric content and range, from 2-D topographic mapping to full 3-D volumetric models which we can present as follows:

2-D digital maps and digital orthophotographs	Low geometric content
Image-based rendering (including panoramic imaging techniques and 2.5D image draping)	↓
Prismatic building models by building footprint extrusion (block modeling)	↓
Block modeling with image-based texture mapping	↓
Modeling of architectural details including roof morphology	↓
Full volumetric CAD modeling	High geometric content

Image-based rendering techniques attempt to extend the use of image data by warping images to enable production of novel viewpoints of the object. Two main techniques have emerged in this category: those based upon panoramic images, and those based on range images draped with photographic texture. Panoramic images provide a highly realistic visualization from static viewpoints within the survey area. If captured with sufficient density, they can provide a very detailed representation of an urban area complete with many of the features often omitted in 3-D CAD models (people, vehicles, street furniture, and so on). It is possible to generate geometrical models from sets of panoramic images but this is still a manual procedure and thus is rarely undertaken. One of the most advanced examples of such models is to be found in the MIT City Scanning project shown below (city.lcs.mit.edu/city/city.html) in figure 1:

Figure 1. Panoramic image from MIT City Scanning Project.

We have developed similar panoramics for Canary Wharf in London's Docklands which will provide an important element of the visualization methodology that we develop later in this paper (Smith, 2000). We show these in figure 2 in stretched panorama form as in figure 1 above.

Figure 2. Stretched panorama of Canary Wharf Square in London's Docklands.

Range-imaging techniques such as LIDAR are based upon camera systems that use a pulsed laser device to record the distance from the camera to each point in the image. Common applications use either ground-based or airborne sensors, the former being suitable for architectural surveys and the latter for small-scale surveys—including City models. Airborne LIDAR is invariably used in conjunction with the Global Positioning System (GPS) to deliver high-resolution Digital Elevation Models (DEM). Range images from such sensors can be treated as surfaces over which high resolution intensity images can be draped, thus enabling the creation of alternative views of the object as in figure 3. Unfortunately it is not yet possible to automatically segment such range images to deliver full 3-D models, although this is an area of very active research and commercial concern.

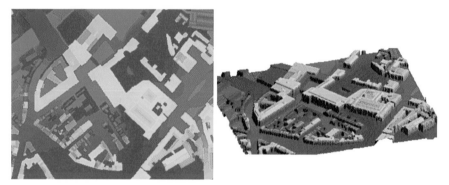

Figure 3. LIDAR-based city models (www.globalgeodata.com/bldgdata.html).

These models often arise from the fusion of 2-D building footprints with range-image data or other height data sources. Using simple GIS technology, it is possible to overlay 2-D building footprints on airborne LIDAR range images and determine the spatial characteristics of the range image within each building footprint. This enables the extrusion of the map data to yield a crude 3-D model such as that for Berlin in figure 4a, but at present, this does not enable the automatic generation of roof morphology. Moreover, some simplification of the outline of building geometry is likely to be required if a model of a manageable size is to be produced.

Prismatic block models lack any significant architectural detail and thus do not convey any compelling sense of the environment. In part this is due to the fact that extrusion based upon aerial data offer little opportunity to detail building façades which are not adequately captured by the near-vertical aerial images. To provide detail on building façades, either oblique aerial or terrestrial images must be acquired. Unfortunately, obtaining suitable viewpoints for image acquisition in a city center poses great logistical problems due to restrictions on helicopter flight paths or access to rooftops for terrestrial survey. Thus, building textures are most commonly generated from ground-level photography which often does not provide optimal unobscured facade coverage. An example for Piccadilly Circus in the West End of London is shown in figure 4b.

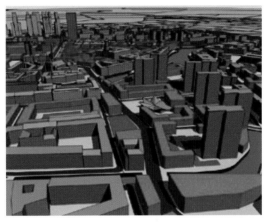

Figure 4a, b. Prismatic models: LIDAR-based Berlin, (top) and texture-mapped Piccadilly Circus, London (bottom).

At present the automated extraction of roof morphology from digital image data remains a formidable research task. Modern digital, or soft-copy, photogrammetric systems enable an operator to recover 3-D surface details more efficiently than previous generations of photogrammetric equipment. Detailed models of either individual buildings or small city blocks are frequently derived from a combination of aerial and terrestrial digital photogrammetry. Leading players in this field use automated search techniques to identify corresponding locations (points, edges, and regions) in multiple, overlapping images and then generate a number of possible "geometries" which can be tested against templates. Even the best of such methods require significant operator intervention in complex areas where buildings do not conform to a limited number of characteristic templates. Thus, the current state of the art demands manual interpretation of roof and other architectural details as we show again for the Canary Wharf development in figure 5.

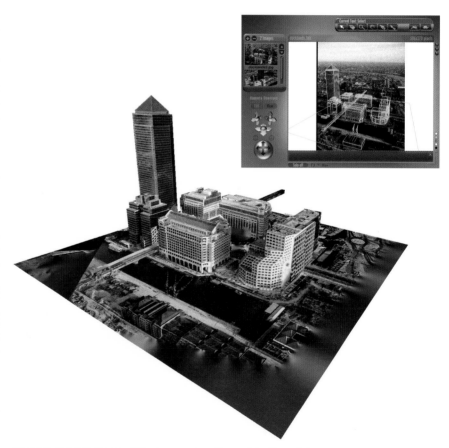

Figure 5. Building Canary Wharf as a prismatic model with roof shapes.

As-built CAD models of individual buildings are frequently under-taken by a combination of measured building survey and terrestrial photogrammetry. The complexity of such models ranges from digital ortho-photographs (in which images are rectified and combined to remove perspective effects) to full architectural detailing. While there are a large number of specialist photogrammetric companies offering such services to architectural clients, it is likely that the cost of such products would be prohibitively expensive for full city coverage. An example is shown in figure 6.

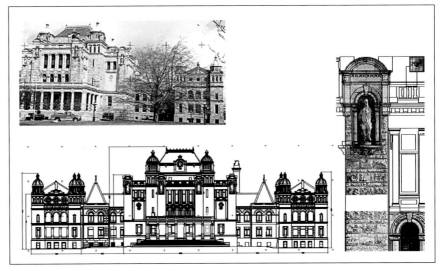

Figure 6. Full architectural CAD modeling by Terrestrial Photogrammetry (www.asfound.com/).

There is a complete class of models now emerging which essentially extrude the third dimension from the 2-D plan form. These models are usually based on extensions to proprietary GIS, a good example being 3D Analyst, an extension to ArcView GIS. The great advantage of these models is that they extend the functionality of GIS to the third dimension in that the attributes associated with the 2-D map can also be queried in the 3-D model. These models also have the ability to be generalized ,in that aggregating the 2-D map is considerably easier and more logical a basis for generalization than directly approaching such scaling within 3-D. In fact, most of these models do not render the 3-D geometry in any detail whatsoever, but for functional purposes this may not be necessary, and such models do provide a useful basis for an appreciation of massing and even crude daylighting calculations. An example of such generalization at the level of the small administrative areas is given in figure 7 below, where we show population density in enumeration districts for the Isle of Dogs and for the entire area of inner London.

Figure 7. 3-D GIS: Population density in docklands and in inner London.

There have been several attempts at developing models which link to GIS but which are composed of special adaptations of proprietary software. Several of the city models which we note below, in New York for example, are based on CAD-like software but have rudimentary GIS functionality. Unlike the London models above, which are quite abstracted, these models are based on building plots with some rendering detail. An example for downtown Manhattan is shown below in figure 8.

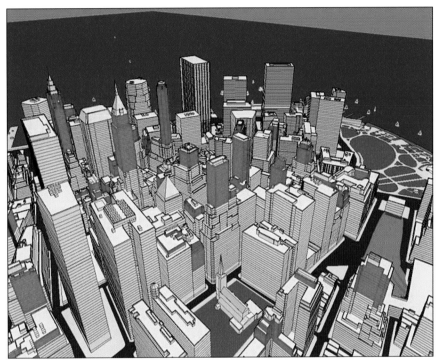

Figure 8. Skyscrapers (in red) Greater than 8000-square-foot floor space, from www.simcenter.org.

We are integrating many of these techniques in building various models of central London, but before we illustrate these, we will return to our review of the field, noting developments in New York and Tokyo, before returning to London and to the prototypes that we are currently developing.

THE MOST DEVELOPED APPLICATIONS: TOKYO AND NEW YORK

The most obvious but also interesting feature of all the models that we surveyed is the almost complete lack of any generalized approach to 3-D city modeling. In fact, there is no general purpose software apart from the 3-D extensions to desktop GIS such as ArcView 3D Analyst. However, where very extensive models have been developed, such as in New York and Los Angeles for example, the software systems themselves, which are composed of more specialist proprietary products, appear to be in the vanguard of the development of general purpose systems for 3-D modeling (Smith 1999). That is to say, this software is being developed with a view to more extensive generalization, probably as much around the particular approaches of the companies involved, as around any specific city modeling project.

Another feature that should be noted is the move to ortho-photos and LIDAR-type systems for recording height data. Most of the models we examined no longer use manual methods for measuring and recording height data. Various kinds of photogrammetry are now judged to be essential in the construction of such models, and therein lies the route to automation of the entire process—a likelihood which is on the horizon. Another interesting characteristic of some model developments is the continued use of physical iconic models, usually constructed from balsa. For example, the City of London relies extensively on its elaborate wooden model which is ported to many places by the economic development unit for marketing purposes. There is some digital imagery associated with it, but the "hands-on feel" that the model gives is still important to its use. In Jerusalem, a digital model has been built alongside the traditional wooden model and there is interaction between the two in usage to evaluate development proposals. One of the main applications in Tokyo, by the Mori Corporation, is based around the extension of a physical model to various kinds of digital display. The authors have also just learned, at the time of this writing, of an effort in Liverpool to build a digital model of the city center from detailed scanning of the traditional wooden model, thus bypassing the need for digital photogrammetry (Padmore 2000). In fact, the notion of developing 3-D models using VR displays acknowledges this role; the idea of building such a model and displaying it within a holobench implies that users would interact with the model using digital simulations of the physical movement of objects, such as buildings, within it.

TOKYO: MANY VARIED APPLICATIONS

The two best-developed sets of applications that we found are in New York and Tokyo, although the UCLA model of Los Angeles is probably still the most elaborate singly developed model to date (Liggett and Jepson 1995; Jepson 2000). In New York, there are four serious applications, one of these being a synthesis of the other three independent commercial efforts by the municipal authority. In Tokyo, there are upwards of 15 different applications, but here we will only refer to eight which we consider to be the most significant. We begin with Tokyo, where there are at least four sets of key players involved in sponsoring 3-D modeling: government at different levels, urban facility services providers such as telecommunications and utility companies, commercial firms in the construction and engineering sectors, and academic and related research centers. Tokyo is so large that there are many models of its various parts at different levels of detail, and the impression is one of great diversity of modeling efforts with little coordination or even recognition that so many competing applications exist.

Asian Air Survey is one of the leading data surveillance companies in Japan. Its model covers the entire area of Greater Tokyo, and is based on an original aerial photo database produced by the company and a highly interoperable proprietary 3-D GIS with nonstandard interfaces. It has been used for various 3-D planning applications which comprise full aerial data linked to GIS attributes. Other uses for landscape planning, telecommunication base station location-allocation, transportation, and disaster simulation have been developed. The application has extensive GIS-type functionality but it needs to be adapted to each particular application. Despite the popularity of its data, it is unlikely that the software could ever be promoted as standard in the Japanese market.

The Tokyo CAD Center has developed 12 different applications in parts of Tokyo as well as the downtown. These models are essentially 3-D CAD with good VR but limited GIS functionality. They are largely used for design review in the architectural and urban design domain but lack interoperability in a GIS environment, and are thus difficult to link to spatial data. Many of their models have good photorealism in that they have exploited recent developments in digital photography and related media. On the other hand, the Mori Corporation has developed the hybrid digital-physical model referred to earlier which, although useful in traditional terms, has limited portability and cannot be extended to embrace spatial data base technologies other than those that relate to photo-realistic media.

The company has constructed 1:1,000 scale models of various cities including the central areas of Tokyo, Manhattan, Yokohama, and downtown Shanghai. They claim that the advancement in IT and digital technologies is beneficial not only for the builders of VR models, but also helps physical model builders through reduced costs and increased time efficiency. Their approach is unique in that they scan the model with a multilens digital video camera which reflects the images on larger screens on a real-time basis. They have used their models quite extensively in public consultation and the models are produced using photo-surveys from which maps and height information is printed for the manufacture of the physical models using foam blocks. They are also developing Web-based applications based on visualizations from such models. Zenrin is another company that has a fully functional 3-D GIS for 298 major cities throughout Japan. They collect their own aerial photographic data and much of their work has been in developing systems for car navigation. In fact, Mori uses Zenrin photographic products which are also used for the production and sale of various paper-based map products.

The Ministry of Posts and Telecommunications has begun very recently to develop 3-D visualization designed for telecommunications applications in all the cities of Japan. Some of the data used has been taken from aerial data produced by the Nakanihon Air Service, which has its own visualizations and digital mapping software. A particularly interesting example is its use of 3-D models to simulate the spread of fire, although the prime focus of the company is on proprietary software and data for digital mapping. Other models are worthy of note, such as the Planet9 Shinjuku model which, like all Planet9 models, is a VRML-based application for virtual tourism. There are applications to Shibuya using Superscape, while, finally, digital panoramas with some 3-D content have been developed by Webscape for parts of downtown Tokyo. These applications are all very diverse and we do not have time to examine them in any real detail. Readers are referred to the appendix, which lists Web sites that contain more content. The range of visualization for two of these is shown in figure 9.

NEW YORK: APPLICATIONS WITH STRONG SPATIAL DATABASE STRUCTURE

The four significant applications in New York are less varied than Tokyo, and all of these are strongly oriented to GIS, that contain elaborate query systems which exploit the 3-D geography and geometry of the city. The New York City Department of Information Technology and Telecommunications (DOITT), part of the municipality, is heavily involved in GIS and spatial data systems for a variety of applications which range from environmental protection to security and crime. The modeling effort is based on a three-pronged approach. The base foundation is the development of an extensive and coordinated GIS for the city that spans several departments and users, and this goal has been all but achieved. Allied to these efforts, a pilot model has been developed for a small area of the city (in conjunction with ASI, another of our New York case studies). Finally, a full 3-D model for the city is planned. It is important to note that DOITT is very much at the cutting edge of all 3-D applications in the city and is involved with the three other commercial players.

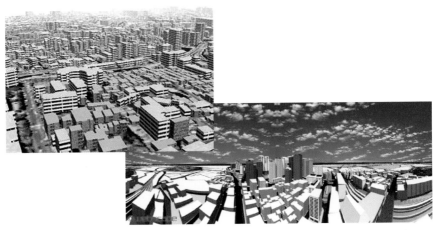

Figure 9a, b. Tokyo: The Asian Air Survey model of Tokyo, top, and Webscape's Digital Panoramic Visualization, bottom.

The first of these is Analytical Surveys Inc. (ASI) Technologies, a large surveying, GIS, and photogrammetric company that has been developing GIS and orthophotography resources for the New York City Department of Environmental Protection (NYCDEP) for the last two years. A by-product of this work is a 3-D model that has been developed for part of Manhattan. This has been constructed using building height data generated during GIS production and by draping orthophotos using ArcView 3D Analyst. So far, this model is a promotional venture for ASI and is not yet used by NYCDEP, although there are plans to develop a full model for a variety of services.

The Environmental Simulation Center (ESC), a quasicommercial spin-off from the New School of Social Research, has been involved in developing various 2-D and 3-D GIS for the city using a variety of proprietary systems. ESC has developed several models of different parts of Manhattan and a number of small towns. The motivation behind the initial 1995 3-D model of Manhattan was to identify commercial floor space that had the potential to be converted into apartments. Most of their more recent models, however, have been largely to view planned buildings in context and hence improve the planning process, and they see their effort encouraging more discussion and public participation in planning and design through 3-D models.

The ESC modeling approach is principally used as a community planning support tool: for site selection (locating proposed developments), and design review. Here the models are used as interactive design tools to visualize developments and to bring the design review process to community groups in a bid to foster citizen participation in the planning process. The ESC see their models as "an environment that people can instantly relate to and move around in." They are also linking their visual 3-D interfaces with predictive simulation models, using their models to predict changes in communities over time. The "CommunityViz" project combines their 3-D visualization model with the agent-based model (The "Policy Simulation Tool") being developed by PriceWaterhouseCooper's Emergent Solutions Group. The project is being applied to a small town—Scutney, Vermont—which has a population of roughly one thousand. The agent-based model simulates the socioeconomic evolution of every individual in the population, building up an incredibly detailed composite profile of the community in terms of ethnic diversity, tax revenue base, growth and decline, cohort survival, and so forth. (ESC 2000).

The fourth effort is in many ways the most impressive. Urban Data Solutions (UDS), started as a commercial venture in 1997, has grown rapidly since then, and is now expert in the provision of 3-D GIS and integrated CAD models for several cities, mainly in the United States. The company prides itself on its "smart models" and has pioneered work in this area with detailed models of Manhattan, Chicago and Washington, D.C., which are all commercially driven.

The founding members worked in CAD modeling for the architectural firm of Skidmore, Owings and Merrill, which pioneered CAD and fly-throughs of cityscapes as far back as the late 1970s (Deken 1983). Since then the applications context has changed, and the wireless telecommunications industry has provided a major commercial drive to develop the models for line-of-sight analysis in locating antennae in cities.

Various other demands for the model have motivated the work still further. These have included providing 3-D visualizations for property developers who wish to visualize what the view would be like from a particular office on a particular floor of a proposed building. It has also included visualizations for newspapers and other media presentations (for example, *The New York Times'* map and visualization of the events of millennium night, and fly-throughs around the New York Stock Exchange). The core application of the UDS models is large-scale modeling of cities for whatever reasons a client might have. This includes visualizing the views of and from planned buildings, management of property data (particularly in the case of buildings with many floors), GIS analysis such as line-of-sight (particularly mobile telecommunications), and the shadow effects of buildings. Once again, as in Tokyo, the range of applications is impressive. To provide some sense of what is being achieved, we show three examples from the commercial ventures in New York City in figure 10.

Figure 10. New York City: (a) Urban Data Solutions—Floor space in downtown Manhattan.

Figure 10. New York City, continued: (b) The Environmental Simulation Center—floor space, (c) ASI—Draping orthophotos on 3-D block models, and (d) ASI—Utility lines beneath the floor-space blocks.

AD HOC ATTEMPTS TO VISUALIZE CENTRAL LONDON'S URBAN LANDSCAPE

Apart from our own prototype, which we sketch in the next section, there are currently six efforts focused on building 3-D city models for parts of London; none, as far as we know, is specifically associated with applications sponsored by government. To some extent, these have all been built to offer proof-of-concept; that is, to demonstrate the potential of such approaches. Consequently none of these models have been developed for as large an area as the entire central area, for example. All of these are what we somewhat euphemistically referred to earlier as examples of forward visualization—attempts to develop models useful to community groups, political and related decision makers, as well as more general tools for virtual tourism. None have been developed for professionals and none have the level of sophistication and functionality of the New York, Tokyo, or Los Angeles models which we noted in the last section. There are also some ad hoc developments, in particular the Planet9 model which is currently offline and being redeveloped, and the Metropolis Street Racer game model developed by Bizarre Creations for the Sega Dreamcast, which has just been released and which includes considerable 3-D content of parts of Westminster.

The Street Racer Game is worth illustrating as evidence of the kind of ad hoc developments that are driving these products. Metropolis Racer is a driving simulation on the Dreamcast gaming console, and its interest here is that it marks a significant point in the use of realism in games. Some screenshots of its realism are captured in figure 11.

Figure 11. Scenes from the London Track of Metropolis Street Racer.

Street Racer includes three cities within the game: London, Tokyo, and San Francisco. Each city has been accurately modeled using photogrammetric techniques, allowing a realistic driving course to be constructed covering two square miles in each city. The preview version of London is particularly well implemented, running in real time at 60 frames per second. The games industry is becoming a major player in the modeling of built form, as demand from the consumer for realistic environments is met by the increase in processing power of the latest gaming consoles. With gaming exceeding cinema in the United Kingdom in terms of consumer spending, developers have a mass-market appeal, allowing games to be developed on budgets often exceeding £2 million. Such budgets allow realistic cities to be modeled, although it should be noted that Metropolis Racer is available only on the Dreamcast console, making it unusable for the range of applications identified in this paper. It may be possible to port the game to other computing platforms and thus enable use for a much wider range of applications.

Unlike other cities such as Chicago, Glasgow, and Los Angeles, the first 3-D digital models of parts of London date from the mid-1990s. The firm of Miller–Hare specializes in the production of high quality photo-realistic visualizations of architectural designs to support planning applications and the marketing of proposed buildings, but their focus is not on 3-D modeling per se. Over the last 15 years, however, they have either undertaken or commissioned site surveys covering the whole of the City of London at various levels of detail (LOD), which they have categorized in decreasing levels (A-G), as set out in the table below.

Level of Detail (LOD)	Description
A	Detailed architectural model including fenestrations
B	Detail equivalent to 1:100 measured building survey
C	Detailed elevations
D	Major details of building elevations
E	Accurate building volumes
F	Roofscape
G	Prismatic Block models—Coarse massing

The city has been divided into city blocks with OS (Ordnance Survey) 1:1250 building footprints heightened (using aerial photogrammetry) to provide a prismatic model corresponding to LOD G in their system. Incremental upgrading of the model has been undertaken on a project-by-project basis with a significant number of sites now being held at LOD A and B. The model is maintained within a package called *Navisworks* (www.navisworks.com) with multiple versions of the model being managed through a file-naming convention. Typical views of the model are shown in figure 12, which illustrates the superb degree of detail of the parcels but also indicates a complete absence of photo-realistic rendering.

Figures 12a, b. Views of the city of London from the Miller–Hare model.

This model was originally designed for a fly-through as part of an exhibition for the Museum of London, but was never actually used. In fact there is no real 3-D content in the model in that it is not backwardly compatible with any spatial database system. A related modeling effort by Hayes Davidson for the Architecture Foundation is even more impressionistic, being based on various collages of urban and building maps and images. This is called London Interactive, and it ". . . consists of a multi-layered digital plan of London generated from aerial photography and an integrated database providing information about contemporary urban design and the Foundation's work—past, present, and future. It offers the public, practitioners, and politicians a dynamic vision and a growing archive of the capital . . . The first layer of London Interactive was entitled 'New London Architecture' . . . The second layer of London Interactive is London 2000 which reviews more than 50 projects which will change the public face of London over the next ten years . . . In London 2000 photographs fade into visualizations to show how schemes will alter the familiar landscape of London . . . digital video and computer animations provide vivid simulations of the exterior and interiors of buildings currently being planned or under construction across the Capital . . ." (http://www.architecturefoundation.org.uk/project2a.htm).

Two other initiatives involve work at University College London (UCL), including our own. A model for virtual tourism that also illustrates the ability to move between different virtual environments has been developed by Steed at University College London's Computer Science Department over the last five years. The motivation underlying the model's development was a proof-of-concept. Steed's group was interested in demonstrating that a building-by-building model of an entire downtown (in this case the West End of central London) could be developed within a virtual environment using their own in-house software. Visually, the model looks dated in comparison to some of the other efforts around the world. The vast majority of buildings in the model are represented as simple blocks; we show a view across central London in figure 13. Key buildings are texture mapped, but again the resolution is quite coarse. The section of the model surrounding UCL is quite well developed, although it still shows its age. A particularly innovative feature of the model is the fact that the computer science building on UCL's campus is fully modeled in such a way that users can enter the building and navigate its corridors. The modeling lab within the building can be entered and its interior design visualized, including furniture and items on desks. The navigator can also gaze out of windows from within the model to view the built environment outside. The model is weak, however, in its functionality for any kind of decision making and analysis. It is not yet tied to a GIS or any modeling although its purpose continues to be as a vehicle to develop virtual environments.

Figure 13. The UCL Computer Science fly-through of Central London. (http://www.cs.ucl.ac.uk/staff/A.Steed/london-demo/vrst99/index.htm)

In CASA, we have developed many different visualizations of parts of central and inner London, largely as part of Andy Smith's work on online planning and community participation (Batty, Dodge, Doyle, and Smith 1998). More recently we have begun to merge some of these ideas with the more professional spatial database technologies being developed by Dave Chapman. Worth noting here is the initial virtual tour that makes heavy use of panoramic imaging called "Wired Whitehall," which is Net-based and enables access to related Web sites through maps and panoramas. A section from this tour is illustrated in figure 14.

Figure 14a, b. Wired Whitehall: Maps and panoramas hotlinked to one another and to related Web sites.

Application	Web Address
Wired Whitehall	www.casa.ucl.ac.uk/vuis
Virtual Tour	www.casa.ucl.ac.uk/olp/panoramic
Hackney Building Exploratory Interactive	www.casa.ucl.ac.uk/hackney
Shared Architecture	www.casa.ucl.ac.uk/olp/3d
Notable Landmark Sites	www.casa.ucl.ac.uk/public/meta.htm
London Bridges	www.casa.ucl.ac.uk/londonbridges
The VENUE Project	www.casa.ucl.ac.uk/newvenue/newvenue.htm

These techniques have been further developed for the Hackney Building Exploratory and for the Museum of London, while prismatic rendering techniques are being developed for block modeling as we showed earlier in figure 5 for Canary Wharf and for the Tottenham Court Road area of London. The table above shows a list of these examples and the Web sites from which users can access the content and the movies, but as in all these examples, the focus is not really on experts and professionals, nor is it on spatial data analysis, but on the community and more general interest groups. The CASA work is noteworthy in that all the examples are delivered over the Web.

The only professionally driven application we have encountered in London was commissioned by Trafalgar House and this is probably the most detailed large scale model of the City that has been produced. It is a 3D MicroStation model produced on an Intergraph ImageStation from aerial photography with roof detail, has a ground level Digital Terrain Model, and a precision of about +/− 0.2m. It is a photogrammetrically derived 3-D model of a corridor north of the Thames between Blackfriars and Tower Bridges which accurately depicts all major roof structures (excluding chimneys—equivalent to Miller–Hare level F). The model took three man months to create in 1996, but it has not been revised or updated since its creation and now requires significant revision. We understand that the model was most recently used by Foster and Partners in the analysis and visualization of the proposed Millennium Tower project and may have been used in support of other Trafalgar house projects. A view of the model from the Tower area is shown in figure 15.

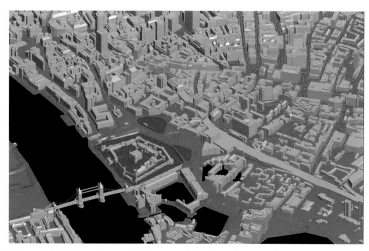

Figure 15: A View of Tower Bridge and Environs from the City University Model.

The City University model, like the Miller–Hare model, has no spatial data functionality and was mainly intended for problems involving aesthetic impact, particularly high buildings. Our last example is more of a 3-D map than a model, but it has been developed by Alan Day's group at University of Bath, which has considerable computer graphic expertise in this area, as developed through their state-of-the-art CAD model of the town of Bath (Day 1994). They have developed a simple model of the Soho area of central London which they bill on their Web site as "The Map of the Future." In essence this is a 3-D map through which users can fly and which provides " . . . a tool for analyzing the relationships between built form and various kinds of data . . ." as well as a " . . . publicly accessible interface to a wide range of urban information." There are various VRML versions of the map through which users can fly at www.bath.ac.uk/Centres/CASA/. as illustrated in figure 16.

Figure 16. "The Map of the Future" from the University of Bath Group.

LOOSE TO STRONGLY COUPLED GIS AND CAD: THE VIRTUAL LONDON PROJECT

Most 3-D models of cities that we have reviewed have not been developed from the perspective of spatial database technologies and associated analytical functionality, but from a mixture of traditional CAD, multimedia, and photogrammetry. What we are doing at present is developing a prototype application for Central London which is based on the view that GIS is essential to such developments but also that new functionality should be developed to deal with the geography of the third dimension. Our focus is thus on developing a GIS base which is robust enough to incorporate other kinds of media, in particular panoramic imagery as well as rapid CAD, based on photorealism. We are following two strategies: an ad hoc process in which we are using a state-of-the-art Internet GIS as the base to deliver spatial data, multimedia, and 3-D imagery across the Internet, and a more traditional approach in which we are using 3-D extensions to proprietary GIS. In the first case, we are strongly reliant on developing our own functionality for analysis of the third dimension, whereas in the more traditional case we are able to use the established functionality of the GIS to undertake analysis.

VIRTUAL LONDON: IMS, RAPID CAD, AND PANORAMIC IMAGING

In our first prototype, we are using ArcIMS® to store, retrieve, and deliver information across the Web for Central London. We have a wide range of data layers that link geometry to geography and progress from the scale of census tracts—enumeration districts that we illustrated in figure 7 above—down to parcel level data that we have culled from a variety of sources such as OS Landline, Cities Revealed data, and so on. We have various raster data on which this geometric and geographic data sits, and we are intending to develop query systems that enable us to intersect geometric with geographic land units. So far we do not have any movement data within the base and the data is largely cross-sectional, being compiled from diverse time slices between 1991 and 1999. With ArcIMS, we can customize the query system within limits, and in the first instance we intend the product to be an example of forward visualization, useful to end users and interest groups, rather than planning professionals per se. We have some experience of Internet map servers for related projects (Doyle, Dodge, and Smith 1998), and an early version was demonstrated for both travel and pollution problems in London. One of the key features of the interface we are developing is that it will be interactive and widely available.

One of the key issues in 2-D mapping and 3-D modeling is that the same product may look forward to the end-user base or back to professional use. This will certainly be a feature of Virtual London. The way the various CAD and multimedia products are woven into the map server is quite innovative. The map server does not serve 3-D geometric information in terms of height data to the CAD visualization, for this is preprocessed using the rapid CAD package Canoma and then delivered using MetaStream across the Internet. Rather, the map server contains key codes to the objects that are already stored in the CAD model. Objects can be moved in the CAD interface and changes in position are then recorded in the map database. We are not able to go into the basics of Canoma although an example of its use was given earlier in the visualization of Canary Wharf in figure 5. In fact the user basically constructs the 3-D object model from photographs and the objects created are thence movable, as we show in figure 17.

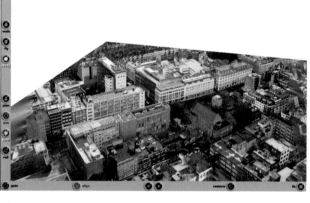

Figure 17. Constructing the CAD model with movable buildings as objects.

This shows a portion of Tottenham Court Road, which was photographed from the BT Tower and then turned into object form using Canoma. The object highlighted in red in the top image is an example of such a block object, and as the lower image shows, it can be moved to another position in the street. When this process takes place on the Web but outside the map server, positional information is sent back to the server and input to the database. At the end of a session, these changes to the original database are stored.

The panoramic imagery is simply activated from the CAD model and in figure 18 below we show a mock-up of the prototype. The panorama is produced as we indicated earlier in figure 2. In figure 18, we show the map server in the upper left-hand window, the CAD model—in this case of the Palace of Westminster (The Houses of Parliament)—in the upper right window, with the panorama of this area below. The various buttons at the bottom of the screen enable the user to operate some rudimentary navigation controls that allow zooming and panning and movement within the various visualizations. We also show a search capability that directs the user to find particular sites and building complexes through the map server.

Figure 18. The Virtual London prototype integrating Internet GIS, rapid CAD, and digital panoramics.

This interface is much more suggestive of virtual tourism than of considered professional use, but the power and flexibility of adding 2-D and 3-D maps, models, and multimedia is clear.

DESKTOP GIS WITH 3-D CAPABILITIES

Our second approach is more classic and this is based on developing the entire model within a proprietary GIS—in this case in ArcView GIS with extensions, particularly 3D Analyst. In fact, we consider that this model will eventually be worked up in ArcInfo, but for the moment, to simply demonstrate what is possible, we are using basic desktop software. It is quite easy to code and import height data into ArcView GIS directly from LIDAR data, produced in this case for the City of London from the UK National Remote Sensing Centre. Figure 19 shows a typical screen shot of the 2-D map alongside the 3-D model, with a special import of St. Paul's Cathedral in LIDAR form. This shows how problematic it is to work with remotely sensed data for irregular objects that are composed of nonstandard polygons. In fact, the geometric integrity of the cathedral is captured by LIDAR but the distortions produced simply illustrate the state of the art. This will of course change—rapidly.

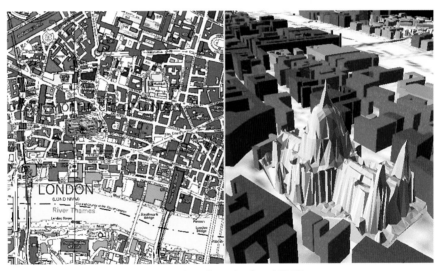

Figure 19. 3-D block modeling of the City of London from LIDAR.

Currently we are adding new layers of data for the subway system, whereupon the model will become useful in querying and analyzing distances that relate to local pedestrian access around tube stations. This is the kind of query that is essential to any kind of transport or telecommunications problem that involves complex urban areas where 3-D form is critical to lines of sight and access. The New York examples shown earlier were fashioned around this kind of application.

We have not shown any kind of completed product here, but what is clear is that the array of different media and database systems now enables us to construct many different kinds of virtual models. In some senses, the diversity that we found in our worldwide review is even greater than we originally anticipated, for there are many new techniques that have not been developed in practice as yet, some of which we have hinted at above.

NEXT STEPS: AUTOMATED VISUALIZATIONS AND REMOTE DELIVERY

Spatial database technologies and remotely sensed geometric data are the two features of 3-D city modeling that are forcing the pace. It is entirely conceivable that 3-D models will be produced on the fly as data is sensed remotely and downloaded into standard packages that generate effective and useful models. In fact, this is not to be doubted, but what is unclear is the extent to which such automation will extend to bespoke applications, particularly those that address professional concerns. In this domain, specialist and unique adaptations of general principles are likely to remain the norm. However, software packages are likely to emerge that will be capable of generating good, standard models. In a sense, this is already the case with the plug-ins and extensions to desktop GIS such as ArcView GIS, and the Evans & Sutherland RAPIDsite 3-D modeling package. More elaborate systems incorporating software from such companies as Multi-Gen-Paradigm, Inc., will also become more generally available, as will software and data systems for producing good remotely sensed data such as LIDAR (Snyder and Jepson 1999).

The way these models will be delivered is also likely to change. CAD and 3-D on the Internet has not moved as fast as expected due to a combination of cumbersome, nonintuitive interfaces and lack of "killer applications" (Leavitt 1999). But these will be resolved as internet commerce begins to pick up fast, elaborate interfaces and as the bottlenecks associated with bandwidth begin to disappear, and as optical fiber takes over (Gilder 2000). Desktop will give way to Internet as IMS- and VRML-like browsers become standard. Remote access of data and software, as well as the generation of content on the fly and over the Internet will become the norm in the next five years. This will open an entirely new way in which users can interact with such models, and it will herald new ways in which the wider public will be able to participate. Our Virtual London prototype is largely designed for such forward visualizations, for community participation across the Internet. What we have demonstrated here is simply a snapshot of what is going on. We have not sought to present a learned treatise on such models but have attempted rather to paint an impressionistic picture of the field of planning support, which is rapidly developing and will clearly aid the planner and public alike in ways that are surprising, exciting, and novel.

REFERENCES

Batty, M. 1979. On Planning Processes. In *Resources and Planning.* ed. B. G. Goodall and A. M. Kirby. Oxford, UK: Pergamon Press: 17–45.

Batty, M., and A. Smith. 2001. Virtuality and Cities: Definitions, Geographies, Designs. In *Virtual Reality in Geography,* ed. P. F. Fisher and D. B. Unwin. London: Taylor and Francis, forthcoming.

Batty, M. M. Dodge, S. Doyle, and A. Smith. 1998. Modelling Virtual Environments. In *Geocomputation: A Primer,* ed. P. Longley, S. Brooks, R. McDonnell, and B. Macmillan. Chichester, UK: John Wiley and Sons: 139–61.

Batty, M., M. Dodge, B. Jiang, and A. Smith. 1999. Geographical Information Systems and Urban Design. In *Geographical Information and Planning.* ed. J. Stillwell, S. Geertman, and S. Openshaw. Heidelberg, Germany: Springer: 43–65.

Day, A. 1994. From Map to Model. *Design Studies,* 15:366–84.

Deken, J. 1983. *Computer Images: State of the Art,* London: Thames and Hudson.

Delaney, B. 2000. Visualization in Urban Planning: They Didn't Build LA in a Day. *IEEE Computer Graphics and Applications,* May/June 2000:10–16.

Doyle, S., M. Dodge, and A. Smith. 1998. The Potential of Web Based Mapping and Virtual Reality Technologies for Modeling Urban Environments. *Computers, Environments and Urban Systems,* 22:137–55.

Fuchs, C. 1996. OEEPE Study on 3D–City Models, *Proceedings of the Workshop on 3D–City Models,* OEEPE (Organisation Europeenne d'Etudes Photogrammetriques Experimentales), Institute for Photogrammetry, University of Bonn, Bonn, Germany.

Gilder, G. 2000. *Telecosm: How Infinite Bandwidth Will Revolutionize Our World.* New York: The Free Press.

Leavitt, N. 1999. Online 3D: Still Waiting After All These Years, *Computer,* July 1999:4–7.

Liggett, R. and W. Jepson. 1995. An Integrated Environment for Urban Simulation, *Environment and Planning B,* 22:291–302.

Lowry, I. S. 1965. A Short Course in Model Design, *Journal of the American Institute of Planners,* 31:158–66.

Morgan, B. A. 2000. *Evaluation of LIDAR Data for 3D-City Modelling.* MSc Thesis in Remote Sensing, Department of Geomatic Engineering. London: University College.

Padmore, K. 2000. *The Liverpool Project,* The Centre for Virtual Environments. Manchester, UK: University of Salford.

Smith, A. 2000. Shared Architecture: Rapid-Modeling Techniques for Distribution via On-Line Multi User Environments. *Arcadia*, 19:1.

Smith, S. 1999. Urban Simulation: Cities of the Future. *A/E/C/Systems* (Architecture, Engineering, and Construction Automation). Summer 1999.

Snyder, L., and W. Jepson. 1999. Real-Time Visual Simulation as an Interactive Design Tool. *ACADIA 99 Conference Proceedings*: 356–57.

Teicholz, N. 2000. Shaping Cities: Pixels to Bricks, *The New York Times*, Technology Circuits, Thursday, December 16, 1999.

APPENDIX

Web addresses for visualization projects in cities with greater than one million population, ranked by size (March 2000):

City	Web address
Tokyo	csis.u-tokyo.ac.jp/links-e.html www.ajiko.co.jp/infocom/index.html www.webscape.com/Worlds/tokyo.html www.zenrin.co.jp/products/Digital/L/Zi2HP/2/2.html www.oyo.co.jp/service/sentan/3d/index.html www.seikabunka.metro.tokyo.jp/english/englishindex.html www.cadcenter.co.jp/01-CG-frame.html www.planet9.com/earth/tokyo/index.htm www.cyber66.or.jp www.nnk.co.jp/skymedia
New York	www.simcenter.org www.u-data.com www.3dmetric.com/cities/Manhatten.JPG www.planet9.com/earth/newyork/index.htm www.3dmetric.com/cities/New%20_York_City.JPG www.esri.com/news/arcnews/summer98articles/03-av3danalyst.html
Mexico City	www.mexico-city-3d-map.com.mx/ETenoc.htm
London	www.cs.ucl.ac.uk/staff/A.Steed/Pictures www.cs.ucl.ac.uk/staff/A.Steed/london-demo/vrst99/index.htm www.bath.ac.uk/Centres/CASA/london www.millerhare.com/page0104.htm www.architecturefoundation.org.uk/project2.htm www.dome2000.co.uk/static/html/3d_dome/model/index.htm www.aerobel.co.uk/urbansim.html www.planet9.com/earth/london/index.htm www.hayesdavidson.co.uk/index2.html
Paris	www.paris-france.org/VR/anglais www.paris-france.org/asp/carto2.asp webscape.com/Worlds/paris.html

City	Web address
Los Angeles	www.planet9.com/lacitymenu.htm www.3dmetric.com/cities/LosAngeles.html www.gsaup.ucla.edu/bill/LA.html www.aud.ucla.edu/~robin/ESRI/p308.html www.ust.ucla.edu www.multigen-paradigm.com/urbsimhm.htm
Chicago	www.3dmetric.com/cities/Chicago_downtown.JPG home.digitalcity.com/chicago www.planet9.com/earth/chicago/index.htm www.uic.edu/cuppa/udv www.u-data.com
Delhi	www.thecpmall.com/virtualvision/VRML/CPvrml_aerial.htm
St. Petersburg	www.mapserv.com/new/e/index.htm
Hong Kong	hkugis.hku.hk/campus www.hku.hk/cc/sp2/software/graphics/dx/html/pages/usrgu015.htm www.centamap.com/cent/index.htm
Philadelphia	saturn.bentley.com/news/97q2/modelcity.htm www.bentley.com/modelcity
Berlin	www.cyberlin.de www.cy-berlin.de/intro/cityframe.htm www.multigen-paradigm.com/echtzeit/echtzeit_story.htm www.artcom.de/contacts/city-and-architecture/berlin.de.shtml www.echtzeit.de/e-berlin/index_e.html
Detroit	www.3dmetric.com/cities/Detroit_Downtown.JPG
Santiago	www.uchile.cl/facultades/arquitectura/urbanismo/articulo/urban.htm
San Francisco	www.abag.ca.gov/bayarea/eqmaps/eqmaps.html www.planet9.com/sfnasa.htm www.planet9.com/sfcitymenu.htm www-laep.ced.berkeley.edu/research/simlab www.planet9.com/bayarea.htm webscape.com/Worlds/sanfrancisco.html www.zenrin.com/pr.html
Boston	www-ims.oit.umass.edu/~umassmp/intergraph/boston.html www.planet9.com/earth/boston/index.htm
Toronto	www.clr.toronto.edu www.clr.utoronto.ca
Sydney	www.cityofsydney.nsw.gov.au/vg_panoramas.asp www.culture.com.au/virtual www.planet9.com/earth/sydney/index.htm www.bentley.com/biuc/awards/psnurban.htm
Washington, DC	www.3dmetric.com/cities/Washington_NW.JPG www.geocities.com/Pentagon/8215/digital.html www.planet9.com/earth/washdc/new/master.wrl
Singapore	www.singapore.vrt.com.sg/sing-1/merlion_frame.htm www.bizarts.com www.ura.gov.sg www.ura.gov.sg/corporate/gallery_main.html

City	Web address
Yokohama	www.ymm21.co.jp/annai/as direction
Houston	www.transamerica.com/Business_Services/Real_Estate/TerraPoint/Technology/demo.asp#
Warsaw	andante.iss.uw.edu.pl/cgi-bin/modzel
Lisbon	ortos.cnig.pt/igeoe/ingles www.marconi-is.com/products
Cleveland	www.3dmetric.com/cities/Cleveland.JPG www-ims.oit.umass.edu/~umassmp/intergraph/cleveland.html
San Diego	www.sci.sdsu.edu/People/Jeff/newhome/phase4.html www.planet9.com/earth/sandiego/index.htm
Seattle	www.wizards.com/rpga/vs/welcome.asp www.download32.com/proghtml/18/1859.htm
Atlanta	www.planet9.com/earth/atlanta/index.htm www-ims.oit.umass.edu/~umassmp/intergraph/atlanta.html webscape.com/Worlds/atlanta.html
Baltimore	www.planet9.com/earth/baltimore/index.htm
Vienna	www.neonet.nl/itc/~oeepe/newsletters/let1_984.html
Amsterdam	www.dds.nl www.xs4all.nl/%7Eavsas/index_v2.html www.xs4all.nl/~avsas/urban_3d_model.html www.zegelaar-onnekes.nl/home/zeno-3d.htm
Frankfurt	www.centricsoftware.com/gallery/frankfurt.html ipb1.ipb.uni-bonn.de/ipb/projects/semi-automatic.html www.frankfurt.de/panorama/deutsch/index.html www.khm.de/~jo/about/about_projekte.html
Glasgow	iris.abacus.strath.ac.uk/glasgow www.glasgow1999.co.uk www.glasgowdevelopment.co.uk www.glasgow.gov.uk
Kyoto	www.digitalcity.gr.jp
Denver	www.planet9.com/earth/denver/index.htm
Vancouver	www.planet9.com/earth/vancouver/index.htm
Portland	www.planet9.com/earth/portland/index.htm www.pdx3d.com/Default.htm www.pdx3d.com/links.htm www.nc3d.com/services.htm#3d%20Modeling www.nc3d.com/links.htm
New Orleans	www.virtualneworleans.com/Main.html www.planet9.com/earth/neworleans/index1.htm www.pb4d.com

ACKNOWLEDGEMENTS

This project on which material in this paper has been based was funded by the Corporation of the City of London and involved a worldwide review of computer visualization projects for cities. Various Web pages support the project at: www.casa.ucl.ac.uk/3dcities/index.htm and www.casa.ucl.ac.uk/3dcities/london3d.htm. The authors gratefully acknowledge Sarah Sheppard's contributions to this project.

AUTHOR AFFILIATIONS

Michael Batty, Steve Evans, Mordechai Haklay, Naru Shiode, Andy Smith, and Paul M. Torrens from the Centre for Advanced Spatial Analysis; David Chapman from the Department of Geomatic Engineering; and Stefan Kueppers of the Bartlett Graduate School, University College London.

CONTACT THE AUTHORS

mbatty@geog. ucl.ac.uk, dchapman@ge.ucl.ac.uk, s.evans@ucl.ac.uk, m.haklay@ucl.ac.uk, s.kueppers@ucl.ac.uk. n.shiode@ucl.ac.uk, asmith@geog.ucl.ac.uk, ptorrens@geog.ucl.ac.uk

www.casa.ucl.ac.uk/3dcities